A Cruel Theatre of Self-Immolations

A Cruel Theatre of Self-Immolations investigates contemporary protest self-burnings and their echoes across culture.

The book provides a conceptual frame for the phenomenon and an annotated, comprehensive timeline of suicide protests by fire, supplemented with notes on artworks inspired by or devoted to individual cases. The core of the publication consists of six case studies of these ultimate acts, augmented with analyses and interpretations hailing from the visual arts, film, theatre, architecture, and literature. By examining responses to these events within an interdisciplinary frame, Ziółkowski highlights the phenomenon's global reach and creates a broad, yet in-depth, exploration of the problems that most often prompt these self-burnings, such as religious discrimination and harassment, war and its horrors, the brutality and indoctrination of authoritarian regimes and the apathy they produce, as well as the exploitation of the so-called "subalterns" and their exclusion from mainstream economic systems.

Of interest to scholars from an array of fields, from theatre and performance, to visual art, to religion and politics, *A Cruel Theatre of Self-Immolations* offers a unique look at voluntary, demonstrative, and radical performances of shock and subversion.

Grzegorz Ziółkowski is a theatre director and Professor of Theatre and Performance at the Adam Mickiewicz University in Poznań, Poland. He has authored monographs on Peter Brook and Jerzy Grotowski, and co-edited special issues of *Polish Theatre Perspectives* (*Voices from Within*), *Performance Research* (*On Performatics*), and *Contemporary Theatre Review* (*Polish Theatre After 1989*).

Routledge Advances in Theatre and Performance Studies

The Bible and Modern British Drama
From 1930 to the Present-Day
Mary F. Brewer

Moving Relation
Touch in Contemporary Dance
Gerko Egert

The Dramaturgy of the Door
Stuart Andrews and Matthew Wagner

Professional Wrestling and the Commercial Stage
Eero Laine

Performing Home
Stuart Andrews

The Dances of José Limón and Erick Hawkins
James Moreno

Shakespeare in Singapore
Performance, Education, and Culture
Philip Smith

A Cruel Theatre of Self-Immolations
Contemporary Suicide Protests by Fire and Their
Resonances in Culture
Grzegorz Ziółkowski

For more information about this series, please visit: www.routledge.com/
Routledge-Advances-in-Theatre--Performance-Studies/book-series/
RATPS

A Cruel Theatre of Self-Immolations

Contemporary Suicide Protests by Fire and Their Resonances in Culture

Grzegorz Ziółkowski
Translated by Jan Szelągiewicz

LONDON AND NEW YORK

First published 2020
by Routledge
2 Park Square, Milton Park, Abingdon, Oxon OX14 4RN

and by Routledge
605 Third Avenue, New York, NY 10017

Routledge is an imprint of the Taylor & Francis Group, an informa business

First issued in paperback 2021

© 2020 Grzegorz Ziółkowski

The right of Grzegorz Ziółkowski to be identified as author of this work has been asserted by him in accordance with sections 77 and 78 of the Copyright, Designs and Patents Act 1988.

All rights reserved. No part of this book may be reprinted or reproduced or utilised in any form or by any electronic, mechanical, or other means, now known or hereafter invented, including photocopying and recording, or in any information storage or retrieval system, without permission in writing from the publishers.

Trademark notice: Product or corporate names may be trademarks or registered trademarks, and are used only for identification and explanation without intent to infringe.

Publisher's Note
The publisher has gone to great lengths to ensure the quality of this reprint but points out that some imperfections in the original copies may be apparent.

British Library Cataloguing-in-Publication Data
A catalogue record for this book is available from the British Library

Library of Congress Cataloging-in-Publication Data
A catalog record has been requested for this book

ISBN 13: 978-0-367-18064-5 (hbk)
ISBN 13: 978-0-429-05937-7 (ebk)
ISBN 13: 978-1-03-223845-6 (pbk)

Typeset in Bembo
by codeMantra

If I give away all I have,
and if I deliver up my body to be burned,
but have not love,
I gain nothing.

(1 Corinthians 13, 3)

Contents

List of figures   xi
Acknowledgements   xii

Introduction   1

The aim, subject, and structure of this book 2
A cruel theatre *of protest self-burnings? 5*
Approach 8
Echoes in contemporary culture 10
Inconclusiveness 13

PART I
Mapping suicide protests by fire   19

Protest self-burnings as suicide protests 20
Some general remarks 23
Reactions, scrutiny, and effectiveness 28
The somatic act of communication and its performative dimension 31
Summary 35

PART II
Chronology: notes and microstudies on
selected protest self-burnings (1963–2017)   39

Republic of Vietnam 41
Republic of India 41
Republic of Vietnam 42
United States of America 42
Republic of Korea 43
Republic of Vietnam 43

viii Contents

People's Republic of China 44
Japan 44
Polish People's Republic 45
Czechoslovak Socialist Republic 45
Hungarian People's Republic 46
Latvian Soviet Socialist Republic – Soviet Union 46
United States of America 46
Socialist Republic of Romania 47
Basque Country – Spain 47
Italy 47
Republic of Korea 48
Lithuanian Soviet Socialist Republic – Soviet Union 48
Canada 49
German Democratic Republic 50
France 50
Federal Republic of Germany 51
Ukrainian Soviet Socialist Republic – Soviet Union 51
Crimea – Soviet Union 51
German Democratic Republic 52
*Switzerland, India, Federal Republic of Germany, United States of
    America, the Philippines, Great Britain 52*
Poland 53
Turkey, Germany, Denmark, Great Britain 53
Turkey 55
Chile 55
South Korea 56
United States of America 56
Romania 57
India 57
Republic of China – Taiwan 57
India 58
United States of America 60
South Korea 60
Great Britain 61
Islamic Republic of Iran 62
Germany 64
United States of America 64
Vatican 65

India 66
China 67
Chile 69
Czech Republic 70
Great Britain, France, Italy, Switzerland, Canada 70
China 71
Pakistan 72
Luxembourg 72
United States of America 73
Israel 73
Afghanistan 73
India 74
United States of America 74
South Korea 75
India 76
Myanmar 76
India, Malaysia, Switzerland 76
Tibet – People's Republic of China 77
India 78
Georgia 79
Tunisia, Algeria, Egypt, Mauritania, Italy, the Netherlands,
*   Ethiopia, Jordan, Bahrain, Morocco 79*
Tibet, India, Nepal, China, France 81
India 85
Indonesia 85
Israel 86
Russia 86
Vietnam 86
Albania 87
Bulgaria 87
Sri Lanka 88
Vietnam 88
United States of America 89
Iran 89
South Korea 90
Republic of Somaliland – Somalia 91
Australia, Nauru, Manus Island – Papua New Guinea 91
Mongolia 92
Poland 93

x Contents

PART III
**Selected contemporary ultimate protests by
fire and their echoes across culture**   101

1   A lotus in a sea of fire: on two self-immolations
     performed during the war in Vietnam   103
     *Under the icon's skin: Thích Quảng Đức's political and sacrificial
        auto-cremation (The Republic of Vietnam, 1963) 107*
     *Skin of flame: Norman Morrison's self-immolation (The United
        States, 1965) 132*

2   Confronting defeat: on two protest
     self-incinerations performed after the Warsaw
     Pact invasion of Czechoslovakia   167
     *Two minutes of silence: the self-immolation of Ryszard
        Siwiec (Poland, 1968) 171*
     *The other Jan: the fiery self-sacrifice of Jan Palach
        (Czechoslovakia, 1969) 192*

3   Sparks: on two self-burnings protesting the
     exploitation of subalterns   227
     *A drop of dew: the self-immolation of Chun Tae-il
        (The Republic of Korea, 1970) 231*
     *The drop that made the cup overflow: the protest self-
        burning of Mohamed Bouazizi (Tunisia, 2010) 247*

     Index   275

Figures

All illustrations are courtesy of the artists.

I.1	Wolfgang Stiller *Matchstick Men* (2010)	1
PI.1	Piotr Wyrzykowski *Self-Immolation* (2014)	19
PII.1	Van Thanh Rudd *No Nauru* (2012)	39
PIII.1	Van Thanh Rudd *Special Forces (After Banksy)* (2008)	101
PIII.2	Kevin Maginnis *Self-Immolation* (2013)	167
PIII.3	Majd Abdelhamid *Bouazizi* (2012)	227
PIII.4	Wolfgang Stiller *Matchstick Men* (2010)	274

Acknowledgements

The book is an abridged and updated version of its Polish original *Okrutny teatr samospaleń: protesty samobójcze w ogniu i ich echa w kulturze współczesnej* (Poznań: Wydawnictwo Naukowe UAM, 2018). The translation by Jan Szelągiewicz (Grammaton Translations) was funded by the Faculty of Polish and Classical Philology of the Adam Mickiewicz University in Poznań. The Polish edition summarised the research project *Samospalenie w kulturze współczesnej: akt-widowisko* (*Self-Immolation in Contemporary Culture: The Act-Performance*, 2014–18), financed by a grant from the Narodowe Centrum Nauki (National Science Centre) under its OPUS 6 Programme, grant no. 2013/11/B/HS2/02873.

I extend my warmest appreciation to Paul Allain – a true friend.

I am greatly indebted to Tomasz Mizerkiewicz, the dean of the Faculty of Polish and Classical Philology of the Adam Mickiewicz University in Poznań, for financing the translation.

I would like to express my deepest gratitude to Laura Hussey from Routledge, who made things happen and took great care of this publication. I direct the words of thanks also to Laura Soppelsa and Jeanine Furino for their professionalism at different phases of work on this project.

Let Jan Szelągiewicz – the book's translator – accept my words of appreciation for his expertise, perceptiveness, and precision. And Augustine Allain-Labon – for his marvellous proofreading job.

I wish to thank Jerzy Fiećko, the deputy dean of the Faculty of Polish and Classical Philology of AMU, for his support.

I would like to thank Marzenna Ledzion-Markowska, the director of the Adam Mickiewicz University Press, for agreeing to the publishing of an English-language version of the book.

I cordially thank the artists: Majd Abdelhamid, Kevin Maginnis, Wolfgang Stiller, Van Thanh Rudd, and Piotr Wyrzykowski for kindly sharing photographs of their works and agreeing to publish them in this volume.

My deepest thanks to Dobrochna Ratajczakowa, Marta Steiner, Tadeusz Kornaś, Magda Hasiuk, Maria Bohdziewicz (Witczak), Maciej Zakrzewski, Leszek Kolankiewicz, Elżbieta Rygielska, Maciej Pachowicz, Agata Rokita,

Mohammad Reza Aliakbari, Claudio Santana Bórquez, Giulio Ferretto Salinas, Monika Blige, Maria Kapała, Marta Pautrzak, Paulina Krzeczkowska, Brygida Pawłowska-Jądrzyk, Joanna Krakowska, Halszka Witkowska, Katarzyna Kuczyńska-Koschany, Agata Siwiak, Ewa Guderian-Czaplińska, Maciej Łuczak, Sławomir Wieczorek, Rafał Rosół, Krzysztof Podemski, Jarosław Siejkowski, Krzysztof Gajda, and Arleta Borowiak. All of them were of great assistance at different stages of the work on this volume.

Before and after the book's publication in Polish, I gave multiple talks and delivered papers on the subject of protest self-burnings at conferences in Poland and abroad (in Chile and Iran). The subsequent discussions helped me clarify some thoughts on various issues related to the main theme, for which I thank the participating attendees.

Last but not least, I would like to express my most profound gratitude to my beloved wife, Iwona Gutowska, and our children – Estera and Kajetan Ziółkowski – for their patience, support, and understanding.

Introduction

Figure I.1 Wolfgang Stiller *Matchstick Men* (2010).

The aim, subject, and structure of this book

This interdisciplinary monograph aims to investigate protest self-burnings and their specific variant, namely fiery self-immolations.[1] Suicide protests by fire are performed publicly, intentionally, and voluntarily to defend the values espoused by persons who decide that resorting to this form of resistance is something worth sacrificing their lives for. Self-immolators also attempt to appeal to the consciences, empathy, emotions, and logic of their witnesses and other spectators (opponents, supporters, and the undecided), in order to demand change, highlight the gravity of their cause and persuade others to it, and/or reinforce their stand.

The broader category of *protest self-burning* encompasses all public self-destructions by fire performed as expressions of dissent, while its *self-immolation* subgroup points to those demonstrative acts which were undeniably motivated by altruism and the desire to preserve supra-individual values. Both are extracted here from a wider group of practices, which also includes the following: (a) self-immolations rooted in religious customs and traditions (for example, *sati* or *suttee* – the Hindu funeral rite wherein widows would follow their deceased husbands onto their funeral pyres) (Weinberger-Thomas); (b) deliberate self-burnings (DSBs), that is suicides or suicide attempts for personal reasons, where fire is used as the vehicle of self-annihilation;[2] and (c) body self-burning stunts which aim exclusively at spectacle (a display of skills)[3] or act on a purely utilitarian level (such as events performed in the process of filming or taking attractive photographs).[4]

The book's second objective is to study the resonances of protest self-burnings in contemporary culture, especially in works of art either inspired by or related to them more directly.

The specificity of the complex phenomenon of protest self-burnings, which themselves can be situated alongside other practices of corporeal *necroresistance* (to borrow Banu Bargu's term),[5] flows from its hybrid, borderline quality which combines an individual, extreme, and passionate act of confronting death with a spectacular fire event carried out with others in mind. Its significance may be associated with its increased prevalence in recent decades, which is itself a consequence of (a) the development of mass media that publicise dramatic incidents of this kind, (b) the widespread availability of flammable substances, and (c) the contemporary *politicization of death* and *weaponization of life* (Bargu, *Starve* 62, 65) as "existing forms of protest and access to political representation have become increasingly useless for those feeling marginalised and oppressed" (Taylor, Dan 6).

Sociologist Michael Biggs estimates that between 1963 and 2002 suicide protests by fire were carried out no fewer than 800 times (with the final tally being potentially three or even four times higher)[6] ("Dying" 174). In the following years, cases of fiery self-annihilation appeared in reports with even greater frequency. In the Middle East and North Africa, for example,

Introduction 3

self-burning has become an important and relatively frequent form of protest after 2010, in the wake of the self-destruction of Mohamed Bouazizi, a young Tunisian street vendor, which stirred civil unrest and ultimately led to the Arab Spring. This particular form of radical dissent has also been practised by Tibetans (monks, nuns, and laypeople) who have carried out self-incinerations since 2011 (totalling more than 150 at the time of writing) in protest against the hardline policies of Communist China in the region.

Suicide protests by fire have a long history (Biggs, "How"; Crosby et al.). However, if we dismiss the self-burnings performed *en masse* by Old Believers in Tsarist Russia in the 17th and 18th centuries, driven by both religious and political motivations (Robbins), then the historical record reveals that they actually had been relatively rare, at least until recently, especially in the so-called "Western cultural sphere."[7]

In the 1960s, they entered the global repertoire of peaceful resistance actions and nowadays are associated mainly with non-violent struggle (the violence is directed towards their performers). Their reception began to shift after an elderly Mahāyāna monk, Thích Quảng Đức, self-immolated on 11 June 1963 at a major intersection in the centre of Saigon to protest the persecution of Buddhists by the government of Catholic President Ngô Đình Diệm. The act – calling on centuries-old religious traditions and meticulously staged by representatives of the Buddhist community who actively sought to make it as public as possible (Taylor, Dan 4) – was immortalised in a series of photographs taken by American reporter Malcolm Browne. The graphic images shocked the public in the US and across the globe. Their content, sheer visual power, and strong reception ended up influencing American policy towards the Washington-backed Diệm regime, itself overthrown less than five months later in a military coup that left the president and his brother Ngô Đình Nhu brutally murdered. The monk's ultimate sacrifice, preceding the escalation of the war in Vietnam, can be considered the founding act of this particular practice of resistance in present times (Biggs, "How" 416–420; Plank 186–188); its photographic representations, meanwhile, can be seen as iconic of the turbulent 1960s, a decade which remains immensely influential in shaping the late modern world.

The Buddhist protest auto-cremations, which continued in Vietnam after Đức's pivotal act, in turn encouraged American peace activists, who began carrying out self-immolations to oppose the war which their government was waging across the Pacific and "perhaps to denounce their country's guilt, perhaps to erase some of it by their sacrifice, perhaps to simply urge an end to the slaughter" (Andriolo 106). These sacrifices included middle-aged Quaker Norman Morrison, who set fire to himself outside the Pentagon in 1965. Vietnamese self-incinerations almost certainly inspired Polish philosopher and accountant Ryszard Siwiec (1968), and Czechoslovak history student Jan Palach (1969), whose self-burnings were intended to decry the Warsaw Pact's 1968 invasion of Czechoslovakia and the apathy of their countrymen, bred

4 Introduction

by the ruthless indoctrination and oppression of their respective regimes. It is also highly likely that the Vietnamese fire protests inspired Chun Tae-il (1970), a young South Korean worker and activist struggling to improve labour conditions, who set himself ablaze to publicise the inhuman treatment suffered by South Korean textile workers in the rapidly developing country. These five acts are widely considered the most striking examples of self-immolations in contemporary history.

This book, however, will append to the list the self-burning of Bouazizi whose act, although admittedly impulsive and prompted by personal reasons (a sense of humiliation and harm), was still performed publicly outside a local magistrate and with multiple eyewitnesses, and will thus be considered an act of suicide protest, too. Besides, as Nicholas Michelsen (87–89) and Bargu ("Why" 28) have convincingly argued, Bouazizi's intentions were secondary to the retrospective understanding of his act in political terms, and also to the fact that it had an extensive ripple effect which brought about wide-ranging changes in the socio-political sphere.

Protest self-burnings have been performed (a) across the globe, (b) mainly outdoors and in public (usually in locations either symbolically charged or associated with authority), but also in prisons, detention centres, and other indoor sites, (c) individually, simultaneously, or in waves, (d) as part of other protest actions (also extreme ones) or by individual (e) women and men, adults, and teenagers of (f) different races, nationalities, class or education backgrounds, and sexual orientations, (g) followers of various religions and atheists, (h) subscribers to a wide spectrum of political views, (i) members of organisations and those without affiliations, all of whom have, at one point or another, decided to express their dissent to (j) a range of different issues. Moreover, although these final acts were (k) often meticulously orchestrated, (l) many eventually turned out to be futile or at least only partly successful as a protest method. In consequence, it is difficult – perhaps even impossible – to squeeze them all into one conceptual frame (Shakya 21). Therefore, rather than provide a comprehensive theoretical background of the phenomenon, Part I of this book will attempt to map it and outline some related notions and perspectives. Indebted to Biggs' sociological argument and drawing on discourses transcending the Foucauldian paradigm of *sovereignty* and *biopower,* these conceptualisations comprise a backdrop for subsequent in-depth studies and, hopefully, help make sense of those borderline actions which so violently contest the biopolitical obligations of self-preservation, productivity, and well-being.

Part II features an annotated timeline of protest self-burnings, supplemented with notes on artworks inspired by a given case (where available). The timeline was compiled from a broad range of printed and online sources, in response to the lack of comprehensive and updated statistical data. It is my presumption that such a calendar may help readers grasp the global dimension of fiery suicide protests, the spectrum of issues raised by self-burners, and whether they were indeed agents of change. In my view, the chronology is more than just a complement: it is in fact a key ingredient that feeds and supports the conceptual section; therefore, it is located immediately after it, instead of near the tail end of the book, as is customary with such compilations. The other reason for my decision to stray from tradition, so to speak, was the desire to impress upon the readers that the configuration of cases discussed in Part III could be different and that many other examples – fiery acts by women chief among them – deserve equal attention and further in-depth studies. Besides, the chronology clearly demonstrates that protest self-burnings have mirrored and amplified many major upheavals that have shaken the world over the past half century.

Part III forms the publication's core and consists of six case studies of the aforementioned final acts, performed for a variety of reasons in different parts of the world. The acts are linked in pairs, arranged in chronological order, and provided with their own complex, multidimensional, and interdisciplinary *thick description* to employ Clifford Geertz's phrase, drawing from a variety of sources, including text, audio, visual, and audiovisual, as well as from disparate discourses, including academic, press, and artistic, to name but a few. Even though I consider these ultimate acts to be consequences of individual decisions, I am aware that they did not happen in a vacuum, therefore I not only focus on the people who performed them and their motivations, but also discuss the contexts involved and the circumstances from which the incidents developed. The choice of individual cases for further study was motivated by four main factors. First, by selecting cases from different countries and cultural backgrounds, I sought to highlight the phenomenon's global reach. Second, my intent was to shed light on the problems that most often spurred protest self-burnings, such as (a) religious discrimination and resultant harassment, (b) war and its horrors, (c) the brutality and indoctrination of authoritarian regimes and the apathy they spawn, and (d) the exploitation of the subalterns and their exclusion from mainstream economic systems. Third, the choice was driven by the availability and reliability of sources. Fourth, the cases discussed in Part III elicited the strongest and, in my opinion, the most valuable reactions in the artistic domain.

As a result, the book is something of a double hybrid. On the one hand, it aspires to cover two areas of study: real acts of ultimate protest by fire and their reverberations across art and culture; on the other hand, it comprises three autonomous parts which can be read independently of one another, but which are arranged to produce a strong synergistic effect. Ideally, they will reinforce each other in the reader's perception and, hopefully, together deliver a meaning greater than the sum of their parts.

A cruel *theatre* of protest self-burnings?

The cruelty intrinsic to a protest self-burning is twofold. The act itself is literally cruel, merciless, and ruthless on both physical and psychological levels. Above all, it is cruel not only to the person who performs it, but also – to some

6 Introduction

extent – to the witnesses of their actions, who might be horrified, shocked, and experience complete stupefaction at the very sight. If the act does not immediately kill the protester, it generally leaves them with grave injuries. Setting oneself ablaze usually yields a burned body – abject flesh which can elicit revulsion and which, at the very least, some of us would fear or hate to touch. The act produces ash and smoke, leaving behind the odour of charred skin and burned fat. But it is also cruel in an Artaudian sense of determination and rigour.[8] For the person performing it, the act may stem from ultimate self-examination and be driven by an unshakeable will to express one's beliefs. It is often committed to stir the spectators, to rouse them from their emotional torpor, and to tear down their tepid morality – to push those who stand witness towards self-analysis, compel them to examine their consciences, and ask themselves the fundamental question: is any cause actually worth sacrificing one's life for?

But is this act ultimately a performance? Is it befitting to talk about the *theatre* of protest self-burnings, a cruel theatre even, in the vein of Antonin Artaud's Theatre of Cruelty? Or is it simply cynical of us to perceive it as a theatrical event or spectacle? (Weiler 125)

Access to Evil, a 2004 documentary directed by Polish journalist, director, and producer Ewa Ewart, features the testimony of one Kwon Hyok, a senior North Korean military intelligence official, who was persuaded by Western intelligence during his 1999 visit to China to defect to Seoul. Prior to his escape, he headed the notorious Haengyŏn Camp, also referred to as Camp No. 22, and his debriefing revealed how the camp was ran and brought to light the fact that its staff was tasked with conducting human experimentation, including testing poison gases and choking agents. To quote from his testimony:

> The scientists sit around the edge and observe the experiment from above, through the glass. The injection tube comes down through the unit … I watched a whole family being tested on suffocating gas and dying in the gas chamber. … The parents were vomiting and dying, but until the very last moment, they tried to save their kids by doing mouth to mouth breathing.[9]
>
> (Kwon Hyok in *Access to Evil*)

Employing the methodologies developed by contemporary humanities and social sciences and later absorbed by performance studies, one could conceive the situation described above as a totalitarian variant of *theatrum anatomicum*: the reactions of the prisoners – who may be perceived as the epitome of Giorgio Agamben's *bare life* (life vulnerable to omnipotent violence) and who performed the imposed roles of human guinea pigs – were studied from behind the glass by researchers and medical doctors. But the people imprisoned in this laboratory or in this *necropolitical space*, to borrow from Achille Mbembe, did not (re)present nor display anything, and perhaps were not even

Introduction 7

aware they were being watched while in extremis. According to the account, they were struggling to save the lives of their kin and their own, and indeed, it is secondary that this horrifying situation – in the fact that their (re)actions and behaviour became the subject of direct observation and live study – was turned into a performative event. By referring to this particular case, I am asserting that applying categories such as *spectacle, show, presentation, theatre*, or *performance* (in its narrow sense related to an event "on display," intended to be watched) to the camp situation would not get us far. On the contrary, these concepts would obscure rather than illuminate the overwhelming truth about the atrocious event that attempted to reduce human life to naked powerlessness and to rob it of dignity.[10] The situation, however, is starkly different in the case of protest self-burnings.

Suicide protests by fire are performances because they (a) aim to be transformative, (b) imply standing out (literally) from a crowd or a group, and (c) are, at their very core, intentional acts of communication that use self-inflicted bodily suffering and the high likelihood of death as their main vehicles for argument. Although underpinned by suicidal intent, the decision to take one's own life in this case is not motivated by stress, depression, frustration, or other emotional problems, but rather by the desire to reach out to an audience, both on site and through media. As a means of inflicting torment and (most often) death or (less often) the permanent mutilation of those who perform them, protest self-burnings are usually watched (in an immediate or mediated manner) and are meant to be watched. They seek to augment the community's collective consciousness and harness the radicalism of the act to unravel the fabric of communal life. Although one of the most drastic ways of drawing attention to social crises and their attendant tensions, they also are an uncompromising attempt to resolve this crises through self-sacrifice. Therefore, they may be seen as an element of *social drama* as conceptualised by Victor Turner, and eventually lead to the emergence of anti-structural communities fostering a sense of *communitas* (togetherness).

As such, they appear to be performative acts (I call them *acts-performances*), because, on the one hand, they are acts of sacrifice and communication, while, on the other, they are performances of dissent which resort to the real, spectacular, and symbolic potency of fire, and which are often orchestrated with considerable attention to detail. Their performers decide the venues of their pleas, pore over prop selection and the phrasing of their speeches, plan scenarios, and define the audiences. They also try to shape the reception of their acts by using banners, pamphlets, and/or farewell letters. The performances themselves feature actions that adjust and adapt to existing patterns (Richard Schechner's *restored behaviour*), such as the distribution of messages and/or slogans or the occasional incorporation of symbolic postures, like the distinctive meditative position, for example. All of the above situate protest self-burnings alongside other types of social, political, and *cultural performances* (as defined by Milton Singer), and – especially – among other *necroperformances*, to borrow Dorota Sajewska's concept.

8   Introduction

The remarks above clearly demonstrate that my usage of the term *theatre* in the title of the book is not merely metaphorical. The theatre, chiefly associated in social and political life with the realm of unreality and illusion, sometimes with pretending, flippancy, and even tomfoolery, is here understood differently: as a synonym for earnest performance and an existential entreaty delivered within the public sphere.

Approach

Since its escalation in the 1960s, the phenomenon of protest self-burnings has been explored across a number of studies and interpretations, drawn up by scholars hailing from disparate academic fields. Psychologists and psychiatrists tend to treat them as suicides resulting from post-traumatic disorder, depression, frustrations, and other ailments of the psyche (Kelly). Sociologists, on the other hand, see in them examples of *altruistic suicide* (Czabański) and consider some cases to be variants of the Werther effect (*copycat suicide*), when an act is prompted by an earlier suicidal death which then becomes a reference point, especially after it had been widely publicised (Coleman). Together with political scholars (Bargu, *Starve*, "Why"; Fierke; Kim; Michelsen), sociologists situate demonstrative self-burnings within a broader spectrum of practices of dissent and forms of politicised self-destruction, such as indefinite hunger strikes and fasts to death, and view them as elements of what Simanti Lahiri calls *suicide mobilisations* and as weapons in struggles for shared values. Some also compare them to terrorist attacks, asserting that protest self-burnings are likewise spectacular and (usually) fatal practices of resistance, but – unlike the attacks – expose to physical danger and destruction only the sacrificant, in most cases at least. Scholars of religions view protest auto-cremations as elements of sacred traditions and locate them alongside other sacrificial actions, including self-mortification and self-harm (Benn; Jan).[11] In the following deliberations, I draw on findings developed within these fields, as well as on historiographical discourse and my own factual research.

Nonetheless, my own inquiry into the subject in question takes place in the wake of the blurring of the genres, to resort to Clifford Geertz's wording, that has occurred within academic discourses expressing diverse configurations of social and cultural thought over the closing decades of the 20th century. It also follows the *performative turn* in the humanities, which included, to quote Polish historian Ewa Domańska's interpretation,

> a disposition towards agency and change produced in reality, the expansion of the understanding of agency to include inhuman entities (post-humanist aspect of the performative idiom), interdisciplinarity or antidisciplinarity of scholarship, and the abandonment of the metaphor of world understood as text in favour of a different one, one that conceived the world as ... a performance that you participate in. (52)

This is why I decided to include in my deliberations the perspectives and notions developed by performance studies, following in the vein of scholars such as Richard Gough in the UK, James Harding and Joseph Shahadi in the US, and Robert Kulmiński and Iwona Kurz in Poland. But that is not my sole reason for doing so.

As aptly contended by Banu Bargu in her illuminating and well-theorised *Starve and Immolate*, a study of fasts to death performed in Turkish prisons in the 2000s, different forms of resistance correlate with the dominant modalities of power relations. Bargu asserts that

> Since subjects are shaped in and through power relations, their practices, including their practices of resistance, carry the stamp of the power regime that molds their subjectivities. As a counterpower, resistance is shaped by and responds to the dominant characteristics of the prevailing power regime and the technologies of violence it deploys upon its objects. (54)

Building upon the Foucauldian slant, Bargu's book made "a case, theoretically and empirically, for *biosovereignty*, which indicates the contradictory amalgamation of sovereignty and biopolitics as the distinguishing feature of contemporary power regimes" (Bargu, *Starve* 26). In other words, power regimes extend their rule over contemporary societies through *both* disciplinary power (applied to individual bodies) and biopower (applied to social bodies). According to Bargu, the prevalence of self-destructive practices as means of resistance in late modernity can be viewed as flowing from the "increased biopoliticization of sovereign power" (27). Therefore, *biosovereignty* is inevitably contested by practices of *necroresistance* which wrench "the power of life and death away from the apparatuses of the modern state in which this power is conventionally vested" (27).

To supplement Bargu's convincing argument, I would like to refer here to Jon McKenzie's penetrating intimations included in his groundbreaking volume *Perform or Else: From Discipline to Performance*, an inquiry into performance paradigms of efficacy (of cultural performance), efficiency (of organisational performance), and effectiveness (of technological performance). McKenzie asserts that in late modernity, *performance* replaced Foucauldian *discipline* as the instrumental force in the construction of subjectivities and their internalised modes of control. In other words, it is performance that drives the contemporary ontological formation of power-knowledge, just like discipline had done in the 18th and 19th centuries. McKenzie explains: "While disciplinary institutions and mechanisms forged Western Europe's industrial revolution and its system of colonial empires, those of performance are programming the circuits of our postindustrial, postcolonial world" (18).

The passage suggests that the turn from discipline to performance should be attributed to the consolidation of the Western capitalist economy, the development of communication technologies, and the rapid growth and expansion of mass media, among other factors. It would seem, therefore, that – as per Bargu's deliberations – both discipline and biopower continue to play an essential role in shaping and controlling the knowledge and behaviour of individuals and populations. However, following McKenzie's reasoning, these modalities of power which form what Bargu called a *biosovereign assemblage* (*Starve* 53) should be supplemented with *performativity* as a substantial dimension underpinning contemporary power relations. Protest self-burnings – in post-Foucauldian language the radical and voluntary reenactments of the violence of biosovereign power – can be thus viewed as responses to, and consequences of, the pressures exerted by performative requirements, which include the aforementioned "(un)holy trinity" of efficacy, efficiency, and effectiveness, further reinforced by the demand for *spectacularity* (intensified visibility) – essential in the context of this study – that permeates the contemporary world. The argument above, therefore, spells out the other reason for this study's turn towards performance studies.

This model interdisciplinary approach sheds light on those events of public life where individuals gather and find themselves involved in dynamic situations in which it is essential to develop means of representing specific notions and of sharing energy. It also provides comprehensive insight into social and cultural phenomena and their symbiotic and synergistic relationship with the realm of artistic creation (Carlson). Hence, my decision to include (and highlight) the views of individual artists in order to potentially enrich prior attempts at explaining the phenomenon and to contribute to its exhaustive understanding. On the other hand, however, I cannot imagine that any study of artworks related to protest self-burnings could be considered complete without the following thorough examination of both the acts themselves – that is without exploring their circumstances and course, their locations and precise dates, as well as the props and phrasing that accompanied them – and their attendant contexts. One must also scrutinise the motivations of their performers, their further reception, and their potential consequences.

Echoes in contemporary culture

Protest self-burnings ignite artists' imaginations. This is, in itself, not surprising since self-burnings stand as proof of the uncompromising nature of human beings, which is embodied here by their capability to sacrifice their lives to amplify the expression of their grievances, dissentions, and objections. Art – as an exemplary space wherein new solutions can be sought, the status quo rejected and transformed, and radicalism and rebellion cultivated – willingly confronts examples of borderline actions. After all, art itself also probes, pushes, and renegotiates limits, edges, and extremes.

Nonetheless, the majority of works produced in response to protest self-burnings commemorate them in a rather conservative manner, as if putting themselves in the service of a far greater cause. Artworks that raise doubts and question clichés are rather rare, since in the artistic domain self-burners are usually glorified, and the heroic dimension of their acts is emphasised and cherished. Provocative or iconoclastic efforts are almost non-existent, as if the artists were intimidated by the drastic nature of such events and their radicalism, and as if they were afraid to trivialise or "desecrate" them. After all, as Polish theatre scholar Grzegorz Niziołek emphatically remarked, "no shock induced by a work of art can be treated as equivalent to someone's traumatic experience" (15).

But there are exceptions, as exemplified by the work of Polish performer and media artist, Piotr Wyrzykowski, who famously designed a virtual protest self-burning kit in 2014. The witty, ironic, and controversial piece comprised a smartphone app and a portable podium that allowed anyone to safely express their objection to anything anywhere (but only once a day) and spread news of the protest via social media outlets. The piece lent credence to the notion that in contemporary culture, especially in its currently prevailing form of pop culture, protest self-burnings no longer occupy an inviolably sacred space protected by unwritten rules of political correctness. There are hundreds of cartoons and graffiti pieces, in both real and virtual spaces, that refer to self-immolation and treat it mainly as an allegory of opposition to various issues.[12] The motif was even exploited in advertising – one example being Pepsi's notorious 2008 campaign, which proved so controversial that the posters had to be withdrawn. The iconic photographs of Thích Quảng Đức engulfed in flames have been repeatedly replicated, remediated, and re-worked, also in a playful and/or ironic manner, as in the case of a neon light installation designed by American visual artist Kevin Maginnis.

The efforts outlined above demonstrate that protest self-burnings continue to occupy a prominent position in the collective imagination, where they function as an equivalent of and synonym for intransigent resistance. As acknowledged by other artworks examined in this volume, suicidal fire protests are seen as gestures of final and solemn dissent, one that cannot simply be ignored.[13] The most worthwhile pieces that I focus on, with regard to the six cases discussed here, stand as expressions of empathy and interrogate the various dimensions of borderline experiences. Rather than reflect upon them in negative terms, using concepts such as "crisis, agony, lack, emptiness, rupture, oppressive power, exclusion, and repression" (Nader 25–26), they instead point to the agency and potency of their subjects.

Obviously, the theme of protest self-burning does not function within the realm of art solely as a response to specific incidents but also at a more general level. To illustrate this, I choose from many examples of such artworks a handful of the most emblematic (in my opinion) and describe them briefly here.

First on the list is Tadeusz Konwicki's 1979 novel *Mała apokalipsa* (*A Minor Apocalypse*), which portrays self-burning as a means of confronting the gloomy and dejected reality of the Polish People's Republic. The self-sacrifice that the protagonist is encouraged to perform by activists from dissident circles is supposed to lay bare society's sin of indifference, but – as Polish literary scholar

12 Introduction

Przemysław Czapliński argued – the act could "never offer deliverance nor redemption to society, as society considers itself blameless" (155).[14]

The second suggestive piece is Andrei Tarkovsky's penultimate film *Nostalghia* (*Nostalgia*, 1983) which culminates in a scene portraying a fiery self-sacrifice performed by a recluse who rejects the cynical and secularised world. Domenico's final gesture, executed on behalf of the powerless and the marginalised, may be read as a solemn act of self-denial or a wholly destructive deed, committed under the influence of a peculiar ideological self-hypnosis or following from mental instability. Rather than outwardly glorifying it, Tarkovsky juxtaposes it with a symbolic, ritualised, and extrainstitutional sacrifice, like that performed by Andrei Gorchakov (another protagonist in the film), which potentially stands as a testament to selflessness and the rejection of egotistical calculation.

Wojciech Smarzowski's 2018 box office hit drama *Kler* (*The Clergy*) also features a depiction of self-immolation that was not based on any real-life event. A critique of the Catholic Church in Poland and the abuses of power committed by its functionaries, the picture – which made quite a stir in both Poland and among the Polish diaspora – concludes with a self-incineration at a mass religious service. The act is performed by a priest suspected of pedophilia, whose prior attempts to inform the media about the extent of the local clergy's transgressions came to nothing. He ultimately decides to embrace self-burning to shed light on the widespread problems that the Church is concealing from the public. It is also possible that the deed was an attempt at expiating his own sins.

In my opinion, however, the clearest and most distinct example of the confrontation between the realm of art and the horror of self-immolation can be found in Ingmar Bergman's seminal 1966 *Persona*. In the film, the real-life fiery protest of a Buddhist monk (Thích Thiện Mỹ) in Saigon is watched on TV by stage actress Elizabet Vogler, who was admitted to an observation ward following an incident where she had stopped speaking mid-performance. Vogler's gesture can be interpreted as a somewhat futile rebuke of the hollowness and duplicity of the world.[15] In a monograph on the work of the Swedish director, Polish film scholar Tadeusz Szczepański wrote that confronted with true terror, the actress once again succumbs to a sense of unreality. Later on, he made a case for that particular scene, arguing that "In *Persona*, Bergman sought to prove that modern art is unable to cope with and bear witness to the horror of 20th century reality, the moral burden of which the artist simply can no longer put up with" (282). With *Persona*, the legendary Swedish filmmaker seemed to argue that in the face of the impossible savagery of the modern world, artists could neither indulge in escapist fantasies nor stay silent.

Bergman's notions would find purchase in the practices of artists–activists (*artivists* in Diana Taylor's vocabulary), such as the Guatemalan-born representative of radical body art Regina José Galindo (active since 1999) or Petr

Pavlensky, a Russian performer who drew on her work (active since 2012). Their transgressive, subversive, and provocative pursuits, straddling the intersection of critical art and political activism, often involved self-injury and self-harm (Taylor, Diana; Kutyła and Walaszkowski). The works of the two *artivists*, with their commitment to the genuine violation of bodily integrity in pursuit of drawing attention to grave political and social issues, seem to come the closest out of all artistic efforts to protest self-burnings. The correlation between the two, however, will not be explored any further here, as the matter demands and warrants a separate and broader inquiry.

Inconclusiveness

In the famous mystical poem *The Conference of the Birds*, penned in 1177 CE by the Persian poet and Sufi theorist, Farīd ud-Dīn Attar tells of three moths who wish to penetrate the essence of candlelight (206). As it turns out, only the one who touches the flame and burns is able to grasp the truth, but that truth is incinerated along with its body. The tale appears near the end of the poem, when the birds, in search of an ideal king, the mythical Simorgh, reach the final valley – the Valley of Poverty and Annihilation. For devout Sufis, their quest is an allegory of the soul's journey to its divine source, while the self-burning moth exemplifies the soul consumed by its love of God.

As it appears, the import of the tale can be applied to other fields, as well. At its core, the story reminds us that if we wish to penetrate into the heart of something, we must commit to the process wholeheartedly, as half-measures may end up leading us astray. Simultaneously, however, success in the search is by no means dependent on the intensity of the passion with which it is undertaken.

As I was putting the finishing touches to this book's original Polish version, on 19 October 2017 Piotr Szczęsny, a chemist and my contemporary, set himself ablaze to protest against the illiberal policies pursued by Poland's majority ruling party. A few hours after his immolation 300 km from where I was passionately typing away, a Warsaw-based friend sent me pictures of the venue of Szczęsny's protest: a spot outside the Palace of Culture and Science in the city centre, once a symbol of the oppressive power of the former Communist regime. In a heartbeat, the broad, abstract issue of protest self-burning transformed for me into a poignant, tangible reality. The tragic event and its disturbing aftermath in Poland, both of which deserve their separate studies, touched me on a deeply personal level and brought to my mind Attar's parable. I felt myself palpably facing the sublime mystery of human power – a mystery I could neither penetrate nor hope to unravel, despite being equipped by my work on the subject with a plethora of explicative conceptualisations. I was perhaps no less confused than Michel Foucault, who pondered the motivations behind the immolations of Tunisian rebel students in 1968: "What on earth is it that can set off in an individual the desire, the capacity and the

14 Introduction

possibility of an absolute sacrifice without our being able to recognize or suspect the slightest ambition or desire for power and profit" (136).

Shocked and saddened by the tragic incident, and frustrated by my impotence and hubris, I thought back to Clifford Geertz's warnings about the limitations of cultural analysis that "is intrinsically incomplete."

> And, worse than that, the more deeply it goes the less complete it is. It is a strange science whose most telling assertions are its most tremulously based, in which to get somewhere with the matter at hand is to intensify the suspicion, both your own and that of others, that you are not quite getting it right.
>
> (Geertz 29)

Therefore, on account of Szczęsny's horrifying act – and Geertz's powerful ideas – I decided to leave the book inconclusive.

Notes

1 Given the Latin etymology (the word *molare* refers to the ritual sacrifice of a salted flour cake, the *mola salsa*), the term *self-immolation* literally means *self-sacrifice*, the sacrificing of one's own life. The phrase was previously applied to fasts to death undertaken by Irish protesters between 1913 and 1923 and later under the Thatcher government in the 1980s (Sweeney), among other events. However, in light of the impact that sacrificial and protest self-burnings that swept Vietnam in the 1960s had on international public opinion, the term's import shifted towards primarily signifying an act of altruistic self-burning (King 148; Park 82). For the purpose of this study, the expression *self-immolation* will be used in its present meaning of *self-sacrifice by fire* and the modifiers distinguishing it from other types of fatal self-sacrifice will not be employed.

2 A vast body of scholarship on this topic (see, for example, Gauthier et al.; Laloë; Laloë and Ganesan; Rothschild et al.) proves that DSB is a suicide method that occurs worldwide, across vastly diverse societies with scant sociocultural or religious overlap. In contrast to other methods of suicide, DSBs are committed relatively rarely (although research indicates that they are more common across Asia, particularly among women). DSB is pursued primarily as a result of mental illness (more frequent in the West) or due to intra-familial tensions and adjustment problems (more frequent in Asia).

3 This particular aspect is well illustrated by attempts to set a new World Guinness Record for the most people performing *full body burns*. One such attempt, held on 19 October 2013, involved 21 stuntmen in special jumpsuits setting themselves alight in a parking lot near the Cuyahoga River in Cleveland, thus breaking the previous record of 17 simultaneous burnings of this kind. The venue chosen for the attempt was not random – back in the 1960s the Cuyahoga was so polluted with crude oil derivatives that it tended to spontaneously combust, thus giving rise to its popular moniker, the Burning River.

4 The artwork for Pink Floyd's 1975 LP *Wish You Were Here* is one example. The cover features a picture of two men shaking hands, one of whom is burning, probably a reference to the colloquial phrase *getting burned*, used in the music industry to describe a situation where a record label would refuse to pay artists for services rendered.

Introduction 15

5 The phrase denotes "the self-destructive practices that forge life into a weapon as a specific modality of resistance." In consequence, these practices transform "the body from the site of subjection to a site of insurgency" (Bargu, *Starve* 27, 85).

6 The fact that only certain countries consider self-burning a separate category in suicide statistics (Poland does, but only since 2017) gives rise to rather fundamental research problems, including the futility of trying to gauge the prevalence of that particular form of protest.

7 James Benn asserts that in medieval China, "self-immolation was not only common but also enduring and largely respected within the tradition" (210). Among the numerous reasons behind the Chinese Buddhists' self-sacrificial practices was the desire to protest against religious persecution.

8 Antonin Artaud, French actor, director, and visionary, wished to liberate the idea of theatre from the oppression of psychologism and tear down its conversational nature by embracing, in the early 1930s, what he called the Theatre of Cruelty. In this particular context, however, cruelty implied "neither sadism nor bloodshed," but "rigor, implacable intention and decision, irreversible and absolute determination" (Artaud 101).

9 Here and elsewhere, quotes from films are sourced directly from their scripts, subtitles, or soundtracks.

10 Lisa Guenther's counter-Agamben argument bears repeating in this particular context: "Even when reduced to a 'naked relation to naked existence,' even when exposed to an unimaginable extremity of need and affliction, even when forced to steal from others in order to secure one's own survival, the subject retains a relation to alterity which provides a starting point, however minimal, for resistance. This relationality remains even when every relation to every particular other has been severed, and it remains even when the subject who would be in relation to others – the I, the ego – has been utterly destroyed" (75).

11 Naturally, self-harm can also be performed as part of a political protest. One particularly suggestive example of such a protest was the lip sewing incident carried out on 19 January 2002 by almost 60 detainees held at the notorious Woomera Immigration Reception and Processing Centre in Australia.

12 Protest self-burning was also unintentionally trivialised by the actions of Polish rapper and music producer Andrzej Żuromski, who, during a 2013 appearance on a current affairs show, doused his sweatshirt with a small amount of a flammable liquid and set fire to himself to show off on television. The stunt proved harmless, as he quickly removed his clothes and the host immediately moved to extinguish the flames.

13 This type of perception of protest self-burnings can also be found in rather unexpected locations, such as detective novels. For example, Swedish author and journalist Mons Kallentoft pointed out in his popular series *Fire Hunters* that people who set themselves on fire often take great pains to secure an audience.

14 The novel was later adapted for the theatre and staged multiple times since its 1982 premiere, including at the anti-establishment Teatr Ósmego Dnia (Theatre of the Eighth Day) in Poznań, where it premiered in June 1985. The novel was also reworked into a film, a 1993 comedy directed by Constantin Costa-Gavras. In the loose adaptation, two left-leaning Parisian intellectuals encourage a Polish writer to self-immolate in order to bring attention to his works and then profit off the subsequent publicity. It bears repeating here that the French director of Greek descent also directed the 2002 film *Amen*, based on Rolf Hochhuth's seminal play *Der Stellvertreter* (*The Representative* or *The Deputy*, 1963), a critical appraisal of the relationship between the Vatican and Nazi Germany. The film opens with the suicide protest of Štefan Lux, who shot himself at the League of

16 Introduction

Nations building in Geneva during the 3 July 1936 session. The Czechoslovak journalist, actor, and director intended for his protest to draw attention to Adolf Hitler's expansionism and to decry virulent Nazi antisemitism.

15 Obviously, as correctly noted by Susan Sontag in her classic essay published in *Styles of Radical Will*, Bergman allows the spectator to interpret Elizabet's silence not only as a deliberate moral decision but also as a nervous breakdown.

References

The online resources identified below were consulted multiple times. All of them were active as of 1 December 2018.

Access to Evil. Directed by Ewa Ewart, BBC, 2004. *YouTube.* www.youtube.com/watch?v=upOhzsSTMDs&index=7&list=PL72678481055B0FD1.

Agamben, Giorgio. *Homo Sacer: Sovereign Power and Bare Life.* Translated by Daniel Heller-Roazen, Stanford UP, 1998.

Andriolo, Karin. "The Twice-Killed: Imagining Protest Suicide." *American Anthropologist*, vol. 108, no. 1, 2006, pp. 100–113.

Artaud, Antonin. *The Theatre and Its Double.* Translated by Mary Caroline Richards, Grove Press, 1958.

Attar, Farid ud-Din. *The Conference of the Birds.* Translated by Afkham Darbandi and Dick Davis, Penguin Books, 1984.

Bargu, Banu. *Starve and Immolate: The Politics of Human Weapons.* Columbia UP, 2014.

———. "Why Did Bouazizi Burn Himself? The Politics of Fate and Fatal Politics." *Constellations*, vol. 23, no. 1, 2016, pp. 27–36.

Benn, James. "Multiple Meanings of Buddhist Self-Immolation in China: A Historical Perspective." *Revue d'Etudes Tibétaines*, no. 25, 2012, pp. 203–212.

Biggs, Michael. "Dying Without Killing: Self-Immolations, 1963–2002." *Making Sense of Suicide Missions*, edited by Diego Gambetta, Oxford UP, 2005, pp. 173–208.

———. "How Repertories Evolve: The Diffusion of Suicide Protest in the Twentieth Century." *Mobilization: An International Quarterly*, vol. 18, no. 4, 2013, pp. 407–428.

Carlson, Marvin. *Performance: A Critical Introduction.* 3rd edition. Routledge, 2018.

Coleman, Loren. "Fiery Copycats." *The Copycat Effect: How the Media and Popular Culture Trigger the Mayhem in Tomorrow's Headlines*, edited by Loren Coleman, Paraview Pocket Books, 2004, pp. 48–66.

Crosby, Kevin et al. "Suicide by Fire: A Contemporary Method of Political Protest." *International Journal of Social Psychiatry*, vol. 23, no. 1, 1977, pp. 60–69.

Czabański, Adam. *Samobójstwa altruistyczne. Formy manifestacji, mechanizmy i społeczne reperkusje zjawiska* [Altruistic Suicides: Forms of Manifestations, Mechanisms, and Social Repercussions]. Nomos, 2009.

Czapliński, Przemysław. *Tadeusz Konwicki.* Rebis, 1994.

Domańska, Ewa. "'Zwrot performatywny' we współczesnej humanistyce" ['Performative Turn' in Contemporary Humanities]. *Teksty Drugie* [Warsaw], no. 5, 2007, pp. 48–61.

Fierke, Karin. *Political Self-Sacrifice: Agency, Body and Emotion in International Relations.* Cambridge UP, 2013.

Foucault, Michel. *Remarks on Marx.* Conversations with Duccio Trombadori, translated by R. James Goldstein and James Cascaito, Semitext(e), 1991.

Gauthier, Saskia et al. "Self-Burning: A Rare Suicide Method in Switzerland and Other Industrialised Nations." *Burns*, vol. 40, no. 8, 2014, pp. 1720–1726.

Geertz, Clifford. *The Interpretation of Cultures: Selected Essays*. Basic Books, 1973.

Gough, Richard. "Burning Bodies: Transformation and Fire." *Performance Research*, vol. 18, no. 1, 2013, pp. 9–23.

Guenther, Lisa. "Resisting Agamben: The Biopolitics of Shame and Humiliation." *Philosophy and Social Criticism*, vol. 38, no. 1, pp. 59–79.

Harding, James M. "Incendiary Acts And Apocryphal Avant-Gardes: Thích Quảng Đức, Self-Immolation, and Buddhist Spiritual Vanguardism." *Performing Arts Journal*, vol. 38, no. 3, 2016, pp. 31–50.

Jan, Yün-hua. "Buddhist Self-Immolation in Medieval China." *History of Religions*, vol. 4, no. 2, 1965, pp. 243–268.

Kallentoft, Mons. *Łowcy ognia* [Fire Hunters]. Translated by Anna Krochmal and Robert Kędzierski, Rebis, 2017.

Kelly, Brendan D. "Self-Immolation, Suicide and Self-Harm in Buddhist and Western Traditions." *Transcultural Psychiatry*, vol. 48, no. 3, 2011, pp. 299–317.

Kim, Hyojoung. "Micromobilization and Suicide Protest in South Korea, 1970–2004." *Social Research*, vol. 75, no. 2, 2008, pp. 543–578.

King, Sallie B. "They Who Burned Themselves for Peace: Quaker and Buddhist Self-Immolators During the Vietnam War." *Buddhist-Christian Studies*, vol. 20, 2000, pp. 127–150.

Konwicki, Tadeusz. *A Minor Apocalypse*. Translated from the Polish by Richard Lourie, Farrar, Straus, Giroux, 1983.

Kulmiński, Robert. *'Tu pali się ktoś...' Ryszard Siwiec, Jan Palach, Zdeněk Adamec* ['Here Is Someone Burning...']. Libron, 2016.

Kurz, Iwona. "Między chrztem a samospaleniem. 'Teatra polskie' drugiej połowy lat 60." [Between Baptism and Self-Immolation: 'Polish Performances' in the Second Half of the 1960s]. *1968/PRL/Teatr*, edited by Agata Adamiecka-Sitek et al., Instytut Teatralny im. Zbigniewa Raszewskiego, 2016, pp. 23–41.

Kutyła, Julian, and Patryk Walaszkowski, editors. *Pawlenski*. Wydawnictwo Krytyki Politycznej, 2016.

Lahiri, Simanti. "Choosing to Die: Suicide Bombing and Suicide Protest in South Asia." *Terrorism and Political Violence*, vol. 27, no. 2, 2015, pp. 268–288.

Laloë, Véronique. "Patterns of Deliberate Self-Burning in Various Parts of the World: A Review." *Burns*, vol. 30, no. 3, 2004, pp. 207–215.

Laloë, Véronique, and Mohan Ganesan. "Self-Immolation a Common Suicidal Behaviour in Eastern Sri Lanka." *Burns*, vol. 28, no. 5, 2002, pp. 475–480.

Mbembe, Achille. "Necropolitics." Translated by Libby Meintjes, *Public Culture*, vol. 15, no. 1, 2003, pp. 11–40.

McKenzie, Jon. *Perform or Else: From Discipline to Performance*. Routledge, 2001.

Michelsen, Nicholas. "The Political Subject of Self-Immolation." *Globalizations*, vol. 12, no. 1, 2015, pp. 83–100.

Nader, Luiza. "Afektywna historia sztuki" [The Affective History of Art]. *Teksty Drugie* [Warsaw], no. 1, 2014, pp. 14–39.

Niziołek, Grzegorz. "Lęk przed afektem" [The Fear of Affect]. *Didaskalia. Gazeta Teatralna* [Krakow-Wrocław], no. 131, 2016, pp. 9–17.

Park, Ben B. C. "Sociopolitical Contexts of Self-Immolations in Vietnam and South Korea." *Archives of Suicide Research*, vol. 8, no. 1, 2004, pp. 81–97.

18 Introduction

Plank, Katarina. "Burning Buddhists: Self-Immolation as Political Protest." *Sacred Suicide*, edited by James R. Lewis and Carole M. Cusack, Ashgate, 2014, pp. 173–191.

Robbins, Thomas. "Religious Mass Suicide Before Jonestown: The Russian Old Believers." *Sociological Analysis*, vol. 47, no. 1, 1986, pp. 1–20.

Rothschild, M. A. et al. "Suicide by Self-Immolation in Berlin from 1990 to 2000." *Forensic Science International*, vol. 124, no. 2–3, 2001, pp. 163–166.

Sajewska, Dorota. *Nekroperformans. Kulturowa rekonstrukcja teatru Wielkiej Wojny* [Necroperformance: Cultural Reconstruction of the Great War Theatre]. Instytut Teatralny im. Zbigniewa Raszewskiego, 2016.

Schechner, Richard. *Performance Studies: An Introduction*. Routledge, 2002.

Shahadi, Joseph. "Burn: The Radical Disappearance of Kathy Change." *TDR: The Drama Review*, vol. 55, no. 2, 2011, pp. 52–72.

Shakya, Tsering. "Self-Immolation: The Changing Language of Protest in Tibet." *Revue d'Etudes Tibétaines*, no. 25, 2012, pp. 19–39.

Singer, Milton, editor. *Traditional India: Structure and Change*. American Folklore Society, 1959.

Sontag, Susan. *Styles of Radical Will*. Anchor Books, 1991.

Sweeney, George. "Self-Immolation in Ireland: Hungerstrikes and Political Confrontation." *Anthropology Today*, vol. 9, no. 5, 1993, pp. 10–14.

Szczepański, Tadeusz. *Zwierciadło Bergmana* [Bergman's Mirror]. Słowo/obraz terytoria, 1999.

Taylor, Dan J. "Sacrifice and the Productive Body of Mohamed Bouazizi." www.academia.edu/3354879/_Sacrifice_and_the_productive_body_of_Mohamed_Bouazizi_.

Taylor, Diana. *Performance*. Duke UP, 2016.

Turner, Victor. "Are There Universals of Performance in Myth, Ritual and Drama?" *By Means of Performance: Intercultural Studies Theatre and Ritual*, edited by Richard Schechner and Willa Appel, Cambridge UP, 1990, pp. 8–18.

Weiler, Christel. "Flying Sparks." *Performance Research*, vol. 18, no. 1, 2013, pp. 123–126.

Weinberger-Thomas, Catherine. *Ashes of Immortality: Widow-Burning in India*. U of Chicago Press, 1999.

Part I

Mapping suicide protests by fire

Figure PI.1 Piotr Wyrzykowski *Self-Immolation* (2014).

Protest self-burnings as suicide protests

Can protest self-burnings be considered suicides if death is, in their case, only a means rather than an end in itself? Naturally, it would be fairly easy to fit them into a number of suicidological concepts which prioritise awareness of the possibility of death and its acceptance as distinguishing characteristics of suicide, while marginalising suicidal intent (Hołyst 81–82). In this particular context, however, it bears repeating that many self-burners themselves firmly rejected the notion that their acts, performed for supra-individual reasons, could be labelled *suicide*.[1]

The question of taxonomy is crucial here, as seemingly interchangeable terms can carry wildly different implications and thus affect the broader reception of the acts themselves. Probing that particular issue, political theorist Banu Bargu emphasised that in politics, the term *suicide* used to denote self-annihilation practices pursued for collective cause has

> the rhetorical function of assigning responsibility solely to the actor who performs the act of self-killing, thereby individualizing the action, obfuscating its political message, and even working against the very purpose of action. ... the choice of vocabulary defining the act clearly shows that the nominal operation is cryptonormative, incorporating a judgement of the cause for which the self-destructive act is performed. (18)

Hence, her coinage of the neutral term *necroresistance* which, stripped of any negative connotations, refers to acts of protest self-destruction performed for political reasons.

The term is a viable alternative for the phrase *suicide protest*, popularised by Michael Biggs, sociologist and author of a number of influential essays on demonstrative self-burnings ("Dying"; "How"; "Self-Immolation"). I ultimately adopted the latter phrase because it emphasises the affinity between practices of altruistic self-annihilation and suicide, and while preserving the possibility of drawing on the vast body of scientific discourse on the subject, it also shifts the underlying meaning from a deliberate, self-inflicted death towards an expression of resistance. Additionally, it allows us to finally retire the term *altruistic suicide*, which underpinned the typology first introduced by Émile Durkheim in his seminal 1897 volume *Le Suicide* (*Suicide*), and was once widely used to refer to protest self-burnings and self-immolations. The term itself is too generic and, as demonstrated by Polish health sociologist Adam Czabański, can stand in for any kind of suicidal act with a pro-community slant, essentially indicating any such act aimed at "improving the quality of life of other people, a specific group, or the entire society (nation)" (Czabański 58). As a result, the term covers protest self-burnings, suicide terror attacks driven by ideological fanaticism or even egoism (for example, when the attack is perpetrated in the hope of being rewarded with entry to paradise), as well as suicides and suicide attempts undertaken by "the elderly and the sick who wanted to relieve the burden to their loved ones," and the extended suicides in which "the perpetrators, intent on shielding their families from hypothetical suffering, humiliation or poverty, first kill their loved ones and then themselves" (Czabański 61).

In itself, the phrase *suicide protest* in no way dismisses the altruistic motivation behind the act, and thus, altruism remains implicit in the term. It accentuates the demonstrative character of the incident and the subject's wish to challenge the status quo and repudiate that which is considered unacceptable. Furthermore, the phrase stresses protest rather than the method used to express it; the obverse would have been true if we were to follow the lead of anthropologist Karin Andriolo and instead use its inversion, namely the term *protest suicide*.

Besides, as keenly pointed out by cultural scholar Joseph Shahadi, altruism implies a high degree of relatedness to society, while often enough fiery suicide protests are performed by alienated outcasts whose sacrifice is the final exemplification of their outsider status (66). Pushing the matter further, Shahadi asked rhetorically: "is it possible to commit an altruistic suicide without the implicit agreement, consent and/or encouragement of your community?" (65) and suggested we call those demonstrative acts of self-annihilation which accentuate the performer's stance on supra-individual issues *performatic suicides*. In his view, they differ from both altruistic suicides and egoistic self-destructions motivated by personal problems, even though they incorporate some distinctive features of both. Like the former, they are performed in service to a cause, but differ in that they grant agency to individuals, allowing them much greater influence over the collective. On the other hand, unlike egoistic suicides, which are typically committed in detachment from the social fabric, they carry with them the potential to disrupt the social equilibrium and the flow of collective energy in the public sphere. A closer look, however, reveals a trace of egoism underlying the concept of performatic suicide, as the act presumes the imposition of will and a specific perception of reality upon a group. In my opinion, however, although Shahadi's observations are merited, the performative aspect is implicit in the phrase *suicide protest* and does not warrant any further qualification.

Biggs argued that an event must meet four criteria to be considered a suicide protest. First, the individual must deliberately carry out an action which may result in their death. Second, the individual must not intend for their act to either kill or harm anyone or cause damage to any property. Third, the act must be public – either performed in a public space or accompanied by a written or otherwise recorded statement or appeal to politicians, other public figures, and/or society, in general or in part. And fourth, the act must be performed on behalf of some collective cause, rather than follow from mental illness or personal problems, such as job loss, financial trouble, adjustment difficulties, or familial misunderstandings (Biggs, "How" 407).

22 Mapping suicide protests by fire

Needless to say, in many cases, unequivocally asserting whether a protest was undertaken for personal or supra-individual reasons is difficult, if not impossible. It is my belief, therefore, that emphasis should be placed on the public character of the act rather than the motivation behind it. That particular angle, however, is not free from ambiguity either. For example, deliberate self-burnings by desperate women from Central and South Asia – whose radical and impulsive acts are often designed to produce a sense of guilt within a specific person or group they deem responsible for the injustices inflicted upon them – are performed primarily at home, in their courtyards, or outbuildings near their houses (Aziz; Laloë; Laloë and Ganesan). However, it is restrictions on free movement that women are subject to in such traditionalist societies that may be ultimately responsible for preventing some of them at least from finding a more public venue to express their dissent, resistance, and despair.

Regardless, the definition suggested by Biggs seems the most feasible as it allows us to separate suicide protests (including demonstrative self-burnings) from (a) other types of suicides; (b) suicide attacks that claim innocent lives; (c) acts of martyrdom, wherein death is inflicted by other people (for example, in the course of protecting others); and (d) cult suicides, wherein some members of a religious group (or the entire community) commit self-murder for religious or ideological reasons (Biggs, "How" 407–408). Furthermore, the term *suicide protest* allows us to sidestep the seemingly irresolvable problem of whether protest self-burnings performed as part of a religious tradition (like Buddhist auto-cremations across Vietnam in the 1960s) should be seen as self-sacrificial gestures or altruistic political actions, thus enabling us to avoid ambiguous and imprecise phraseology.

Protest self-burnings situate themselves alongside other forms of protest self-annihilation, including jumping from tall structures or under trains, ingesting poison, self-inflicted shooting or throat slashing, or self-stabbing.[2] They are also a part of the broader spectrum of liminal protest efforts that includes hunger strikes (also indefinite ones) and subversive acts committed by radical environmentalists who chain themselves to heavy machinery or trees slated for felling, or peace activists employing similar means of non-violent resistance to halt the transfer of ordnance or arms, to name some examples.

Scholars investigating forms of non-violent protest usually juxtapose self-burnings and hunger strikes as two similar methods of communication based on self-inflicted suffering. Biggs adopts a similar approach, but cautions that the majority of people undertaking hunger strikes do not intend to continue them to their death ("How" 408). Naturally, some hunger strikes do end in death,[3] but that does not change the fact that they presume – and enable, given their potential duration – the possibility of negotiation and conciliation, whereas suicide protests by fire preclude dialogue. (Threats or negotiation prior to the act itself are another matter.) In the case of protest self-burnings, death is not contingent upon a change in behaviour or concessions from those at whom the protest or entreaty is aimed, as statistical data indicates that setting oneself ablaze is usually fatal – over 70% of deliberate self-incineration incidents end in death (Laloë and Ganesan 476).

Drawing on Andriolo, we may contend that protest self-burnings and hunger strikes differ in two other respects. First, in the case of the former, the individual loses control of the event and its popular reception, which is fundamentally important to both the effectiveness and the subsequent scrutiny of these types of acts (a notion I will come back to later). Second, self-burning is much more spectacular and, consequently, captures public attention to a much greater degree. As Andriolo rightly noted, "Individual hunger striking gleans scant publicity, unless the performer – as in the case of Gandhi – brings to it his own preestablished prominence" (103). Hunger strikes and fiery suicide protests are similar in that they are often undertaken to further a joint cause. In other words, one person pays the price (injury or death) so that others can reap the benefits (Biggs, "How" 408).

In such a context, self-burning can also be situated alongside aforementioned protests of environmentalists and peace activists. In these cases, we are able to assert that it is the pursuit of supra-individual causes that carries risk of injury or even death (and some have indeed been wounded or killed in the course of their action). As is the case with hunger strikes, however, the course of these actions is charted mostly in response to the reaction of the other party to the conflict, thus making them fundamentally different from protest self-burnings.

Some general remarks

Drawing on Biggs' sociological scholarship, rooted in his systematic study of press reports from 1963 to 2002 ("Dying"), as well as my own factual research featured in the timeline section of this book (Part II), I would like to formulate some general remarks on protest self-burnings. Due to the lack of comprehensive statistical data on the phenomenon itself, these observations may carry a measure of imprecision.

Self-burning may be performed for a variety of reasons, but only some of these touch on principles widely considered fundamental, such as political repression or threats to basic liberties. In many cases, the reasons behind individual incidents can seem trivial to outsiders, or at least inadequate to warrant an act that may very well end in death. The decision to embrace that particular form of protest may be driven by a desire to preserve values seen as worth sacrificing one's life for and/or may be a consequence of the violation of one's dignity. These motivations may be further amplified by despair resulting from the realisation that other forms of dissent either have failed or will fail. Another motive, related to the above issues, is the desire to reclaim individual agency when it is felt to be lost, in order to demonstrate that some decisions still lie solely with the individual. Furthermore, in most

24 Mapping suicide protests by fire

cases, the decision is driven by a plethora of intertwined motivations, and it is essentially impossible to isolate the one prevailing factor that spurred the individual to embrace such violent form of dissent.[4] Consequently, in some situations, protest self-burning becomes a mask that may conceal personal problems or even egoistic motivations, such as a desire for fame or the wish to absolve oneself of past transgressions (Biggs, "Dying" 196).

Citing Marcel Mauss' seminal concept of the gift, Andriolo asserted that self-burnings are governed by the principles of the exchange economy. According to the logic of the gift, which emerged in pre-modern communities and continues to hold true in contemporary societies, sacrificing one's own life demands a reaction, a response, a repayment (107). The anthropologist also posited that contemporary self-immolators see their self-burning as an offer that they hope cannot be refused (109). And although I cannot eliminate the possibility of such an assumption (either conscious or not) being true in many cases, broadening the notion to encompass the phenomenon in its breadth seems unwarranted to say the least. For example, Tibetans who decide to lay down their lives for a cause must reckon with the possibility that the other party – the authorities in Beijing – will not be swayed by their death, just as it had not been by their predecessor's sacrifices, and thus rendering their actions futile. They also need to consider the possibility of their efforts being ignored as "the world has grown indifferent to ever new reports of human torches setting themselves ablaze the world over," thus "transforming further sacrifices into mere statistics" (Stefanicki 374). They continue to embrace self-burnings, however, as apparently they are unable to remain acquiescent and refrain from responding to what they consider oppression.[5] This, in turn, demonstrates that in some cases, the immolators reject clearheaded and calculated judgement and instead decide to follow through with self-burning on impulse, without succumbing to any illusions as to the political effectiveness of their final actions.

As a practice, fiery suicide protests are understandably associated with non-violence and are very rarely embraced by groups focused on violent tactics, including those pursuing suicide terrorist attacks (Biggs, "Dying" 183).[6] By no means does that imply, however, that they are a safe method of expressing dissent that never endangers onlookers or passersby, as clearly evidenced by a number of incidents.[7] Furthermore, on closer inspection, the historical record of self-burnings reveals at least a handful of questionable incidents which could have potentially been suicide attacks performed with the intent of hurting a third party.[8] Regardless, the prevailing rule is that self-burners do not aim to either start fires or inflict suffering on those caught up in their protest, willingly or otherwise.

The age span of protest self-burners is quite broad – ranging from teenagers to senior citizens. Their ranks include, as has already been pointed out in the introduction, both atheists and people of faith, people of all races, classes, nationalities, and sexual orientations. The majority seem to be male;

however, due to the fact that many countries do not possess relevant data on the subject, it has been impossible to determine unequivocally whether the ratio of males to females in a population is similar to that observed for deliberate self-burnings (in the West, this ratio is around 65 male to 35 female). In contrast to deliberate self-burnings (DSBs), protest self-burnings are usually performed outdoors, although there have been exceptions, including incidents performed inside a car, a prison, a detention centre, an office complex, a church, and even individual rooms (for example, during a video conversation or a press conference). The venue is usually selected for maximum symbolic impact to amplify the message behind the protest, and presumably to allow the incident the greatest possible media reach and penetration.

It is difficult to pinpoint the exact factors that heighten the likelihood of a self-burning. Biggs contended that statistical data from over 30 countries he pored over revealed no correlation between the overall suicide rate and the number of protest auto-cremations ("Dying" 186). Nor could such a correlation be identified between this number and the extent of a society's propensity for other forms of protest or its tolerance for divorce. The latter serves as an apt illustration of the degree of social integration, a particularly ephemeral variable which, in Durkheim's view, tends to determine the types of suicides pursued by individuals within a given society. Religion remains the only relevant determinant to exhibit a correlation with the incidence of protest self-burnings. As explained by Biggs,

> Durkheim emphasized the intensity of religious belief rather than the content of religious doctrine. For self-immolation, however, the extent of religiosity – measured for instance by belief in life after death – does not matter. What matters is the proportion of Hindus and Buddhists.
>
> ("Dying" 186)

In other words, most self-burnings take place in locations where these two faiths are dominant, which, in Biggs' opinion, is mostly a product of their cultural background rather than doctrine, as religions in general tend to be unfavourably disposed towards suicide ("Dying" 187).[9] The key point here is that cultures with strong Buddhist and/or Hindu traditions usually espouse a plethora of cremation practices, including corpse incineration, which are in turn rooted in these traditions' veneration of fire as a purifying agent, a holy power that can cleanse mistakes and ignorance. The significance of a given society's cultural background, of which the predominant religion and its attendant rituals are a crucial part, is best illustrated by South Korea, where a number of politically motivated self-burnings were performed between the 1970s and the 1990s by radicalised activists and students with strong leftist views. In their case, principles of religious doctrine were not nearly as significant as the cultural context, shaped primarily by the culture's Buddhist underpinnings.

26 Mapping suicide protests by fire

Biggs also posited that when trying to determine the most frequent locations of protest self-burnings, we must not overlook the question of the political power structure in these settings. Drawing on the Polity data series, a data set containing information on the level of democracy in most independent states that goes as far back as the year 1800, Biggs concluded ("Dying" 187) that most fiery suicide protests take place in countries that are anocratic (that is partly democratic, partly authoritarian), and are quite rare under unambiguously totalitarian regimes. In his opinion, this could be explained by the fact that in authoritarian dictatorships, would-be protesters necessarily expect their immolation to fail to produce the desired results, as the regimes remain in full control of the media and either do not trouble themselves too much with the public opinion or dismiss it outright. It bears repeating here, however, that Biggs based his calculation on data compiled prior to the many suicide protests that transpired in the course of the Arab Spring, which swept across the authoritarian regimes of North Africa and the Middle East, as well as prior to the recent spate of self-immolations in Tibet. Besides, for most of the second half of the 20th century, the level of democracy in the Republic of Vietnam and South Korea, both sites of multiple acts of self-burning, was relatively low due to the authoritarian inclinations of their governments. Furthermore, we ought to remember that many ultimate protests undertaken under totalitarian governments would necessarily remain unacknowledged, as classifying such reports or framing their performers as mentally unstable is standard practice for these regimes. Conversely, suicide protests by fire are rarer in countries with strong democratic traditions, as these allow citizens to express their opinions freely and pursue political agendas by other, less radical means.

The tendency to accumulate in certain points in time is another distinctive characteristic of protest self-burnings. Nearly a fifth of all the cases Biggs examined appeared in correlation with at least one other self-burning incident ("Dying" 188). The historical record includes a number of self-incinerations that openly referenced a prior incident, one which typically had electrified public opinion. We also know of situations where one self-burning sparked a wave of follow-up acts of ultimate protests using fire and other means. In a fashion similar to what has been observed for suicides, successive protest self-burnings can be prompted by the Werther effect (*copycat suicide*). Waves of self-burnings that end up claiming the lives of dozens of protesters, meanwhile, may also be motivated by subsequent immolators' desires: (a) not to let the sacrifice of their predecessors come to nothing, (b) to live up to the example set by those who decided to lay down their lives in fiery protest, and (c) to make their own ultimate contribution to a struggle they consider worth dying for.

Some protest self-burnings take place after lengthy contemplation and preparations, including prayer, fasting, drafting demands for the authorities or appeals addressed to fellow citizens; others are driven by impulse rarely preceded by much forethought. In this particular context, we would do well to mention that it is difficult to unambiguously determine whether a self-burning protest can actually be "staged," that is whether it is possible to design the event to minimise the risk of death or injury, although some cases seem to suggest exactly such a course.[10]

Biggs correctly noted that suicide protests by fire are rarely preceded by threats or declarations ("Dying" 190). This is probably owing to the fact that a significant portion of these incidents are undertaken on impulse. Furthermore, pre-emptive announcement of intent could potentially result in attempts to interfere with or thwart the incident, for example by law enforcement. Biggs argues that the primary reason behind this reticence is the would-be burners' fear of being publicly discredited. Multiple incidents seem to suggest, however, that this fear by no means precludes such declarations, threats, or attempts at negotiation.[11]

A self-immolation does not require extensive logistical preparation or planning, as is the case with most terrorist attacks. Neither does it demand any technical skills (in contrast, for example, to the Japanese practice of *seppuku*, which entails highly ritualised disembowelment) nor much coordination with other members of a group or a command-and-control centre. All the act requires is a committed individual, equipped with a flammable substance, boundless determination, and nearly unimaginable courage (Biggs, "How" 422).

By no means, however, does that imply that self-burnings happen in isolation, with no connection to other people, and it should be noted that in many instances they have been performed during a demonstration (which does not necessitate that the immolator coordinated their protest with the organisers). History, naturally, knows situations where a self-burning incident entailed the synchronised or coordinated actions of many. Some would-be immolators who were part of monastic orders or religious organisations consulted their superiors to ask for permission. In some instances, the incidents included a number of helpers, either to assist with the act or to obstruct the efforts of police or firefighters. It is also sensible to suspect that in many cases, third-party involvement in the planning or execution of an ultimate act of resistance is kept secret to shield these accomplices from future charges of either failing to prevent or aiding suicide. It bears emphasising, however, that self-burning is typically a result of an individual decision, and it is hard to imagine anyone being actively encouraged or coerced into performing it. That is probably why Gene Sharp's seminal manual of non-violent action, *From Dictatorship to Democracy*, does not list self-burning as one of the instruments in the struggle against unjust regimes.

Self-burning produces unimaginable suffering, comparable maybe only to the agony of *seppuku*, but the latter ends with the performer's head being lopped off to cease their pain. A peculiar analogy could possibly be drawn between the South Korean practice of following self-immolation with jumping off a tall building, undertaken either to shorten the agony, to ensure that the act ends in death or, potentially, to amplify the impact of the protest (or all three reasons together). The suffering may also be cut short or alleviated by loss of consciousness or the cauterisation of nerve endings. It is quite telling that aside from a couple of incidents,[12] those who survived their self-incineration never undertake another attempt at that sort of protest. As already pointed out above, self-burning has a very high mortality rate. Death can occur on site, usually as a result of asphyxiation, or later – mostly due to multiple organ failure brought on by extensive burns to the skin and respiratory system.

Reactions, scrutiny, and effectiveness

As an inherently unpredictable, irreversible, and shocking act rooted in the actuality of death, a self-burning calls routine behavioural patterns into question. In short, it is a derailing spectacle. When put on the spot, some bystanders or accomplices of the performer usually move to snuff out the fire or to render help. Others photograph or film the event. Most witnesses, however, are shocked, bewildered, horrified, even stupefied, or disoriented. The staggering impact of a self-burning may be amplified by the fact that a person who is unafraid of death and entails a maximum amount of suffering can be also perceived as an innocent victim.

The broad spectrum of emotional reactions to a self-burning ranges from compassion, a sense of solidarity, and even grief, to revulsion, anger, and, in some extreme cases, the perverse pleasure of voyeurs, whom Susan Sontag called "adepts of proximity without risk" (111): consuming images of suffering as spectacle and deriving satisfaction from watching someone else's experience of pain.[13] The aforementioned anger can be vectored against the regime, opponents of a given cause, or against the very protester, coercing the public to heed their cause, becoming in its eyes almost an emotional blackmailer, capable of resorting to methods some would consider terrorist.

However, if the protester were to be acknowledged as a hero, they would most likely also become an object of veneration. Their grave, the symbolically marked site of their self-burning, and/or memorials erected to honour them may, in such a case, become places of commemoration, pilgrimage sites, venues for vigils, prayer assemblies, or demonstrations, while the date of the incident and/or their death may be elevated to the status of a properly observed anniversary. These practices may be carried out by entire communities centred around the liminal act, with their size, character, staying power, and internal dynamics determined primarily by broader sociocultural, historical, and political processes, different for different contexts. These communities may emerge in both real and virtual spaces, brought together either by their approval of the protester's deeds or by their rejection of such violent methods of dissent and/or the actual issues which sparked the protest. Like all borderline acts, self-burning has the power to polarise both direct and indirect audiences.

Following a self-burning, most leaders of the causes for which the immolators perished usually call on the public to refrain from further violent acts. Reactions like these may be driven by moral concerns, but we have to consider the possibility that they are just unscrupulous political calculations, since failing to deliver such a statement could be seen as promoting or, at worst, encouraging suicide, and thus lead to severe backlash. This approach is more or less an inversion of the strategy typically embraced by terrorist groups which publicly declare their readiness to conduct further attacks in order to amplify their message.

Given the recurring presence of self-immolation in mass media and its reach across different cultural contexts in past decades, people who witness such acts are usually capable of rationalising the horror and thus reducing their initial shock relatively quickly. That does not change the fact, however, that such acts are still perceived (particularly in the West) as manifestly extremist and deviant, a testament to the self-burners' irrationality (Kelly) and their surrender to pre-logical and pre-modernist atavisms (Michelsen 85). Self-immolation is also seen as a waste of human life and potential that could be harnessed in a much more productive way. Such appraisals are issued primarily in the wake of acts that proved futile or ineffective. Furthermore, suicide protest is often considered a "shortcut," a throwaway gesture deployed in lieu of a long-term strategy of constructive, incremental resistance. Self-burners are sometimes seen as suffering from the Messiah complex, meaning they aspire to single-handedly save the world, without first looking for alternative methods, particularly those that involve collaborating with other members of the community.

Self-burning is ambivalent enough to avoid straightforward moral judgements. On the one hand, it stands as a testament to its performer's audacity, their triumph over fear of pain and death, and their embrace of self-sacrifice (sometimes in service to a cause that some part of society may view as questionable). On the other, it violates religious taboos and as such cannot be considered a moral benchmark to aspire to, unlike other acts that the public opinion sees as praiseworthy. Although usually pursued in defence of supra-individual values, it still exposes others – family, relatives, and friends – to suffering. That is why it is so often rejected outright, even if it may inspire a measure of admiration and engender a sense of the sublime.

Protest self-burners are treated as vehicles through which the collective problems of society, its tensions and crises, are exposed. Moreover, they are usually seen as burdened with inordinate sensitivities, as so attuned to potential violations of norms and values that they cannot help but feel them more intensely (with critics going so far as to label them oversensitive), while their involvement with their cause is considered so profound as to prevent them from seeing things objectively. Others see them as unflinching champions of their cause, ready to cleave themselves from their earthly ties, and take the final step.

30 Mapping suicide protests by fire

Evaluating the effectiveness of suicide protests mostly depends on the criteria we adopt for the purpose of the process. If we focus on whether the self-immolators' demands become reality in the wake of their act, then we must admit that most self-burnings fail. Even those incidents that were followed by real political change are usually hard to classify as successful, since the self-burnings were most probably not the single decisive factor that motivated the shift. Objectively tangible results of some of the protest self-burnings may include mass demonstrations that erupt in their wake or the outpouring of public grief at funerals or other memorial events. In some cases, the sheer impact of the act may precipitate the radicalisation of public sentiment or, as we have already discussed above, inspire others to perform follow-up auto-cremations or other self-sacrifices. Naturally, the longevity of the impact and its character are rather debatable, and probing them would require approaching each case individually, all the more because many protest self-burnings have passed into legend, their performers since enshrined as heroes; from such a point onwards, the impact of their actions is determined primarily by the principles governing mythologised heroic narratives. Sometimes, despite producing a public response and resonating on a symbolic level, the incident nevertheless fails to yield real political consequences (Michelsen 86). Although some incidents may reveal their inspirational potential in later years, in principle, society (or a significant portion of it) remains mostly unmoved by the actions and entreaties of self-burners, and usually manages to come up with a number of justifications for its own inaction, such as judging the form of protest too radical or unsuitable for the situation. Nevertheless, on a more personal level, self-immolations tend to have a profound, sometimes decisive, impact on individual lives, choices, and value systems.[14]

A complex plethora of factors may ultimately decide that one self-burning produces a genuine wave of public outcry, whereas another fizzles out with scarcely an echo.[15] Each case would require a separate enquiry to untangle the web of historical, political, and sociocultural ramifications. In principle, however, two things seem key: media attention and relevant spokespersons capable of constructing an appropriate interpretive frame, since, to quote Martin Kovan on Tibetan self-immolations, "It always depends on the living what kind of Phoenix rises from the ashes" (422). That particular issue was also pointed out by Andriolo, who wrote that self-burning can never be self-sustaining because "others are needed to take up the torch" (107). In other words, for protest self-burnings to be perceived as honourable immolations, they need to be presented in secular or religious narratives as acts of martyrdom rather than fanatical self-destructions (Hedges 802). The incidents may be justified and lent legitimacy by oppressive situations and restrictions on other forms of protest, as well as by the "self-identification between those receiving or creating the mythic narrative and the actor" (Hedges 802).

The somatic act of communication and its performative dimension

Contrary to hunger strikes, protest self-burnings are difficult to count among persuasive practices, understood here as verbal and non-verbal (and often allusive) efforts aimed at gradually persuading others to adopt a given view or position. They should be seen as a prescriptive strategy aimed at (a) opponents, to whom it reveals the power of the convictions driving a person willing to lay down their life for a cause; (b) supporters, to whom it lends moral assistance or whom it guilts into stepping up their efforts, as the cause is worth every sacrifice; (c) bystanders and other third parties, often undecided, to whom it signals the gravity of a given problem and the determination of those who confront it (Kim 549). Although some protesters employ a breadth of means to express their demands or make themselves heard prior to the act of self-burning (they surround themselves with banners, read off their manifestos, distribute pamphlets, shout slogans, leave farewell notes, etc.), it is extreme suffering that is their primary vehicle for communication. Here, the suffering, or even death, amplifies their message, emphasises its gravity, and lends credibility to their individual testimony. The far-reaching repercussions of these processes and their impact on communication itself were explored by Young Cheon Cho in his illuminating dissertation, *The Politics of Suffering in the Public Sphere*, which I will draw on below.

The theory of the public sphere, formulated by German philosopher and sociologist Jürgen Habermas, defines it as space dominated by post-Enlightenment rational discourse and concepts such as dialogue and critical polemics, rooted in logical verbal declarations: a space in which we can be seen and heard. In other words, the public sphere is the sphere of the *logos*, a liberal democratic utopia where the continuous negotiation of positions offers citizenship to people willing to abide by its rules. As correctly noted by Cho (4), protest self-burning subverts that logocentric model, questioning the privileged status of debate as the public sphere's primary participatory medium. It can be read as a radical gesture of severance, the opposite of mediation and negotiation. In modern societies, where life is regulated by a range of social compacts, such as legal systems, violence and its application are the domain of the state. A person who decides to self-burn (or pursues another form of suicide protest) violates that monopoly at a fundamental level, and thus subverts the rule of law, that is the prerogative of the ruling powers to decide the course of events and determine standards of conduct. In other words, individuals bestow upon themselves the sovereignty to make decisions emanating from their conscience, their sense of dignity, and their system of values, thus reasserting their own subjectivity. Crucially, they do so by embracing bodily suffering as the primary vehicle of their dissent and focusing on "neglected forms of communication that are visual, spectacular, violent, unruly, and physical" (Cho 3).

This extraverbal, confrontational, and anarchic form of communication is usually adopted by (genuinely or seemingly) marginalised or ignored individuals, stripped of their voice and excluded from political participation, the unseen, subservient, and/or disenfranchised. In such a context, self-burning seems a profoundly democratic gesture, i.e. one that does not make the ability to protest conditional upon education, manners, gender, wealth, social standing, sexual preferences, or skin colour. Bodily suffering, therefore, is the price of admission into the public sphere, a ticket that has to be purchased by the (genuinely or seemingly) marginalised who either cannot or do not want to abide by the principles of *ratio* and *decorum* (Cho 86). The phrasing in this case is far from figurative: for the poor, who cannot afford airtime or advertising space in the press, self-annihilation by fire is a way to attract media attention and broadcast the self-burner's message to a much broader audience.

As Cho emphasised (36), many political theorists, German thinker Hannah Arendt chief among them, relegated pain to the private realm, since suffering exposes the language of discourse to the likelihood of incommunicability. In spite of that, pain is eagerly embraced by those who lack representation in systems and structures they live under. It becomes the last recourse of individuals and their causes against being ignored or erased. The burning flesh thus embodies the suffering individual's objection to its own disappearance, amplifying their own visibility and the visibility of the problems they stand up for. A suicide protest by fire, therefore, is a peculiar paradox which transforms deliberate self-annihilation into amplified, augmented appearance (Gough 9; Shahadi 55).

Self-burning encourages a closer look at the agency of the individual body – at its active role in the body-power relationship. It promotes a diagnosis of the extent to which the subject can use their body for the purposes of political protest. As sociologist of the body Chris Shilling rightly pointed out, "body matters have moved to the centre of public and academic debate" (ix) already in the early 21st century, a shift driven, among other factors, by the pioneering work of Michel Foucault, who focused primarily on the impact of discursive strategies of punishment on the body (*Discipline*). The French scholar believed that the body was formed and formatted by power and stood as a reflection of the control that power held over it. The mutual permeating of the political and the physical can be gleaned, for example, through inquiry into issues related to biopower, such as nutrition policies, mandatory vaccinations, or demographic planning. Shilling emphasised that Foucault's notions were the "most influential source of social constructivism" (77) by implying that "the body is not only given meaning by discourse, but is *wholly constituted by* discourse: it vanishes as a biological entity and becomes an infinitely malleable and highly unstable socially constructed product" (77–78). Although feminist critiques drew extensively from Foucault and focused on those discourses which comprised the stage of the struggle between power relations, and which forced specific, unique bodies into normative templates, they continued to argue for the materiality – and sexuality – of the body. Sociologist Bryan Turner was another influential theorist to critique the French thinker, who focused particularly on what Turner saw as Foucault's disregard for the phenomenology of embodiment.

This issue is related to the fact that the anguish of a particular individual frustrates the generalisations and abstractions (including those pertaining to the body) enshrined in the foundations of democracy which itself, in turn, demands that we see through the eyes of others and distance ourselves from the personal and the particular. In anguish, the body demands that attention be given to the individual, indivisible features of each case. Instead of accentuating the disembodied and impersonal, pain stresses the particular and the physical. Physical pain, as Austrian philosopher and essayist Jean Améry wisely noted in reference to torture, "is the most extreme intensification imaginable of our bodily being" (33), and it resists being demoted to a mere common denominator. Instead of generalising, it stresses the singular and the unique.

When publicly displayed, the anguished body draws on bodily rhetorical values which had been identified in the West already in Ancient Greece and which later found substantiation in the practices of medieval religious martyrs. These observations were compiled by Edmund Burke in his seminal treatise *A Philosophical Enquiry into the Origin of Our Ideas of the Sublime and Beautiful* (1757), which seems to confirm the intuition that the appearance of a body in anguish is imbued with a power that can strike terror into the hearts of mankind; terror, as the Irish philosopher put it, is "the heart of the Sublime" (xxi), and as such is capable of piercing the sphere of the symbolic. Consequently, bodily suffering is crucial to amplifying the power of a given argument. This, in turn, refers to the notion of bodily frailty, which can be seen as the fundamental premise of all human understanding. It is the body's vulnerability that lies at the heart of empathy, understood here as the ability to interpret the emotions of others and identify with them. Paradoxically, although all pain is unique, individual, and impossible to distil into shareable experience, it can still be common ground on which to build understanding, as others may still have or may have had similar experiences.

It is this potential that hunger striking prisoners of conscience draw on, as do radical environmentalists whose argumentation is not rooted in the power of their words, but in the vulnerability of their flesh. Therefore, if – as Foucault demonstrated – the strategies and efforts of the ruling powers entail the disciplining of the body, then this "domination can also be resisted first and foremost by the body" (Cho 109). It seems that self-burners follow precisely that particular strategy, although perhaps not always intentionally.

Even though it may seem that the suffering body is stripped of a voice beyond moans, screams, and cries of pain, protest self-burnings clearly demonstrate that even when in anguish, the body can still communicate meanings and appeal to emotions, it can "speak" and be expressive. In this

34 Mapping suicide protests by fire

sense, such an act is "a performative critique of disembodied rationality" (Cho 122). The voice of suffering flesh may seem irrational or emotional, but we must remember that it is often the only one available to people who decide to embrace that form of protest. Consequently, self-burners "make a forceful statement of conviction by dramatizing their bodies in pain" (Cho 123). Here, the intrinsically devastating element of fire sheds a light on what constitutes the essence of resistance and – often enough – the entrenched positions that the opposing party in the conflict is not willing to renegotiate.

The power inherent in self-burning, however, can be used against the immolators. The act lays bare the frailty of bodily communication, which is susceptible to ambiguity and dependent on interpretive frames that imbue specific incidents with particular undertones. Self-burnings require words – to make up manifestos or farewell letters, to explain the motives driving the protesters, to complement the narrative, to provide justifications, and to strip away any remaining ambiguities. In other words, the performance of bodily argumentation and the embodied praxis of dissent are neither self-sufficient nor self-sustaining. The suffering flesh communicates, but the message is only ostensibly unequivocal and clear across all its aspects. It shocks, pleads for compassion, and does so aggressively, resorting to what amounts to (in the eyes of some people) emotional blackmail. Voluntary suffering, however, is proof only of the gravity of the cause that drove it, and not much more. Protest self-burnings, therefore, are not at all as plain and manifest as it would seem at first glance, and may ultimately be considered a hermeneutic problem, demanding explanation and interpretation. Addressed to a scrutinising public, the protest is mindful of and even open to critical appraisals, and as such is infused with a particularly "democratic flavour" (Cho 130).

Self-burnings' special status in the repertoire of contention is reinforced by the spectacle and dramatics that they engender. The anguished body, engulfed in flame and smoke, is a striking and deeply shocking image. It is meta-quotidian at its very core. Its appearance is always invasive. Like a catastrophe, it is sudden and tragic, a "rupture, an interruption, a stain" on the illusory vision of the world (Kosiński 38). It is unexpected and unpredictable, even more so than a terrorist attack that can be discovered and thwarted. Like such an attack, a self-burning is a brief and violent affair (usually it takes a few, maybe a dozen minutes). The shock may be amplified by poised screams, which provide an aural layer and become a crucial element of the entire act. Naturally, the protest can be accompanied by assorted displays, such as banners or placards, for example; often enough, however, a single gesture leads straight into the climax of the incident.

The anguished body of the self-burner becomes "a self-destructive performance site," which "denounces injustice by enacting its fatal consequences" (Andriolo 110). Thus, self-immolation becomes a borderline act which uses

Mapping suicide protests by fire 35

the suffering flesh as a medium with which it exposes to the public the injustice inflicted upon an individual or a community (Fierke 38). It is performative because it strives (sometimes successfully) to bring about real political and social change, but also on account of its irreversibility. In its aftermath, nothing is truly ever the same. Contrary to a protest letter, which can be withdrawn or its postulates renegotiated, or a worker strike, which can be cancelled or suspended, a self-burning sharply brings into focus the fact that something irreversible has truly happened.

Summary

A self-immolation is an individual transgression, a drastic, public display of excess, provocative, and radical. It is a spectacular *act-performance*, giving rise to ambivalent emotions and lying open to extensive scrutiny. In such an act, discourse is relegated to the background by visual elements and bodily action. In the eyes of the established power structures, against which self-burnings are usually performed, the act itself may seem a revolutionary attempt to subvert the existing order. It cannot be predicted, and as such cannot be controlled or mollified (only its reception and interpretation can be moulded). Therein – alongside its existential aspect – lies the primary source of its subversive power.

Even when part of a bigger wave, the act of self-burning goes against the notion of power in numbers and stresses the particularity of human existence. It is a penetrating expression of faith in personal agency, the voice of individuals, and their right to make their own decisions. By embracing self-immolation, particular individuals stand up for values they consider paramount in their lives and – often enough – the lives of others, in what amounts to a projection of personal notions onto the community's hierarchy of values. Aside from the performative dimension, it is this particular quality that situates self-burning at the intersection of the individual and the collective. Although the act usually proves futile and ineffective on a macro scale, at an individual level, it is perfectly capable of upsetting existential foundations and leading to extensive moral reevaluations.

By obliterating "instrumental rationality" and standing as "a commentary on the meaning of life" (Bargu 16), the act itself points to metaphysics. And as such, it seems to hold "a grain" of mystery – a mystery of human will, capable of overcoming the most basic self-preservation instincts, the fear of suffering and death, and entrenched cultural and religious taboos, all in the name of a cause considered worthy of sacrificing one's life for and cherished far more than doctrines and laws. That is why a self-burning could be considered not only a gesture of emotional blackmail, but also a profoundly creative act, opening itself unto others and encouraging them to strike up empathetic relationships with self-immolators – which, in turn, makes their sacrifices paradoxically future-oriented.

Notes

1 For example, on his deathbed, Jan Palach's demanded that his protest be referred to as an "action" (Palata 2). The Tibetan activist and author Tsering Woeser embraced a similar approach when she called Tibetan self-burnings a "sacrifice for a greater cause, and an attempt to press for change" (43) and categorically rejected any phraseology that might suggest that they were mere suicides.

2 One of the most widely publicised examples of that type of protest was undertaken by the President of the Federation of Farmers and Fishermen of Korea, Lee Kyung-hae, who stabbed himself on 10 September 2003 at the World Trade Organization conference in Cancún, Mexico, to protest against neoliberal globalist policies, which he believed were impoverishing individual farmers. The stabbing was performed during a demonstration, in front of witnesses and numerous cameras. Around his neck, Lee hung a placard with the words "WTO kills farmers," and intended his act to be a literal illustration of the charge (Andriolo 102; Cho 131–134).

3 This was the case of the 1981 strike launched by Roibeard Gearóid Ó Seachnasaigh (Bobby Sands) and his fellow IRA fighters, which led to the death of ten prisoners. The protesters called on the Thatcher government to recognise them as political prisoners and refrain from treating them as common criminals. Sands and his protest were explored at length in Steve McQueen's remarkable 2008 picture *Hunger*.

4 See, for example, the protests of Homa Darabi (1994) and Kathy Change (1996) described in Part II of this volume. Although both women articulated undeniably political demands, in both their cases personal problems played significant roles in driving them to self-immolation; the former was suffering from depression, while the latter had a history of suicide attempts.

5 Woeser pointed out that "Tibetans in Tibet are not primarily seeking international support" (57), and argued that they prefer addressing their message directly to fellow Tibetans (their goal being the strengthening of Tibetan unity and national identity) and the Chinese authorities.

6 One exception was the practices adopted by the Kurds from the Workers' Party of Kurdistan in Turkey, who used both forms of protest in pursuit of statehood and their right to self-determination.

7 See, for example, the protests of Chan I-hua (1989) and Valentina Gerasimova (2012). The self-immolations of Tibetans can also be a threat to others, albeit indirectly, as since 2012, the Chinese authorities have been treating self-burning incidents as criminal offences and using collective punishment to prosecute and harass the immolators' families, relatives, and even entire villages and monasteries (Woeser 13–17).

8 See the self-burnings of Joseba Elósegi Odriozola (1970) and Musa Mamut (1978).

9 Both Hinduism and Buddhism are much less categorical than monotheist Abrahamic religions and do not forbid self-sacrifice in service of a higher goal. Furthermore, Buddhism actually emphasises that the motivation driving the sacrifice is crucial, meaning that if motivated by noble intentions, the act of self-annihilation cannot be considered a sin.

10 Similar suspicions were raised, for example, with regard to Neusha Farrahi's (1987) and Rajiv Goswami's (1990) protests.

11 See, for example, the protests of Hartmut Gründler (1977) and Maggy Delvaux-Mufu (2004). Another such case was particularly tragic. On 19 January 2011, outside the provincial government building in M'Sila, Algeria, a 54-year-old man by the name of G. Seguir wrapped himself in the Algerian flag, doused himself, his 11-year-old son, and eight-year-old daughter with petrol and threatened to set the

whole family alight. After an hour of negotiations, he let his children go free and eventually set only himself ablaze. The fire was quickly put out, and Seguir was taken to hospital. He was driven to self-immolation by poverty and the prospect of losing electricity and utilities due to unpaid bills. There is a possibility, however, that the wave of social unrest that was sweeping North Africa and the Middle East at the time, played a considerable part in his decision.

12 See protests by Rajiv Goswami (1990, 1993) and Sarwar Bhund (2004).
13 For more on the subject of emotional response to protest self-burnings, see Lahiri.
14 For example, the self-immolation of Piotr Szczęsny (2017) proved such a pivotal moment for hairstylist Gabriela Lazarek that two days later she found herself reading the self-burner's final message out loud at the old market square in Cieszyn. She was soon joined in her performance by members of Obywatele RP, a civic movement formed to safeguard democracy and the rule of law in Poland. The public readings have been carried out more than 300 times as of the time of writing.
15 This was the case of the middle-aged Japanese businessman's political self-immolation performed on 29 June 2014 at the Shinjuku Station in Tokyo. As pointed out by Kyoko Iwaki, his act "vanished from the public discourse literally overnight" (206) mainly because "for people in Tokyo, it was one of the many carnivalesque events to be consumed and forgotten" (204). The scholar convincingly suggested that "Since the city dwellers perpetually receive an overdose of stimuli, their rusted senses were not able to perceive the magnitude of the event fully" (204).

References

Améry, Jean. *At the Mind's Limits: Contemplations by a Survivor on Auschwitz and Its Realities.* Translated by Sidney Rosenfeld and Stella P. Rosenfeld, Indiana UP, 1980.

Andriolo, Karin. "The Twice-Killed: Imagining Protest Suicide." *American Anthropologist*, vol. 108, no. 1, 2006, pp. 100–113.

Aziz, Nahid. "What Self-Immolation Means for Afghan Women." *Peace Review. A Journal of Social Justice*, vol. 23, no. 1, 2011, pp. 45–51.

Bargu, Banu. *Starve and Immolate: The Politics of Human Weapons.* Columbia UP, 2014.

Biggs, Michael. "Dying Without Killing: Self-Immolations, 1963–2002." *Making Sense of Suicide Missions*, edited by Diego Gambetta, Oxford UP, 2005, pp. 173–208.

———. "How Repertories Evolve: The Diffusion of Suicide Protest in the Twentieth Century." *Mobilization: An International Quarterly*, vol. 18, no. 4, 2013, pp. 407–428.

———. "Self-Immolation in Context: 1963–2012." *Revue d'Etudes Tibétaines*, no. 25, 2012, pp. 143–150.

Burke, Edmund. *A Philosophical Enquiry into the Origin of Our Ideas of the Sublime and Beautiful.* Oxford UP, 1990.

Cho, Young Cheon. *The Politics of Suffering in the Public Sphere: The Body in Pain, Empathy, and Political Spectacles.* Dissertation, U of Iowa, 2009.

Czabański, Adam. *Samobójstwa altruistyczne. Formy manifestacji, mechanizmy i społeczne reperkusje zjawiska* [Altruistic Suicides: Forms of Manifestations, Mechanisms, and Social Repercussions]. Nomos, 2009.

Durkheim, Émile. *Suicide: A Study in Sociology.* Translated by John A. Spaulding and George Simpson, Free Press, 1951.

Fierke, Karin. *Political Self-Sacrifice: Agency, Body and Emotion in International Relations.* Cambridge UP, 2013.

Foucault, Michel. *Discipline and Punish: The Birth of the Prison.* Translated by Alan Sheridan, Vintage Books, 1995.

Gough, Richard. "Burning Bodies: Transformation and Fire." *Performance Research*, vol. 18, no. 1, 2013, pp. 9–23.

Hedges, Paul. "Burning for a Cause: Four Factors in Successful Political (and Religious) Self-Immolation Examined in Relation to Alleged Falun Gong 'Fanatics' in Tiananmen Square." *Politics and Religion*, vol. 8, 2015, pp. 797–817.

Hołyst, Brunon. *Suicydologia* [Suicidology]. 2nd edition. LexisNexis, 2012.

Iwaki, Kyoko. "The Politics of the Senses: Takayama Akira's Atomized Theatre after Fukushima." *Fukushima and the Arts: Negotiating Nuclear Disaster*, edited by Barbara Geilhorn and Kristina Iwata-Weickgenannt, Routledge, 2017, pp. 199–220.

Kelly, Brendan D. "Self-Immolation, Suicide and Self-Harm in Buddhist and Western Traditions." *Transcultural Psychiatry*, vol. 48, no. 3, 2011, pp. 299–317.

Kim, Hyojoung. "Micromobilization and Suicide Protest in South Korea, 1970–2004." *Social Research*, vol. 75, no. 2, 2008, pp. 543–578.

Kosiński, Dariusz. *Teatra polskie. Rok katastrofy* [Polish Performances: The Year of the Catastrophe]. Instytut Teatralny im. Zbigniewa Raszewskiego, Znak, 2013.

Kovan, Martin. "Thresholds of Transcendence: Buddhist Self-Immolation and Mahāyānist Absolute Altruism." *Journal of Buddhist Ethics*, part 2, vol. 21, 2014, pp. 378–423.

Lahiri, Simanti. "Choosing to Die: Suicide Bombing and Suicide Protest in South Asia." *Terrorism and Political Violence*, vol. 27, no. 2, 2015, pp. 268–288.

Laloë, Véronique. "Patterns of Deliberate Self-Burning in Various Parts of the World: A Review." *Burns*, vol. 30, no. 3, 2004, pp. 207–215.

Laloë, Véronique, and Mohan Ganesan. "Self-Immolation a Common Suicidal Behaviour in Eastern Sri Lanka." *Burns*, vol. 28, no. 5, 2002, pp. 475–480.

Michelsen, Nicholas. "The Political Subject of Self-Immolation." *Globalizations*, vol. 12, no. 1, 2015, pp. 83–100.

Palata, Luboš. "Pochodnia numer jeden" [Torch No. One]. *Ale Historia*, the history supplement of *Gazeta Wyborcza* [Warsaw], no. 2 (361), 14 Jan. 2019, pp. 2–3.

Shahadi, Joseph. "Burn: The Radical Disappearance of Kathy Change." *TDR: The Drama Review*, vol. 55, no. 2, 2011, pp. 52–72.

Sharp, Gene. *From Dictatorship to Democracy: A Conceptual Framework for Liberation.* Albert Einstein Institution, 1993.

Shilling, Chris. *The Body and Social Theory.* 3rd edition. Sage, 2012.

Sontag, Susan. *Regarding the Pain of Others.* Picador, 2003.

Stefanicki, Robert. *Czerwony Tybet* [Red Tibet]. Agora, 2014.

Woeser, Tsering. *Tibet on Fire: Self-Immolations against Chinese Rule.* Translated by Kevin Carrico. Verso, 2016.

Part II

Chronology

Notes and microstudies on selected protest self-burnings (1963–2017)

Figure PII.1 Van Thanh Rudd *No Nauru* (2012).

40 Chronology of protest self-burnings (1963–2017)

The below timeline comprises notes and microstudies on selected contemporary protest self-burnings, arranged in chronological order. The entries include accounts of artist reactions and the specific methods of commemorating the people who had engaged in auto-cremation. The chronological order is interrupted at times, particularly when a given event spawned one or more follow-up incidents or when some subsequent self-burnings either invoked the original protest or drew attention to the same problem. The notes and microstudies also include abridged accounts of each individual act and, where source material allowed, some additional context that may assist with understanding the origins of the incidents and – in specific cases – their consequences.

Using academic sources as well as press clippings and agency cables, mostly sourced from reputable, high-profile newsrooms and agencies, I tried to establish the full names of the self-burners, precise dates, and locations where their protests occurred, as well as the ultimate fates of the casualties. Although verified through various sources, the data (names, dates, and locations) is still incomplete or unreliable in places. Nonetheless, the record I managed to compile will be of help to people interested in investigating these incidents or locating additional information or iconographic materials, recordings, or video footage. In the course of my work, I consulted the "List of Political Self-Immolations" Wikipedia entry, the "Living Torches" website, and other sources, some of which are identified below the notes and microstudies.

The compilation includes, first and foremost, self-immolations performed for political reasons, cases motivated by altruism (or at least seemingly so), as well as fiery suicide protests motivated socially – by poverty, unemployment, job loss, or adverse judicial decisions. I have included both types in the record primarily because the lines between protests self-burnings as expressions of frustration and as articulations of uncompromising personal beliefs and moral urgency are often difficult to draw. I ultimately decided to choose the location of the act as the primary classification criterion. In other words, if the incident occurred in a public place, such as a square, the street outside a local or state government office, or a court building, I included it in the list – even if reports alleged that the act itself was motivated chiefly by personal problems. The decision was prompted by the fact that if a person chose to self-burn in a publicly available place, then the message they tried to send in so violent a manner was probably important enough to warrant a circle of witnesses broader than immediate family or friends. There were exceptions, obviously, including auto-cremations by incarcerated political prisoners, as well as individual acts undertaken in a car, an office, a church, and even during a video conversation or a press conference. These exceptions may demonstrate how difficult it is to draw generalisations when it comes to suicide protests by fire.

The list I managed to compile is by no means complete, but including more cases may have had adverse effects on the structure of the book. When selecting individual incidents, I was driven primarily by the desire to present as broad a spectrum of issues pertaining to these borderline acts as possible. Aside from that, I wanted the list to feature the most important waves of self-burnings, as well as situations where one suicide protest inspired a number of follow-up events.

Republic of Vietnam

11 June 1963 – in Saigon, **Thích Quảng Đức** (aged 66), a Mahāyāna Buddhist monk, self-immolated in protest against the persecution of Buddhists by the US-supported South Vietnamese government of Ngô Đình Diệm. News of the act spread far and wide distributed across the globe by international press agencies and mass media, while the iconic photographs of the monk engulfed in flames, taken by the AP reporter Malcolm Browne, became one of the symbols of the war in Vietnam and the 1960s in general.

The event inspired a number of self-burnings, in Vietnam and across the globe, committed for personal and supra-individual reasons. Up until 2 November 1963, when the Diệm regime finally fell in South Vietnam, at least five Buddhist monks and one nun committed auto-cremations. Prior to that, the desire to perform self-immolation in the name of the Buddhist cause was expressed by two members of the royal family, sisters and nuns Thích Nữ Diệu Huệ and Thích Nữ Tu Diệu, but neither of them ultimately followed through with the threat. Self-incineration was not the only radical form of protest employed at the time across the Republic of Vietnam. Aside from mass protests, marches, and sit-downs, dissidents also engaged in hunger strikes, and on 13 August 1963, an 18-year-old Buddhist attempted to cut her arm off to stress the urgency of her pleas to the president to stop the persecution.

(Biggs, "How"; Chân; Halberstam, *The Kennedy, The Making*; Karnow; "Thuviengdpt"; Topmiller, "Struggling," *The Lotus*)

Republic of India

25 January 1965 – a Tamil peasant from Kizappazuvur by the name of **Chinnasamy** (aged 27) set himself on fire in the Trichy region of Madras State in southern India. The incident was part of a wave of Tamil protests against rising Hindu domination and government plans of imposing Hindi as an official language across the country, including in majority Dravidian areas calling for autonomy. Inspired by Chinnasamy's example, before the end of 1965 at least six more Tamils immolated themselves. Over the following months, New Delhi authorities ultimately withdrew from their plans to implement legislation suppressing the use of the Telugu language. Most of the protest self-burnings that took place across India in subsequent years were attributed to the Chinnasamy Effect, while Dravidian political parties celebrated the anniversary of his death as a day of martyrdom for the cause of defending the native tongue.

(Nalankilli)

Republic of Vietnam

26 January 1965 – popular youth leader **Đào Thị Yến Phi** (aged 17) set herself on fire in Nha Trang in the Khánh Hòa province, during a hunger strike of 200 Buddhists protesting against the war and calling for a ceasefire. The same cause inspired **Thích Giác Thanh**, a young Buddhist monk, to auto-cremate on 20 April in the Tỉnh Gia Định province.

("Thuviengdpt")

United States of America

16 March 1965 – protesting against the arms race and the escalation of the war in Vietnam, peace activist **Alice Herz** (aged 82) set herself on fire in Detroit. The incident took place shortly after the commencement of Operation Rolling Thunder, a sweeping bombing campaign against North Vietnamese targets, and the landing of US Marines on the beaches of Đà Nẵng. She was the first in the US to self-immolate in protest against the war, but both the act and her death ten days later barely registered in the news. The public reaction differed considerably following the death of **Norman Morrison** (aged 31), a Quaker, and husband and father of three, who immolated himself outside the Pentagon on 2 November 1965, in front of his daughter Emily, barely one-year-old at the time. A week later, Morrison was followed by **Roger LaPorte** (aged 22), former Trappist seminarian and member of the Catholic Worker Movement, who on the morning of 9 November 1965 sat down in the lotus position outside the UN complex in New York and set himself aflame. Before dying in the hospital the following day, he confessed that he had acted in protest against the war and the hatred sweeping the world.

The following years saw a spate of pacifist self-burnings across California. **Florence Beaumont** (aged 56), anti-war activist, mother of two, and former English teacher, set herself on fire on 15 October 1967, outside the Federal Building in Los Angeles. Her husband described her as an ordinary person who empathised deeply with the victims of the war in Vietnam. In her car, the authorities found anti-war literature and brochures. On 10 May 1970, in protest against the American incursion into Cambodia, senior year history major **George Winne** (aged 23) auto-cremated a couple of days after receiving his draft card. Next to him stood a sign with anti-war slogans. Before dying in the hospital the following day, he asked his mother to write to President Richard Nixon and plead with him to end the conflict. A week after his death, the anti-war movement began gaining serious momentum, with mass protests and student sit-ins breaking out across the country in the wake of the killing of four and wounding of nine Kent State University students by the Ohio National Guard. At the 11 May vigil for the Kent State victims, philosopher Herbert Marcuse encouraged the assembly to take up Winne's call and escalate the protests.

The aforementioned cases by no means exhaust the list of people who self-incinerated or attempted to do so in the US over the course of the war in Vietnam. The list also includes **Celene Jankowski** (aged 24) who set herself ablaze shortly after Morrison, on 11 November 1965, in her home in South Bend, Indiana (she survived), and **Ronald Brazee** (aged 16), a high-school student who self-immolated on 19 March 1968, outside the Cathedral of the Immaculate Conception in Syracuse, New York (the teenager died in the hospital on 27 April). It is generally assumed that both cases were inspired by reports from Vietnam, among other factors.

(Coburn; Cooper; Ryan; Zaroulis and Sullivan)

Republic of Korea

21 July 1965 – **Huh Jik** (aged 63), a Korean politician and leader of one of the smaller opposition parties, self-immolated on the steps of the National Assembly in Seoul to protest against the treaty reestablishing relations between Korea and Japan. The treaty, signed by the Park Chung-hee cabinet on 22 June 1965, was hotly contested by the opposition, especially the people's parties, as well as college professors and students who believed that the document would encourage Japan to seek to subjugate Korea once again. Hundreds of people took to the streets of the capital and major cities to demonstrate their disapproval of the treaty and its provisions, and decry the refusal of the Japanese to extend an official apology for the crimes perpetrated during their occupation of the Korean Peninsula (1905–45).

(*Keesing's*)

Republic of Vietnam

29 May 1966 – the Buddhist nun **Thích Nữ Thanh Quang** (aged 55) auto-cremated in protest against the policies of the head of Saigon government, General Nguyễn Cao Kỳ, and his dismissal of General Nguyễn Chánh Thi, a figure popular with the Buddhists in South Vietnam, two months prior. The nun left two letters – the one addressed to Lyndon B. Johnson implored him to withdraw American support for the South Vietnamese government, while the other, addressed to Prime Minister Kỳ, requested the government cease its harassment of the Buddhist community. Her death sparked a series of mass protests against the prime minister, accusing him of seeking to entrench his position and pursuing the escalation of the war. This ultimately inspired a spate of follow-up self-immolations (at least eight) of both lay and monastic people in 1966, most of which were performed by women. As the incidents continued, one Buddhist leader, Thích Trí Quang, called on his fellow believers to cease the self-burnings. Contrary to 1963, the protests failed to sway Washington, and the US ultimately chose to stand by General Kỳ as he guaranteed that the South Vietnamese government would continue its war against the Communist

North, a policy that the Buddhist protests stood to undermine. Additionally, in contrast to their position three years prior, the Buddhists were no longer seen as victims of authoritarian persecution due to their support of, or active involvement with, the independent-minded military leaders from the Đà Nẵng and Huế areas, where the unrest led to the burning of the US Information Service building and the US consulate. These events ultimately prompted Washington to accept Kỳ's June 1966 suppression of the Buddhist unrest, seeing it as a necessary step towards stabilising the country's internal situation.

In the following years, anti-war protests, including self-burnings, continued unabated. On 16 May 1967, **Nhất Chi Mai (Thích Nữ Diệu Huỳnh**, aged 30) set herself ablaze outside the Từ Nghiêm pagoda in Saigon. Her funeral attracted nearly 50,000 people. Another wave of auto-cremations swept through the country in October and November 1967, after the government prevented Buddhist activists from voting in parliamentary elections and later claimed majority victory despite receiving less than 35% of the vote.

Until the capture of Saigon by the North Vietnamese and the end of war in 1975, Vietnam was stage to many more self-burnings, performed by nuns, monks, and laypeople. Self-immolation was also used after the war to protest against the oppressive policies of the new Communist authorities. For example, in November 1972, 12 monks and nuns, led by **Thích Hue Hien**, performed a collective auto-cremation in Cần Thơ. Appeals were made to authorities to respect the population's freedom of worship. Auto-cremations in the name of religious liberty, performed by Buddhists as well as Hòa Hảo adherents, were not uncommon in the following decades too.

(Chân; Karnow; Topmiller, "Struggling," *The Lotus*)

People's Republic of China

12 June 1966 – the early days of the Cultural Revolution in China were stage to the auto-cremation of **Liangqing** (aged 70), the abbot of Famen Temple in Shaanxi province, who refused to let the Red Guards (Hunweibin) destroy the Buddhist shrine in his care. His sacrifice proved a Pyrrhic victory, as the invaders left the pagoda of the main temple complex untouched, but smashed many of the valuables. Thirty years later, the abbot's sacrifice was honoured with a ceremony during which his ashes were buried in the temple.

(Vilkaite)

Japan

11 November 1967 – Japanese radio engineer, anti-war activist, and Esperantist **Yui Chūnoshin** (aged 73) set himself aflame in Tokyo, outside the offices of Prime Minister Satō Eisaku, to protest against his government's foreign policy, which supported US presence and conduct in Vietnam. Yui also demanded the government take a tougher stance in its negotiations with

the Americans regarding the return of administrative control over Okinawa and the Ogasawara Islands to Japan. Before his self-immolation, he sent letters to a number of press outlets. The *Tokyo Shimbun* daily published the letter in its entirety, while other major papers ended up running excerpts. Yui's act also prompted several subversive actions, including a restaging of his self-immolation with an effigy by the Zero Jigen (Zero Dimension), one of the most prominent performance art groups of the era, which took place at a well-known 1960s protest site at Shinjuku Station.

The man's final protest and death the following day inspired a number of followers: **Shirakawa Kazuo** (aged 17), who lit himself on fire in 1968 outside the US consulate in Osaka to protest the war in Vietnam, and **Funamoto Shūji** (aged 29), who followed suit outside the gate of Kadena Air Force Base on Okinawa in June 1975, in protest against the visit of Prince (later Emperor) Akihito to the Island, planned to take place the following month.

(Andrews; Marotti; Norimatsu)

Polish People's Republic

8 September 1968 – **Ryszard Siwiec** (aged 59), a philosopher working in Przemyśl as an accountant, set himself ablaze at Warsaw's main sports stadium during the summer harvest festival, in front of high-ranking officials and Party members, and 100,000 people in attendance. Despite so many witnesses, Siwiec's gesture languished in historical obscurity until the release of Maciej Drygas' 1991 documentary *Usłyszcie mój krzyk* (*Hear My Cry*). Siwiec opposed Communist indoctrination, widespread violations of the rule of law, and the restrictions placed on individual liberties, and denounced the August 1968 invasion of Czechoslovakia by Warsaw Pact forces, including Polish People's Army detachments. He died in the hospital four days later. Siwiec was the first person in the Soviet Bloc to self-immolate for political reasons.

(Blažek)

Czechoslovak Socialist Republic

16 January 1969 – **Jan Palach** (aged 20), a history major at Charles University's Department of Philosophy, set himself aflame outside the National Museum at Wenceslas Square in Prague, intent on shocking society out of the torpor it has succumbed to following the crushing of the Prague Spring in 1968. In the letters he left, he demanded the authorities abandon censorship and forbid the distribution of the newspaper circulated by the occupying forces, and called for his fellow countrymen to hold a nationwide strike to force the government to concede to the demands. Although he signed the letters "Torch No. 1," suggesting that his immolation was only the beginning of a concerted clandestine effort, all available evidence indicates that he acted alone. He died in the hospital three days later. His death received a great deal

46   Chronology of protest self-burnings (1963–2017)

of publicity abroad, while his 25 January funeral drew thousands and turned into a major patriotic demonstration. The social impact of his death was so profound that it inspired numerous followers in Czechoslovakia and other countries. His protest became a symbol of resistance against the Communist regime; in contemporary Czechia, Palach serves as a symbol of the country's post-1989 democratic turn.

Hungarian People's Republic

21 January 1969 – **Sándor Bauer** (aged 17) self-immolated on the steps of the National Museum in Budapest in protest against the occupation of Czechoslovakia and the presence of Soviet troops in Hungary, and in solidarity with Palach. He died two days later. Although the Hungarian national press agency reported his death, the despatch called him mentally unstable. This characterisation resulted in Bauer's act being mostly ignored and forgotten. Only in 1989 did the director Zsolt Balogh introduce Bauer's story to a broader audience with his documentary *1968*, which featured statements from Bauer's friends and witnesses of the self-burning.

Latvian Soviet Socialist Republic – Soviet Union

13 April 1969 – gifted mathematics student of Latvian Jewish descent, **Ilya Aronovich Rips** (aged 20), who learned of Palach's self-immolation from Radio Free Europe, unrolled a banner saying "I protest against the occupation of Czechoslovakia" under the Freedom Monument in Riga, then doused himself with fuel and lit the flame. The fire was put out quickly by passersby, leading to Rips suffering only minor burns to his neck and arms. Following an extensive interrogation, he was first transferred to a psychiatric hospital and later placed in a "reeducation" facility, where he spent two years. The authorities decided to release him when pressure from international public opinion began to mount. Rips emigrated to Israel in 1972, where he went on to a distinguished career in science. Years later, he explained that he did not intend to spark mass protests, but rather wanted to release pent-up bitterness and deal with his loss of hope in the collapse of communism.

United States of America

30 May 1969 – **Bruce Mayrock** (aged 20), a student at Columbia University, lit himself on fire outside the United Nations Headquarters in New York City, in order to draw attention to the suffering of the Biafran people during the Nigerian Civil War (1967–70). Next to him was a poster calling for intervention and putting a stop to the genocide. He died in the hospital on the same day.

(Onyekachi)

Socialist Republic of Romania

13 February 1970 – **Márton Moyses** (aged 29), a member of the Hungarian minority, set himself on fire in Braşov in Transylvania, outside the headquarters of the Romanian Communist Party. During the Hungarian Revolution of 1956, he attempted to cross over into Hungary with three friends to join the rebels. The Securitate arrested him in 1960 for writing poems deemed anti-state by the authorities. Tortured and afraid of giving up his friends under interrogation, he cut his tongue out with thread. After his self-immolation, he was shipped to the hospital where the doctors were ordered to deny him any analgesics. He died after three months of horrifying agony.

("Márton Moyses")

Basque Country – Spain

18 September 1970 – **Joseba Elósegi Odriozola** (aged 54), a Basque separatist, self-immolated in San Sebastián (Donostia) in protest against the repressive policies of the Francisco Franco regime. In 1937, while fighting in the Spanish Civil War, he witnessed the bombing of Guernica. Sentenced to death for fighting alongside the Republicans, he escaped the noose thanks to a prisoner swap. During World War II, he joined the French resistance. In 1946, he unfurled the Basque flag from the tower of the San Sebastián Cathedral. He set himself aflame during the opening ceremony of an international pelota championship presided over by Franco himself. Jumping from the second story of the stadium gallery, he bellowed "Long live the free Basque country!" and allegedly tried to embrace the dictator. He survived the attempt and was sentenced to seven years in prison (of which he served three).

In later years, he was elected to the Spanish parliament from the province of Gipuzkoa. In his memoirs, Odriozola indicated that his act was inspired by Buddhist auto-cremations in Vietnam and the self-immolation of Palach. The incident eventually became a symbol of the struggle for Basque autonomy.

Elósegi was celebrated in song (such as folk ballad by the Etxamendi eta Larralde named after him) and became the subject of a number of documentaries.

(Etxamendi; "Joseba Elósegui")

Italy

19 September 1970 – Greek engineering student **Kostas Georgakis** (aged 22) set himself ablaze on the Giacomo Matteotti Square in Genoa in protest against the reign of the neofascist junta headed by Georgios Papadopoulos, which took power in a military coup in April 1967. Letters sent by the Greek consulate in Italy clearly show that the authorities worried Georgakis would be seen as the Greek Palach, and that his death could lead to widespread protests. Fearing civil unrest, the government allowed the family to bring

48 Chronology of protest self-burnings (1963–2017)

Georgakis' remains to his native island of Corfu only four months after the incident. The student's violent act of protest made the world realise the extent of the Greeks' disapproval of the Regime of the Colonels, which was eventually deposed in 1974.

Two Greek poets wrote verses in his honour. In 2000, a Genoa publisher released *Il grande sì* (*The Big Yes*), Costantinos Paputsis' book on the incident. The following year, Andreas Apostolidis directed a documentary *Mia fora kai enan kairo ypirhan iroes* (*Once Upon a Time There Were Heroes*), which featured students discussing Georgakis' sacrifice at a university debate in Athens. A commemorative plaque sits near the site of his self-immolation, and his family town of Kerkyra has erected a statue of his likeness.

("Kostas Georgakis")

Republic of Korea

13 November 1970 – Korean labourer, **Chun Tae-il** (aged 22), self-burned in Seoul in protest against the brutal exploitation of textile workers. His death drew considerable attention to horrible working conditions and widespread abuse of the lower social classes, ultimately leading workers, students, clergymen, and media figures to unite in the struggle for worker rights and laying the foundation for the establishment of independent labour unions in South Korea. Indirectly, his protest was also aimed against the authoritarian rule of General Park Chung-hee, who forcibly modernised the country without regard for the staggering social costs these changes incurred. Chun died in the hospital later that same day, and his death inspired many followers, mostly drawing from radicalised leftist activists, who protested against the government, whose authoritarian grip on the country only eased off in 1993.

(Cho Y-r.; Park)

Lithuanian Soviet Socialist Republic – Soviet Union

14 May 1972 – **Romas Kalanta** (aged 19), a night school student, worker, and Komsomol member intent on becoming a clergyman, set himself aflame in protest against the Soviet occupation in a square near one of Kaunas' main avenues, outside the State Musical Theatre, where the Soviets proclaimed the incorporation of Lithuania into the Soviet Union in 1940. His choice of venue was doubly symbolic: aside from its 1940 connotations, the square was also situated across the street from the Municipal Executive Committee, the local arm of Soviet authority. Kalanta was presumably inspired by Palach's immolation and allegedly yelled "Freedom for Lithuania!" moment before lighting the flame. Unconscious and suffering from extensive burns, he was brought to a hospital where he died the following day. Although the funeral was set for 18 May and the official date was released to the public, the authorities

Chronology of protest self-burnings (1963–2017) 49

clandestinely sped up the burial. Realising the deception, a crowd of despondent protesters began a two-day riot that ultimately had to be put down by force, leading to the arrest of 400 protesters, of whom seven were handed three-year prison sentences for "disturbing the public order." Hundreds of other detainees were expelled from schools or sacked from their jobs.

Although opposition to the Soviet-backed authorities in Lithuania was not unheard of prior to Kalanta's self-burning, it was his act and burial that galvanised public resistance. According to a 1972 report produced by Lithuanian state security, as many as 13 people followed in Kalanta's footsteps. In order to discredit his image, in 1972, a specially appointed medical commission retroactively diagnosed him as *non compos mentis*. In spite of these efforts, Lithuanians considered Kalanta a symbol of resistance against Soviet occupation. They kept bringing flowers to the site of his immolation, while authors who wrote poems and pamphlets honouring his memory found themselves persecuted by Soviet authorities. In 1989, his case was re-examined by medical professionals and his prior diagnosis was officially dismissed.

On the 30th anniversary of his death, a memorial to Kalanta was unveiled at the site of the incident, and city authorities announced that a street and a school would be named after him. Commissioned by Lithuanian filmmaker Raimundas Banionis, Polish director Maciej Drygas wrote the screenplay for *Vaikai iš Amerikos viešbučio* (*The Children from the America Hotel*), a feature film set in Kaunas in spring 1972, which tells the story of a group of youths living under a totalitarian regime who yearn for free, unrestrained expression. The picture was shot in Lithuania after it declared independence in 1990, a decision the Kremlin responded to by imposing a lengthy economic blockade on the country. In 1999, Banionis and Andrius Šiuša produced a documentary about Kalanta, *Fontano vaikai* (*The Children's Fountain*). The title is a reference to a popular youth hangout near which Kalanta immolated himself. The incident inspired numerous other politically motivated self-burnings across the country.

(Dorr; Drygas; Vardys)

Canada

4 June 1972 – Francophone Canadian poet, **Huguette Gaulin Bergeron** (aged 28), self-immolated on Place Jacques-Cartier in the Old Montreal neighbourhood, likely in response to the political events unfolding at the time. She died two days later. As she set herself ablaze, she yelled: "Vous avez détruit la beauté du monde!" ("You have destroyed the beauty of the world!"), inspiring Luc Plamondon to write his pro-environmental ballad *Le monde est fou* (*The World is Mad*, 1973). A new version of the song, *Hymne a la beauté du monde* (*The Hymn to the Beauty of the World*), became hugely popular thanks to Diane Dufresne (1979). In later years, the song would be repeatedly reinterpreted by Québécois artists.

("Huguette Gaulin")

German Democratic Republic

18 August 1976 – **Oskar Brüsewitz** (aged 46), an Evangelical pastor and rector of the Drossdorf-Rippicha parish, self-immolated outside the Church of St. Michael in Zeitz near Leipzig, in protest against the persecution of Christians in the German Democratic Republic (GDR) and what he saw as the Evangelical Lutheran Church leadership's acquiescence to the Communist regime. The pastor was known for his rather unorthodox approach to evangelisation. When in 1975 the Party unveiled its slogan, "We will still harvest our crop in the morning, without help from God or sunlight," the pastor wrote "Without rain and God, the whole world will go bankrupt" on his horse-drawn carriage and took it down the road to Zeitz, creating a huge traffic jam. These highly symbolic forms of protest brought him to the attention of the authorities, which finally leaned on the Church to move Brüsewitz to another rectorate. In summer 1976, superiors ordered him to vacate the parish; presumably feeling abandoned by his fellow clergymen, the minister decided to self-immolate in public. He affixed a banner with an anti-Communist slogan to his Wartburg and wrote a farewell letter, in which he called for the faithful to abandon the "feigned peace." He died four days after the incident. Officers of the Ministry for State Security first prevented his wife from visiting him and later made attempts to conceal the event from the public and discredit the pastor. Despite these efforts, however, news of Brüsewitz's violent protest reached the West, where it was interpreted as a desperate call for help from persecuted Christians. Initially critical of the incident, the Lutheran Church leadership eventually acknowledged the pastor and his cause, mostly as a result of mounting pressure from church members and international public opinion, the latter familiarised with the case through the efforts of the Oskar Brüsewitz Centre established in the Federal Republic of Germany (FRG) in 1977.

Recognised as a symbol of resistance against the GDR regime, the pastor became known as "Das Fanal von Zeitz" ("The Torch of Zeitz"). Matthias Koeppel's 1977 painting *Die Selbstverbrennung des Pfarrers Brüsewitz* (*The Self-Immolation of Pastor Brüsewitz*), inspired by the incident, is currently on display at the Checkpoint Charlie Museum in Berlin.

(Czabański and Czabańska-Rosada)

France

10 February 1977 – **Alain Escoffier** (aged 28), a member of the far-right Parti des Forces Nouvelles (Party of New Forces), set himself aflame at an Aeroflot office during an anti-Communist demonstration in Paris. He died in the hospital a couple of hours later.

Later that same year, the Italian right-wing band Compagna dell'Anello dedicated a song to the protester, naming it after him (the alternative title is *Champs Élysées*) and linking his death with Palach's self-immolation in the lyrics. Alejandro Rex recorded a Spanish-language version of the song in 2013.

("Alain Escoffier")

Federal Republic of Germany

16 November 1977 – on the Protestant Day of Prayer and Repentance, **Hartmut Gründler** (aged 47), a member of the West German environmental movement, high school teacher, and proponent of Gandhi's non-violent resistance, set himself aflame in Hamburg, just before the commencement of the Social Democratic Party of Germany (SPD) congress on the development of the nuclear power programme. He protested against what he saw as misinformation on energy policy spread by the Helmut Schmidt government. Earlier, the teacher attempted other means of protest, including hunger strikes. Before the incident, he wrote to the Chancellor and other politicians to inform them of his plans, attaching his political testament to the letter. He also printed pamphlets announcing the self-immolation and distributed them for two days before the incident, which he himself called "an appeal against the atomic lie." Over 1,000 people attended his funeral.

("Hartmut Gründler")

Ukrainian Soviet Socialist Republic – Soviet Union

21 January 1978 – **Oleksa Hirnyk** (aged 64), a Ukrainian independence activist and former political prisoner, self-immolated by the tomb of Taras Shevchenko on a hill near Kaniv, then stabbed himself in the heart. Before the incident, he scattered pamphlets in which he railed against Soviet domination. His body was found by a police patrol, who picked up the pamphlets before anyone had a chance to find them.

His death was first reported to the public after Ukraine became independent in 1991. In 2007, President Viktor Yushchenko awarded him the country's highest honour, the order of Hero of Ukraine.

("Oleksa Hirnyk")

Crimea – Soviet Union

23 June 1978 – **Musa Mamut** (aged 47), a Crimean Tatar, doused himself with petrol and set himself on fire outside his home in Besh-Terek near Simferopol. In accordance with Joseph Stalin's 1944 decree accusing Crimean Tatars of collaboration with the Nazis, he had been deported at the age of 13, along with his entire family, to Uzbekistan. The Soviet authorities' decision to rescind the treason charge in September 1967 launched a gradual return of Tatars to Crimea, but once there, they usually encountered many

52 Chronology of protest self-burnings (1963–2017)

administrative difficulties. Such was the case of Mamut, who purchased a house in 1975 but was refused notary certification, which prevented him from obtaining a residence permit. He moved into the house regardless, an offence that sent him to prison for two years and gave his wife a suspended two-year prison sentence. Mamut was released after a couple of months and the rest of his sentence was commuted to forced labour in a refinery. In later years, he was often subject to similar harassment and repeatedly petitioned higher authorities to complain against local officials. When law enforcement arrived to arrest him, he ran outside and set himself on fire (an act he allegedly pondered already a year prior). It is possible that he intended the self-immolation to be a suicide attack that would claim the life of an arresting officer. Mamut died in the hospital five days later.

His act became a symbol of the Crimean Tatars' struggle for justice, and his funeral sparked a mass protest. In a letter to Leonid Brezhnev, Andrei Sakharov argued that Mamut's death should become the first step towards reconciliation with the Tatars. Reshat and Mustafa Dzhemilev reported news of the incident to the king of Saudi Arabia and the international community, asking for help ending the persecution of the Tatars.

(Allworth; Aydın; Cemilev; Uehling)

German Democratic Republic

17 September 1978 – protestant pastor **Rolf Günther** (aged 31) set himself on fire during mass in front of 300 parishioners in Falkenstein in Saxony, next to a banner with the words: "Awaken already!" The congregation fled the church, and no one else was hurt. A couple of months before the incident, the minister sent a fellow theologian a letter in which he critiqued the Communist system. His protest, however, was presumed to have been brought on by a conflict with a group of other priests he accused of sectarian practices. Less than two weeks before the incident he was dismissed from his parish, presumably as a result of his continued insubordination towards the Church leadership, which sided with his detractors. Church and state authorities kept his death a secret, and Stasi ultimately used it to weaken the position of the Church in the GDR.

(Czabański and Czabańska–Rosada)

Switzerland, India, Federal Republic of Germany, United States of America, the Philippines, Great Britain

2 October 1978 – **Lynette Phillips** (aged 24), an Australian national, self-immolated outside the United Nations Office at Geneva, in protest, according to her farewell letter, against the injustice and irrationality of modern society. Initially, she planned to set herself aflame outside the British

Parliament, but was arrested by law enforcement and deported from British territory. The daughter of a mining magnate, she was a member of the international Ánanda Margá organisation, established by Prabhat Ranjan Sarkar in Bihar (then East Pakistan) in 1955 to promote a range of ideas, including self-actualisation and the socio-economic Progressive Utilisation Theory (PROUT). In 1971, its founder was arrested in Patna on charges of ordering the killing of 18 former members, and in 1975, Ánanda Margá was officially labelled a dangerous sect and banned by the Indira Gandhi government, which the organisation opposed. To protest Sarkar's imprisonment and the persecution of the organisation's rank-and-file, seven members self-immolated in India, the FRG, the US, and the Philippines. Phillips took her own life soon after the sect leader's release from prison on 2 August 1978. Before leaving for Europe, she sent a letter to the Ánanda Margá chapter in Australia, in which she repeated calls for social justice. Her death was widely reported by the media in Great Britain and other Commonwealth countries, inspiring many others to follow in her footsteps, mostly for personal reasons.

(Ashton and Donnan; Balderstone; Coleman)

Poland

21 March 1980 – on the 40th anniversary of the Katyń massacre, retired baker and bibliophile, former Home Army Soldier **Walenty Badylak** (aged 76) chained himself to a well on Krakow's Main Square, doused himself with petrol, and lit himself aflame. As he burned, he warned those who ran to extinguish the fire to stay away, saying the fuel bottles he hid underneath his coat would soon start exploding. From his neck hung a metal plate on which he etched a denouncement of the Communist authorities. He died within minutes. The government tried to keep the incident a secret, while the local newspaper published a report the following day that painted Badylak as a long-time mental patient. The locals kept placing candles and flower at the site of his immolation, which state security collected time and time again.

In 1981, Eugeniusz Waniek, a professor at the Krakow Academy of Fine Arts, painted *Zdarzenie* (*The Event*), a depiction of Badylak engulfed in flames. His sacrifice was also commemorated by the poet Bronisław Maj in a 1986 poem which opens with the line "It only takes a couple of minutes." The incident is also the subject of the 2011 documentary *Święty ogień* (*The Holy Fire*), produced by Jarosław Mańka and Maciej Grabysa. Today, the site is marked by a commemorative plaque.

(Fijałek)

Turkey, Germany, Denmark, Great Britain

18 May 1982 – four activists of the leftist Kurdistan Workers' Party (PKK), an organisation striving to establish an independent Kurdish state, **Eşref Anyık,**

54 Chronology of protest self-burnings (1963–2017)

Ferhat Kurtay, **Necmi Öner**, and **Mahmut Zengin**, set themselves on fire in anti-government protest inside the Diyarbakır high-security prison in southeastern Turkey. After the military *coup d'état* on 12 September 1980, Turkish prisons were quickly filled with members and supporters of the PKK, and the inhumane conditions inside the penal facilities were decried by inmates, who staged hunger strikes in protest. On 4 March 1981, three days after IRA fighter Bobby Sands began the hunger strike that would end in his death, Diyarbakır detainees started their own protest that would last 45 days. On 21 March 1982, the day of the Nowruz holiday marking the Persian New Year, when Kurds traditionally light bonfires to ward off evil (a custom rooted in Zoroastrian traditions), **Mazlum Doğan**, a member of the PKK's Central Committee, set fire to his cell and then hanged himself. The self-immolation of the four prisoners that took place shortly after has come to be known among historiographers as "Dörtlerin gecesi" ("The Night of the Four"). Self-incineration as protest later transcended the walls of the prisons, in 1988 three mothers set fire to themselves to draw public attention to the terrible conditions of their sons' detainment.

The spread of self-immolations and other suicidal forms of protest (including suicide bombings) among the Kurds could have been influenced by the ideal of the new Kurd, obedient, reasonable, responsible, and ready to make the highest sacrifices for the cause, an image cultivated by left-leaning party ideologues, including PKK founder Abdullah Öcalan. Self-burnings were often undertaken in response to military or political defeats to draw international attention to the plight of the Kurds. That was the case after the PKK was outlawed in Germany in November 1993, an event that resulted in 12 Kurds setting themselves ablaze in different cities. Between May and October 1996, shortly after Öcalan was marked a terrorist by both Turkey and Israel, the Kurds were responsible for three suicide bombings and nine self-immolations.

The two biggest waves of these protests were triggered by Öcalan's 1 August 1998 declaration of a ceasefire and his arrest on 15 February 1999. The Kurds responded with mass protests held across the globe. They occupied and blockaded diplomatic facilities, and often took hostages. They also frequently threatened self-immolation and actually followed through with the threats in Berlin, Copenhagen, and near Stuttgart. The incidents continued despite Öcalan himself categorically proscribing such forms of protest, and after his arrest his younger brother Osman emphasised that the Kurds should set their enemies ablaze rather than themselves. Estimates indicate that 92 Kurds self-immolated between 1988 and 1999, of whom only a handful died because most were quickly put out by their comrades. This was the case of **Nejla Coşkun** (aged 14), born on Cyprus into a family of Kurdish refugees living in Great Britain since 1993. The girl set herself aflame in the centre of London during a protest held the day after Öcalan's arrest. She survived the attempt and three years later, in an interview with *The Guardian*, said that the act was supposed to draw international attention to the terrible fate of her fellow Kurds.

Research conducted by psychiatrists among Kurdish refugees living in the West indicate that in 2002 most of them doubted the efficacy of self-immolation as an instrument of political struggle. This seems different for some Kurds in the Middle East though, as evidenced by the self-immolation of a Kurdish actor and a militant from the ranks of the Hêzên Parastina Gel (the People's Defence Forces, a military wing of the PKK), **Erdoğan Kahraman**, who set himself on fire on 27 March 2004 (World Theatre Day) in Aleppo for the Kurdish cause. His sacrificial act has become a symbol for Kurdish performance artists in Syria who, in 2015, decided to name the first theatre festival in Qamishli in northeast Rojava after Kahraman's *nom de guerre*, Yekta Herekol.

("First"; Grojean; Husni et al.; "'I Would Do'";
Othman; Rasool and Payton)

Turkey

10 August 1982 – **Artin Penik** (aged 61), an Armenian living in Turkey, set himself on fire on Istanbul's Taksim Square, because he was unable to accept the deaths of the victims of an attack on Esenboğa International Airport perpetrated by the Armenian Secret Army for the Liberation of Armenia (ASALA). Between 1973 and 1986, ASALA conducted a series of attacks (primarily against Turkish diplomats) across Western Europe, the US, and Canada, attempting to force the Turkish government to acknowledge its responsibility for the Armenian Genocide in 1915, pay reparations, and cede territory to Armenia. The 7 August 1982 attack at Ankara airport, during which the assailants detonated an explosive and opened fire on unsuspecting passengers, killing nine and wounding 72, was the first to target innocent bystanders. In the hospital, Penik was visited by the Armenian Patriarch of Constantinople, Shenork I Kaloustian, who declared Penik's act a symbol of the Armenian people's repudiation of the slaughter. In a filmed interview two days before his death, Penik asserted that if he could go back in time, he would still set himself ablaze, without a moment's hesitation. His funeral was reportedly attended by both Armenians and Turks.

("Armenian Issues")

Chile

11 November 1983 – Chilean construction worker **Sebastián Acevedo Becerra** (aged 52) self-immolated on Independence Square outside the Immaculate Conception Cathedral in Concepción. Two days earlier, unknown assailants abducted his son and daughter from a mass protest against the authoritarian dictatorship of Augusto Pinochet. Suspecting that his children were taken by Central Nacional de Informaciones (CNI), the president's secret police force, the father launched a desperate search effort. Powerless against the shadowy agency, Acevedo eventually doused himself with fuel

56 Chronology of protest self-burnings (1963–2017)

and threatened to immolate himself if he did not receive information about his children or was not taken to see them. When a police patrol attempted to remove him from the square, Acevedo set himself ablaze. He died hours later in the hospital.

His desperate act became a symbol of the pain and suffering of those whose loved ones or relatives disappeared in suspicious circumstances during the Pinochet era. The Chilean poet Gonzalo Rojas wrote verses in Acevedo's memory. The incident also inspired a number of protest songs. Today, the site of Acevedo's sacrifice in Concepción is marked with a commemorative cross.

("Sebastián Acevedo")

South Korea

15 August 1985 – on the 40th anniversary of the liberation of Korea from Japanese occupation, a construction worker by the name of **Hong Ki-il** set himself ablaze after visiting the government offices in Gwangju, where he petitioned the government to tell the truth about the massacre of students and civilians perpetrated there by government forces, acting on Chun Doo-hwan's orders, between 18 and 27 May 1980. The incident took place during mass protests against the Chun dictatorship, which came into power in a *coup d'état* on 12 December 1979. Before Hong made the final decision, a wave of protests swept through the country on the fifth anniversary of the Gwangju Uprising. Over 40,000 students marched at 80 universities, demanding the truth about the tragic events. A week later, 73 students staged a four-day sit-in at the US cultural office in Seoul and demanded the US withdraw their support of the authoritarian regime.

(Park)

United States of America

20 September 1987 – Iranian bookseller **Neusha Farrahi** (aged 31) set himself aflame outside the Federal Building in Los Angeles in protest against the appearance of Ayatollah Khamenei at the UN General Assembly. Friends surrounded him as he burned, to prevent law enforcement from putting out the fire. According to other reports, however, Farrahi had a fire extinguisher prepared nearby. Ultimately, the man suffered extensive burns and died in early October. The protest, during which the incident took place, gathered less than 1,000 people, most of whom came from two groups that were at odds with each other. One comprised proponents of reinstating the monarchy in Iran, the other included liberals who opposed both the theocratic regime and the authoritarian rule of Iran's former shah, Mohammad Reza Pahlavi, deposed in the 1979 Islamic revolution. Farrahi belonged to the latter, and once co-edited a book cataloguing the human rights violations committed by the regime of the Ayatollahs. He left a farewell letter intended for public release,

in which he emphasised that he opposed the Khamenei regime, as well as the right-wing foreign policy of Ronald Reagan and the monarchists, who sought to use the crimes perpetrated by the fundamentalists as justification for the reinstatement of the Pahlavi dynasty. The Farrahi incident was a highly controversial subject for the US-based Iranian diaspora. Some progressives saw the bookseller as a martyr and his act as an expression of the suffering borne by the victims of the Islamist regime; conservatives, on the other hand, considered him an attention-seeking poser.

(Becklund; Himmel)

Romania

2 March 1989 – **Liviu Cornel Babeş** (aged 47), a Romanian painter and sculptor working as an electrician, self-burned in a clearing near Braşov in protest against the Communist regime. The incident took place more than eight months prior to the overthrow and execution of Nicolae Ceauşescu and his wife Elena. Babeş left a farewell note saying: "Stop Mörder! Braşov = Auschwitz." Eighteen months earlier, a massive worker protest broke out in Braşov on 15 November 1987, the day of the local government elections, with thousands of people taking to the streets to decry wage slashing and employment cuts. The protest, which later came to be known as the Braşov Rebellion, was brutally put down by the Securitate and the military (300 people were dragged off to jail after the crackdown).

In 1997, Babeş was recognised as a hero of Romania and a street in his hometown was named after him.

("Liviu Cornel Babeş")

India

24 March 1989 – **Kailash Pawar**, one of the thousands of victims of the Bhopal industrial disaster that took place on the night of 2–3 December 1983 in the centre of Bhopal, set himself on fire in protest against the public's indifference to the fate of those who either died or suffered the horrifying consequences of the gas leak from the pesticide plant owned by the American chemical giant Union Carbide.

Republic of China – Taiwan

7 April 1989 – Taiwanese publisher and pro-democratic activist **Cheng Nan-jung** (aged 41) self-immolated in his office in Taipei, in protest against the violation of civil liberties. Cheng was born six months after Taiwan was swept with a wave of anti-governments protests against the repressive policies of the Kuomintang (1947). The events, which have come to be known as the February 28 Massacre, gave birth to the White Terror, a range of repressive

58 Chronology of protest self-burnings (1963–2017)

measures pursued under the guise of martial law, the longest in recorded history (1949–87). In March 1984, Cheng founded the *Freedom Era Weekly* and declared he would not be making any concessions to government that would be detrimental to free speech or freedom of the press; as a result, the weekly was repeatedly closed. In 1989, after he printed a draft of the constitution for the Republic of Taiwan (the island state's official name is the Republic of China), he was charged with inciting sedition and a warrant was issued for his arrest. When law enforcement appeared in his office, Cheng sealed himself inside and set himself on fire.

His funeral on 19 April was the stage of another self-immolation; when the police stopped the cortège from passing by the presidential palace, another Taiwanese pro-democratic activist, **Chan I-hua** (aged 32), set himself ablaze, injuring a number of nearby mourners.

("Cheng Nan-jung")

India

19 September 1990 – **Rajiv Goswami** (aged 19), a commerce student at Delhi University, set himself on fire in protest against plans to introduce legislation that would reserve a number of positions in the civil service and public universities for people from the Other Backward Classes (OBC).

Although a special report drafted in 1979–80 by a committee headed by Bindheshwari Prasad Mandal recommended that a minimum of 27% of positions be reserved for the OBC members, the Indira and Rajiv Gandhi governments summarily ignored its findings. The recommendations were unearthed in 1990 by Prime Minister Vishwanath Pratap Singh, but plans to implement them encountered such resistance from the privileged classes that he was forced to abandon them entirely and eventually compelled to resign. Opponents of the solution saw the government formula as unjust, because historically, the lowest classes, the Scheduled Castes and Tribes (SC and ST), namely dalits (the "untouchables," among others) and adivasis (members of indigenous tribes), were already guaranteed at least 22.5% of seats in colleges across the country. In their view, reserving an additional 27% for the OBC, who stand slightly higher in the social hierarchy than SC and ST, was too great a concession and threatened to discriminate against talented college candidates who would find themselves without a seat because of the quotas. It should be noted here that some Indian states, such as Tamil Nadu or Andhra Pradesh, introduced their own local changes that followed the Mandal recommendations, but these new plans presumed nationwide reforms.

Goswami's act sparked a wave of mass protests which saw youths, mostly across northern parts of India, express their dissatisfaction in a multitude of ways – including demonstrations, strikes, sit-ins, street blockades, forced store closures, blackouts, obstructing public transit routes, and suicides in different forms (by fire and others). At the time, protests of the most radical form (i.e. suicide) were pursued by a record high number of people (both men and women). Estimates indicate that between 24 September 1990, when **Surinder Singh Chauhan**, Goswami's fellow student, set himself on fire, and the end of November, at least 130 people committed self-burnings, with the number reaching as high as 220 in the following months, making it the biggest wave of protest self-incinerations in history. A subsequent psychiatric study (Singh et al.) revealed that out of 22 examined protesters (12 males and ten females, of whom nine set themselves on fire and the rest ingested poison), all but one were free of manifest mental disorders and the majority of them demonstrated high aspirations and hostility, and felt alienated.

Goswami survived his attempt and died in 2004, aged 33, from organ failure, probably brought on by the severe burns he sustained. The Goswami incident was also highly controversial due to the circumstances it took place in – the student set himself aflame at an anti-government demonstration, in front of journalists and photographers. Fellow students were to form a circle around Goswami to prevent law enforcement from reaching him in time. Initially, he intended only to douse his legs, which would allow his co-conspirators to quickly put out the fire, but as soon as he saw the police, Goswami doused himself from head to toe and lit the flame, while his friends scattered in the crowd. Three years later, Goswami undertook another attempt at self-burning, but was quickly thwarted by the police; as a result, he was singled out as a poser and his act was widely considered a hoax.

In 2006, the government reintroduced the 27% quota proposal, triggering another wave of protest self-burnings. The 27 May incident took place at a mass rally of pharmacists, doctors, and medical students, at a location in New Delhi where the annual Ramlila ceremony was usually held. The victim was **Rishi Gupta** (aged 23). It is not known whether he self-burned in protest against the government's plans, as he himself was not a student, while the rally organisers quickly distanced themselves from him and his action. Gupta was taken to the hospital, and his condition stabilised. Doubts about the motives driving the decision to self-burn also appeared in the case of **Surendra Mohanty**, a postgraduate medical student from Cuttack in Orissa, who set himself on fire that same day. The general student strike which commenced on 12 May, as well as mass protests breaking out across the country, ultimately compelled Prime Minister Manmohan Singh to promise to expand the number of seats in the most popular medical and engineering colleges, and in the top six business schools.

In 2010, the Indian TV channel Imagine TV broadcasted a series titled *Armanon Ka Balidaan-Aarakshan* (*Arman's Sacrifice-Reservation*) set against the backdrop of the turbulent events of the early 1990s. The political thriller garnered much controversy, primarily due to its graphic depiction of violence and self-immolation.

(Biggs, *Dying*; "Immolation"; Singh et al.; "Student")

United States of America

9 December 1990 – barely four months after the Iraqi invasion of Kuwait, the impending American intervention precipitated the self-burning of **Timothy Brown** (aged 48) on the steps of an abandoned factory in Isleton, California. In anti-war pamphlets he left behind, he portrayed himself as a Vietnam veteran and warned against involving the US in another conflict.

A little more than a month after the commencement of Operation Desert Storm, two more people set themselves ablaze in Massachusetts for similar reasons: **George Levely** (aged 30) lit himself on fire in Amherst on 18 February 1991, and **Raymond Moules** (aged 33) who followed suit three days later in Springfield.

("Man's"; Verhovek)

South Korea

29 April 1991 – **Park Sung-hee** (aged 20), a college student, set herself on fire at a rally at the Chonnam National University campus in Gwangju, where over 1,000 people gathered in response to the tragic events that took place three days prior in Seoul. During a protest calling for democratic reforms and lambasting President Roh Tae-woo's refusal to publicly acknowledge the truth of the Gwangju massacre, plainclothes police officers attacked a protester, Kang Kyung-dae (aged 20), with steel pipes as he tried to leap over a fence. He later died from injuries. So did Park Sung-hee, nearly three weeks later. These incidents triggered another wave of self-immolations across South Korea.

Unwilling to heed neither the sheer size of the protesting crowds that gathered across the country nor the petitions of the college professors and clergymen, the government refused to disband the universally detested riot police units, and later announced that Kang's death was an accident and a result of an isolated case of police misconduct. Thousands continued to march in protest, and strikes began breaking out across the country; at a 1 May rally at Andong National University, a student by the name of **Kim Young-kyun** (aged 19) doused himself with paint thinner, set himself on fire, and ran towards the protesters, bellowing calls for freedom. He died in the hospital the following day. In the wake of his death, the number of people embracing the most violent forms of protest rose significantly. **Chun Sae-yong**, a student in Seongnam, set himself on fire at a demonstration on 3 May. Engulfed in flames, he jumped off the roof of a building, yelling anti-regime rhetoric on his way down. The same *modus operandi* was followed on 8 May by one of the leaders of the protests, **Kim Ki-sul** (aged 27), who leapt off the five-story building of Sogang University in Seoul, dying on impact. The authorities accused his friend, the dissident Kang Ki-hoon, of forging Kim Ki-sul's last will, and after a handwriting expert corroborated the charges, Kang Ki-hoon was sent to prison for three years, but was eventually cleared of all wrongdoing in 2008 by the Truth and Reconciliation Commission established by President Kim Dae-jung.

At the time, protests escalated to include hunger strikes among prisoners and clergymen, as well as overnight university sit-ins carried out by college professors. Students stood accused of forming suicide groups, which would allegedly hold lotteries to select the next immolator. Some even suspected the malign influence of North Korea, supposedly inciting the suicide protests. In defiance of the government's ban on free assembly, 200,000 people poured into the streets in 23 cities on 10 May 1991, demanding the dismissal of the cabinet and the disbanding of the militarised riot police. At the Chonnam National University in Gwangju, **Yoon Yong-ha** (aged 20), a university student, set himself aflame in the toilets and rushed into a lecture hall, yelling anti-Roh Tae-woo rhetoric. Also around that time, 80 clergymen began a hunger strike in Inchon and were soon joined by 500 students. Trying to defuse the untenable situation, the president ordered the release of 200 political prisoners. On 18 May, the day of Kang Kyung-dae's funeral and the anniversary of the Gwangju Uprising, as police clashed with over half a million protesters in the streets (during the biggest protests since the beginning of Roh Tae-woo's term), three people self-immolated in three different locations across the country. The corporate media, owned by the *chaebol*, conglomerates with deep ties to the government, portrayed the protests as a symptom of the immaturity of Korea's democracy, where coercion was used where dialogue was called for. Escalation of violence was usually blamed on both the protesters and the riot police, but never on the government. Protesters were portrayed as people craving the status of heroic martyrs, uninterested in earthly life, a position that pro-government reporters ascribed to the protesters' embrace of "terrorist" or "fascist" beliefs. Dissident groups maintained that the spate of self-immolations was a direct result of the government's uncompromising stance, while opposition leaders called on the protesters to avoid resorting to extreme measures.

Ultimately, the manifestations brought about the dismissal of Prime Minister Roh Jai-bong and a cabinet reshuffle. The changes, however, failed to placate the aggrieved crowds, and the unrest ended only after public opinion turned against the protesters in the aftermath of 3 June 1991, when acting Prime Minister Chung Won-shik was prevented from speaking at the Hankuk University of Foreign Studies and pelted with eggs and flour by angry students. Photographs of the humiliated politician were a worldwide sensation and rallied the Koreans, traditionally respectful towards the elderly on account of their Confucian beliefs, to the prime minister's defence.

(Cho Y.Ch.; Katsiaficas and Na; Kim; Park)

Great Britain

29 April 1993 – **Graham Bamford** (aged 48), an unemployed man from Macclesfield, set himself on fire outside the British Parliament, demanding

62   Chronology of protest self-burnings (1963–2017)

the government take immediate action to stop the rampant ethnic cleansings in Bosnia and Herzegovina. His death later that day in the hospital went largely unnoticed in Britain, presumably because the media highlighted the depression he went into after the breakup of his marriage, and ignored the overt political import of his protest. However, in a letter written to a relief organisation shortly before his death, Bamford stressed that he had been compelled to act by a picture of a crying Balkan girl that was the same age as his daughter. In his farewell letter, he drew attention to the plight of the innocents caught up in the Bosnian conflict.

In 1997, Croatian film and theatre director Nenad Puhovski produced the documentary *Graham and I – a True Story*, a meditation on Bamford, his final act, and the lack of public attention given to his death in Great Britain and the Balkans. The following year, the film was screened in the British Parliament. In 2006, the director shot additional footage for the documentary featuring Bamford's father, who previously refused to comment on the matter.

(Steele)

Islamic Republic of Iran

21 February 1994 – **Homa Darabi** (aged 54), a paediatrician and psychiatrist, set herself on fire in Tajrish Square in north Tehran, pleading for women's rights in Iran under the rule of Ayatollah Ali Khamenei.

In college, Darabi became involved with dissident circles opposing the dictatorship of Shah Mohammad Reza Pahlavi and was briefly imprisoned. In 1963, she married a classmate and opened her own practice in a small village after graduating from Tehran University. She soon travelled to the US to study psychiatry, and eventually stayed there for nine years, going so far as to obtain American citizenship. She returned to Iran in 1976 to repay the debt she felt she owed to the country which gave her the opportunity to study medicine. As one of the few trained psychiatrists in Iran, she was appointed the head of a paediatric psychiatry clinic in Tehran.

Like many of her fellow Iranians, she initially supported the Islamic revolution of 1979, believing in Ayatollah Ruhollah Khomeini's assurances that he would hand power over to secular politicians shortly after the overthrow of the Shah and focus on matters of faith. She even met with the first President of Iran, Abolhassan Banisadr, and presented him with a list of women's demands. Khomeini, however, soon removed Banisadr from power and moved to curtail the rights of women, introducing, among other directives, the compulsory wearing of the *hijab* in public. For a long time, Dr. Darabi refused to comply with these regulations. After her transfer to the Imam Hussein Hospital, the facility's fundamentalist director demanded she wear a *chador*, but she refused, arguing that such an outfit would make patient examination impossible. In response to her dismissal, she sued the hospital, but the case would drag on for four years. Alongside her hospital duties, she continued to work in her private practice, where she offered young girls accused of indecency and sentenced to flogging the possibility of being certified legally insane (the diagnosis was a last resort, however, as it severely hampered their chances of continuing their education, finding a partner, and putting their life in order). Her patients were often subject to intimidation and reprisals, which ultimately compelled her to close her practice.

In 1991, her younger sister Parvin, a graduate of a US engineering school who decided to stay in America, came back to Iran to help Homa leave the country. Homa's husband, however, refused to let her leave (under Sharia law, the husband must formally consent to his wife's travels abroad). In January 1994, the government completed the construction of a children's psychiatric hospital designed according to her specification, but when the regime gave her a chance to lead it, provided she conform to religious laws, she still refused.

Deeply depressed, she decided to self-immolate, and screamed anti-regime and patriotic rhetoric as she burned. She died in the hospital several hours later and her funeral drew thousands. Iranian fundamentalists tried to discredit her by claiming she was insane, while her sister attempted to draw the attention of American media but was ultimately unsuccessful, because she could not provide them with pictures or footage of her sister in flames. Later, Parvin Darabi established the Homa Darabi Foundation to monitor women's and children's rights violations. Together with her son, Romin Thomson, she wrote a biography of her sister, showing her life against the backdrop of social and political changes in contemporary Iran, where self-immolation rates among women remain one of the highest in the world.

This fact was explored in *Bemani* (*To Stay Alive*) – a 2002 Iranian feature film directed by Dariush Mehrjui. The film tells the story of three young women with no chance to lead normal lives in the ultraconservative society. The title character, a teenager, is forced to marry a simple, boorish farmer. In an act of desperation, she immolates herself on the night of the wedding, emulating Nasi, a medical student, whose traditionalist father intended to marry her off to a much older man to get her away from "evil" temptations. The third character, Madina, is beheaded by her brothers to purge the shame that has descended upon the family after her alleged affair with a young soldier.

In 2013, the issue of self-burning in response to domestic violence was taken up by two female artists, playwright Farzaneh Soheyli and theatre director Samaneh Zandinejad, in a play titled *Dolls in Silence*, produced by the Madreseh Theatre in Tehran. The text was based on a true story of two sisters who were arrested by police after a date. After their father brings them home from the police station, he kills them both and cuts their heads off in a fit of rage. A witness to the horror, their mother then sets herself ablaze and dies. Statistical data indicates that in Iran familicide, where wives, daughters, or sisters are murdered by husbands, fathers, and brothers, is most prevalent in the two western provinces of Ilam and Kermanshah, where social structures are based around clan relationships. Islamic law also plays an important role,

64 Chronology of protest self-burnings (1963–2017)

as it states that children belong to their fathers, who can kill them with impunity. In order for *Dolls in Silence* to receive the censor's approval, the authors decided to portray the father as a mentally ill man who forgets to take his medication. After the tragedy, he keeps meeting his wife and daughters every night in the cemetery, as if in a nightmare. The play ends with one of the girls saying: "You have been coming here for ten years and we haven't grown even a centimetre."

(Darabi and Thomson; Shelley)

Germany

25 April 1995 – on the 50th anniversary of the surrender of Nazi Germany, **Reinhold Elstner** (aged 75), a former Wehrmacht soldier hailing from the Sudetenland, set himself aflame in Munich's Lenbachplatz. The letter he left indicated that, like David Irving, he denied the Holocaust had ever happened and protested against what he called a merciless campaign to slander and demonise an entire nation, Zionist legal revanchism, and attempts to divide Germans by criminalising the deeds of their fathers and grandfathers. Elster died in a Bavarian hospital 12 hours after the act.

("Reinhold Elstner")

United States of America

22 October 1996 – **Kathleen Chang** (**Kathy Change**) (aged 46), a political activist and performer, set herself ablaze in front of the Peace Symbol on the University of Pennsylvania campus in Philadelphia, in protest against the imperialist policies of the US government, the dominant Western economic paradigm, as well as the cynicism and passivity afflicting the populace. She died in the hospital 30 minutes later.

Chang was born into a family of Chinese intellectuals who immigrated to Ohio. Her parents divorced when she was a teenager, leading to her first suicide attempt. When she was 14, her mother took her own life. A "flower child" of the hippie era, Chang rebelled against the strict behaviour norms and the work ethic of her immigrant family, a conflict which ended in her being renounced by her relatives. She was married for five years to Frank Chin, an American writer and playwright of Chinese descent, widely considered a pioneer of Asian-American theatre. After the marriage broke up, Chang again unsuccessfully attempted to take her own life. She later moved to Philadelphia where, in the early 1980s, she used the university campus and the Philadelphia Museum of Art to stage her political solo performances, dancing in extravagant DIY costumes, singing, waving flags, playing the guitar and the keyboard, and giving impassioned speeches. In her performances, she warned the government and society against sparking another war and an impending financial crisis, called for the decriminalisation of marijuana, the implementation of direct democracy measures, and the introduction of a cooperative, barter-based economy. She changed her name from Chang to "Change" to emphasise the need for a transformation of both society and individual consciousness. Considered a radical and a politically naïve eccentric, she ultimately failed to capture the attention of college students whom she considered her target audience. Her performances were often mocked – although tolerated because of their obvious references to 1960s counterculture and anti-war movements, they failed to establish a clear connection with contemporary reality.

The media coverage after Chang's death interpreted her auto-cremation as an act of self-destruction rooted in existential problems and mental instability, ignoring her overt political message. Although the woman sought psychiatric treatment, it is unclear whether she had actually been diagnosed with any mental disorder. Chang herself mockingly claimed to have suffered from a "Messiah complex" and said that she would have been labelled a paranoiac because of certain passages in her notes and journals, in which the artist accused law enforcement and intelligence services of deploying mass surveillance against ordinary citizens. Her writings also included radical social and political notions, as well as warnings against the US involvement in conflicts in the Middle East.

Her left-leaning, pro-environmental stance, and fiery demise proved inspiring to many of her fellow artists, mostly painters and musicians. In 2015, dancer and performer Soomi Kim collaborated with Suzi Takahashi to produce the documentary performance *Chang(e)* at New York City's HERE Arts Center, in which Kim would play the titular protagonist. The performance used Chang's notes and a recorded 1995 radio interview with the artist. The hybrid spectacle, blending dance, text, video footage, and a custom musical score portrayed the artist-activist (*artivist*) as a modern-day Cassandra, repeating unheeded warnings about the dangers of neoliberalism, which she believed was eroding the very fabric of modern society.

(Fisher; King, A.; Shahadi; Tony)

Vatican

13 January 1998 – **Alfredo Ormando** (aged 39), a gay writer, poet, and native of Sicily's San Cataldo, set himself aflame outside St. Peter's Basilica in Vatican to protest the Catholic Church's conservative and uncompromising stance on homosexuals, which Ormando felt stigmatised gay catholics. He died 11 days later. His coming out took place in 1995 and coincided with the release of his autobiographical novel, *Il fratacchione (Fat Monk)*, an account of the two years Ormando spent in a monastery, where he tried to get closer to God and rid himself of his "unclean" desires. The Church authorities dismissed his radical protest, claiming that Ormando was mentally ill and plagued by family problems.

66 Chronology of protest self-burnings (1963–2017)

Ormando's sacrifice and message are commemorated every year with manifestations at St. Peter's Square held by the Italian LGBT group Arcigay. In 2013, Andy Abrahams Wilson produced the documentary *Alfredo's Fire*, featuring passages from Ormando's writings and interviews with his friends and acquaintances. The film explores the acceptance of otherness and the consequences of the lack thereof.

India

27 April 1998 – **Thupten Ngodup** (aged 60) becomes the first Tibetan national to self-immolate after setting himself ablaze in New Delhi in protest against the political situation of Chinese-occupied Tibet.

In his youth, he had been a monk at the Tashi Lhunpo Monastery near Xigazê (Shigatse) in south Tibet. After the 1959 Tibetan uprising, he fled to India alongside thousands of his compatriots; later on, he joined the army and got involved in a variety of dissident activities – between 1995 and 1996, for example, he took part in peace marches from Dharamsala (a key centre of the Tibetan exile community, as well as the location of the official residence of the 14th Dalai Lama and the headquarters of the Tibetan Government in Exile) to New Delhi. In 1998, he joined an open-ended hunger strike organised in the Indian capital by the Tibetan Youth Congress (TYC), an organisation which advocated fighting for Tibetan independence, also using armed means – its position standing in stark contrast to the rather moderate stance of the Dalai Lama and the government-in-exile, who renounced violence and called for Tibetan autonomy rather than independence.

Emboldened by the release of Wang Dan, a key dissident figure, and Bill Clinton's upcoming state visit to China, the 1998 strikers demanded the UN reopen debate on the status of Tibet, send observers to monitor human rights violations, and organise a referendum that would decide the future of the region. Before leaving for New Delhi, Ngodup, certain of his fate, instructed his friend to donate all of his possessions to the TYC, sign over the house to the Dharamsala monastery, and offer a prayer for the Dalai Lama. During the hunger strike, he cared for the six protesters, as he was in line to pick up the strike after the first group perished. Forty-eight days into the protest, just before the historic visit of the Chinese top military commander to India, Indian policemen forcibly entered the tent and took three protesters to the hospital, where they were given intravenous glucose drips. When the following day the police arrived to pick up three more strikers, Ngodup hid in a nearby toilet and then doused himself with petrol, lit himself on fire, and ran out onto the street, shouting pro-freedom rhetoric. He was soon taken to the hospital, where he died two days later. Before his death, he was visited (as were his fellow protesters) by the Dalai Lama, who later declared that he cannot ask the strikers to end their protest, as he did not have anything to offer them instead, but reiterated that although he admired the valour and determination of those who chose to self-immolate, he advised against taking such radical steps. The hunger strike continued after Ngodup's death, and a service was held for him in New Delhi. His body was later taken to Dharamsala where he was given a proper burial, and his funeral became an opportunity for the Tibetans to demonstrate their patriotism. Ultimately, the hunger strike was suspended on the Dalai Lama's request, who wrote a personal letter to each protester. In Dharamsala, Ngodup was commemorated with a small statue. The Tibetan diaspora in the US holds an annual basketball tournament in his name, and Techung, a popular Tibetan artist, has dedicated a song to his memory.

(Stefanicki; *Storm*)

China

23 January 2001 – on the eve of Chinese New Year, five people set themselves ablaze on Tiananmen Square in Beijing, four of whom were allegedly women: **Liu Chunling** (aged 36), her daughter **Liu Siying** (aged 12), **Hao Huijun** (around 50), her daughter **Chen Guo** (aged 19); the women were accompanied by a man, **Wang Jindong** (aged 51). All were quickly extinguished by law enforcement. According to state media, Liu Chunling died on the square, while her daughter passed away in the hospital a few weeks later. The reasons behind the incident remain shrouded in controversy. The Chinese news agency Xinhua portrayed the victims as deluded members of the banned Falun Gong movement and interpreted their deed as cult suicide. Representatives of the movement, however, emphasised that they oppose violence and instead suggested that the incident was a ruse concocted by the Chinese government in order to discredit the organisation.

Falun Gong (or Falun Dafa) is a syncretic spiritual practice and a rigorous moral system that draws on Buddhism, Daoism, and folk beliefs. It combines meditation-in-movement *qigong* exercises with a philosophy based around honesty, compassion, and forgiveness. *Qigong* – rooted in traditional Chinese philosophy, medicine, and martial arts – is a method of cultivating and balancing *qi*, or internal vital energy, in order to maintain good health. The origins of the Falun Gong date back to 1992 and the teachings of *qigong* master Li Hongzhi from China, which gained popularity in the wake of the *qigong* boom that swept China in the 1980s. *Qigong*, which stresses personal development, was seen as a substitute for religion in the spiritual vacuum left by the Cultural Revolution (1966–76). It is estimated that by the end of the 1990s, Falun Gong had tens of millions of adherents, mainly elderly people, including many members of the Communist Party, some even in high-ranking positions. After Li Hongzhi started teaching abroad in 1995 and received permanent resident status in the US in 1998, the movement began to develop dynamically outside China. The Communist Party of China allows only five recognised religions (Buddhism, Catholicism, Daoism, Islam, and Protestantism) and, like past imperial rulers, monitors all religious organisations

68 Chronology of protest self-burnings (1963–2017)

operating in the country. The authorities initially supported Falun Gong, but when it grew enough to threaten their rule, it was decided that the movement had to be suppressed. On 25 April 1999, a meditation protest with 15,000 followers in attendance took place outside government offices in Zhongnanhai, Beijing. It was the first protest of this size in the Chinese capital since the brutally suppressed 1989 student demonstration and was met with a similarly harsh reaction of the authorities. The official ban on the organisation, issued on 19 July 1999, marked the beginning of a harassment campaign against Falun Gong. The movement was named *xiejiao* (heterodox tradition or illegitimate organisation), which was then translated as "evil cult" in order to turn international public opinion, which saw Falun Gong adherents as unjustly persecuted peaceful meditators, against the group. Tiananmen Square soon became the stage of peaceful protests by Falun Gong followers, who adorned it with banners and used it to hold group meditation sessions. Human rights organisations reported that protesters were persecuted, detained without charge, tortured, and subjected to "reeducation" in prisons and forced labour camps. Allegedly, many of them became involuntary organ donors for the illegal transplant market in China. However, for over 18 months, it was impossible to clamp down on Falun Gong because it enjoyed far too much public support.

The fiery incident became a turning point in the propaganda campaign. The joint self-immolation was immediately turned into a domestic and international media event. On 31 January 2001, the Chinese Central Television (CCTV) broadcast a special edition of the current affairs programme *The Forum*, featuring footage allegedly taken by security cameras in Tiananmen, which argued that out of the seven protesters that planned to self-immolate, two changed their minds in the last instance. According to the official narrative, all of them were from Kaifeng and were "deluded" by Li Hongzhi. The programme focused on Liu Siying, who seemed to be convinced that self-burning would pave her a painless way to heaven. The immolators allegedly accused Li Hongzhi of lying, while Wang Jingdong mentioned a "final test" they had to pass. In an immediate response, the movement quickly distanced itself from the incident. Some independent journalists also began to question the official narrative and even the event itself. In the January 2002 documentary *False Fire: Staged Self-Immolation at Tiananmen*, journalists from the New York City-based New Tang Dynasty Television pored over the footage broadcast by official government outlets and identified a number of discrepancies that, in their view, proved that the whole incident was a hoax. Sometime later, six Falun Gong followers from Changchun hacked the satellite link and broadcast *False Fire* nationwide across China. All six were subsequently rounded up and allegedly died in prison.

Speculation about the dramatic events in Tiananmen Square continues to this day. The most probable explanation is that the incident was a genuine protest undertaken by desperate movement members in the wake of their leaders' absence, who wished to focus international attention on the harassment they were subject to. Regardless of the interpretation, the official government narrative, which stressed the intense fanaticism of the perpetrators, managed to turn the public against the movement and paved the way for a crackdown that crushed the movement in China in barely six months. The ruthless persecution of the Falun Gong resulted in hundreds of victims which the government labelled suicides, further reinforcing the official narrative portraying the movement as a harmful cult. In April 2002, the authorities held a press conference with the would-be immolators, who outright rejected the notion that the incident was a ruse and showed their scars as evidence. Responding to a question about the motive behind the immolation, Hao Huijun explained that confronted with repressions, the movement had to resort to more drastic measures than their usual fare of protest letters and banners. They all condemned Falun Gong and toed the party line.

Before the conference, on 17 February 2001, another Falun Gong adherent, **Tan Yihui** (aged 25), set himself on fire outside a military office in western Beijing. Although law enforcement quickly extinguished the flames, the young man died. The incident took place only a few days before the visit from the International Olympic Committee (IOC), which would evaluate Beijing's candidacy as host of the 2008 Summer Olympics. Although human rights groups kept publicising the brutal repression of the Falun Gong and called for the IOC to dismiss Beijing's candidacy, their pleas fell on deaf ears. The self-burnings, on the other hand, continued: on 1 July 2001, Falun Gong member and college student **Luo Guili** (aged 19) set himself ablaze in Nanning in southern China and died the following day.

(Chang; Farley; Hedges; Human Rights Watch; Ownby; Zhao)

Chile

30 November 2001 – **Eduardo Miño Pérez** (aged 50) of Santiago, a member of the Communist Party of Chile and father of three, set himself on fire and stabbed himself in the stomach outside the La Moneda presidential palace. In a pamphlet he distributed to passersby before the incident, he stressed that he was of sound mind and identified himself as a member of the Chilean Association of Asbestos Victims. In the pamphlet, he brought up the plight of people suffering from black lung, unemployed and destitute, and protested against imperialist wars and pervasive globalisation. He later died from the injuries sustained in the incident.

In 2002, the Chilean rock band Los Bunkers released a song about the incident, titled *Miño*, joining a number of groups that have penned music in his honour. In the commune of Maipú, a monolith was erected to commemorate Miño's protest.

("Eduardo Miño Pérez")

70 Chronology of protest self-burnings (1963–2017)

Czech Republic

6 March 2003 – **Zdeněk Adamec** (aged 19), a student from Humpolec, invoked the memory of Jan Palach by self-immolating in the very same spot. On his body, the authorities found a document titled *Action Torch 2003*, which contained direct references to his predecessor from 1969. The young man railed against the imperfections of democracy, corruption, rampant commercialisation, and violence, all of which he considered side effects of universal globalisation. His self-immolation (which killed him less than 40 minutes later) took place two weeks before the 2003 invasion of Iraq, a time when international tensions were running particularly high. His decision may have also been prompted by the upcoming presidential inauguration of conservative politician Václav Klaus. Law enforcement declared Adamec to have been mentally unstable and revealed that he had been charged in the past with inciting attacks against public institutions and aiding and abetting Darkers (a youth gang that blacked out entire neighbourhoods by disrupting power lines), a misdemeanour which carried a two-year sentence. The media portrayed Adamec as a young man with a rather poor grasp of his own life, who frequently ran into trouble with the law, while the official narrative about the reasons behind the incident was peppered with a variety of moral or political motives.

Adamec was also the subject of the final part of Polish reporter Mariusz Szczygieł's 2006 book *Gottland*, an anthology of essays on the Czech Republic, which was translated into Czech the following year and has since gone on to achieve considerable success in the country. 2011 saw the release of two plays about Adamec based on *Gottland*: one was produced in Ostrava, the other in Prague. Three years later, a series of short documentaries based on Szczygieł's essays were released – the film focused on Adamec, directed by Klára Tasovská, portrayed him as deeply unhappy, lonely, sensitive, and misunderstood. His self-burning was one of at least seven similar incidents that took place in the Czech Republic between March and April 2003.

(Green; Sabatos; Stojaspal; Szczygieł)

Great Britain, France, Italy, Switzerland, Canada

18 June 2003 – a Tehran-born Canadian national, **Neda Hassani** (aged 26), set herself on fire outside the French Embassy in London to protest against the arrest of over 150 members of the National Council of Resistance of Iran (NCRI) and its close affiliate, the People's Mujahedin of Iran (MEK), by the French police on suspicion of preparing terrorist operations against Iranian interests in Europe. Hassani was a member of the NCRI – a coalition of dissidents opposing the authoritarian rule of the ayatollahs in Iran. On 17 June, law enforcement raided the organisation's Paris offices and arrested its President Maryam Rajavi (wife of MEK leader, Massoud Rajavi). Hassani, in the United

Kingdom at the time of the raids, joined a crowd of students protesting outside the French Embassy against the possibility of Rajavi and other NCRI members being deported to Iran, where they would undoubtedly find themselves in grave danger. Much of the Iranian diaspora in Europe believed that the Chirac cabinet struck a deal with the Iranian regime to secure the sale of French arms and military tech to Iran. Politicians, on the other hand, believed that the MEK sought to strengthen its position in France after losing their influence in Iraq in the wake of the American invasion. After the demonstration began to disperse, Hassani doused herself with a flammable liquid and set herself on fire. She died in the hospital on 23 June. The woman was one of the dozen or so people who self-immolated in protest against Rajavi's arrest across Great Britain, France, Italy, Switzerland, and Canada.

Released on 1 July 2003, Rajavi later called on protesters to refrain from pursuing such radical acts of protest, thus attempting to distance herself from accusations of inspiring the suicides, as at the time MEK was considered a terrorist organisation by a number of countries, including Great Britain and France.

("Burning"; Vasagar)

China

22 August 2003 – **Weng Biao** (aged 39) set himself on fire in Nanjing's municipal evictions office, where he was petitioning the government for restitution. When he was notified that his property was scheduled for demolition, Weng held out for more favourable resettlement terms. Unwilling to negotiate, the authorities first cut off his electricity and water supply and then bulldozed his home with the family's belongings still inside. Across China, many similar incidents were taking place, a side effect of the country's rapid development. Left with no other recourse, thousands of people from the rural countryside streamed into the capital to protest in Tiananmen Square and draw attention to their plight (many were wrongfully terminated from their jobs, had their wages withheld, or were unlawfully expropriated). Those most desperate among them sometimes pursued more radical forms of protest.

One of the most widely known incidents involved **Tang Fuzhen** (aged 47), a Chengdu native. On 13 November 2009, she refused to leave her house and kept hurling Molotov cocktails for over three hours at construction crews tasked with demolishing her home. Cornered, she finally set herself on fire, and later died on 29 November. It seemed that the incident would stem the tide of resettlements and demolitions, as the public opinion unanimously sided with her and began openly questioning the sustainability of the resettlement policy. Under pressure from the public, the State Council eventually moved to revise relevant legislation, but the adjustments have not made any tangible impact on the practices of real estate developers and local government officials.

(Deng; Yu; Zhang)

Pakistan

18 January 2004 – **Dhani Bux Memon**, a Pakistan Peoples Party (PPP) activist, set himself on fire during a party demonstration outside the police headquarters for the Lakhi Dar area in the Shikarpur District (Sindh province). The protesters demanded the release of Asif Ali Zardari, at the time serving a death sentence, and the dismissal of corruption charges against his wife, former Pakistani Prime Minister Benazir Bhutto, which prevented her from moving back home from abroad. In critical condition, Memon was transferred to Karachi where, in the presence of the media, party members, and the party spokesman, he threatened to set himself ablaze again, this time outside the building of Parliament or the Islamabad residence of President Pervez Musharraf. Although aware of the fact that the party leadership did not support his act, he nevertheless reasserted his willingness to lay down his life for the cause. He later died of injuries sustained in the incident.

His example was followed by another PPP member **Sarwar Bhund**, who first attempted to self-immolate during the 7 June 2004 protest in the Dadu District (Sindh province), but was prevented from going through with his plan by other protesters. Bhund suffered only minor injuries and went home, where he repeated the attempt, this time with fatal results.

("Activist"; "Self-Immolation Bid")

Luxembourg

5 October 2004 – **Maggy Delvaux-Mufu** (aged 44), a Belgian of Congolese descent, wife and mother of three, set herself on fire in the crowded Place d'Armes in the centre of Luxembourg City. She later died in the hospital in Metz. Before the incident, she sent a letter to the Luxembourg-based weekly *Le Jeudi*, expressing her staunch anti-violence stance and enumerating the many instances of discrimination against her and her family by the administration of the Luxembourg Prime Minister, Jean-Claude Juncker. The letter also revealed her plan to self-burn and offered the precise date and location of the event, putting local law enforcement on high alert, but Delvaux-Mufu eventually changed the venue of her protest at the last possible moment. Before lighting the flames, she allegedly yelled that her act was a protest against racism. Sometime before the incident, Delvaux-Mufu and her husband took out a loan to open a business, but were soon left unable to repay it, as the business stalled due to their inability to secure the necessary permits. The couple tried to appeal the administrative decision but were ultimately unsuccessful.

The American artist Alex Lilly immortalised her sacrifice in his painting *Protesting Racism – Luxembourg City*, which he based on a picture of Delvaux-Mufu engulfed in flames. The painting is part of his series depicting notorious self-immolations.

("La flamme")

United States of America

15 November 2004 – **Mohamed Alanssi** (aged 52), a Yemeni national, set himself ablaze outside the White House in Washington, D.C. As a confidential informant for the Federal Bureau of Investigation (FBI), Alanssi assisted with over 20 terrorism investigations. He wanted to travel back to Yemen to visit his cancer-stricken wife, but was prevented from doing so, because he was scheduled to testify in court against Mohammed Ali Hassan Al-Moayad, a Yemeni cleric charged with conspiring to raise funds for Hamas and Al Qaeda. *The Washington Post* later revealed that Alanssi was dissatisfied and his relationship with his FBI handlers soured, particularly after his passport was seized.

("Mohamed Alanssi")

Israel

17 August 2005 – **Yelena Businov** (aged 54), a resident of Kedumim, an Israeli settlement in the West Bank, set herself on fire to protest Ariel Sharon's unilateral peace plan, which presumed the expulsion of Israeli settlers from the Gaza Strip, the withdrawal of military forces from the area, and the evacuation of four settlements from the West Bank. Five years earlier, Businov and her mother immigrated to Israel from Odessa, where the woman was involved with Memorial, the human rights association working to raise awareness of Soviet-era terror and its victims. Active in Odessa's Jewish community, she was known for helping the sick and elderly. In her new homeland, she took classes in Jewish history and philosophy, and participated in courses for people interested in converting to Judaism. She opposed the forcible relocation policy and joined right-wing radicals in calling for a nationwide referendum on the matter. She published her writings on the subject online and once held a hunger strike outside the Knesset. Ultimately, she decided to embrace the most radical form of protest. Businov died nine days after her self-immolation. Sharon's plan was implemented, and all resettlement efforts were completed by 22 September 2005.

(Galili)

Afghanistan

15 November 2005 – **Ghazi Anwar**, a refugee from Gilgit-Baltistan, the Pakistan-occupied portion of Kashmir, set himself ablaze in Kabul, outside the offices of the United Nations Assistance Mission in Afghanistan (UNAMA) to protest against the UN's indifference towards the tragedy of his people. Anwar was the treasurer of the Karakorum National Movement, an organisation supporting the pro-independence aspirations of the region, which has been a flashpoint between India and Pakistan for decades. Kept under surveillance by Pakistani secret services, he was forced to flee Gilgit.

He was one of 17 refugees from northeastern Kashmir, who fled to Afghanistan in the span of 18 months and requested asylum there. UN officials rejected four of the 17 applications, including Anwar's. Not long after, the man was severely beaten by the police, and before his self-immolation he allegedly declared that he preferred death to humiliation.

("Pakistani")

India

11 June 2006 – **Pravin Joshi** (aged 30), a labourer from Rajkot in the state of Gujarat, set himself on fire to prevent the screening of *Fanaa* (*Destroyed in Love*), a Bollywood production and one of India's biggest box office successes of 2006. The release in Gujarat was mired in controversy after the lead, Aamir Khan, called on then-Prime Minister of the state, Narendra Damodardas Modi, to provide restitution to families who had been re-settled away from their homes to make room for the Narmada river dam project. The Bharatiya Janata Party, Modi's key political base, demanded the actor issue a formal apology, and when Khan refused, state authorities officially banned the film from distribution, while locals began burning effigies of the performer and posters with his likeness. Given the possibility of civil unrest, many cinema owners refused to screen the film in their establishments. In response, the film's distributor petitioned the Supreme Court of India to extend some form of protection to those theatres which refused to cancel the screenings. The court ultimately dismissed the case, arguing that if someone felt threatened, they could always call on the police. This was the case of a privately owned cinema in the coastal city of Jamnagar, where the film was screened with armed law enforcement officers in the audience. Despite their efforts, however, the film was still pulled from distribution after Joshi went to the toilet during the intermission, doused himself with a highly flammable substance, and set himself on fire. He died nine days later.

("Fanaa")

United States of America

3 November 2006 – **Mark 'Malachi' Ritscher** (aged 52), an anti-war activist, musician, devoted fan of the Chicago music scene, and one of its most prolific chroniclers, immolated himself in order to shock the American society out of the complacent stupor it had found itself in following the 2003 invasion of Iraq. His self-burning took place a couple of miles from the centre of Chicago, under Leonardo Nierman's steel sculpture *Flame of the Millennium*. The spot was rather inaccessible to pedestrians, but in excellent view of passing cars. Ritscher set himself on fire in the morning, in order to make the biggest impact on people making their commute. He wrapped his

head in an American flag and placed a placard with anti-war slogans next to his person. Although he self-immolated in front of a video camera, the police seized the footage and handed it over to the family, who refused to release it to the public. Local media clearly condemned the act. Although Ritscher, who lived alone, uploaded a pacifist-themed farewell letter to his personal website, wrote notes to his friends, and even drew up his own obituary, his self-sacrifice failed to find purchase among similarly minded activists and artists in America until much later.

In 2007, Theatre 5.2.1 produced ten performances of *The Silence of Malachi Ritscher*, a play written by the Theatre's own Kevin Kilroy. After completing the run, the authors burned the script and destroyed all its digital copies, while vowing never to stage the play again. In 2008, the Florida band Less Than Jake released a song about Ritscher's death, titled *Malachi Richter's Liquor's Quicker*. The lyrics featured passages from Ritscher's farewell letter, while in the background Morse code spelled out the message: "We may lose hope, but there's always hope." Later that year, David Lester, the guitarist for the band Mecca Normal, designed a poster commemorating Ritscher for his original series *Inspired Agitators*, a collection of portraits of over 25 political activists and cultural luminaries. Two years later, Mecca Normal released a single featuring the song *Malachi*. In 2011, Tyrone Williams dedicated a collection of poetry, titled *Howell*, to Ritscher's memory – a section of the volume featured poems named after the songs Ritscher recorded in Chicago clubs.

(Fischer; *Inspired*; "War Protester's")

South Korea

1 April 2007 – **Heo Se-uk** (aged 54), a taxi driver and labour union activist, set himself on fire outside the Hyatt hotel in the centre of Seoul, where officials were concluding free trade agreement negotiations between South Korea and the US. He died 15 days later, while the United States-Korea Free Trade Agreement was signed on 30 June 2007 and entered into effect in March 2012. The agreement was met with violent opposition from entrepreneurs and farmers, who feared the influx of cheaper, subsidised foodstuffs. Before the incident, Heo collected press clippings on the agreement and participated in protest rallies, finally launching a solitary protest outside the residence of President Roh Moo-hyun on 29 March. His political awakening came about in 1995, after he witnessed the assault on an activist protesting on behalf of evictees, whose houses were scheduled for demolition to make room for a new housing community. Spurred to action, he joined a number of progressive organisations. He also tried to draw public attention to a 2002 incident, in which an American military vehicle ran down two middle-schoolers.

("Man")

India

2 July 2007 – **Jaswinder Singh** (aged 26) set himself on fire in Sirsa, in the northern state of Haryana, the seat of Dera Sacha Sauda, a religious organisation founded in 1948. The incident took place during an open-ended hunger strike held by 25 members of the organisation in protest against the arrest of its leader. Gurmeet Ram Rahim Singh was detained after appearing in public wearing the attire of Guru Gobind Singh (1666–1708), the tenth Sikh Guru, supposedly offending the religious sensibilities of the Sikhs.

A week later, another Dera Sacha Sauda member, **Shyam Sunder Bansal**, self-immolated outside the *gurudwara* (Sikh temple) in the Punjabi city of Bathinda to protest against the pressure exerted upon him and his fellow members by their families and the local community to leave the organisation. Both men died. The rising tensions between the Sikhs and Dera supporters protesting against the rule of Parkash Singh Badal in Punjab soon turned into open riots that had to be put down by the police.

(IANS, "Another," "Dera")

Myanmar

23 March 2008 – **Thaw Zin Naing** (aged 26) set himself on fire outside the Shwedagon Pagoda in Rangoon, the country's former capital. He protested against widespread poverty caused by economic decline under the military junta headed by General Than Shwe. During the incident, he supposedly chanted anti-regime slogans. The site of his self-immolation was previously the stage for a number of protests against British colonial administration and then the dictatorial junta, which has held power in Myanmar since the 1962 *coup d'état*.

(Sarkar)

India, Malaysia, Switzerland

29 January 2009 – **Kumar Muthukumar** (aged 26), a journalist and activist from Tamil Nadu, set himself ablaze in Chennai in protest against the slaughter of the Tamil minority in Sri Lanka, prompted by the January 2008 government offensive, one of the final large-scale operations of the 1983–2009 Sri Lankan Civil War.

At the time, around 200,000 civilians found themselves trapped between Sinhalese forces and units of the Liberation Tigers of Tamil Eelam (LTTE). The former were accused of indiscriminate bombardment and herding Tamils into concentration camps, while the latter were suspected of using civilians as human shields and forcibly conscripting them into their ranks. Muthukumar immolated himself outside the Shastri Bhawan, the central seat of government in Chennai. In the pamphlets he had prepared beforehand, he outlined his opposition against Indian support of the Sinhalese government in Sri Lanka and called on the international community, including Barack Obama, to intervene on behalf of the persecuted Tamil minority. His self-burning sparked a wave of civil unrest, strikes, and demonstrations aimed against the central Indian government, which labelled the Tamil Tigers a terrorist organisation following the 1991 assassination of Prime Minister Rajiv Gandhi (a decision later followed by over 30 countries, including the US). Muthukumar's funeral turned into a mass demonstration, with 100,000 people in attendance to show their support for Tamil Tiger leader Velupillai Prabhakaran, including activists, students, and representatives of leading Tamil political parties. To show solidarity with the protesters, locals pasted over storefront windows and burned the billboards of politicians affiliated with the central government. Protesters clashed with law enforcement and riot police units, and chanted slogans calling for independent Eelam, the portion of Sri Lanka inhabited by the Tamil minority. Balasingham Nadesan, the head of the LTTE's political arm, paid homage to Muthukamar and called his self-immolation an act of heroism. He was followed in his praise by Kanthar Nallathamby Srikantha, the then-leader of the Tamil National Alliance (TNA), a political coalition of moderate Tamil national parties and former members of militant organisations. For the Tamil Nadu, the fiery suicide soon became a symbol and inspired others to rise in protest, sometimes in its most violent and radical forms.

Muthukamar's example was followed by many others at home and abroad (in Malaysia and Switzerland), who sacrificed their lives to call for justice and peace for Eelam. The Sri Lankan Civil War came to an end a couple of months later, after the LTTE leader was killed in the particularly bloody clashes of May 2009.

(Jones; King T.; "Poignant")

Tibet – People's Republic of China

27 February 2009 – **Tapey (Lobsang Tashi)** (aged ca. 20), a monk from the Kirti Gompa monastery located in an autonomous prefecture in China's Sichuan province, set himself on fire after Chinese authorities banned the celebrations accompanying the annual Monlam Prayer Festival. A few hundred monks were intent on violating the ban, but ultimately abandoned their plans under pressure from their superiors and local authorities, as such a blatant display of dissent could have brought about a severe government response. Tibetan officials claimed that after the monks dispersed back to their quarters, Tapey headed out towards an intersection near the local market. There, in the middle of a major concourse, he supposedly unfurled a Tibetan flag adorned with the Dalai Lama's likeness, began calling on the authorities to allow the Tibetan spiritual leader to return to his homeland, and then finally doused himself with a flammable liquid and set himself ablaze. Some reports claimed

that Chinese policemen first opened fire on the blazing figure and then, after seeing Tapey collapse, rushed to extinguish the flames and take the man away. Tapey's fate remained unclear for several days. Eventually, on 5 March 2009, the Xinhua News Agency reported that Tapey was alive and denied ever having been fired upon by police.

In May 2012, a period when Tibetan self-immolations were particularly frequent, CCTV broadcast a documentary which alleged that Tapey tried to take his own life to reclaim his honour, supposedly marred by accusations of him sitting out the earlier (brutally suppressed) protests that swept Lhasa and Ngawa in March 2008, months before the Summer Olympics in Beijing. The broadcast also featured footage that the authorities alleged depicted the incident, and a brief interview with Tapey, who spoke in Chinese about the physical pain he was suffering and the limited mobility of his severely burned arms. His mother, also interviewed for the programme, added that her son was deeply regretting his decision. It is possible that both of them decided to speak on camera, because refusal would result in the authorities discontinuing or curtailing Tapey's treatment. According to reports from Tibetan sources, the authorities planned to amputate the monk's right arm (in which he was allegedly shot) to destroy evidence of police misconduct.

Tapey's fate remains unknown, but it is possible that his hospital stay eventually turned into an involuntary hold or outright imprisonment. The Tibetan writer and blogger Tsering Woeser disclosed that no one has seen or heard from the monk in five years. She added, however, that another monk, Sangko, was sentenced to a six-year prison term for publishing pictures of Tapey's self-immolation online.

(Storm; Woeser)

India

29 November 2009 – **Kasoju Srikanth Chary** (aged 24), a physical therapy student and member of the Telangana Rashtra Samithi (TRS) party's youth wing, set himself on fire to protest the imprisonment of Kalvakuntla Chandrashekar Rao, who fought to establish a Telangana state in southeastern India. Chary died on 4 December.

On the recommendation of the States Reorganisation Commission, which worked primarily on linguistic criteria, the Indian authorities established the state of Andhra Pradesh, by merging the state of Andhra with Telangana, a region where Telugu was the dominant language. For years, leading political figures in Telangana insisted the decision be rolled back and Telangana be established as a separate state. Separatist movements were particularly active in 1969, 1972, and 2009.

The open-ended hunger strike that Rao began after his imprisonment in 2009 was one of many means of protest employed by the separatists. Mass demonstrations of support for the pro-independence aspirations of the people of Telangana were another. Shortly afterwards, on 9 December 2009, the central government announced that it would be commencing the process of establishing a new state, but soon withdrew from the plan due to unrest breaking out in the wake of the decision in other parts of Andhra Pradesh. The withdrawal, in turn, prompted a wave of counter-protests across Telangana, including riots, demonstrations, sit-ins, and public suicides – mostly self-burnings. It is estimated that over 600 people laid down their lives in pursuit of the establishment of a new state (ultimately formed in 2014). Many of them chose auto-cremation to do so.

(Rao)

Georgia

27 October 2010 – **Nana Pipia** (aged 46), an Abkhazian woman, set herself on fire outside the Georgian Ministry of Internally Displaced Persons from the Occupied Territories, Accommodation and Refugees in Tbilisi. She later died from her injuries.

Prior to the incident, she camped out in a makeshift tent city set up outside the Ministry offices with a few dozen like-minded protesters, who demanded Minister Koba Subeliani's help with settling in the capital, as they were dissatisfied with Georgian authorities' earlier offers to find the displaced new homes in the western part of the country, where employment prospects were much bleaker. According to Amnesty International, as of August 2010, there were nearly 250,000 refugees living in Georgia, most of them displaced by the war in Abkhazia in the early 1990s and the South Ossetian conflict of August 2008. Most people who came over with the initial (bigger) waves of refugees were placed in either disused schools, hospitals, or huts unsuitable for long-term habitation. In 2010, nearly half of them still lived in these facilities, while the rest roomed with relatives or friends, or lived in rental apartments. The protesters also accused the minister of embezzling a portion of the funds raised by international NGOs for helping the expatriates.

("Self-Immolation Incident")

Tunisia, Algeria, Egypt, Mauritania, Italy, the Netherlands, Ethiopia, Jordan, Bahrain, Morocco

17 December 2010 – **Mohamed Bouazizi** (aged 26), a Tunisian street vendor, set himself on fire outside the magistrate building in Sidi Bouzid, after local police approached him on suspicion of trading without necessary permits, confiscated his goods, which he had purchased on credit, along with his electronic scales, and after the magistrate refused to file his complaint. After the flames were put out by passersby, Bouazizi was taken to the hospital, where he succumbed to his injuries on 4 January 2011. Before his death, he was paid a visit in the burn ward by President Ben Ali, who was growing

80 Chronology of protest self-burnings (1963–2017)

worried about the rising tide of social unrest, which erupted in the country-side shortly after Bouazizi's self-burning.

After his death, the protests exploded from the provinces and swept across the country, eventually forcing Ben Ali, who had been ruling Tunisia for the past 23 years, to flee the country on 14 January 2011. These events sparked what is now called the "Arab Spring," a series of mass protests and armed uprisings that rocked a sizeable portion of the Arab world from 2011 to 2013. For the most part, these revolts were driven by popular discontent with de-teriorating living standards, food price hikes, rising unemployment rates, overall lack of prospects, rampant corruption in government, and the severe curtailing of civil liberties by dictatorial regimes. Many of the grassroots pro-tests that decried collapsing living standards were soon expanded to include purely political demands. Even though Bouazizi's protest was not inherently political, his self-incineration set off a sweeping wave of transformation. Re-gardless of his intentions, the Tunisian vendor became a symbol of the pop-ular revolt spreading throughout the Arab world and has been posthumously honoured both at home and abroad.

Bouazizi's death triggered a wave of self-burnings across many Arab and some European countries. Estimates indicate that over 100 similar incidents took place in Tunisia in the six months following his death, most of which involved young, isolated, and poorly educated males from the country's poorer areas.

Many instances of self-immolations were also recorded in neighbouring Algeria, particularly in the early months of 2011. On 12 January, **Mohamed Aouichia** (aged 26) set himself ablaze outside the building housing the *dajrat* (prefecture) administration in Bordj Menaïel. Similar cases were reported nearly every day for the next two months.

Self-burnings were also becoming frequent in Egypt. The lethal series began on 17 January 2011, when **Abdou Abdel-Moneim Jaafar** (Gaafar) (aged 49), a restaurant owner from El Qantara, set himself on fire outside the building of Parliament in Cairo, after failing to receive bread coupons promised by the local government. He was quickly extinguished and did not sustain any life-threatening injuries. The incidents sparked a series of widespread protests which eventually forced Hosni Mubarak to resign the presidency on 11 February 2011.

On 17 January 2011, **Yacoub Ould Dahoud** (aged 41) set himself on fire in Nouakchott, the capital of Mauritania, in a car parked outside the palace serving as the residence of President Mohamed Ould Abdel Aziz. In a communiqué released through a social network, Dahoud called on the au-thorities to enact democratic reforms, release prisoners of conscience, stamp out corruption, and introduce a number of amendments to the constitution – including one that would prevent current and former military officers from running for presidential office. Dahoud died in a Moroccan hospital on 23 January, and the authorities delayed repatriating his remains in fear of escalating the protests that erupted across the country after his death.

Chronology of protest self-burnings (1963–2017)

The widespread protests that spread across the country after the self-burning of **Hasan Ali Alekh** (aged 25) in Al-Hasakah in eastern Syria soon gave rise to what has since become a devastating civil war.

In February 2011, **Fadoua Laouri** (aged 25), an unwed mother of two, tried to take her own life outside the municipal administration building in Souk Sebt in Morocco, after city officials refused to arrange social housing for her and her family. She died on 23 February in a Casablanca hospital.

The wave of self-burnings soon reached the shores of Europe. On 11 February 2011 in Palermo, Sicily, a Moroccan street vendor by the name of **Noureddine Adnane** (aged 27) set himself aflame in what was a near-mirror image of Bouazizi's protest. The man died five days later. On 6 April 2011, Iranian national **Kambiz Roustayi** (aged 36) self-incinerated on the steps of the National Monument on Dam Square in Amsterdam, after he was refused political asylum in the country. Having spent 11 years in the Netherlands, he was afraid of being deported and persecuted in his native land.

In the wake of these events, on 25 October 2011, the Dawro Zone in the south of Ethiopia became the stage of protests against the dictatorial rule of President Meles Zenawi. In response, law enforcement set up a media blockade and moved to cordon off the area to stave off the possibility of the protests sparking a nationwide revolt, similar to the riots that spread across the Maghreb and other Arab countries. As the protests raged, teacher and local activist **Yenesew Gebre** (aged 29) set himself on fire in Tercha on 11 November 2011. Gebre fervently opposed the brutal repressions against 50 young protesters and called for their release. He died in the hospital two days later. The authorities first forbade his family and friends from visiting him in the hospital and then tried to prevent the local community from attending his funeral, fearing further escalation of unrest.

In January 2012, self-burnings were reported in Jordan, Bahrain, and Rabat, the capital of Morocco, among other locations.

(Citton; Khosrokhavar; LeVine and Reynolds)

Tibet, India, Nepal, China, France

16 March 2011 – a monk from the Kirti Monastery, **Rigzin Phuntsog** (aged 20), set himself on fire on the third anniversary of the brutally suppressed riots in nearby Ngawa. The Phuntsog incident took place during a Buddhist demonstration (since the riots, the monastery has been cordoned off by law enforcement and its denizens subject to "reeducation"). According to Tibetan sources, before setting himself on fire the young monk demanded the authorities allow the Dalai Lama to return to Tibet and was subsequently beaten by the police after the flames engulfed him. Brought to a hospital, he was refused admission. To save the man's life, he had to be handed over to the authorities. The hospital was eventually permitted to treat him after a couple of hours, but the delay allegedly resulted in the monk's death later that night. In response

82 Chronology of protest self-burnings (1963–2017)

to the incident, the Chinese enacted a range of repressive measures against the recalcitrant monastery, but the approach ultimately backfired, further radicalising Buddhist attitudes and forms of protest. It also triggered one of the biggest waves of politically motivated self-immolations in history.

The farewell letters left behind clearly indicate that the Tibetan self-immolations were not mere acts of desperation driven by complicated or unbearable personal circumstances. Although these do appear in every fifth letter, they are usually accompanied by ulterior motives. In her book *Tibet on Fire*, Tsering Woeser asserted that her countrymen set themselves ablaze in the name of faith and liberty, and categorically denied that the deaths were suicides, calling them sacrifices instead. Likewise, during his 2011 testimony before the Tom Lantos Human Rights Commission of the US House of Representatives, the abbot of the Kirti Gompa monastery called the self-incinerations an appeal to the Chinese authorities and the clearest expression of opposition to their rule that still abides by the principles of non-violence.

As reported by the International Campaign for Tibet, between the Tapey incident in February 2009 and November 2018, 153 people – 125 men and 28 women – self-immolated in the Tibet Autonomous Region (TAR) and in areas populated by Tibetans in the Chinese provinces of Qinghai and Sichuan. Of the 153, no fewer than 122 incidents ended in death, and 26 victims were 18 years old or younger, with people under 30 making up the core of the rest. Self-burnings were carried out by both monks and nuns, but over half of the incidents involved laypeople (both men and women), including teachers, students, and itinerant shepherds. The youngest person to self-immolate was 15 years old. The majority of the listed incidents, over 80 cases altogether, took place in 2012, of which 28 happened in November, during the 18th National Congress of the Communist Party of China, when the reins of government were taken over by a new generation of Party functionaries, a clear indication of whom the protests were intended to reach. Additionally, most were carried out outside the TAR and its capital, Lhasa. Ten incidents took place outside Tibet (outside the TAR and the Amdo and Kham provinces incorporated by China), in Nepal and India. At this point, we cannot eliminate the possibility that the British-born Buddhist monk **Lobsang Tonden** (**David Alain**, aged 38) who set himself ablaze on 15 November 2012, in the Nalanda Monastery in Labastide-Saint-George, a village in the south of France, did so to further the Tibetan cause. The websites for the International Campaign for Tibet and Free Tibet feature comprehensive lists of people who self-immolated in the name of free Tibet, accompanied by brief biographic notes, as well as exhaustive info packages that contain detailed descriptions of the tragedy playing out at the Roof of the World.

The Tibetans who even today light themselves on fire demand the Dalai Lama's safe return to Tibet and the release of the 16th Panchen Lama, abducted by the Chinese in 1995, when he was just five years old (the Panchen Lama serves a crucial role in the process of selecting the new Dalai Lama), and continue to urge China to respect human rights, freedom of speech, and the independence of Tibet, even though they recognise that they stand virtually no chance of either overcoming China or changing its policies regarding Tibet. They do it primarily in defence of Tibetan dignity, powerless to fight for the welfare of their nation by any other means. They call for unity and preserving Tibet's unique cultural identity, and preach temperance, agreeableness, and avoiding vice. They oppose the deliberate undermining of religion and tradition, the removal of Tibetan language from schools and curricula, and the destruction of the environment wrought by China's blatantly extractive approach to Tibetan natural resources. Because most self-immolations are usually widely reported by foreign press outlets (despite the sophisticated media blockade enforced by China) and thus undermine the official narrative portraying Tibet as rapidly modernising and economically developing, Beijing deploys misinformation and propaganda campaigns that characterise the immolators as mentally disturbed or failures with a history of trouble with the law, gambling, prostitution, or drugs, sometimes even going so far as to label them terrorists. Furthermore, the authorities often persecute not only the immolators, but also their families and communities. Those who survive the flames are detained, and their further fates usually remain unknown. Protocol also confers severe punishment on people suspected of assisting the protesters. Bodies of self-immolators who die of extensive burns are usually quickly cremated to make traditional burial impossible. Local communities are threatened with hefty fines for organising prayer meetings or rendering assistance to the protesters' families. The Chinese also continue to argue that "Dalai," which is what they call the Dalai Lama, and his "coterie" encourage their fellow countrymen to embrace self-immolation as a form of protest. Although the Tibetan spiritual leader has not issued an unambiguous call for his supporters to cease sacrificing their lives, he repeatedly expressed his deepest regret over the incidents and emphasised that he has never actively encouraged anyone to engage in self-burning.

Robert Stefanicki, a Polish journalist, noted that Tibetans themselves are divided over their view of self-immolations. Some of them (particularly those in exile) affirm them as a silver bullet that both satisfies the need for resistance and abides by principles of non-violence – and thus consider self-immolators unquestioned heroes. Others, however, condemn suicide protests, asserting that each such death is a loss for the small nation of barely six million people. Instead, they suggest embracing other forms of dissidence, such as *lhakar*, that is "White Wednesday," a practice aimed at strengthening the Tibetans' national identity through speaking pure Tibetan, listening to independent radio stations, eating traditional Tibetan food, and buying only from Tibetan-owned businesses. Self-immolations have also met with considerable rejection due to their ultimate futility as a form of protest against the Beijing regime and because they exacerbate the marginalisation of Tibet's government-in-exile. In 2012, Wang Lixiong, a Chinese dissident, writer, and Woeser's husband, argued that self-incinerations – which he saw as an expression of profound heroism and unspeakable valour – should be ceased, while the courage they unleashed should eventually be channelled into more productive usage.

Tibetan auto-cremations have been explored by plenty of artists, both in Tibet and abroad (also in China), working across different media and genres, including poems, paintings, sculptures, graffiti, and installations. Selected works have been discussed by Leigh Sangster in her 2012 article *The Work of Art in the Age of Self-Immolation*. Also in 2012, Françoise Robin examined the poems that were appearing in the Tibetan-speaking blogosphere after each self-incineration. One of the first was *Mya ngan zhu ba* (*Mourning*), written in October 2011 by an author hiding under the *nom de plume* Sangdor. The scholar pointed out that tight censorship forced Sangdor and his fellow writers to rely on heavily metaphorical language. In these particular instances, choosing the literary form was supposed to help express emotions, join others in shared mourning, and reaffirm one's own identity. Only one of the examined authors chose to question the validity of embracing such a violent method of protest. The rest portrayed the self-burnings with empathy and respect, countering the official narrative that labelled the victims "criminals," "terrorists," "outcasts," and "mentally deranged."

The plight of the Tibetans also inspired many artists abroad. On 3 March 2012, Justyna Jan-Krukowska, a Polish visual artist, staged a piece of performance art entitled *Flame*. In Wrocław's Market Square, she set up an installation comprising six sheets of rusty metal forming a cuboid, with the outline of a person from the waist up, arms thrown up in a dramatic gesture, cut out from the wider rectangular sides. After a flame was lit inside, the cuboid, representing a human engulfed in flames, became a peculiar furnace; the installation was rounded out with a Tibetan flag stuck next to it. The performance was accompanied by a debate, *Art and Human Rights*, set up in collaboration with the Freedom and Peace Foundation.

Also in March 2012, Canadian visual artist Alexandrine Capolla Beauregard staged *Imaginary Self-Immolation*, a performance piece carried out at sunset on the roof of a Montreal apartment building. The artist performed it with no audience in attendance and in utter silence, symbolically taking the whole city as witness. She sat down cross-legged next to a petrol can, then split the match she was holding in half, lit the two halves, and let them burn down to the nub while holding her hands down on her knees in a meditative position. Next, she took the can and doused herself with fuel, and pulled out another match, holding it with her eyes closed. With the unlit match in hand, she then meditated over the plight of the Tibetan people, paying symbolic homage to the 32 people who had met a fiery end in the cause of free Tibet up until the day of the performance.

(Beauregard; Buffetrille and Robin; McGranahan and Litzinger; Robin; Sangster; Stefanicki; *Storm*; Whalen-Bridge; Woeser)

India

28 August 2011 – two years after the last wave of protest self-burnings, the Tamil community was rocked by another incident, carried out outside the administrative headquarters of Kanchipuram District by **Senkodi** (aged 27), who demanded the release of three convicts sentenced to death in 1998 for their involvement in the preparations for the suicidal attack on Rajiv Gandhi. The former PM of India was killed in 1991 at an election rally in Sriperumbudur, around 40 km from Chennai. The bombing also killed the assassin, Thenmozhi Rajaratnam (Dhanu), and 14 bystanders. The attack was blamed on the Tamil Tigers, because Gandhi was responsible for despatching Indian peacekeepers to Sri Lanka, who then stayed on the island for three years. The 1998 trial of the perpetrators produced 26 death sentences, but successful appeals reduced the number of convictions to four. One of the plotters, S. Nalini Sriharan, had her sentence commuted to life in prison in 2000 when Rajiv's widow, Sonia Gandhi, interceded on the woman's behalf after the former bore a daughter in prison. In August 2011, Indian President Pratibha Patil refused clemency to the remaining three conspirators, who were to be hanged on 9 September at the penal facility in Vellore. In the light of numerous petitions (written by, among others, the daughter of Nalini and one of her fellow suspects, Shrinan; the daughter herself was a UK resident) and a wave of protests that rocked Tamil Nadu in the wake of the sentencing (and Senkodi's self-burning), the execution was postponed.

Eventually, all three death sentences were commuted to life in prison. Then, in a surprising move, on 19 February 2014, state authorities decided to release all three death row inmates. Aside from them, early releases were also granted to Nalini and three other convicts serving life sentences for their involvement in the attack.

(Shekhar)

Indonesia

7 December 2011 – **Sondang Hutagalung** (aged 22), a law student at the Bung Karno University in Jakarta, set himself on fire outside the entrance to the presidential palace in the capital. He died three days later. Before the incident, he took part in demonstrations commemorating Munir Said Thalib, the founder of the Indonesian human rights group Kontras, poisoned using arsenic while flying from Singapore to Amsterdam in 2004. Hutagalung also mailed letters to President Susilo Bambang Yudhoyono in which he discussed the rampant corruption and human rights violations in Indonesia. The incident was possibly the first recorded instance of politically motivated self-immolation in Indonesia.

("Indonesia")

Israel

14 July 2012 – **Moshe Silman** (aged 57), a social justice activist, set himself on fire at a protest in Tel Aviv and died six days later. Prior to the incident, he made a couple of abortive attempts at opening a business, which landed him in dire financial straits. He was also threatened by homelessness, as municipal authorities refused him social housing. Silman involved himself with protest movements and began appearing at demonstrations decrying the policies of the Netanyahu government that spread across Israel in 2011. He called for the establishment of a new opposition party and suggested seizing vacant housing. In his farewell letter, he accused the prime minister and finance minister of humiliating disadvantaged and underprivileged Israelis like himself. His death was picked up and widely reported by the local media, inspiring several followers who self-burned due to adverse economic situations.

(Kaufman)

Russia

19 July 2012 – **Valentina Gerasimova** (aged 57) set herself ablaze in the waiting room of the regional offices of the ruling United Russia party in Novosibirsk after trying to obtain legal assistance in the case she brought against a dishonest construction contractor. She died in the hospital. Four bystanders were hospitalised for burns while the party offices were evacuated of over 80 staffers. The resulting fire consumed a portion of the building's second floor.

The act became a symbol of the popular struggle against bureaucracy and the soullessness of government officials. Graffiti with Gerasimova's likeness began appearing on walls across the city, and the local black metal band Devilgroth dedicated one of its songs to the woman.

("Police")

Vietnam

30 July 2012 – **Bà Đặng Thị Kim Liêng** (aged 64) made an attempt on her life outside a government building in Bạc Liêu to protest the continued detainment of her daughter, Tạ Phong Tần, an ex-police officer and former member of the Communist Party of Vietnam, arrested in 2011 and charged with "anti-government propaganda" for running a blog containing detailed accounts of government corruption, human rights violations, and overly violent conduct of law enforcement officers. Liêng finally set herself on fire a week before her daughter's trial, after a prolonged harassment campaign waged against her by the authorities. She died en route to the hospital, and her funeral drew considerable crowds, despite government efforts to frustrate popular attendance.

After the incident, the trial of her daughter (and two other bloggers) was postponed indefinitely for apparently no reason. Tần was ultimately sentenced to ten years in prison at a one-day trial on 24 September 2012. She was released early after three years due to pressure from the international community and human rights groups. After her release, Tần left for the US where her indomitable spirit brought her widespread recognition, including the International Women of Courage Award from the US Department of State.

("Tạ Phong Tần")

Albania

8 October 2012 – **Gjergj Ndreca** (aged 51), a former dissident active in the struggle against dictator Enver Hoxha, set himself on fire in Tirana in protest against repeated delays in the disbursement of settlements to former political prisoners. He was followed two days later by **Lirak Bejko** (aged 47). Both were a part of a 20-man group that launched a hunger strike in September 2012 in protest against the government's failure to provide proper redress to victims of the former regime. Pursuant to a 2007 law, former political prisoners were entitled to state compensation amounting to around 20 USD per day of imprisonment. Ndreca survived the incident and returned to Tirana from a Thessaloniki hospital, where he was subsequently informed that the strike was disbanded by court order. Bejko succumbed to his injuries in a hospital in Bari, Italy.

("Albania")

Bulgaria

20 February 2013 – **Plamen Goranov** (aged 36), photographer, mountaineer, construction worker, and social activist, self-immolated in Varna outside the city council offices demanding the resignation of corrupt mayor Kiril Yordanov and his associates. He died in the hospital on 3 March. Three days later, faced with mass protests, Yordanov resigned. At the site of the incident, Varna locals erected a makeshift memorial stone cairn topped with flowers and Bulgarian flags.

The mass protests that erupted across Bulgaria in February 2012 were an expression of the widespread disapproval of the staggering social costs of the economic transformation that the country undertook after the fall of the Communist regime. The protests ultimately resulted in the collapse of the Boyko Borissov cabinet and the prime minister's resignation, which he tended on the day of Goranov's self-burning (the politician later retook the office). Although Goranov was one of six men who carried out self-incinerations around that time, his was the only one to receive widespread public attention (the media went as far as to call him "the Bulgarian Palach"), probably due to his suprapersonal, universal motivations, allegedly evinced by his prior attempts at public protest, often quite unconventional. In 2012, he climbed three 10-m-tall female statues, a part of a memorial to Soviet-Bulgarian friendship, and put coloured hoods over their heads. The act was a demonstration of solidarity with the Russian feminist protest punk group Pussy Riot following their notorious action in Moscow's Cathedral of Christ the Saviour.

Goranov's self-immolation has been explored by *Flame* (the Bulgarian name "Plamen" translates to "flame"), a documentary from the NYC-based production company Dress Code.

(Flame; "Plamen Goranov")

Sri Lanka

24 May 2013 – the Buddhist monk **Bowatte Indarathana Thera** (aged 30) self-burned in protest against Muslim ritual slaughter practices and the forced conversion of Buddhists to Christianity and Islam. He carried out his protest outside the Temple of the Tooth, a Buddhist shrine in Sri Lanka allegedly holding one of Buddha's teeth. The incident was captured on video by a reporter from a local private broadcaster, whom the monk informed of his plans beforehand. The footage shows the monk dousing himself with flammable liquid in a crowded square near a busy street and shouting protest rhetoric. Then, we see another man running up to the monk and lighting both the monk and himself on fire. Engulfed in fire, the monk lurches towards a nearby market stall, where onlookers put out the flames in under two minutes, place the monk on a board, and put him inside a nearby jeep, which then takes him to a hospital. Despite immediate medical attention, the monk died. After the authorities refused to grant him a state funeral, dozens took to the streets of Colombo in protest.

("Bowatte"; "Sri Lanka")

Vietnam

23 May 2014 – **Lê Thị Tuyết Mai** (aged 67), member of an outlawed Buddhist movement, set fire to herself outside the Reunification Palace in the centre of Hồ Chí Minh City. Banners calling for respecting the Dharma and carrying rhetoric protesting against Chinese territorial claims on the South China Sea were found near the body. On 2 May 2014, China installed an oil rig in contested waters near the Paracel Islands, triggering a wave of strikes across Vietnam and causing thousands to pour into the streets in protest against the move. Initially, the Communist regime treated the demonstrations as an expression of Vietnamese patriotism and did not move to neutralise the unrest. But when protesters began assaulting Chinese workers, wrecking factory facilities, and raiding industrial parks belonging to foreign investors, the government cracked down on the radicals to maintain domestic security and protect the country's international position. In response to attacks from

Vietnamese protesters which left over 100 people injured, the Chinese authorities recalled 3,000 of its citizens home. The patriarch of the Unified Buddhist Sangha of Vietnam, Thích Quảng Độ, called on the Vietnamese government to embrace democratisation. News of the protests spread abroad thanks to the Vietnamese diaspora, and demonstrations were held in Australia, Europe, the Philippines, and the US, primarily outside Chinese embassies and consulates. On 16 July 2014, the Chinese removed the drilling platform from disputed territory, while the Vietnamese government moved to preserve the presence of foreign business in the country, offering tax reliefs, rent reductions, and credit lines to companies that sustained damage or losses during the protests. Following Mai's self-burning, two more people attempted to self-incinerate, in all likelihood in service to the same cause.

("Vietnamese")

United States of America

23 June 2014 – **Charles Moore** (aged 79), a minister of the United Methodist Church (UMC), set fire to himself in a shopping centre parking lot in his hometown of Grand Saline in east Texas. Moore died on arrival at the hospital. Inspired by self-immolations among Tibetans, he decided to lay down his life to draw public attention to his own struggle for social justice and the abolition of the death penalty, and to protest the treatment of gays and lesbians by the UMC hierarchy. In 1995, during the UMC bishops' conference in Austin, Texas, Moore staged a 15-day hunger strike with similar objectives in mind, and ended it only after the Church hierarchy admitted to stigmatising and discriminating LGBT people. Years spent working on behalf of the Ecumenical Institute, first in the more challenging areas of Chicago and later in the slums of Mumbai, in Africa, and the Middle East, sensitised the minister to issues of social justice, poverty, and iniquity to such a degree that he became, in his own words, a "social justice fundamentalist." In a note he left behind, he wrote that his decision to self-immolate in his hometown was driven by the painful memories of racism and prejudice that he witnessed in childhood. The note also denounced the crimes of the slavery era and the disgraceful efforts of the Ku Klux Klan. His death was profoundly misunderstood by his fellow locals – most reports indicated that he may have been driven to martyrdom by insanity. The minister, however, foresaw these reactions and said in the note that he made the decision while of sound mind and body, and added that his only regret was that he was unable to do more to advance the cause of human rights.

("Charles R. Moore"; Hall)

Iran

14 March 2015 – street vendor **Younes Asakereh** (aged 34) set himself ablaze outside the municipal building in Khorramshahr in southwestern Iran

90 Chronology of protest self-burnings (1963–2017)

after his fruit stand, his only source of income, had been confiscated by local authorities. His act and his subsequent funeral eight days later offered an opportunity for the Ahvazi Arabs to manifest their dissatisfaction with central government policies, which openly discriminated against ethnic minorities. On 17 March, 100 protesters were arrested for chanting anti-regime slogans and posting banners saying "We are all Younes" at a football game. Demonstrations that broke out in Khorramshahr and Ahvaz after Asakereh's funeral gathered crowds in the thousands, but were quickly put down by law enforcement. The Iranian government is very serious about any and all symptoms of cultural or political independence exhibited by Arabs populating this oil- and natural gas-rich region, incorporated into Iran only in 1925. The regime has been particularly vigilant since a series of bombings carried out in 2005–06 in the capital of the region by the Arab Struggle Movement for the Liberation of Ahvaz (ASMLA), a group that the central government considers a terrorist organisation. Asakereh was not the first Ahvazi to self-burn in protest against the persecution of his people, as similar incidents have happened in the region before.

(Karami)

South Korea

12 August 2015 – **Choi Yeon-yeol** (aged 80) set fire to himself outside the Japanese embassy in Seoul, at a protest demanding justice for Korean "comfort women" (*ianfu*). A weekly demonstration calling for Japan to provide redress to Korean women sexually enslaved and abused by Japanese soldiers during World War II has been held in the South Korean capital since 1992, with each gathering drawing sizeable crowds. In 2011, at the 1000th manifestation, South Korean activists set up a small bronze monument of a young woman dressed in traditional Korean garb sitting with bare feet on a chair. The chair next to her was empty to indicate that another person was missing. The Japanese demanded, unsuccessfully, that the sculpture be removed, while the former *ianfu* renewed their demands for official apology and redress. The Tokyo government rejected these claims as lacking legal basis pursuant to the provisions of the 1965 Treaty on Basic Relations between Japan and the Republic of Korea, but the women argued that the agreement concerned inter-state rather than personal grievances. Finally, in December 2015, Japan and South Korea agreed on compensation in order to, paraphrasing the words of Japanese Prime Minister Shinzō Abe, refrain from passing the problem on to future generations. The redress issue was pressing, as the remaining Korean "comfort women" are all advanced in years – in 2015 alone, nine out of the surviving 47 passed away. Abe issued an official apology, and his government transferred 8.3 million USD to Korean authorities. This, however, did not satisfy the surviving victims, because the contract had not been consulted with them and the redress fund would be administered by the state.

The following year, activists erected a replica of the contentious sculpture in front of the Japanese consulate in Pusan, to which Japan responded by temporarily recalling its envoys. To ease diplomatic tensions, Korean police forcibly removed the sculpture, but after the Japanese Minister of Defence visited the controversial Yasukuni Shrine in Tokyo, where Japanese war dead, including the notorious war criminals, are commemorated, the piece was quickly returned to its former spot.

("Japan"; "Japan Recalls")

Republic of Somaliland – Somalia

5 October 2015 – **Mohamed Jehad** (aged 25), a Yemeni national, set himself aflame outside the UNHCR offices in Hargeisa, the capital of the self-declared and internationally unrecognised Republic of Somaliland. The self-burning was an act of desperation, the last resort of a man who allegedly did not receive the humanitarian aid he was promised. At the time, Hargeisa held around 1,500 refugees in similar straits, mostly from war-torn Yemen. Ever since the start of the Yemeni Civil War in March 2015, thousands of civilians have fled the country seeking refuge in Somalia and Somaliland, a reversal of what was seen as the typical direction of migrations in the region (earlier it was predominantly Somalis moving to the Arabian Peninsula for work). Although many of the Yemeni refugees in Somaliland were former migrant workers, most were native Yemenis so desperate to flee the civil war that they decided to seek refuge in the African self-declared state, ravaged by years of war and drought.

(Maruf)

Australia, Nauru, Manus Island – Papua New Guinea

18 October 2015 – **Khodayar Amini** (aged 30), an Afghani refugee, set himself on fire in the Melbourne suburbs during a meeting with his lawyers. After being charged with stalking and making death threats against the employees of an aid organisation, Amini was waiting for a meeting with immigration officials and a trial. His death drew international attention to the horrid conditions in refugee detention centres on Christmas Island, Nauru, and Manus Island, where self-mutilation was rampant. As the Australian authorities pursued a policy of securing its borders, incoming refugees were officially warned that self-harming behaviour would not in any way increase their chances of being granted entry into the country. In 2012, an Australian artist of Vietnamese descent, Van Thanh Rudd, took action on the bank of the Yarra River in Melbourne, where he burned his own lifelike effigy. The mannequin was clad in a T-shirt emblazoned with the phrase "No Nauru," the title of the event. It was the artist's protest against the reopening

of the Australian detention facility which was stage to a number of protest self-incinerations.

To protest against the Australians' hardline approach to immigration, Iranian national **Omid Masoumali** (aged 23) self-burned on 27 April 2016, during a visit of UNHCR officials to the Nauru camp, where he was detained. Masoumali was taken to a Brisbane hospital, where he died two days later. He was soon followed by **Hodan Yasi** (aged 21), a Somali national, who set herself alight on 2 May. In the week separating the two incidents, at least six people attempted to take their life: some swallowed razors or laundry detergents, others hanged themselves with bed sheets.

(Davidson and Doherty; Hasham)

Mongolia

13 November 2015 – **S. Erdene**, leader of the Mongolian labour union Ev Sanaany Negdel, called a press conference in Ulaanbaatar to discuss upcoming changes to work contracts for miners employed by the state-owned mining company Erdenes Tavan Tolgoi (ETT). After revealing his misgivings, he doused himself with a flammable substance and set fire to himself in front of his fellow union leaders and journalists. Footage of the incident shows his colleagues' fruitless attempts to snuff the fire out with their jackets, followed by one of the onlookers finally putting the flames out with a fire extinguisher. With severe burns to nearly half of his body, Erdene was quickly driven to a hospital. Before the incident, the union official was heard saying that Mongolia was selling off its own citizens to a foreign power, a reference to the state-owned company's decision to transfer over 200 of its employees to Tavan Tolgoi, a sprawling mining operation that was to be partially sold off to a Chinese consortium: a move that would have likely resulted in layoffs and a decline in working standards. Before the union boss decided to protest the plan by self-burning, he and his fellow miners tried to oppose the decision by whatever means at their disposal.

After the tragic incident, ETT Executive Director Tuur Bilgee promised that the miners' working time limits would remain unchanged and guaranteed their employment through the next 33 months. He also promised bonuses, and that the new work contracts would be given to the miners in Mongolian, reversing an earlier decision that presumed that the agreements would be drafted solely in English. Following the incident, Mongolian Prime Minister Chimed Saikhanbileg obliged the ETT to cover all of Erdene's medical costs and announced that an investigation into the company would be launched – but backpedalled on the decision the following day, after labelling Erdene's protest a terrorist act. In spite of Saikhanbileg's accusations, however, no charges were ultimately brought against Erdene, even though his self-incineration resulted in a fire that caused significant property damage and endangered the lives of the people who were in the building at

Chronology of protest self-burnings (1963–2017)   93

the time. It is possible that Erdene's ensuing popularity mitigated some of the punishment he would have otherwise faced. Despite widespread shock and admiration that his actions have elicited among his countrymen, some soon began arguing that instead of attempting to take his own life, the union boss should have attempted to assassinate one of the corrupt politicians who were allegedly behind the deal Erdene protested against.

(Menard; "The Horrifying")

Poland

19 October 2017 – **Piotr Szczęsny** (aged 54), a chemist who worked as a coach holding training seminars for businesses and local government officials, set himself on fire outside the Palace of Culture and Science in the centre of Warsaw. Near his body stood a bottle with traces of flammable liquid, a megaphone, a portable loudspeaker, and pamphlets suggesting that Szczęsny immolated himself in protest against the majority rule of the Prawo i Sprawiedliwość (PiS) (Law and Justice) party. The pamphlets also contained Szczęsny's 15-point manifesto, which outlined the motives behind his violent protest, including the authorities' alleged efforts to curtail civil liberties, abrogate the rule of law, and undermine democracy, and their silent acquiescence in the depredation of the environment, the discrimination of minorities, and their role in entrenching societal divisions. His clear-eyed and highly suggestive analysis of the political situation in Poland bore no indication that its author may have suffered from any mental problems or could be considered a fanatic, but instead revealed a well-developed social conscience. Szczęsny set himself ablaze to the tune of *Kocham wolność* (*I Love Freedom*), a rock song that was quickly adopted as one of the hymns of the protests which swept the country in July 2017, when thousands of citizens took to the streets to demand that the rule of law be respected and to convince the Polish president to veto the courts reform bill that PiS steamrolled through parliament earlier that summer. Szczęsny was taken to the hospital, where doctors fought for his life for the next ten days. He finally died on 29 October, and his death quickly became a symbol of popular opposition to the rule of PiS.

The day following Szczęsny's self-sacrifice, Jarosław Mikołajewski – a writer, poet, and translator of Italian literature – published a poem online, written in the form of a letter addressed to the immolator. Not long after, musician Piotr Bukartyk recorded a song about Szczęsny's self-burning under the name *W środku miasta* (*In the Middle of the City*). Another song about the incident was recorded by Jacek Kleyff, a musician and poet, who co-founded the cabaret Salon Niezależnych (The Independents' Salon) in the late 1960s and was harassed by Communist authorities for the political undertones in his work. Kleyff's song was called *Piotr S.*, which was how the media referenced the self-burner after his family refused to release his name in the immediate wake of the incident.

(Żuk and Żuk)

94 Chronology of protest self-burnings (1963–2017)

References

The online resources identified below were consulted multiple times. All of them were active as of 1 December 2018.

"Activist Who Set Himself on Fire Shifted to Karachi." *Dawn*, 23 Jan. 2004. www.dawn.com/news/348936.

"Alain Escoffier." it.wikipedia.org/wiki/Alain_Escoffier.

"Albania Ex-Dissident Dies After Self-Immolation Protest." *BBC*, 2 Nov. 2012. www.bbc.com/news/world-europe-20189444.

Allworth, Edward. *The Tatars of Crimea: Return to Homeland.* Duke UP, 1998.

Andrews, William. "Self-Immolation and Suicide as Protest in Japan." 30 Jun. 2014. throwoutyourbooks.wordpress.com/2014/06/30/self-immolation-and-suicide-as-protest-in-japan/.

"Armenian Issues in History: He was an Armenia: Artin Penik." *Turkish Journal*, 28 Oct. 2011. www.turkishjournal.com/i.php?newsid=361.

Ashton, John R., and Stuart Donnan. "Suicide by Burning as an Epidemic Phenomenon: An Analysis of 82 Deaths and Inquests in England and Wales in 1978–1979." *Psychological Medicine*, vol. 11, no. 4, 1981, pp. 735–739.

Aydın, Filiz Tutku. *Comparative Cases in Long-distance Nationalism: Explaining the 'Émigré,' Exile, Diaspora and Transnational Movements of the Crimean Tatars.* Dissertation, U of Toronto, 2012.

Balderstone, Simon. "An Heiress Dies…" *The Age* [Melbourne], 4 Oct. 1978, p. 1. news.google.com/newspapers?nid=1300&dat=19781004&id=vu1UAAAAIBAJ&sjid=W5IDAAAAIBAJ&pg=4366,774485&hl=en.

Beauregard, Alexandrine C. "Imaginary Self-Immolation." *Liminalities. A Journal of Performance Studies*, vol. 12, no. 3, 2016, pp. 1–6.

Becklund, Laurie. "Hundreds Pay Respects at Service: Iranian Who Set Himself Afire Interred." *Los Angeles Times*, 11 Oct. 1987. articles.latimes.com/1987-10-11/news/mn-13481_1_iranian-exile.

Biggs, Michael. "Dying Without Killing: Self-Immolations, 1963–2002." *Making Sense of Suicide Missions*, edited by Diego Gambetta, Oxford UP, 2005, pp. 173–208.

———. "How Repertories Evolve: The Diffusion of Suicide Protest in the Twentieth Century." *Mobilization: An International Quarterly*, vol. 18, no. 4, 2013, pp. 407–428.

Blažek, Petr. *Ryszard Siwiec 1909–1968.* English translation Dominika Ferens, Instytut Pamięci Narodowej, 2010.

"Bowatte Indarathana Thera Full Video." Uploaded by Sandaeliya. *YouTube*, 21 Jun. 2013. www.youtube.com/watch?v=9jA6dc0LKPQ.

Buffetrille, Katia, and Françoise Robin, editors. "Tibet is Burning: Self-Immolation: Ritual or Political Protest?" *Revue d'Etudes Tibétaines*, no. 25, 2012.

"Burning with Conviction." *Independent*, 1 Jul. 2003. www.independent.co.uk/news/uk/home-news/burning-with-conviction-111104.html.

Cemilev, Reşat, editor. *Musa Mamut – Human Torch: Collection of Documents.* Crimean Foundation, 1986.

Chân, Không. *Learning True Love: How I Learned and Practiced Social Change in Vietnam.* Parallax Press, 1993.

Chang, Maria Hsia. *Falun Gong: The End of Days.* Yale UP, 2004.

"Charles R. Moore." en.wikipedia.org/wiki/Charles_R._Moore_(minister).

"Cheng Nan-jung." en.wikipedia.org/wiki/Cheng_Nan-jung.

Cho, Young Cheon. *The Politics of Suffering in the Public Sphere: The Body in Pain, Empathy, and Political Spectacles.* Dissertation, U of Iowa, 2009.

Cho, Young-rae. *A Single Spark: The Biography of Chun Tae-il.* Translated by Chun Soon-ok, Dolbegae Publishers, 2003.

Citton, Yves. "Politics as Hypergestural Improvisation in the Age of Mediocracy". *The Oxford Handbook of Critical Improvisation Studies*, edited by George E. Lewis and Benjamin Piekut, vol. 1, Oxford UP, 2016, pp. 160–181.

Coburn, Jon. "'I Have Chosen the Flaming Death': The Forgotten Self-Immolation of Alice Herz." *Peace & Change: A Journal of Peace Research*, vol. 43, no. 1, 2018, pp. 32–60.

Coleman, Loren. "Fiery Copycats." *The Copycat Effect: How the Media and Popular Culture Trigger the Mayhem in Tomorrow's Headlines*, edited by Loren Coleman, Paraview Pocket Books, 2004, pp. 48–66.

Cooper, Kim. "Flames of Peace." 20 Jan. 2010. insroland.org/2010/01/20/florencebeaumont/.

Czabański, Adam, and Małgorzata Czabańska-Rosada. *The Self-Immolation of Oskar Brüsewitz Compared to Other Suicides Committed as a Political Protest.* Peter Lang, 2017.

Darabi, Parvin, and Romin P. Thomson. *Rage Against the Veil: The Courageous Life and Death of an Islamic Dissident.* Prometheus Books, 1999.

Davidson, Helen, and Ben Doherty. "Iranian Refugee Critically Ill After Setting Himself on Fire on Nauru During UN Visit." *Guardian*, 27 Apr. 2016. www.theguardian.com/australia-news/2016/apr/27/iranian-asylum-seeker-severely-burnt-after-setting-himself-on-fire-on-nauru.

Deng, Annie. "Dousing the Flames: The Tang Fu Zhen Self-Immolation Incident and Urban Land Takings Reform in the People's Republic of China." *Southern California Interdisciplinary Law Journal*, vol. 20, no. 3, 2011, pp. 585–617.

Dorr, Jeanne. "The Young Man with the Mesmerizing Eyes." 4 Mar. 2012. web.archive.org/web/20120304165318/http:/www.lithuanian-american.org/bridges/bal99/dorr.html.

Drygas, Maciej. *Dzieci z Hotelu Ameryka* [Children from the America Hotel]. *Dialog* [Warsaw], no. 3, 1991, pp. 15–49.

"Eduardo Miño Pérez." es.wikipedia.org/wiki/Eduardo_Mi%C3%B1o. Etxamendi eta Larralde. *Joseba Elósegi.* Uploaded by Gabi de la Maza. *YouTube*, 17 Sep. 2014. www.youtube.com/watch?v=loXRwRsocyE.

"Fanaa." en.wikipedia.org/wiki/Fanaa_(film)#cite_note-15.

Farley, Helen. "Death by Whose Hand? Falun Gong and Suicide." *Sacred Suicide*, edited by James R. Lewis and Carole M. Cusack, Ashgate, 2014, pp. 215–233.

Fijałek, Krzysztof. "Śmierć bez metafory" [Death without Metaphor]. *Gazeta w Krakowie* [Krakow], local ed. of *Gazeta Wyborcza* [Warsaw], 21 Mar. 2000, p. 5.

"First Theater Festival in Rojava." *Dicle News Agency*, 28 Mar. 2015. www.diclehaber.com/en/news/content/view/450289?page=1&from=4132442070.

Fischer, Marc. "Malachi Ritscher". *Public Collectors*, Mar. 2014. www.publiccollectors.org/Malachi_Ritscher_Whitney.pdf.

Fisher, Ian. "The Manic and Messianic Life of a Troubled Idealist." *The New York Times*, 27 Nov. 1996. www.nytimes.com/1996/11/27/nyregion/the-manic-and-messianic-life-of-a-troubled-idealist.html.

Flame. Directed and produced by dress code, 2013. www.plamengoranovfilm.com/.

Galili, Lily. "For the Land She Loved to Death." *Haaretz*, 30 Aug. 2005. www.haaretz.com/1.4937340.

Green, Peter. "Student's Suicide Leads Czechs to Bout of Soul-Searching." *The New York Times*, 12 Mar. 2003. www.nytimes.com/2003/03/12/world/student-s-suicide-leads-czechs-to-bout-of-soul-searching.html.

Grojean, Olivier. "Self-Immolation by Kurdish Activists in Turkey and Europe." *Revue d'Etudes Tibétaines*, no. 25, 2012, pp. 159–168.

Halberstam, David. *The Kennedy Years: From the Pages of The New York Times*. Abrams, 2013.

———. *The Making of a Quagmire: America and Vietnam during the Kennedy Era*. Revised edition, Rowman and Littlefield, 2008.

Hall, Michael. "Man on Fire." *Texas Monthly*, Dec. 2014. www.texasmonthly.com/articles/man-on-fire/.

"Hartmut Gründler." en.wikipedia.org/wiki/Hartmut_Gr%C3%BCndler.

Hasham, Nicole. "Asylum Seeker Self-Immolation Amid Fears He Would be Sent Back to Detention, Senate Hearing Told." *Sydney Morning Herald*, 20 Oct. 2015. www.smh.com.au/politics/federal/asylum-seeker-selfimmolates-amid-fears-he-would-be-sent-back-to-detention-senate-hearing-told-20151020-gkd81v.html#ixzz47bc7tRH0.

Hedges, Paul. "Burning for a Cause: Four Factors in Successful Political (and Religious) Self-Immolation Examined in Relation to Alleged Falun Gong 'Fanatics' in Tiananmen Square." *Politics and Religion*, vol. 8, 2015, pp. 797–817.

Himmel, Nieson. "Man Sets Self on Fire to Protest Iranian's Visit." *Los Angeles Times*, 21 Sep. 1987. articles.latimes.com/1987-09-21/news/mn-5998_1_burning-man.

"Huguette Gaulin." en.wikipedia.org/wiki/Huguette_Gaulin.

Human Rights Watch. "Dangerous Meditation: China's Campaign Against Falungong." Jan. 2012. www.hrw.org/reports/2002/china.

Husni, Mariwan et al. "Kurdish Refugees' View of Politically Motivated Self-Immolation." *Transcultural Psychiatry*, vol. 39, no. 3, 2002, pp. 367–375.

"'I Would Do It Again'." *The Guardian*, 18 Feb. 2002. www.theguardian.com/world/2002/feb/18/gender.uk.

IANS. "Another Dera Follower Attempts Self-Immolation." *Hindustan Times*, 8 Jul. 2007. www.hindustantimes.com/india/another-dera-follower-attempts-self-immolation/story-InHMpymaQL9P7RGSTjuogL.html.

———. "Dera Follower Attempts Self-Immolation, Is Serious." *Two Circles*, 2 Jul. 2007. twocircles.net/2007jul02/dera_follower_attempts_self_immolation_serious.html.

"Immolation Bids in Cuttack, Delhi; Docs' Stir Gathers Steam." *Times of India*, 27 May 2006. timesofindia.indiatimes.com/india/Immolation-bids-in-Cuttack-Delhi-docs-stir-gathers-steam/articleshow/1580129.cms.

"Indonesia: Activist Dies After Self-Immolation in Front of Palace." *Global Voices*, 29 Dec. 2011. globalvoices.org/2011/12/29/indonesia-activist-dies-after-self-immolation-in-front-of-palace/.

Inspired Agitators. Poster Series by David Lester. blackdotmuseum.wordpress.com/inspired-agitators/.

"Japan and South Korea Agree on WW2 'Comfort Women' Deal." *BBC*, 28 Dec. 2015. www.bbc.com/news/world-asia-35188135.

"Japan Recalls Korean Envoy Over 'Comfort Women' Statute." *BBC*, 6 Jan. 2017. www.bbc.com/news/world-asia-38526914.

Jones, Sam. "Tamil Killed Himself 'to Guide Others to Liberation'." *Guardian*, 19 Feb. 2009. www.theguardian.com/world/2009/feb/19/tamil-suicide-protest-geneva.

"Joseba Elósegui." es.wikipedia.org/wiki/Joseba_El%C3%B3segui.

Karami, Arash. "Iranian Vendor Dies After Setting Himself on Fire." *Al-Monitor*, 24 Mar. 2015. www.al-monitor.com/pulse/originals/2015/03/iran-younes-asakere-fruit-vendor-self-immolation.html.

Karnow, Stanley. *Vietnam: A History*. Revised and updated edition, Viking Penguin, 1991.

Katsiaficas, Gregory and Na Kahn-chae, editors. *South Korean Democracy: Legacy of the Gwangju Uprising*. Routledge, 2006.

Kaufman, Ami. "Moshe Silman's Self-Immolation Is a National, Not Just a Personal, Tragedy." *Guardian*, 18 Jul. 2012. www.theguardian.com/commentisfree/2012/jul/18/moshe-silman-self-immolation.

Keesing's Contemporary Archives, 18–25 Sep. 1965, p. 20972. web.stanford.edu/group/tomzgroup/pmwiki/uploads/1346-1965-09-KS-a-GK.pdf.

Khosrokhavar, Farhad. "The Arab Revolutions and Self-Immolation." *Revue d'Etudes Tibétains*, no. 25, 2012, pp. 169–179.

Kim, Hyojoung. "Micromobilization and Suicide Protest in South Korea, 1970–2004." *Social Research*, vol. 75, no. 2, 2008, pp. 543–578.

King, Anita. *The Official Kathy Change Website*. www.kathychange.org.

King, Tim. "The Questionable Effectiveness of Lighting Yourself on Fire." *Salem-News*, 8 Feb. 2012. www.salem-news.com/articles/february082012/tamil-immolation-tk.php.

"Kostas Georgakis." en.wikipedia.org/wiki/Kostas_Georgakis.

"La flamme du désespoir." 12 Dec. 2004. www.congovision.com/nouvelles/kongo-fire1.html.

LeVine, Mark and Bryan Reynolds. "Theatre of Immediacy, Transversal Poetics." *Performance Studies: Key Words, Concepts and Theories*, edited by Bryan Reynolds, Palgrave, 2014, pp. 201–214.

"List of Political Self-Immolations." en.wikipedia.org/wiki/List_of_political_Self-Immolations.

"Living Torches." www.janpalach.cz/en/default/zive-pochodne.

"Liviu Cornel Babeş." en.wikipedia.org/wiki/Liviu_Cornel_Babe%C8%99.

"Man Who Immolated Himself in Protest of FTA Dies." *Hankyoreh*, 16 Apr. 2007. english.hani.co.kr/arti/english_edition/e_national/203235.html.

"Man's Self-Immolation Is Protest of U.S. Mideast Policy." *AP*, 11 Dec. 1990. apnews.com/abe37303443713e8e8d3c7fd2ca01fad.

Marotti, William. "Japan 1968: The Performance of Violence and the Theater of Protest." *The American Historical Review*, vol. 114, no. 1, 2009, pp. 97–135.

"Márton Moyses." pl.wikipedia.org/wiki/M%C3%A1rton_Moyses.

Maruf, Harun. "No Aid Drove Yemeni Man to Self-Immolation, Friends Say." *VOA*, 6 Oct. 2015. www.voanews.com/a/no-aid-caused-yemeni-man-to-set-up-self-afire-say-friends/2993758.html.

McGranahan, Carole, and Ralph Litzinger, editors. "Self-Immolation as Protest in Tibet." *Cultural Anthropology*, 2012. www.culanth.org/fieldsights/93-Self-Immolation-as-protest-in-tibet.

98 Chronology of protest self-burnings (1963–2017)

Menard, Aubrey. "Why Did Mongolia's S. Erdene Set Himself Alight." *Open Democracy*, 4 Dec. 2015. www.opendemocracy.net/aubrey-menard/why-did-mongolia-s-s-erdene-set-himself-alight.

"Mohamed Alanssi." en.wikipedia.org/wiki/Mohamed_Alanssi.

Nalankilli, Thanjai. "Self-Immolation Against Hindi Imposition in Tamil Nadu (1965)." *Tamil Tribune*, Jan. 2004. www.tamiltribune.com/04/0101-anti-hindi-Self-Immolations.html.

Norimatsu, Satoko Oka. "Suicide as Protest: Two Self-Immolations Under the Abe Regime." *The Asia-Pacific Journal*. apjjf.org/-Satoko-Norimatsu/4810/article. html.

"Oleksa Hirnyk." en.wikipedia.org/wiki/Oleksa_Hirnyk.

Onyekachi, Chima. "Biafra Heroes Day: Bruce Mayrock 'The Hero in Flames'." www.thebiafraherald.co/2016/05/biafra-heroes-day-bruce-mayrock-hero-in. html.

Othman, Nasih. "Suicide by Self-Burning in Iraqi Kurdistan: Description and Risk Factors." *Archives of Suicide Research*, vol. 15, no. 3, 2011, pp. 238–249.

Ownby, David. *Falun Gong and the Future of China*. Oxford UP, 2008.

"Pakistani Asylum-Seeker with Burn Injuries Rushed to Dushanbe." *Pajhwok Afghan News*, 18 Nov. 2005. wikileaks.org/gifiles/attach/32/32121_Critical%20 Self-Immolation%20in%20News.doc.

Park, Ben B. C. "Sociopolitical Contexts of Self-Immolations in Vietnam and South Korea." *Archives of Suicide Research*, vol. 8, no. 1, 2004, pp. 81–97.

"Plamen Goranov." en.wikipedia.org/wiki/Plamen_Goranov.

"Poignant Acts of Self-Immolation." *TamilNet*, 14 Feb. 2009. tamilnet.com/art. html?catid=79&artid=28412.

"Police Probe Self-Immolation Act in Ruling Party's Office in Siberia." *RadioFreeEurope*, 18 Jul. 2012. www.rferl.org/a/police-probe-self-immolation-in-siberia/24649072. html.

Rao, Srinivasa A. "Telangana Erupts as Activists Take their Own Lives." *India Today*, 4 Apr. 2012. www.indiatoday.in/opinion/a-srinivasa-rao/story/telangana-erupts-as-activists-take-their-own-lives-98028-2012-04-04#close-overlay.

Rasool, Izaddin A., and Joanne L. Payton. "Tongues of Fire: Women's Suicide and Self-Injury by Burns in the Kurdistan Region of Iraq." *The Sociological Review*, vol. 62, no. 2, 2014, pp. 237–254.

"Reinhold Elstner." www.fpp.co.uk/online/02/03/Elstner_Letter.html.

Robin, Françoise. "Fire, Flames and Ashes: How Tibetan Poets Talk About Self-Immolations Without Talking About Them." *Revue d'Etudes Tibétains*, no. 25, 2012, pp. 123–131.

Ryan, Cheyney. "The One Who Burns Herself for Peace." *Bringing Peace Home: Feminism, Violence, and Nature*, edited by Karen J. Warren and Duane L. Cady, Indiana UP, 1996, pp. 16–32.

Sabatos, Charles. "The 'Burning Body' as an Icon of Resistance: Literary Representations of Jan Palach." *Gender and Sexuality in 1968: Transformative Politics in the Cultural Imagination*, edited by Lessie Jo Frazier and Deborah Cohen, Palgrave Macmillan, 2009, pp. 193–217.

Sangster, Leigh. "The Work of Art in the Age of Self-Immolation." *Cultural Anthropology*, 25 Mar. 2012. culanth.org/fieldsights/113-the-work-of-art-in-the-age-of-Self-Immolation.

Sarkar, Shyamal. "Self-Immolation in Myanmar Against Military Dictatorship." *Buddhist Channel.* 23 Mar. 2008. www.buddhistchannel.tv/index.php?id=82,6089, 0,0,1,0#.W9ajVzGNx2F.

"Sebastián Acevedo." es.wikipedia.org/wiki/Sebasti%C3%A1n_Acevedo#cite_note-5.

"Self-Immolation Bid by Worker Shocks Benazir." *Dawn,* 10 Jun. 2004. www.dawn. com/news/361431/self-immolation-bid-by-worker-shocks-benazir.

"Self-Immolation Incident Highlights Desperation of Georgian IDPs." *Caucasus Report,* 29 Oct. 2010. www.rferl.org/a/SelfImmolation_Incident_Highlights_ Desperation_Of_Georgian_IDPs/2204833.html.

Shahadi, Joseph. "Burn: The Radical Disappearance of Kathy Change." *TDR: The Drama Review,* vol. 55, no. 2, 2011, pp. 52–72.

Shekhar, G. C. "Suicide to Stop Hanging: Protests Against Rajiv Killers' Execution Grow in Tamil Nadu." *Telegraph,* 29 Aug. 2011. www.telegraphindia. com/india/suicide-to-stop-hanging-protests-against-rajiv-killers-execution-grow-in-tamil-nadu/cid/357315.

Shelley, Martha. "A Sacrificial Light: Self-Immolation in Tajrish Square." *On The Issue,* Fall 1994. www.ontheissuesmagazine.com/1994fall/tehran.php.

Singh, S. P. et al. 'A Psychosocial Study of 'Self-Immolation' in India.' *Acta Psychiatrica Scandinavica,* vol. 97, no. 1, 1998, pp. 71–75.

"Sri Lanka Buddhist Monk Dies After Self-Immolation." *BBC,* 26 May 2013. www. bbc.com/news/world-asia-22677058.

Steele, Jonathan. "Ultimate Sacrifice." *Guardian,* 20 Jan. 1999. www.theguardian. com/theguardian/1999/jan/20/features11.g22.

Stefanicki, Robert. *Czerwony Tybet* [Red Tibet]. Agora, 2014.

Stojaspal, Jan. "A Suicidal Spring." *Time International,* no. 16, 28 Apr. 2003, pp. 40–42.

Storm in the Grasslands: Self-Immolations in Tibet and Chinese Policy. International Campaign for Tibet, 2012. www.savetibet.org/wp-content/uploads/2013/06/ storminthegrassland-FINAL-HR.pdf.

"Student Attempts Self-Immolation at 'Desh Bachao' Protest Rally." *One India,* 29 May 2006. www.oneindia.com/2006/05/27/student-attempts-Self-Immolation-at-desh-bachao-protest-rally-1148884140.html.

Szczygieł, Mariusz. *Gottland.* Czarne, 2006.

"Tạ Phong Tần." en.wikipedia.org/wiki/T%E1%BA%A1_Phong_T%E1%BA%A7n.

"The Horrifying Moment Mongolian Union Boss Sets Fire to Himself in Protest to Coal Mine Sales." *Yahoo News,* 17 Nov. 2015. uk.news.yahoo.com/horrifying-moment-mongolian-union-boss-114616232.html?guccounter=1.

"Thuviengdpt". thuviengdpt.info/lam-su/tieu-su-thanh-tu-dao/.

Tony, Mike. "Kathy Change: Her Legacy Burns on." *The Daily Pennsylvanian,* 30 Apr. 2014. www.thedp.com/article/2014/05/kathy-change-legacy-burns-on.

Topmiller, Robert. "Struggling for Peace: The Unrecognized Sacrifices of Buddhist Women During the Vietnam War." *Journal of Women's History,* vol. 17, no. 3, 2005, pp. 133–157.

———. *The Lotus Unleashed: The Buddhist Peace Movement in South Vietnam, 1964–1966.* UP of Kentucky, 2002.

Uehling, Greta. "Squatting, Self-Immolation, and the Repatriation of Crimean Tatars." *Nationalities Papers,* vol. 28, no. 2, 2000, pp. 317–341.

Vardys, Stanley. "Protest of Lithuanians not Isolated." *Lituanus: Lithuanian Quarterly Journal of Arts and Sciences,* vol. 18, no. 2, 1972. www.lituanus.org/1972/72_2_01.htm.

Vasagar, Jeevan. "Parents Mourn 'Brave Girl' Who Set Herself on Fire in Memory of Uncle." *Guardian*, 25 Jun. 2003. www.theguardian.com/uk/2003/jun/25/world. iran.

Verhovek, Sam Howe. "Amherst Journal; Candles in the Snow Honor Suffering." *New York Times*, 20 Feb. 1991. www.nytimes.com/1991/02/20/us/amherst-journal-candles-in-the-snow-honor-suffering.html.

"Vietnamese Woman Self-Immolates in Anti-China Protest." *Radio Free Asia*, 23 May 2014. www.rfa.org/english/news/vietnam/self-immolation-05232014155743. html.

Vilkaite, Ruta. "Chinese Author Hu Ping Analyses Tibet Self-Immolation Actions." 20 Aug. 2012. www.thetibetpost.com/en/outlook/reviews/2789-chinese-author-hu-ping-analyses-tibet-Self-Immolation-actions.

"War Protester's Fiery Suicide Provokes Question." *ABCNews*, 27 Nov. 2006. www. nbcnews.com/id/15916765#.W9YngzGNx2F.

Whalen-Bridge, John. *Tibet on Fire: Buddhism, Protest, and the Rhetoric of Self-Immolation*. Palgrave Macmillan, 2015.

Woeser, Tsering. *Tibet on Fire: Self-Immolations Against Chinese Rule*. Translated by Kevin Carrico, Verso, 2016.

Yu, Hua. *China in Ten Words*. Translated by Allan H. Barr, Pantheon Books, 2011.

Zaroulis, Nancy, and Gerald Sullivan. *Who Spoke Up? American Protest Against the War in Vietnam, 1963–1975*. Doubleday, 1984.

Zhang, Li. *In Search of Paradise: Middle-Class Living in a Chinese Metropolis*. Cornell UP, 2010.

Zhao, Yuezhi. "Falun Gong, Identity, and the Struggle over Meaning Inside and Outside China." *Contesting Media Power: Alternative Media in a Networked World*, edited by Nick Couldry and James Curran, Rowman and Littlefield, 2003, pp. 209–224.

Żuk, Piotr, and Paweł Żuk. "An 'Ordinary Man's' Protest: Self-Immolation as a Radical Political Message in Eastern Europe Today and in the Past." *Social Movement Studies*, vol. 17, no. 5, 2018, pp. 1–8.

Part III

Selected contemporary ultimate protests by fire and their echoes across culture

Figure PIII.1 Van Thanh Rudd *Special Forces (After Banksy)* (2008).

Chapter 1

A lotus in a sea of fire

On two self-immolations performed during the war in Vietnam

The title of the chapter references the seminal 1967 book *Vietnam: Lotus in a Sea of Fire*, which the Buddhist monk, poet, and peace activist Thích[1] Nhất Hạnh wrote to provide Western readers with a proper context for the horrifying and devastating war that raged in Vietnam, and explain the motives behind the wave of self-burnings sweeping through the country at the time. The cover of the publication featured Malcolm Browne's iconic photo of Thích Quảng Đức burning in the streets of Saigon on 11 June 1963.[2] As already mentioned, that particular incident permanently fixed the concept of self-burning in the public consciousness and prompted its introduction into the arsenal of the contemporary protester, a process in which the Associated Press photographer's pictures played a crucial part.

Born in 1926 in the city of Đà Lạt, Thích Nhất Hạnh (birth name Nguyễn Xuân Bảo) entered the novitiate at the age of 16 (Alter, "Vietnamese" 3). After receiving training in the Mahāyāna and Thiền traditions, he was ordained a monk in 1951. He met Thích Quảng Đức while still an adolescent, and later practised at his side in Central Vietnam and in his temple near Saigon (Nhat, *Peaceful* 160). Upon graduating from his philosophy and literature studies, Nhất left for the US, where he began teaching philosophy of religion at Princeton in 1961, transferring to Columbia University two years later to lecture in the history of Buddhism. In the light of the rising tensions in Southeast Asia, he returned to the Republic of Vietnam to pursue anti-war activism. Nhất was a proponent of Engaged Buddhism, which combined traditional religious practice with social activism, renouncing involvement in the conflict in favour of tending to the casualties and those in need. In 1964, together with Cao Ngọc Phương (who took the name Chân Không after ordination), Nhất Hạnh founded the School of Youth for Social Service (SYSS), an organisation that would go on to run schools and hospitals, rebuild destroyed villages, and provide support to the homeless. Around that time, Nhất Hạnh also established the Tiếp Hiện religious assembly, later renamed the Order of Interbeing, which allowed the monk to focus "on an ecumenical approach to ending the war by reaching out to other groups like South Vietnamese Catholics" (Topmiller, "Struggling" 149).

On 1 June 1965, Nhất Hạnh wrote his famous open letter to Martin Luther King, Jr., *In Search of the Enemy of Man*, in which he attempted to elucidate the motivations behind the self-burnings of monastics and laypeople taking place across South Vietnam. The letter stressed that the greatest enemy of man was not his fellow man, but intolerance, hate, and discrimination. In the letter, the monk criticised both the Communist regime in the North and the US-supported Catholic government in the South, and offered a synthesis that fused the tenets of European existentialist philosophy with Buddhist pacifism (Alter, "Vietnamese" 3).

In 1966, Nhất Hạnh returned to the US to lead a symposium on Buddhism and continue his anti-war efforts. Soon afterwards, he published a brief foreword to a volume of his anti-war poetry, which succinctly outlined his views on politics, literature, philosophy, and religion. Following the publication, he was barred from re-entering South Vietnam, as under the military junta which took power in a 1965 coup, advocating pacifism was punishable by lengthy prison or even death. In a gesture of solidarity, prominent Trappist monk Thomas Merton, whom Nhất Hạnh had met in the US, penned an open letter titled *Nhat Hanh Is My Brother*. Around that time the monk also met with Dr. King whom he asked to publicly condemn the war. The pastor had eventually done so, coming out in support of the anti-war movement and denouncing the war in Vietnam as immoral in a January 1967 essay he wrote for *The Chicago Defender* and later, on 4 April 1967, during his famous Riverside Church speech in New York City. He called the conflict a massive drain on resources that could otherwise have been used to finance the social programmes making up Lyndon B. Johnson's flagship domestic reform agenda, the Great Society. Later that year, King, himself the recipient of the 1964 Nobel Peace Prize, nominated Thích Nhất Hạnh for the award, writing to the Nobel Committee: "Here is an apostle of peace and non-violence, cruelly separated from his own people while they are oppressed by a vicious war which has grown to threaten the sanity and security of the entire world" (King, M.).[3]

One of Nhất Hạnh's students, Nhất Chi Mai, a teacher at primary schools and orphanages, was one of the first laypeople to be ordained in the Order of Interbeing on 5 February 1966, taking the name Thích Nữ Diệu Huỳnh. On 16 May 1967, the day of the Vesak holiday, which marks the Buddha's birthday, she set herself on fire outside the Từ Nghiêm Pagoda in Saigon to protest against the escalation of the war. Earlier, she had suggested that ten young people engage in a protest culminating in self-disembowelment, realising that hunger strikes and protest self-burnings were no longer making an impression on either the authorities or public opinion (Chân 97). In a farewell note to her mentor, at the time living in exile in Paris, she wrote: "Thầy [master], don't worry too much. We will have peace soon" (qtd. in King, S. 127). Although press reports of her death were censored, her funeral still drew thousands of mourners.

Nhất Hạnh enshrined her sacrifice, a testament to radical pacifism, in a recitative play which drew on traditional Vietnamese performance forms (Alter, "Vietnamese"). The play was published in English in 1972, as *The Path of Return Continues the Journey*, by Hoa Binh [Peace] Press, a small imprint affiliated with Thomas Merton's Life Center. The foreword for the book was written by Father Daniel Berrigan, a Jesuit priest, poet, and leading figure of the US anti-war movement.

A few years prior, the priest delivered a eulogy at the funeral of Roger LaPorte, the 20-year-old philosophy student, former Trappist seminarian, and member of the Catholic Worker Movement, who had sought to protest against the war by setting himself on fire outside the UN Dag Hammarskjöld Library in New York City on 9 November 1965. Rather than condemn the young man or dismiss him as a suicide, Berrigan called his death an act of self-sacrifice, similar to stepping in between an aggressor and his victim and dying in the act. Dorothy Day, the co-founder of the Catholic Worker Movement, journalist, revered human rights activist, and declared pacifist, whose participation in numerous anti-war protests often landed her in jail (Forest), described LaPorte's death in similar terms (Ryan 17). Although she remained rather tight-lipped about the first anti-war self-burning in the US, performed by Alice Herz on 16 March 1965, she believed LaPorte's act to have been a testament of the student's faith, his profound empathy, and his love for his fellow man. Merton, however, saw the matter differently; so profound was the shock of the protest that he temporarily withdrew from the Catholic Peace Fellowship, an educational organisation he had co-founded, claiming that the practice of self-immolation had little to do with the spirit of non-violence and was not only fundamentally immoral, but ultimately irrational (Ryan 19).

Berrigan's aforementioned eulogy drew a sharp reaction from the conservative Cardinal Francis Spellman, a proponent of the US intervention in Vietnam, who decided to discipline the liberal Jesuit by sending him on a mission to South America. Thanks to the intercession of NYC's Catholic community, Berrigan was brought back after only three months abroad, and Spellman's move ultimately backfired, as the mission only radicalised the priest further.

On 17 May 1968, Berrigan, along with eight other Catholic activists, staged a raid on the draft board offices in Catonsville, Maryland, from which they stole a few hundred draft cards that they later publicly burned with homemade napalm. The incident took place around a month and a half after the assassination of Reverend King, and is widely considered the catalyst for the nationwide mobilisation of the American people against the war in Vietnam. In 1970, Father Berrigan authored a one-act play in free verse, *The Trial of the Catonsville Nine*, based on courtroom transcripts from the trial that ultimately sent him to prison for nearly three years.

In 1975, long after the withdrawal of US combat troops, Nhất Hạnh and Berrigan published *The Raft Is Not the Shore*, a record of their lengthy conversation on a broad spectrum of issues. In the passages where the two discussed self-burnings, Nhất Hạnh wrote that although acts like these could not be publicly affirmed for fear of encouraging others, neither could they be justifiably condemned, as they are, at their core, expressions of individual wills. Self-immolation, the Buddhist monk explained, was performed to awaken the consciences of others (62).

As a metaphor for the war ravaging the lotus country, the sea of fire evokes a plethora of images, including carpet bombing and napalm strikes, people burning in anti-war protests, and draft cards burned by those with enough courage to refuse participation in the bloodshed. In my view, drawing up a list of relevant people, augmented with the above explanations, would provide the necessary backdrop for the chapter dedicated to two self-burnings performed on both sides of the Pacific Ocean as the conflict in Vietnam raged on.

The first part of the chapter deals with the emblematic self-burning of Thích Quảng Đức in protest against the religious intolerance of the Ngô Đình Diệm regime. Carried out in Saigon prior to any major commitment of US troops, the monk's act proved pivotal, as its impact, and attendant international publicity, significantly contributed to the redrawing of US foreign policy on South Vietnam and thus to the reshaping of the course of events in Indochina. The protest in Saigon and Browne's emblematic photographs of the incident played an important part in the emergence of pacifist movements and the coalescence of public discontent and opposition to American military involvement in that part of the world (Zaroulis and Sullivan 12). Robert Hariman and John Lucaites argued that such archetypal pictures instigate and channel specific emotions, and are thus capable of inducing political action (7). We must remember, however, that the mass production of imagery and its distribution in the media (both processes intrinsic to liquid modernity) have either reduced or entirely negated the power, which iconic images may have once commanded (Alter, *Vietnam* 80). Hence, to quote the religious scholar Russell McCutcheon, "the image of the monk burning has by now become so decontextualized that it has been commodified; it is now a consumer item in popular culture" (176). Accordingly, I decided to use a considerable portion of this chapter to sketch out some political and religious contexts for the self-burning of Thích Quảng Đức which, I believe, will help the reader penetrate the "skin" of the icon and better understand the act whose contemporary reception is mediated primarily by its photographic depictions. A portion of my deliberations, meanwhile, will explore the impact of the monk's self-burning and its attendant renderings not only on the political or public spheres, but also on the realm of art and the rather unceremonious treatment of Browne's depiction at the hands of mass culture.

The other subchapter is an inquiry into the most well-known of American anti-war self-burnings, that of Norman Morrison, a Quaker who set himself alight on the steps of the Pentagon in Arlington on 2 November 1965, a full week before LaPorte. The subchapter will also explore Peter Brook's anti-war performance *US* (1966) and his later film *Tell Me Lies* (1968), in which the sacrifices of Đức and Morrison played prominent parts. The title of that section, *Skin of flame*, is a direct quote from the memorial poem *Norman Morrison*, penned by leftist poet Adrian Mitchell, often called the British Mayakovsky. Mitchell was part of the team effort that eventually paved the way for *US*, while a passage from his famous poem *To Whom It May Concern*[4] was used by Brook for the title of the film. Morrison's self-immolation had a profound impact on a number of artists, poets chief among them, but Brook's Royal Shakespeare Company (RSC) performance and subsequent film warrant particular attention. After all, the questions they ask about the role of art in confrontation with the savagery of reality, and about potential strategies of representation to pursue in the light of the widespread availability of horrific imagery, are still highly relevant today.[5]

Under the icon's skin: Thích Quảng Đức's political and sacrificial auto-cremation (The Republic of Vietnam, 1963)

The act-performance

The self-burning of the 66-year-old[6] Thích Quảng Đức (born Lâm Văn Túc), a monk who occupied a prominent position in the Vietnamese Buddhist community, was a meticulously planned performance, designed to achieve particular political goals and, simultaneously, an act of self-sacrifice situated in a broader, unorthodox religious tradition. If we intend to grasp the hybrid nature of the incident and unearth its meaning, we must first trace its course and outline the historic and cultural contexts against which it took place. Gauging its impact, meanwhile, will require a closer look at its political consequences and its most important echoes across culture.

According to Thích Giác Đức, who in 1963 was a major figure in the resistance against the Saigon regime, Quảng Đức himself implied he would be willing to sacrifice his life for the Three Jewels – the Buddha, the way of the Dharma, and the community of the faithful – but the suggestion was refused by his superiors (Biggs, "Dying" 179).[7] It is possible, however, that this and similar reports were spread intentionally to quash budding suspicions that the self-immolator was picked for the act by a third party, which could seriously impact the public reception of the incident, as well as its legal implications.[8] It is likely that we will never get to the bottom of the matter, but it is difficult to imagine Đức being persuaded, much less coerced, to sacrifice his own life.[9] It is conceivable, however, that his superiors from Huế, the spiritual centre of the Mahāyāna community in Central Vietnam, ultimately granted him permission to self-sacrifice after the intercession of Thích Đức Nghiệp, the liaison between the Buddhist hierarchy and Western journalists, who

108 Selected contemporary ultimate protests by fire

represented the Saigon Xá Lợi Pagoda, the hub of Buddhist opposition to the Diệm regime (Chanoff and Doan 140, 142).

Before he performed the auto-cremation on the morning of 11 June 1963, the monk spent many days immersed in prayer, meditation, and spiritual anguish. When he finally received word about permission from his superiors, his self-immolation was then designed for maximum impact. The act-performance was intended for the regime, local Saigon residents, and representatives of international media, who were supposed to publicise the incident, emphasising the regime's harassment campaign against the Buddhists, answered by their continued struggle for equal treatment of all religions. Despatches from reporters and declassified US State Department documents[10] clearly demonstrate that the incident was planned down to the smallest detail and meticulously executed.

The self-burning was performed at a busy intersection of two key Saigon thoroughfares: the Phan Đình Phùng (since renamed Nguyễn Đình Chiểu) Boulevard and Lê Văn Duyệt (now Cach Mạng Thang Tam) Street, a location which guaranteed publicity. Furthermore, the incident took place near the embassy of the Kingdom of Cambodia, whose ruler, Norodom Sihanouk, openly sympathised with the plight of the Vietnamese Buddhist community. The night before, Thích Đức Nghiệp informed foreign correspondents that a special event was planned for the following morning and instructed them to pay a visit to the Ấn Quang Pagoda,[11] in the centre of Saigon, at 7 am (Browne, "The Story"). Only a few reporters heeded the call, including David Halberstam of *The New York Times*, Simon Michaud of AFP, UPI's Nguyễn Ngọc Rao, and AP's Ha Van Tran and Malcolm Browne. Since his arrival in Saigon in 1961, Browne had managed to get a good feel for the Buddhist community and even befriended a few monks.[12] Sometime earlier, he heard gossip about the monks planning a spectacular suicide protest, during which one volunteer was supposed to self-immolate, while another would perform a self-disembowelment. Browne argued that the monks were perfectly aware of the impact such an act would have had. One of them, Thích Quảng Lien, was a Yale graduate and knew the degree to which mass media shaped American public opinion (Browne, "Viet Nam"). When the American reporter arrived at the pagoda, the ceremony was already underway and the assembled monks and nuns were chanting a mournful dirge. "At a signal from the leader, they all started out into the street and headed toward the central part of Saigon on foot" (Browne, "The Story").

In 2013, on the 50th anniversary of taking the iconic pictures, AP released online, for a limited time only, a set of ten black-and-white pictures documenting the incident. A handful of other photographs continue to circulate online. Set alongside reports by Browne and Halberstam, and much less known pictures taken by Nguyễn Văn Thông ("Nguỵ"), a photographer working for the South Vietnamese authorities, the images allow us to retrace the course of the incident.

Browne's photos show the aforementioned gathering in the pagoda, as well as a large, orderly procession of Buddhist monks and nuns, wearing traditional garb and trailing an Austin Westminster. The next shot depicts a slender figure of a man sitting cross-legged, head shaved down to the skin, leaning slightly forward, and holding something in his hands. Also in the frame is another monk, dousing the sitting figure with a liquid from a white, plastic canister, the liquid pooling on the ground. Browne's account revealed that the monks experimented prior to the incident to determine the best possible ratio of petrol to diesel fuel for maximum flame duration (*Muddy* 9). In the background, we see a car, parked far enough so that the self-immolation would not explode its tank. The bonnet is open, suggesting that the car simply broke down and came to a sudden stop. The vehicle was also how Đức and two assistants arrived at the site. One helped Đức out of the car and laid down a pillow in the middle of the intersection, on which the senior monk sat down in the lotus position and began reciting the *Nianfo* mantra ("Homage to Amitābha Buddha"), while the other doused him with the flammable mixture. Around them, nuns and monks came together into a tight cordon over 20 m in diameter, which was supposed to ensure the safety of the crowd and other onlookers, "drafted into the role of affirming witnesses in a traumatic ritual complex" (Harding 39). Obviously, the cordon was also set up to prevent law enforcement officers, secret police, and firefighters from interfering with the performance. This is corroborated by one of Browne's photographs, depicting four monks using their own bodies to block a fire engine from reaching the site. Of particular importance are those photographs that portray Thích Quảng Đức himself performing the auto-cremation at around 9.20 am.

On another of Browne's photos – one of the two most recognisable ones – the monk, captured in profile, sits upright, with eyes closed and lips barely parted, his figure engulfed by tall flames. A breeze blows left (from the self-immolator's perspective), briefly revealing one side of his body. Next to him sits the empty canister, still untouched by the flame. In the background is the car and behind it is a post with road signage. Monastics and laypeople stand around, their gazes locked on the spectacle unfolding before them. One of the younger monks – captured as he moves right – stares, seemingly hypnotised, at the burning figure. In his hands, at chest height, is a camera, a clear indication of the Buddhists' own intention to document the act, possibly in case no reporter turned up.

The next picture shows the fire reaching the canister amidst plumes of black, billowy smoke. One of the monks is running to the right with his arms up, clearly shouting. Văn Thông's photographs, depicting the same moment from a different angle, reveal the circle of monastics closing ranks behind the vehicle. The flames and the pillar of smoke tower over the scene, covering nearly a third of the frame. We see individual police caps in the back of the crowd, but no law enforcement officers are present in the foreground.

110   Selected contemporary ultimate protests by fire

Another of Browne's iconic images – the one which brought him the World Press Photo of the Year Award – shows the monk, unperturbed, sitting inside the fireball, the flames reaching straight up, the smoke already cleared away. His head is blackened, and burn welts cover his face and forehead. A few individuals kneel or bow down to him. The plastic canister, deformed by the immense heat, lies on the ground nearby. Halberstam wrote of that moment:

> As he burned he never moved a muscle, never uttered a sound, his outward composure in sharp contrast to the wailing people around him. I had never felt such conflicting emotions: one part of me wanted to extinguish the fire, another warned that I had no right to interfere, another told me that it was too late, another asked whether I was a reporter or a human being.
> (*The Making* 128)

Browne – conceivably to shield himself from similar dilemmas[13] – instead focused on the technical aspects of shooting the pictures. Years later, he admitted that the incident left him with considerable guilt, stemming not from regret that he failed to intervene, as the fire was too great to do so anyway and the cordon around the monk was practically impenetrable, but from the realisation that

> a kind old man who probably would not have done what he did – nor would the monks in general have done what they did – if they had not been assured of the presence of a newsman who could convey the images and experience to the outer world. Because that was the whole point – to produce theatre of the horrible so striking that the reasons for the demonstration would become apparent to everyone.
> (Browne, "The Buddhist")

Another photograph shows the burning monk on his back, with his arms splayed out. Beside him, most of the *sangha* (Buddhist community) are kneeling, their palms pressed together as if in prayer. Browne mentioned that he did not register the monk's death, because Đức had not uttered a single cry of pain and his face had remained placid throughout ("The Story"). Chân Không, who was present at the immolation and herself pondered either performing a self-burning or undertaking a fast to death, pointed out the contrast between the burning monk, completely still and seemingly unperturbed by earthly woes, and the surrounding crowd, most of whom were sobbing or falling to their knees before him (38).

The following photographs portray the monk's charred remains. The fire is nearly out, and the Buddhists making up the circle are now sitting cross-legged on the ground. Behind them, we see a crowd of laypeople. According to estimates, the self-burning was observed on site by around 350 monks, plus assorted laity (Jacobs 147). The pictures taken by Browne and Văn Thông better illustrate just how big the assembled crowd really was.

Other pictures show the Esso petrol station in the background and the crowd of onlookers who climbed on top of its roof to get a better view. Only in one of Văn Thông's photos, the one depicting three monks bowing to the smouldering remains of the monks, do we see a handful of police officers, with their backs turned to the scene, as if looking out for reinforcements coming down the street in the background.

In the subsequent photograph, a few monks are covering the charred remains. Reporters recounted that after the fire had died out, the monks covered the smouldering corpse with a saffron-coloured cloak and then placed it in a pre-arranged wooden box that they later took to the Xá Lợi Pagoda. They had not been able to bend the corpse's limbs, so one arm continued to stick out (Jacobs 148). In the same photograph, two young novices standing in the middle of the broad alley are holding a banner, turning it to face anyone who might have been coming down the street. The thoroughfares in the background, however, are empty, with a crowd visible only farther away. It was widely reported that incidental witnesses and correspondents were handed pamphlets with Đức's farewell note, translated into English, which included a conciliatory message to the president, pleading with him to respect the equality of all faiths (Chanoff and Doan 143).

Asked about details of the incident that photography could not capture or convey, Browne said that the intersection was shrouded with a mix of incense, petrol fumes, and the stench of burning flesh. There was wailing everywhere, blanketed with the cries of firefighters, unable to reach the burning monk, coming through the PA system ("The Story"). At that point, one of the monks started speaking into a microphone in the vein of a seasoned reporter or sports commentator, repeating: "A Buddhist priest burns himself to death. A Buddhist priest becomes a martyr" (qtd. in Jacobs 148). Browne read this rich aural landscape as utter chaos. It is clear that the monks themselves had a plethora of explanations of the unprecedented act for the crowd assembled on site.

The fateful day was capped by events outside the Xá Lợi, where a crowd of students gathered, holding banners with the slogan "A Buddhist priest burns himself for our five demands" (qtd. in Jacobs 149) spelled out in two languages. Around 1.30 pm, nearly 1,000 monks and nuns assembled on the pagoda grounds to hold a brief assembly, with the students outside serving as security. After the meeting concluded, the crowd dispersed, leaving around 100 people in the temple. They reconvened later in the afternoon at the site of the auto-cremation, since secured and surrounded by police, who then tried to separate the monks from the laypeople. The American Embassy reported that around 6.00 pm, approximately 30 nuns and five monks were taken into custody for refusing to move the group prayer session inside the Xá Lợi. Following the arrests, law enforcement officers wearing riot gear sealed off the site, granting access only to locals attempting to reach their homes (Jones 270).

112 Selected contemporary ultimate protests by fire

Historical and political contexts

Had Ellen Hammer, the American expert on Vietnamese history, been correct to assert that "objectively, no single act of the Saigon government seemed to have justified the sacrifice of Thích Quảng Đức" (145)? In order to examine that question and gain additional insight into the monk's actions, we first need to take a closer look at the historical and political contexts of the incident.

In the early 1960s, South Vietnam had been the site for a conflict between the Communist-controlled National Liberation Front (NLF), popularly called the Việt Cộng, and the Army of the Republic of Vietnam (ARVN), supported by American troops who at the time were in Vietnam mostly in an advisory and training capacity. The Buddhist community found itself caught between the two, but despite being patronisingly seen by Washington as rather detached from reality, the monks nevertheless continued their mostly peaceful struggle for equal treatment of all faiths in Vietnam.

The mass influx of Catholics into South Vietnam after the 1954 partition, and Diệm's favouritism towards fellow Catholics who essentially formed his power base, further exacerbated the tensions between the Buddhist community and the regime, which treated the followers of Dharma as second-class citizens. A survey conducted in 1961 in Saigon by The Asian Foundation revealed that over 80% of the 14 million citizens of the Republic of Vietnam declared themselves to be adherents of Buddhism, whereas 13% professed to be Catholics, and only 3% to be followers of Confucianism (Topmiller, *The Lotus* viii). Most diplomats and intelligence officers stationed in Saigon, however, pointed out the highly syncretic nature of religious belief among the Vietnamese, which, particularly in rural areas, was a blend of Buddhism, Confucianism, Daoism, and animism. Only Mahāyāna Buddhism "has tried more than the other creeds to adopt the trappings of a formal religion – partly in reaction to past repression and partly under the tutelage of modern reformers" (Karnow 294).

Although the Buddhists had the numbers, the Catholics held more power. They were a well-organised community, with well-educated members who were extensively involved with public and charity efforts, such as running hospitals and orphanages. Thanks to the patronage of the president, many of them ascended into political and economic elites, were appointed to the National Assembly, and amassed sprawling estates. The Diệm regime considered the Catholic Church a full-fledged religious organisation, whereas Buddhists were only permitted to form associations, the leading one of which was the General Association of Buddhism, established in 1951. The injunction was inherited from the French colonial authority, which moved to curtail Buddhist influence in the country and instead promote Catholics or Catholic converts to official positions.[14] The Diệm government also upheld a 1950 decree that the Emperor Bảo Đại was pressured to introduce by the colonial regime, which banned Buddhists from purchasing land for new temples and forced them to repeatedly petition the government for permits to operate in the public sphere. The Catholic Church was the largest landowner in Vietnam, and its estates were excluded from government land reforms. Furthermore, Catholics were exempt from rendering corvée under the government's Strategic Hamlet Program and from resettlement to potentially worse quality land. Disbursement of firearms for rural self-defence units and US financial support were also tied to religious affiliation. Moreover, it was easier for Catholics to advance in virtually all spheres of public life, and even two newly established universities, in Huế and Đà Lạt, were headed by self-professed Catholics. Additionally, in 1959, the president – to the outrage of the majority of the population – solemnly entrusted the country to the Virgin Mary, a feat followed two years later by the Vietnamese bishops' move to designate the Church of Our Lady of La Vang a National Marian Centre.[15] John XXIII reaffirmed the designation by elevating the church to a minor basilica in August 1961.[16]

In short, affiliation with the Catholic Church usually entailed lending support to the regime and reaping tangible benefits in return. According to Nhất Hạnh, the South Vietnamese associated Catholicism with the French and perceived it as coercively transplanted from overseas in order to facilitate the subjugation and colonisation of Vietnam, while Diệm was widely seen as a puppet imported from the US, actively supported and manipulated by the foreign power (*Vietnam* 122). It should come as no surprise, then, that the majority of the Buddhists, many of whom suffered at the hands of the colonial authorities and were veterans of the struggle for independence, felt deprived of a say in the future of their own country.

The followers of Dharma, however, refused to acquiesce and accept their second-class status, and strove to swell their ranks and match the Catholic Church in influence (Karnow 295). Although they mostly shunned politics, the South Vietnamese decision-makers – including the president's elder brother, the Archbishop of Huế, Ngô Đình Thục – often portrayed the Buddhists as puppets in the hands of the NLF. Even if we acknowledge that some of the monks had purported ties to the Việt Minh, the Buddhist movement had its own identity and because it ultimately sought to equate Buddhism with being Vietnamese, it generally discouraged the Vietnamese population from indiscriminately adopting foreign concepts (Chanoff and Doan 136). Buddhism offered a third way, and as such stood against the peculiar reinterpretation of Emmanuel Mounier's personalism, which the president – along with his younger brother, Ngô Đình Nhu, the chief ideologue of the Diệm regime – advanced as a genuine alternative to both Communist-flavoured totalitarianism and capitalist individualism. The conflict between the Buddhist leadership and the Ngô[17] clan, however, quickly grew beyond the ideological sphere. "Their antipathy towards Diệm might have remained latent had he not committed a blunder which, given his own intransigence, was probably inevitable" (Karnow 295).

The clashes of 8 May 1963 in Huế, which claimed the lives of eight people, most of them teenagers and children, killed in all likelihood by government forces and probably as a result of a provocation,[18] would mark a watershed moment in the conflict. The massacre took place on the Vesak holiday, and was a bloody coda to mass protests sparked by the government's ban on waving Buddhist flags during the celebrations. Fearing a backlash from the international community and wary of destabilising the ARVN, which included many Buddhists in its ranks, the Kennedy administration pressured Diệm to negotiate with the *sangha*. Although the two factions ultimately sat down together on 15 May 1963, Diệm had no intention of conceding to Buddhist demands, which included rescinding the ban on Buddhist flags, granting the Buddhist community the same rights enjoyed by the Catholic minority, putting a stop to mass arrests and harassment, guaranteeing freedom of religion, and providing redress to victims of the Huế massacre. He stayed the course, believing in his ability to regain control over the situation, a feat he had repeatedly accomplished in the past,[19] while seeing any concessions as detrimental to his own position, and a drain on his political capital which could end up breathing new life into the opposition, including sects such as Hòa Hảo and Cao Đài, and national political parties.

The Buddhists, however, refused to back down. On 30 May, inspired by the elderly Thích Tịnh Khiết of Huế, the Superior of the General Association of Buddhism (which made him the leading figure of the Vietnamese *sangha*), the Buddhist community launched hunger strikes in Saigon and Huế to draw public attention to their protest. Aside from the fast, they held a demonstration outside the National Assembly, an event which ended up having a major impact, mostly because it was the first anti-government outcry in quite some time (Halberstam, *The Making* 123). Tensions ran high, culminating in another violent incident – on 3 June in the city of Huế, forces under the command of the president's younger brother, Cẩn, unleashed a chemical attack against a 1,200-strong student protest, injuring 67 people. William Trueheart, then-*chargé d'affaires* at the American Embassy in Saigon, reported to the State Department that the incident involved officers pouring poisonous chemicals onto the heads of the protesters, who held a prayer assembly after hearing rumours of the alleged death of charismatic Buddhist leader Thích Trí Quang (Keefer and Smith, no. 146). The cruel treatment of protesters arrested at the time further exacerbated the conflict. Although a state of emergency had been declared in the city, 200 Buddhists began a hunger strike at the Từ Đàm Pagoda to protest against the regime's brutality and continued religious discrimination. Government forces surrounded the temple and sealed it off with barbed wire, refusing access even to medical services. The blockade continued through early June.

After another wave of civil unrest in Saigon, the Americans increased the pressure on Diệm and threatened to officially withdraw their support. Responding with a conciliatory gesture, the president established the

Interministerial Committee on 4 June to reach a settlement with the Buddhist leadership. When it seemed the crisis would finally be resolved, Ngô Đình Nhu and his wife Trần Lệ Xuân, commonly referred to as Madame Nhu, began sabotaging the compromise, accusing the Buddhists of supporting the Communist insurgency, among other misdeeds. Cables sent home from the American Embassy may give the impression that a settlement with the authoritarian regime was possible right up to Đức's self-burning. But the Buddhist community must have been desperate with frustration at the president's unwillingness to follow through on his promises. Worse still, a key pagoda in Huế was cordoned off, leaving those detained inside vulnerable to persecution. Less than a week earlier, government forces used chemicals against protesters, later arresting dozens. Thus, Hammer's argument that the decision to perform the self-burning had not been driven by any legitimate reasons seems, in my view, to lack validity. All the more so because the monk's sacrifice was situated in a continuum of a centuries-spanning tradition, albeit an unorthodox one, or, to borrow a term coined by religious scholar James Benn, an "apocryphal" one ("Where").

The religious dimension of the act

Russell McCutcheon believed that the monk's altruistic gesture was, first and foremost, a political declaration and an attempt to reclaim agency undertaken by a group that had hitherto been subjected to marginalisation (172). Framing the event thus implies that the monk took a stand against a US-sponsored regime and, indirectly, against the legacy of colonialism and American imperialism.[20] That is indeed true, but omitting the religious aspect of the protest ignores a key component of it. Examining it from a religious angle reveals to us its paradoxical character, as "the renunciation of politics in a spiritual gesture of suicide was a supreme spiritual sacrifice and yet nonetheless an unparalleled political gesture" (Harding 35).

Responding to an oft-repeated argument which questioned why the followers of Dharma so eagerly took their own lives when their belief system abhorred violence, either directed at others or the self, religious scholar Jan Yün-hua published an essay in 1965 on the Buddhist tradition of sacrificing one's own life or flesh in medieval China.[21] He pointed out that although Buddhist doctrine indeed forbade suicide, historical records include a number of instances of the proscription being flouted (244). Further corroboration can be found in highly popular biographies of esteemed Buddhist monks published in the past. Chinese hagiographers considered the actions of people who laid down their lives in defence of their faith to be worthy of imitation as they were driven by noble motivations. Furthermore, the monks' sacrifices were testament to their profound capacity for self-denial, an essential element of the Buddhist *credo*. Jan identified three mutually linked reasons behind the decision to self-sacrifice: (a) the wish to follow the example of the bodhisattvas, who proved themselves ready to sever themselves from earthly cares, (b) the wish to issue a statement of faith, (c) and the desire to honour the Buddha. He did not, however, dismiss the possibility that they could have also been motivated by (d) disgust with their own flesh, or (e) abhorrence of earthly existence as a whole. Still another group comprised monks who sacrificed their lives for (f) politico-religious reasons, to protest against repression and religious persecution. The faithful – monks, nuns, and laypeople – sacrificed themselves in a variety of ways: "from death by fire, to drowning, jumping from a height, self-inflicted wounds, fasting, or being devoured by animals" (246).

The majority drew inspiration from the Jātaka tales, highly popular Buddhism-promoting stories that delved into the past incarnations of the Shakyamuni Buddha and portrayed him as capable of the greatest sacrifice. That is precisely how he was characterised in the story of Prince Sattva, who let himself be devoured by a starving female tiger to prevent the predator from eating its young. Monks were similarly encouraged by stories of the bodhisattvas, who did not hesitate to sacrifice themselves for a higher purpose, such as rescuing villagers from starvation, roving bandits, or hungry predators. A key source of such inspiration was found in the *Lotus Sutra*, one of the most popular and influential Mahāyāna sutras, translated from Sanskrit into Chinese in the year 286 CE. For centuries, monks strove to imitate the bodhisattva Bhaishajyarāja, the Medicine King, renowned for his healing powers, about whom the Buddha speaks in Chapter 23. In his past incarnation, the King venerated the Buddha's holy remains so ardently that he mastered a meditation that allowed him to manifest all physical forms. After he set his body on fire to express gratitude for that gift, it continued to burn for 1,200 years. In his subsequent incarnation, he attained the status of awakened and was granted a new name.

Jan believed that the specifically Chinese approach implied a literal reading of the legends and treating their characters as role models, rather than poetic metaphors (the latter outlook prevailing in India). This attitude was reinforced by traditionally Confucian filial piety and attendant virtues, to be safeguarded even at the price of one's own life.[22] Such *modus operandi* ultimately led Chinese Buddhist hagiographers to see instances of self-sacrifice as moral. He also argued that the scribes who compiled these hagiographies in the end became the voice for beliefs and notions that were considered mainstream and commonly held in Mahāyānist China.

The above insights were further expanded and corroborated by James Benn, a scholar of canon and apocryphal texts and inscriptions, in which he identified hundreds of accounts detailing bodily sacrifices, both partial and complete, and underpinned by a multitude of religious and secular motivations, such as raising funds, paying homage to a mentor, or making a political statement. In the monograph *Burning for the Buddha*, Benn contended that "Although some monks did offer their bodies in periods of relative prosperity and peace, we

A lotus in a sea of fire 117

have seen a marked coincidence between acts of self-immolation and times of crisis, especially when secular powers were hostile towards Buddhism" (199). In his opinion, the self-immolation incidents, first recorded in China in the late 4th century, were an indigenous phenomenon rather than a continuation of practices imported from India, and were rooted in shamanic pre-Buddhist practices such as auto-cremations or exposing the body to sunlight in order to bring rain ("Multiple" 207; "Written" 411).

Benn's work confirms that self-burners found their main source of inspiration and point of reference in both canon texts (the *Lotus Sutra* first and foremost) as well as apocryphal hagiographies extolling the feats of Chinese Buddhist monks, who followed in the footsteps of the Medicine King. Admiration was also afforded to the self-sacrifices of the *mahāsattvas* (the great beings), which contravened the doctrinal monastic principles laid out in the *Vinaya Pitaka*, the Basket of Discipline, one of the three *piṭaka*, or baskets, of the Pāli Canon. According to the scholar, an essential role in the adoption of auto-cremation practices in China was played by two apocryphal texts, the first of which – a compilation of basic principles called *Fanwang jing* (*The Book of Brahmā's Net*) – was drafted between 440 and 480 CE, while the other – the meditation sutra *Shouleng'yan jing* (*Śuraṃgama-sūtra*, or *The Book of Heroic-march Absorption*) – dated back to the early 8th century. Both were written in order to justify and support the practice of self-burning. The apocryphal scriptures outlined the Buddha's teachings on the capacity for self-denial as a pre-requisite for attaining enlightenment. Without these, Benn asserted, self-burning would have been reserved in Buddhist consciousness only for mythical figures, which could be venerated, but not necessarily imitated in practice ("Where" 297). Sacrificing only a portion of one's body soon grew so popular among both monastics and the laity that in 955 Emperor Shizong, seeing it as an expression of undue piety, issued an edict that banned the burning of fingers tied with incense and the piercing of flesh with hooks from which lamps were hung. But opposition also arose from Buddhists who abided by the principles and proscriptions laid out in the Vinaya.

Benn pointed out that self-burning, one of the rarest forms of self-sacrifice, "frequently took the form of a dramatically staged spectacle," pre-announced and performed in the presence of a crowd, and assembled at the pre-arranged location precisely for the purpose of spectating ("Multiple" 204). It was an act-performance, one used by the protagonist to channel their beliefs and convictions and, hopefully, draw the faithful back to the way of the Dharma or persuade the authorities to rescind their persecutory edicts. Auto-cremation became a universal practice available to all Buddhists, as it acknowledged the bodily aspect of the act and equated it with other practices which tended to favour the mind, such as meditation or the study of sacred scriptures. "[S]omatic devotions of self-immolators are best understood not as aberrant, heterodox, or anomalous," as, at their core, they were serious, solemn practices, imitating many classical patterns, the ultimate goal of which was transforming the

118 Selected contemporary ultimate protests by fire

immolator into a bodhisattva (Benn, "Multiple" 207). Although the reactions the practice elicited were rarely unambiguous, we can presume that it was relatively widespread and respected, while being persistent enough to be considered a part of a sacred tradition.

And it was exactly this tradition, Benn wrote, that the scholar monk Quảng Đức, whose daily rituals included the recitation of the *Lotus Sutra*, continued with his act. Like his predecessors,[23] he combined the spiritual and the political in his act, or – to borrow James Harding's phrase – the act "eschewed the social-political even as it embraced it" (37). Like them, he did so publicly, showing neither fear nor pain, an attitude which stood as testament of not only the power of his belief in the temporality of his own corporeal frame, but also the sheer power of his will and the gravity of the cause for which he was taking a stand. Many Buddhists believed that the monk (Nhat, *Peaceful* 160), who was considered particularly advanced on his road to enlightenment, had not committed suicide,[24] but instead attempted to bring others closer to the source of good that fed his own spirit – both the oppressed and the oppressors, whom he yearned to inspire to engage in a moral self-examination (King, S. B. 140–141). His act "was a demonstration of seeming transcendence – of mind over body. It publicly demonstrated that religious repression and intolerance could not contain or thwart Buddhist enlightenment" (Harding 37).

The role of Đức's self-immolation and its image in Diệm's fall

As Thích Quảng Đức was being engulfed by flames, the president, along with his associates, the head of the National Assembly, and assorted members of the diplomatic corps, sat down to say morning mass for Pope John XXIII (Dommen 516), who died on 3 June 1963. The following afternoon, Diệm released a statement in which he announced that the Interministerial Committee has managed to restore much needed peace, but its efforts were subsequently nearly undone by people "poisoned by seditious propaganda," whom Diệm then accused of being responsible for that "tragic death" (qtd. in Joiner 918).

By that point, some of the photographs snapped by Browne at the incident were already making their way to the US, and back then shipping negatives across the globe was no easy feat – not in the least because of the distance, which was effectively nullified with the invention of phototelegraphy. The key obstacle in sending cables or photos abroad was having to use the government's own telecommunications centre, as the South Vietnamese authorities were actively hostile towards foreign correspondents who were not necessarily interested in repeating the official propaganda line and delayed communications the regime deemed unfavourable or suspect for 24 hours or more.[25] Browne knew that if his photos were to reach the US, they would have to be smuggled out of Vietnam.

In 2013, AP published an infographic that outlined the path that the photos travelled in record short time. The negatives were brought to the AP bureau in Saigon by Ha Van Tran barely 20 minutes after the incident. An hour later, some of them were already aboard a plane heading to Manila, where they eventually arrived after a three-hour-long flight. Copies developed from the negatives in the Philippine capital were then wired to the AP offices in San Francisco, and two hours later to the AP's New York office. In New York, selected pictures were captioned and distributed to associate agencies and newsrooms. The entire operation took 15 hours and 20 minutes, and was wrapped up before the morning edition went to print. A veritable techno-logical feat in itself, its success could have been measured by the impact the photo of the burning monk made initially on the news and photo editors, the majority of whom refused to publish the picture they saw as too ghastly,[26] and then on the readers, who first saw it in the *Philadelphia Inquirer* on the morning of 12 June.

The photo was also seen that morning by President Kennedy (JFK) who, allegedly, shrieked "Jesus Christ!" at the sight while discussing the tensions in Alabama with his brother over the phone (Jacobs 149). Some reports claimed that one of the photos was on JFK's desk in the Oval Office on 15 August 1963 when the president met with newly appointed US ambassador to Viet-nam, Henry Cabot Lodge, Jr., prior to the latter's flight to Saigon. Years later, the diplomat revealed that the president used the famous photo to illustrate the precarious situation in Vietnam, reportedly adding that "no news picture in history has generated so much emotion around the world as that one" (qtd. in Zi 61).

We need to keep in mind that in the early stages of the conflict despatches from Vietnam rarely made the news. Much of the public's attention was in-stead focused on the struggle against racial segregation. On the day of Đức's self-burning, George Wallace, the governor of Alabama, blocked two African American students – Vivian Malone and James Hood – from enrolling at the University of Alabama, eventually backing down only after the Deputy Attorney General, Nicholas Katzenbach, appeared at the campus, flanked by National Guardsmen, to enforce the law. The following morning, Medgar Evers, a civil rights activist from Mississippi, was murdered by a Ku Klux Klan member. The auto-cremation in Saigon, however, moved Vietnam – both the conflict between Diệm and the Buddhist community, as well as the escalating war against the NLF – to the front pages of newspapers across America, where it would stay until the very end of the conflict.

As demonstrated by Lisa Skow and George Dionisopoulos, the portrayal of Vietnam in the American press in 1963 was far from one-dimensional. The scholars analysed the information battle over the "Buddhist crisis" that raged all throughout the summer and early autumn 1963 across American dailies and weeklies, and the attendant debate over the meaning of Browne's noto-rious photographs. The two argued that in the case of images portraying an

120 Selected contemporary ultimate protests by fire

incident the public perceived as culturally foreign, a key role was played by the event's discursive background, offering approachable explanations for the unprecedented act. Liberal titles painted the self-burning as a consequence of the discriminatory practices of the regime in Saigon, the violence against the Buddhist community, and the incompetence of the sycophant-dominated government. Against such a background, the photographs became a symbol of the violation of rights the majority of Americans saw as essential and inalienable, including liberty and religious tolerance.[27] Accounts of the regime's blundering incompetence suggested that the Buddhists, like the monk featured in Browne's photos, were "blameless, helpless scapegoats for the brutal, nonrepresentative government in Saigon" (Skow and Dionisopoulos 400).

Conservative outlets, on the other hand, characterised Buddhist demands as unreasonable, unjustified, and motivated by political self-interest. While the government in Saigon, besieged by a Communist insurgency, was portrayed as innocent and undeservedly vilified, the Buddhist community was labelled a "fifth column." In such a frame, the self-burning seemed an act designed to coerce the government into making undue concessions, self-destructive and uncalled for, particularly in the light of the alleged pettiness of the reason behind the immolation (the Buddhist flag ban). Multiple op-eds not only questioned whether suicide was a legitimate avenue of protest, but challenged the social utility of Buddhist teachings as a whole. Many outlets also asserted that the conflict was motivated by politics rather than religion, and benefited the Việt Cộng more than anyone else. Framed against these charges, the self-burning was interpreted as a deliberate attack on American interests in Southeast Asia and a fanatical act of self-destruction, bent on sowing terror in the hearts of its witnesses.

Skow and Dionisopoulos believed that the public ultimately threw its support behind the Buddhist cause for two reasons. One was the power residing in Browne's pictures,[28] the other were the outrageous remarks of Trần Lệ Xuân, who called the self-burning incident a "barbecue."

In early August 1963, Madame Nhu gave an appalling interview to CBS News, during which she spoke the following words, sparking widespread public uproar:

> What have the Buddhist leaders done? ... The only thing they have done, they have barbecued one of their monks, whom they have intoxicated, whom they have abused the confidence [sic]. Even that barbecuing was done not even [sic] with self-sufficient means because they used imported gasoline.
> ("Madame")

Although Xuân's grasp of English was far from expert, lack of education could not account for the shocking nature of her remarks, as the interview she gave on 8 August 1963 to the *Times of Vietnam*, an English-language propaganda broadsheet published in Saigon, was similar in both content and phraseology. Not long afterwards, in a conversation with Marguerite Higgins, Diệm's sister-in-law explained that she used shocking language to wake the world out of the trance in which it looked at Vietnam (Demery 145). She indeed succeeded in that quest, but her remarks were very poorly received in the US. Her subsequent explanations that the term "barbecue," reportedly repeated to her by her daughter who, in turn, heard it from an American GI at a hot dog stand, seemed to her a "perfectly harmless Americanism" ("Nation"), fell on deaf ears. After 23-year-old Thích Nguyên Hương set his body alight on 4 August 1963 by the war memorial in the centre of Phan Thiết, and after Thích Tịnh Khiết issued a ban on further self-immolations – "unless necessary" (qtd. in Jones 295), Madame Nhu told *The New York Times*: "I would clap hands at seeing another monk barbecue show, for one cannot be responsible for the madness of others" (qtd. in Zi 64).

She did not have to wait long. On 13 August, the courtyard of the Phước Duyên Pagoda outside Huế became the stage for the self-burning of 18-year-old Thích Thanh Tuệ, soon followed by the immolation of 27-year-old Thích Nữ Diệu Quang in Nha Trang (who set herself ablaze probably because law enforcement forcibly seized the remains of her predecessor). On 16 August, they were followed by the self-sacrifice of Thích Tiêu Diêu. Madame Nhu's parents, both of whom held diplomatic office, quickly distanced themselves from their daughter's antics in a radio interview with the *Voice of America*, and after martial law was introduced in the Republic of Vietnam on 21 August 1963, they resigned their posts and disowned her. In October 1963, just as the UN sent a fact-finding mission to investigate the persecution of Buddhists in South Vietnam, Madame Nhu left for a tour of the US, which quickly devolved into a public relations nightmare after the South Vietnamese President's sister-in-law began hurling accusations of betrayal at the Americans, sparing neither the Kennedy administration, nor the liberals, nor the monks themselves. American journalists quickly realised that the notorious Dragon Lady – "unfortunately too beautiful to ignore," to quote the sexist description of Xuân uttered by a Kennedy administration official – was easily provoked, so her US tour kept feeding the media circus, while Nhu herself kept appearing on the covers of popular magazines (Demery 173).

Diệm – despite repeated calls from the American Embassy and the White House – refused to denounce his relative. Neither was he willing to accept Washington's suggestions that it would be best for Vietnam and himself to force the Nhus out to a diplomatic post abroad. The president certainly had to reckon with the couple as they held considerable influence in Saigon and controlled the secret police along with a number of other organisations that were loyal only to them (Jones 293). After Madame Nhu's verbal barrage, however, American public opinion felt quite sure who to side with in the Buddhist crisis.

Zi Jun Toong argued that the press – both American and international – played an essential part in shaping the events in the Republic of Vietnam. Swayed by reports of unrest in Huế and Saigon, further amplified by the macabre picture of the burning monk, Kennedy began seriously pondering a redefinition of his administration's approach to its South Vietnamese ally.

122 Selected contemporary ultimate protests by fire

As the crisis deepened and public pressure continued to mount, Kennedy started distancing himself from the regime, eventually abandoning Diệm and his coterie altogether. Although the press indeed contributed to Diệm's fall from grace, the *coup d'état* that overthrew the South Vietnamese government on 1 November 1963 and led to the brutal murder of the president and his brother Nhu the following day[29] could probably have been prevented if it were not for the ruling clan's penchant for ill-advised schemes and comments.

Shortly after midnight on 21 August 1963, Colonel Lê Quang Tung, commander of the ARVN Special Forces, launched an attack on temples across Vietnam on orders from Ngô Đình Nhu. Around 1,400 monks were detained, 30 were killed, hundreds were injured and missing. Many temples had holy shrines destroyed and precious artefacts stolen. From the Xá Lợi Pagoda, soldiers confiscated the charred heart of Thích Quảng Đức, which survived the cremation of his remains intact, a feat which led to the monk being posthumously recognised as a bodhisattva. The soldiers failed to seize his ashes only because Thích Trí Quang, assisted by another monk, absconded with the urn and sought refuge in the US Operations Mission building nearby. To justify the night raids, Diệm claimed the temples were used as sanctuaries by the Việt Cộng and offered weapons, ammunition, and documents allegedly found on temple grounds as proof of a Communist-Buddhist conspiracy. The true objective of the raids, however, was to neutralise the Buddhist opposition and silence the regime's critics within the military.

For all intents and purposes, the Buddhists seemed defeated, and the two final 1963 self-burnings performed in October[30] may be read as an expression of the desperation that gripped the *sangha* (Joiner 924). At that point, Diệm may have believed that he emerged victorious from yet another power struggle, but the night raids against the pagodas would ultimately prove to be the final nail in his coffin. Soon afterwards, State Department officials recommended looking for alternative leadership options for Vietnam. The top-secret Cable 243, sent from Washington, D.C., on 24 August 1963, informed the American ambassador that he was hereby authorised to give ARVN officers the green light to launch a coup if Diệm were to refuse to remove Nhu from power. President Kennedy outlined his position in an interview with CBS News on 2 September 1963:

> In my opinion in the last two months the government has gotten out of touch with the people. The repressions against the Buddhists, we felt, were very unwise. Now, all we can do is to make it very clear that we don't think this is the way to win.
>
> ("Cronkite")

Kennedy's remarks had to seem damning to Diệm and Nhu, as the two men – fully aware of Washington's clandestine contacts with ARVN top brass – decided to open negotiations with Hanoi, a move which probably sealed their fate (Karnow 307).

In the short term, the coup marked a victory for the Buddhists – after the regime was purged, hundreds of nuns and monks were released from prisons in November 1963. Furthermore, in this reshaped political landscape, they were now a force to be reckoned with – all the more because the crisis had united the highly splintered and factious Buddhist movement. On the other hand, the overthrow led to widespread political and social instability. Karen Fierke argued that "The coup against Diệm produced a political vacuum that was filled by the United States, resulting in an escalation of the war, which was an outcome the Buddhists had wanted to avoid at all costs" (179). And indeed, following the 30 January 1964 coup led by Nguyễn Khánh which deposed the General Dương Văn Minh government, power would change hands five times before June 1965. In the light of the political revolving door in Saigon, the Americans were forced to abandon their planned gradual withdrawal of combat troops and instead increase their commitment. When Lyndon B. Johnson took over the presidency following the Kennedy assassination on 22 November 1963, he chose to significantly increase US troop presence in Vietnam, intending to bring a quick and decisive end to the conflict. Alas, the war would rage on for over a decade.

However, Fierke's attempt to trace a causal relationship between the Diệm-Buddhist conflict, the subsequent coup, and escalation of the war in Southeast Asia seems too much of a simplification. Not unexpectedly, it is nearly impossible to judge whether Diệm could have allowed himself to be more conciliatory in dealings with the *sangha*. But we may presume that had he taken responsibility (or at least shouldered some of it) for shootings in Huế, salvaging the situation would still have been possible. The first auto-cremation, however, burned the last bridge, so to speak, and made reconciliation virtually impossible. The Buddhists had to expect that restoring the status quo would have been extremely difficult following such a drastic act. Neither can we assert with any degree of certainty that Diệm would have successfully suppressed the Communist insurgency, assiduously aided and abetted by the North, had he stayed in power. It is possible that a large-footprint US intervention would have been inevitable anyway. Furthermore, as already mentioned, numerous plots against Diệm had been hatched within the ARVN ranks even before the outbreak of the Buddhist crisis, culminating in two failed attempts on his life. We have no way of knowing whether the escalating NLF insurgency could have affected the plans of the ARVN top brass, hungry for power and outraged with the president's nepotism and rampant corruption. It is possible that the dispute with the Buddhists only accelerated the process that would eventually lead to the ousting of the president. Besides, fomenting a coup did not have to result in political chaos, while responsibility for the ousting lay with the factions that failed to reach a settlement.

Ultimately, the Buddhist crisis revealed the president's true colours, and "the well-choreographed atrocity of Quảng Đức's violent death," which "signified the wide chasm that had opened between the moral ideal and the

124 Selected contemporary ultimate protests by fire

immoral reality, greatly increasing the chances of a coup" (Jones 269), proved one of its key flashpoints.

The ripple effect in culture

The Buddhist crisis of 1963 was widely commented on in the international press, as was Thích Quảng Đức's self-burning – the latter mostly thanks to Browne's famous pictures, which were not only carried on the front pages of many press titles published in the US and the West in general, but were also distributed by China and the Democratic Republic of Vietnam as part of the two regimes' propaganda efforts (Browne, "Viet Nam").

Proof of the impact that the Saigon incident had on international public opinion can be found in the fact that it was reenacted in the Italian film *Mondo cane 2 (A Dog's Life 2)*, probably to boost the picture's appeal. The reenactment was later repeatedly picked up by news reports as actual footage of the event.[31] The film was an official sequel to the 1962 documentary *Mondo cane*, directed by Paolo Cavara, Gualtiero Jacopetti, and Franco Prosperi. A critical and commercial success, the film was nominated for a Palme d'Or at the Cannes Film Festival and is credited with singlehandedly launching the *shockumentary* genre, a style of exploitation documentary that relied upon imagery designed to shock and appal the audience. In the US, the picture was released under the title *Tales of the Bizarre: Rites, Rituals and Superstitions*, which better illustrated its character and content, the latter a loose collection of visuals allegedly depicting actual cultural practices from all over the world. The sequel, also known as *Mondo pazzo (Mad World)*, shot by Jacopetti and Prosperi in colour a year after the first instalment, presented a veritable kaleidoscope of shocking rituals and customs. Like its predecessor, the film – first released in Italy on 30 November 1963 – drew accusations of pandering to vulgar tastes, misrepresenting facts, and engaging in deception by shooting reenactments filmed to look like the actual events they depicted (Staples and Kilgore 117).

Unlike most of the documentary, the Vietnam sequence – starting 38 minutes into the film and running just over 7 minutes long – maintains a serious tone. As the section opens, the music turns solemn, while the off-screen commentary drops its shock-jock facade and instead attempts to encourage self-examination. Within the framework of the film, it was preceded by a sequence depicting Hindu fakirs walking across a courtyard lined with hot coals; thus, the two segments are linked only by a loose reference to fire, which was par for the course for the strategy adopted by the authors, to create a montage of individual "attractions" in the quasi-documentary. The Vietnam sequence features footage of modern Saigon interspersed with incidents of Buddhist protests. The voiceover that accompanies the images of Saigon streets emptied of civilians (replaced by police and military troops) speaks of the regime's brutality and stresses the fact that after 2,500 years, the followers of Dharma finally turned away from the principles that underpinned their faith by responding to violence with more violence. Later, we see ordinary citizens shaving their heads to express solidarity with their priests. The image is supplemented with the following commentary: "From now on, they will oppose the steel helmets of Diệm's soldiers with their cropped heads," and many of them will enter monasteries to rediscover "their lost faith which teaches one to create silence within oneself and to listen to it; to kill all passion and desire within oneself and to enjoy the perfect happiness of the dying flame."

These last words appear before footage of the self-immolation, running nearly 90 seconds long, which itself immediately followed a brief shot of a huge, golden statue of the Buddha. This is just another manipulation, as we cannot exactly expect the average Western viewer to know that the statue sits in the temple in the city of Nakhon Pathom in Central Thailand, nearly a 1,000 km from Saigon. To reinforce the impression that we are in South Vietnam, the segment included footage of Madame Nhu, widely seen as a celebrity at the time.

The self-burning is shot handheld, with the cameraman standing at the back of the crowd assembled on site. The view is obscured by police officers who, batons at the ready, are pushing the crowds back and away from the immolator. Their actions are immediately suspicious, as logic would dictate that in such a situation law enforcement would try to disperse the protesters and prevent the monks from setting fire to their brother (such a suggestion appears in the film). Furthermore, the voiceover misspells the name of the immolator and misdates the incident to well before the Huế massacre (2 May 1963). Finally, comparing the footage against Browne's pictures dispels any remaining doubt as to the veracity of the segment. The petrol station depicted in the film looks completely different from the one in the photographs, while the building visible behind and to the left of the burning monk is altogether absent from the footage. The pole just behind the car is also a poorly made replica, cut off at the top, whereas the actual one doubled as a utility post supporting municipal power lines. A handful of other details (the wrong police uniforms, for example) also suggest that the footage is an elaborate deception.

The scene was frequently referenced by the renowned Polish theatre director Jerzy Grotowski, whose work strongly influenced theatre explorations worldwide in the last half of the 20th century. Summarising his own artistic endeavours at a series of lectures delivered at the Collège de France in 1997–98, the director repeatedly brought up the self-burning of the Buddhist monk who laid down his life in what Grotowski believed to be a protest against the war in Vietnam. The artist used this particular reference to emphasise a distinction between the positions of the theatrical spectator and those of the witness, and to highlight the distinctive qualities of the theatrical work of the Laboratory Theatre which Grotowski headed from 1959. The director asserted that we are granted the status of witness when we encounter something genuine and real – as real, he argued, as the act of utmost dedication, sincerity, and total revelation that underpinned the performance of Ryszard Cieślak, one of the Laboratory Theatre's principal actors, in the role of the eponymous religious martyr in *The Constant Prince*. Grotowski stressed, however, that a sense of proportion had to be kept and that ultimately theatrical performances were not final in the sense that self-immolations were. On the other hand, his works shared with self-burning incidents the silence following the final act. And silence essentially was the reaction he wanted his work to elicit – because when it fell, it stood as proof that the performance had not only been delivered on stage, but was also accomplished and fulfilled as an act of sacrifice, one that touched on something nestled even deeper than reason or emotion in the audience, something that could be associated with the conscience, an individual moral sense perhaps.

In Paris, Grotowski referenced a documentary about Vietnam, which he first saw soon after he had realised that his initial experiments with turning the audience into active participants in a theatrical event by pulling them directly into the action were dry and lacked the necessary precision. By his own admission, only then had he understood that the term "witness" would best describe the role he intended for the audience in his theatre. In Grotowski's retelling of the scene from the documentary, a seated monk, surrounded by three rows of his unmoving companions, is then approached by a fellow monk, who douses the immolator with kerosene, sets him alight, and withdraws. The assembled crowd watches the scene with no reaction at all, only their breathing patterns seem different.

I initially presumed that Grotowski was speaking about the aforementioned sequence from *Mondo cane 2*, as it seems that the only self-burning performed in Vietnam in the early 1960s captured on video[32] was the Thích Thiện Mỹ incident, which took place on 27 October 1963, but the set-up was completely different there. Mỹ acted alone, whereas the secular onlookers who were either curious or wanted to show respect to him – as some certainly have – assembled spontaneously into a small crowd after he was already engulfed in flames.[33] In all probability, Grotowski was not aware of the fact that the footage he saw was staged for the purpose of filming *Mondo pazzo*. Although this puts in a different light the reflections of the artist, who placed such an emphasis on the authenticity of the theatrical act, the very fact that the self-immolation he believed to be genuine was staged, ultimately, has no bearing on the validity of his conclusions regarding witnessing borderline events.

It is my conviction that the Vietnamese Buddhists' auto-cremations were, for Grotowski, an important reference point during his work on *The Constant Prince*. The performance, which featured an exceptional equivalent of the ultimate sacrifice, and which simultaneously was a provocation aimed at the viewers, who were supposed to follow the lead performer in, to quote Grotowski, carrying out "an act of self-penetration" (35) – an attempt to reach some truth about oneself – premiered on 1 April 1965 in Wrocław, but Grotowski had begun working on it back in spring 1964, while still in Opole. The idea must have already come up in his 1963 conversations with his then-assistant director Eugenio Barba, given that it was mentioned in what would come to be known as *The Theatre's New Testament*, one of Grotowski's most important dialogues from that period:

> If the actor, by setting himself a challenge publicly challenges others, and through excess, profanation and outrageous sacrilege reveals himself by casting off his everyday mask, he makes it possible for the spectator to undertake a similar process of self-penetration. If he does not exhibit his body, but annihilates it, *burns it*, frees it from every resistance to any psychic impulse, then he does not sell his body but sacrifices it.
>
> (34; emphasis – G.Z.)

With regard to the concept of the "holy actor," embodied by Cieślak in his performance as the prince in many a critic's opinion, the director spoke here of "the attitude of giving and receiving which springs from true love: in other words, self-sacrifice" (35), adding that he was not attaching any religious meaning or undertone to the phrase, a prudent and reasonable approach in Communist Poland. His seminal 1965 manifesto, "Towards a Poor Theatre," also features a passage on the body that – in line with the principle of elim- inating unnecessary obstacles – must be "annihilated," "burnt," reduced to "only a series of visible impulses" (16).

In my opinion, Grotowski's ideas on acting and the philosophy of theatre were profoundly affected by the Quảng Đức incident. *The Constant Prince*, which embodied the ideas of the poor theatre and the total act, strongly in- fluenced the burgeoning theatrical neo-avant-garde of the 1960s and was – as Paul Allain and Jen Harvie have argued – "central" not only to Grotowski's *oeuvre*, but to "the world theatre of the 20th century" (106). Following the *Prince*, French critics hailed Grotowski as "the natural son of Artaud," the theatre visionary who strove to interrogate the essence of human nature through the theatre and encouraged the rescinding of cultural norms which he believed petrified life.

Writing in the 1930s, the French artist advocated against settling for me- diocre forms and instead encouraged embracing the path of heretic "victims burnt at the stake, signaling through the flames" (13). The theatre underpin- ning this suggestive image was supposed to be "iconoclastic as well as evan- gelical in its fervor" (Sontag, *Under* 29). Rather than focusing on the aesthetic, it was expected to serve more of a soteriological function. Artaud's writings collected in *The Theatre and Its Double*, published in English in 1958, made a profound impact on the theatrical and performative experiments that would be undertaken over the course of the following decade. As rightly pointed out by James Harding, the image of signalling through the flames – rooted in Christian discourse and underpinning Artaud's inquiries – was further am- plified by the depiction, at once related to and essentially incompatible with that of the self-burning of Quảng Đức,[34] which "possessed a magnetism that over the years has consistently pulled the interest of experimental and mainstream performance practitioners into it" (32).[35] The performance scholar has suggested that

> what linked Artaud's work and Thích Quảng Đức's self-immolation is that, as experimental artists in the West turned to the works of Artaud in search of strategies for rethinking the foundations of theatre and performance, so too were these same artists frequently drawn to the shocking death of Thích Quảng Đức as a potential trope that they could appropriate within their own anti-war performances.
>
> (Harding 48–49)

Harding, however, did not take into consideration Grotowski's seminal performance, in which "Cieślak recalled Artaud's vision of the martyred actor … communicating even in his death throes" (Allain and Harvie 106). Seven years after first learning of Artaud in 1960 (Kolankiewicz 170–173, 271–272), Grotowski published a brief essay called *He Wasn't Entirely Himself* – a sober (critical yet appreciative) evaluation of the French visionary's intuitions that would be included in the 1968 edition of *Towards a Poor Theatre* (117–125). In this text, Grotowski argued that the images of burned heretics ostensibly confirmed the approach of his own theatre, emphasising the activation of one's entire being within the precise frame of the physical action score: an approach, I reiterate, strongly conceptually indebted to the famous fiery self-sacrifice and its photographic representation. But that was only one of the many avenues of influence of that paradigmatic 1963 self-burning.

Michelle Murray Yang maintained that Browne's two most famous photographs are used in the US primarily "as a graphic reminder of the casualties of a horrific war in which peace with honor would come much too late for far too many" and "a cautionary warning to future generations about entering into entangling alliances abroad" (20). It is my contention that their intrinsic power transcends the purely geopolitical context, following from the fact that they show the figure at their centre as capable of overcoming suffering and illustrate the indomitability of the human spirit. In the first photograph, despite being engulfed in flames, the monk is uncannily still, his body locked in the lotus position. His closed eyes suggest that he is immersed in meditation. It is the placid look on his face that draws our attention, becoming a Barthesian *punctum* – the pinprick that jabs at the viewer, making it impossible to simply look away. It also lets the image speak to those who have no idea about the political and historical context of the situation in the picture. Usually taken for an anti-war demonstration, Đức's act can be perceived as a symbol of protest against the harassment and persecution of the weak, the outcasts, and the voiceless. And it was in this role that his image was usually cast. But it was not this particular aspect of the picture – or at least not just that one – that drove it to such staggering notoriety.

It ought to be reiterated that, *de facto*, the first of the two famous frames does not implicitly portray suffering. We presume that the monk is in agony, but his demeanour suggests otherwise; therefore, it is possible that he truly transcended earthly misery and ascended to a realm that is beyond the reach of mere mortals. The composition of the picture itself is near perfect. The roaring flames and the pillar of smoke serve as a counterbalance to the stillness of the human figure they envelop. The fury of the fire seems offset by the tranquillity of the monk's features. The petrol can, the car, and the crowd swarming the intersection seem to anchor this somewhat phantasmagorical scene in reality. The picture is horrifying, but not without a peculiar beauty. The other photograph, however, is markedly different in character and seems dominated by horror. No wonder, then, that in consumer culture, prone to aestheticisation of suffering, the former was used much more frequently.[36]

It graced, among other pop cultural ephemera, the cover of Rage Against the Machine's 1992 debut LP, where it was cropped to leave out the car and the assembled crowd, while the part of the frame with the petrol can was moved to the back cover. We see the monk in a close-up and a part of the car, but those unfamiliar with the original crop would find it difficult to surmise what the background held. The blazing flames dominate the frame. Near the bottom edge sits the name of the band (and the self-titled album) which can be also seen as a caption for the picture. The photograph quickly became the emblem of the left-leaning band, whose songs openly denounced the establishment and the corporate soul of America. "This is what *rage against the machine* (i.e., the system) looks like," the cover seemed to say. The fire ostensibly engulfing the cover art also served to emphasise the incendiary nature of the band's music and lyrics.

This decontextualisation performed by the band, whose rise to international stardom was relatively quick, helped "unstick" the picture in the minds of the public from the incident from which it arose. Over time, processes of reification that underpin popular culture have transformed it into an empty vessel, carrying whatever meaning one decides to pour into it. As information networks began spanning the globe, the picture of the burning monk became subject to endless multiplication, remediation, and reconfiguration, eventually becoming a mere pop cultural trinket.[37] The Internet carries a veritable flood of its copies – with added colour, transmitted in a variety of formats through a variety of media. The monk engulfed in flames is now a tattoo motif, a design printed on T-shirts and sweatshirts.[38] The image adorns smartphone cases, mugs, even snack crisps bags to imply that the contents are... flaming hot. The RATM cover became a template for neon signs, comic books, cartoons (one implies that ninja warriors won't be able to find you if you're a burning monk in Vietnam), and photomontages (one features Thích Quảng Đức set against Jimi Hendrix, the latter "burning" with the fire of his own passion) that can be purchased and downloaded as computer wallpapers. Many visual and graphic artists have crafted images and photograms referencing or drawing on Browne's celebrated photos. Some, like Randall Stoltzfus, have dedicated their works to Đức and his memory, while others reworked the famed pictures in their own, original way, like Dustin Spagnola, a mural artist from North Carolina, who recreated a large-scale replica of the photo on the façade of an Asheville warehouse. The creativity exhibited in this particular area by artists, designers, and run-of-the-mill Internet users seems boundless.

The scene has also been recreated a number of times using toys (particularly LEGO), primarily for purposes of photographic documentation. One example can be found in a 2010 mini-installation created by Mike Stimpson, an artist who specialises in reenacting iconic photographs and other highly popular images with LEGO bricks. It should be noted that artists – like Zbigniew Libera, the Polish author of a controversial LEGO concentration camp (Sienkiewicz) – usually make use of mass-produced sets, rather than custom bricks. Unlike Libera's efforts, however, these works carry only a negligible critical potential, which is mostly eclipsed by their decorative aspect. Although they do indeed juxtapose macabre imagery with the carefree frivolity of play, and allude to the notion of being a pawn moved around the board by supraindividual, unseen forces which steer our fates from the shadows, these installations are, at their core, still just emanations of mass culture and its proclivity for exploiting the mainstream.

That is precisely the character of the Vietnamese motif in Martin McDonagh's 2012 dark comedy *Seven Psychopaths*, which includes a direct reference to the notorious self-burning in Saigon. In the film, this reference is found in the idea for a scene outlined by one of the eponymous psychopaths to the protagonist, a screenwriter suffering from a bout of writer's block. The original incident is subject to similar treatment in the adult animated series *South Park*. In the 55th episode, *Chef Goes Nanners* (2000), the Chef character tries to protest against the titular town's racist flag by burning Browne's photo. Here, the visage of Quảng Đức engulfed in flame was treated consistently with what was proved to be the dominant pop culture approach to the photo – as an instantly available icon of protest, which can be endlessly reused outside of its original context (Vågnes). The media usually took a similar tack, often using the photograph when reporting on contemporary incidents without iconographic material to fall back on. In such cases, Browne's photos are utilised as substitutes, becoming, seemingly at random, a symbolic representation of all sorts of other suicide protests.

Contemporary visual culture knows of works that do not abide by the mainstream approach to Browne's photos. One such example of the emblematic picture (the WPP-winning shot, to be more precise) being used in a more contentious manner can be found in the work of Australian artist Van Thanh Rudd. His oil and acrylic 2008 painting *Special Forces* is a critique of the creeping McDonaldisation of contemporary culture. The 220-by-170 cm piece portrays Ronald McDonald, the official mascot of the fast-food giant, next to the burning monk and holding a torch in his hand, implying that he either set the monk on fire or lit the torch from his burning body.

Initially, those critics who missed the subtitle of the piece, *After Banksy*, decried it as blatantly ripping off the British street artist's *Napalm (Can't Beat That Feeling)* (Battersby). In the famous 2004 piece, Mickey Mouse and Ronald McDonald hold hands with a terrified, naked girl – a reference to the Pulitzer-Prize winning photo taken by Nick Ut (Huỳnh Công Út) on 8 June 1972 near the village of Trảng Bàng. In the picture, children, many of them marked with deep burns, are fleeing down a road and towards the camera after a napalm bombardment, with the naked Phan Thị Kim Phúc dead centre in the frame. Banksy's poster-like piece, with the instantly recognisable figures against a uniformly grey background, confronts two symbolic realities. On the one hand, drawing on the iconic photo, the piece represents the horror of war, destruction, and the suffering of children. On the other, the symbols of American corporate power and popular culture seem to stand in for the highly processed, pre-digested consumer feed that is contemporary entertainment. Twisted in anguish and horror, the lips of the naked girl stand in stark contrast to the forced smiles worn by Mickey and the red-nosed clown. The juxtaposition can be read as an unambiguous denouncement of consumerism, here seen as a prelude to the inferno of warfare. The piece seems an illustration of the incontrovertible truth that the insatiable greed intrinsic to capitalism tends to both conceal and make light of the consequences of the kind of politics that favours and facilitates bloodshed, ultimately leading to pictures like Nick Ut's *The Terror or War*.[39]

Rudd's piece also relies on referential poetics and is similarly critical of our contemporary, globalised reality; but because the piece was created to protest against the 2008 Summer Olympic Games in Beijing, it seemed to have distributed its emphases somewhat differently. The artist stressed that it was an ironic paradox that the international fast-food giant would sponsor a major sports event (Van). But the jarring incongruity underpinning his piece is remarkable for a number of other reasons. Here, the restaurant chain, known for low wages and aggressive expansion policies, serves to conjure up references to the Chinese economic miracle, rooted in incessant exploitation of labour. The image also brings up the inextricable and morally questionable union of big money, sports, and international politics that shapes a considerable portion of our reality. Today, Rudd's piece can also be seen as carrying furtive references to the self-immolations of Tibetans, who have been burning themselves to protest against Chinese subjugation. Harnessing the unexpected juxtaposition of the regimes of suffering and entertainment, Van's highly political and subversive piece helps the worn-out, fatigued icon reclaim a portion of its original potency within the deeply mediatised reality, "bombarded" with images of cruelty and wartime horror.

In Saigon, since renamed Hồ Chí Minh City, Thích Quảng Đức today has a street named after him, while next to the site of his self-burning

132   Selected contemporary ultimate protests by fire

stands a huge, two–part monument. In the foreground, a large likeness of the monk sits surrounded by a halo of flame, while in the background looms a semi–circular bas–relief based on Browne's iconic photo. In a somewhat ironic turn of events, the Communists commemorated the Buddhist monk, best known for his protest against religious repression, with a monument, but did so because it aligned with the party line, which itself sought to emphasise all forms and instances of resistance against the former imperialist regime. And thus, the monk's deeply hybrid act has been ground down by the millstones of not just popular culture, but history-based politics as well.

Skin of flame: Norman Morrison's self-immolation (The United States, 1965)

The analysis of the family scene in **Far from Vietnam**

The family scene in *Loin du Vietnam* serves as a focal point for a number of issues related to the other prominent self-burning performed as the war continued in Vietnam. But before we discuss this scene and its (absent) protagonist, we must first dive a little into the background of this unusual documentary, or film essay, to be more precise, produced in 1967 by French left-leaning director and theatre enthusiast Chris Marker, and the artistic collective made up of leading figures of the French New Wave.[40]

The film is highly heterogeneous, and features documentary footage of combat operations captured aboard an American aircraft carrier, as well as in North and South Vietnam, a historical review, clips of anti-war protests in Paris and New York, and interviews with Hồ Chí Minh and with Fidel Castro on guerrilla warfare in Cuba. The picture also includes two short etudes. One, directed by Alain Resnais,[41] depicts a French leftist intellectual undertaking a brilliant, self-critical, but ultimately futile analysis of his own lack of involvement and interest in the war in Vietnam. The other, Jean-Luc Godard's[42] *Camera-Œil* (*Camera-Eye*), is a peculiar meditation on the impossibility of shooting a film in a country to which the director failed to secure a visa, which ultimately leads him to look for "Vietnams" within ourselves. Marker considered the group effort an expression of solidarity with the Vietnamese struggle for self-determination. It seems obvious, however, that he was not interested in creating a balanced, objective documentary, but wanted instead to provoke a reflection on the war that many French artists saw as an extension of American imperialist practices. As such, the documentary can be considered an example of politically involved filmmaking and read as a propaganda piece, abetting the Communist government in Hanoi and the forces of the NLF fighting in the South.[43] But it can also be viewed as a pacifist manifesto or an expression of outrage felt by individuals who judged the war from moral rather than political positions.

A lotus in a sea of fire 133

Both readings are reinforced by a 7-minute-long sequence, located about 85 minutes into the film, which tells the story of the self-burning of Quaker Norman Morrison, husband and father of three, who followed the example of Thích Quảng Đức – of whom he had naturally heard (Morrison Welsh 3, 55) – and set himself alight outside the Pentagon on 2 November 1965.[44]

The sequence, called *Ann Uyen*, juxtaposes the testimony of Anne Morrison, the Quaker's widow, and Uyen [Nguyễn?], a Vietnamese woman who fled from her homeland with her children to Paris. But comparing the fates of the two women, both of whom were single mothers to three children, is not supposed to show them as two sides of the same coin (the reasons for Uyen's flight from the country remain unexplored, neither do we know whether she was fleeing North or South Vietnam), but rather to trace the impact of Morrison's act and its meaning and implications.

In a voiceover, the narrator informs us that his sacrifice still goes rather unappreciated at home, in contrast to its reception in Vietnam, where the people not only heard the message behind his protest, but understood it in their own way. Later on, Uyen explains in French that Morrison's decision to sacrifice his life and the well-being of his own family in service to the Vietnamese cause was perceived in Vietnam as something unique and very special, as it told them that they were not alone in their struggle against the superpower and that even in the US there were people who believed the war in Southeast Asia unjust. Thereby, Morrison became a highly respected figure in Vietnam, while his sacrificial act became a foundation upon which the two sides might one day build reconciliation.

As Uyen speaks in voiceover, the footage shows Anne playing with her children, Benjamin, Christina, and Emily, outside their Baltimore home, and then sitting down to eat with friends. As the meal begins, people gathered at the table first pick up chopsticks (presumably to show their solidarity with the Vietnamese), and only then reach for their knives and forks. Holding Emily on her lap, Anne explains that Norman decided to incinerate himself after reading a newspaper article in which a Catholic priest spoke about the American bombing of a village where he had led a parish, an operation which claimed the lives of innocent civilians, many of them children. As she speaks, Emily fusses and repeatedly tries to draw her mother's attention. Moments later, we are shown a peaceful, idyllic vision of Anne playing ball with her children in her backyard garden. From off screen, we hear Uyen admit how deeply she admires Anne for accepting her husband's sacrifice and maintaining equanimity in the face of such horror. Anne herself later adds that she understood Norman's decision, because she knew what sort of man he was. As she speaks, we see two anti-war posters adorned with Morrison's likeness. Anne continues:

> Part of what he must have wanted to say was: this is how it feels to be burnt. As we're burning people, women and children, and men. Every day. I knew that Norman was a kind of person who was willing to make

134 Selected contemporary ultimate protests by fire

a sacrifice for others if it seemed necessary. To do otherwise would be unbearable. For some people it was an act of affirmation that one person can care that much for humanity to give his life.

(from the documentary *Far from Vietnam*)

As the film cuts to Uyen, we are given the impression that she is intently listening to Anne's argument. The editing suggests that the women are engaged in a remote conversation – a conversation which probably would have had no chance of taking place under wartime conditions. Moreover, the juxtaposition itself stands as an assertion that despite some cultural differences, people are similar – both mothers want to feed their children, and give them shelter and an opportunity to realise their potential. Anne later recounts that the day after Norman burned himself, she told her two elder children what had happened. Upon hearing the news, Christina allegedly said: "Daddy has died but now his love has spread." In closing, Uyen proclaims that Morrison's sacrifice crystallised the attitudes of those people who, up until then, had held no clear position on the conflict. Anne, on the other hand, directs her final remarks at a man sitting next to her, as if seeking his reassurance – seemingly going against their very thrust: "I know one thing for absolutely sure that individual lives have been changed by this, changed in some cases dramatically towards concern for society and I think it has been worth it. I mean, he would say this, I mean, a thousand times over."

What meaning emerges from this idyllic yet disturbing sequence? While Morrison's sacrifice is deeply appreciated by the Vietnamese, his wife, having accepted his death, has busied herself with bravely raising their children, secure in the belief that the sacrifice was dictated by higher necessity. The reading of that particular segment changes significantly, however, when we realise that Emily, barely two years old at the time of filming,[45] was present for her father's self-immolation. Not even one, she accompanied him to the Pentagon for reasons unknown.

The scene looks different still to anyone familiar with the incredibly moving and honest memoirs of Anne Morrison Welsh, which stand as proof of how drawn out and arduous the process of accepting his death and reconciling with him truly was. Her published writings, first collected in the 2005 pamphlet *Fire from the Heart* and later in the 2008 book *Held in the Light* – which remains the definitive source on Morrison – reveal how profound a shock the Quaker's self-sacrifice was to his family. Years later, his daughter Christina also revealed that all she could feel immediately following her father's death was utter shock and recounted how affected she was by the fact that he did not leave any farewell letter for his family that could possibly help them cope with their loss and work through their grief (Morrison Welsh 163). Only decades later, during a trip to Vietnam in April 1999, did Morrison's widow manage to fully forgive her husband and cleanse herself of conflicting emotions (Morrison Welsh 120).

It also bears noting that nowhere in her books does Anne Morrison bring up her participation in the French documentary, despite mentioning several other works (mostly poems)[46] that reference her husband's death. Although it might be chalked up to simple forgetfulness, I would risk arguing that she may have felt manipulated by the filmmakers and decided to ignore the film's existence. Why manipulated? Because the sequence closes out with the camera moving over the inscription "Nguyen Van Troi – Morrison," and then panning up to show a memorial to the two men, their faces, in relief, sitting next to each other. To understand the meaning underlying the shot, we must first take a closer look at the man portrayed next to the American immolator.

A Việt Minh fighter, Nguyễn Văn Trỗi, attempted to assassinate American secretary of defence Robert McNamara and future American ambassador to Vietnam, Henry Cabot Lodge, Jr., during their visit to Saigon in May 1963. Captured in the attempt, he was tried and sentenced to death by firing squad; the execution was postponed, however, after Venezuelan guerrillas kidnapped Michael Smolen, a colonel in the US Air Force, in Caracas on 8 October 1964, and threatened to kill him if Trỗi was to be put to death. The sentence was eventually carried out at Chí Hòa prison (and filmed), a week after the kidnappers released the American serviceman. The 24-year-old Trỗi was the first Việt Minh member to be publicly executed, and was subsequently hailed as a martyr and national hero in North Vietnam. A year later – two weeks before Morrison's protest – the NLF released a commemorative stamp to honour Trỗi, but his execution went grossly unreported in the US.

By the North Vietnamese, Morrison was seen as a martyr for the cause whose sacrifice was no smaller than that of the guerrillas fighting to rebuff the American invasion and occupation. And it was that propaganda image of the Quaker that was ultimately adopted by the filmmakers behind *Far from Vietnam*. Anne Morrison, meanwhile, emphasised that because of his faith, her husband was a declared pacifist who cared "deeply, passionately, and finally desperately – about the things he believed: peace and nonviolence, human rights, and an equitable sharing of the world's resources" (xii).

The performer, his immolation, and its reception in the US and in Vietnam

On the day of his self-incineration, Norman Morrison wrote: "The life is mightier than a book that reports it. The most important thing in the world is that our faith become living experience and deed of life" (qtd. in Morrison Welsh xi). The words were accordant with the principles of the Quaker worldview, which demanded the faithful embody the tenets of their faith.[47]

The Quakers emphasise the prominent role of inner, continuous revelation and the unmediated presence of God, which they believe can be experienced through introspection, performed, for example, during assemblies called *silent worship*, which stress expectant waiting. The practice requires striving to be attentive to divine presence and waiting, in focused silence, until guidance is offered. The Quakers follow the Bible and what they call

136 Selected contemporary ultimate protests by fire

the Inner Light, which can be seen as a metaphor for Christ derived from the Gospel of John (8:12) (King, S. B. 132). In *Albion's Seed*, an inquiry into the ideological foundations of the US, David Fisher stressed that for the Quakers, "a believing Christian had a sacred duty to stand against evil in government, and that individual conscience was the arbiter of God's truth" (590–591). Morrison's efforts were part and parcel of these traditions. With his wife and fellow members of his congregation, he prayed for peace, held vigils and debates, and evaded paying taxes which he believed would go to financing the war. He also wrote letters to newspapers and the authorities, including President Lyndon B. Johnson, demanding a stop to combat operations in Vietnam.

Soon after the Việt Cộng assaulted a US helicopter base near Pleiku in February 1965, the president ordered the military to commence Operation Rolling Thunder, a sustained bombing campaign against targets in North Vietnam. The first phase of the operation, launched on 2 March, was eventually halted in a bid to encourage Hanoi to begin peace talks. On 8 March 1965, two battalions of US Marines landed on the beach in Đà Nẵng to augment the security component at the nearby airbase. In the US, the draft continued to pull military age men into service overseas, and by December, the US had nearly 200,000 troops on the ground in Vietnam (Karnow 696). The media, meanwhile, continued to report on the rising number of civilian casualties,[48] deaths of US servicemen shipped home in seemingly endless streams of body bags, protest self-burnings, the mining of the Haiphong harbour, the tactical use of Rainbow Herbicides against vegetation in rural and jungle areas, napalm bombings, and controversial military strategies, such as the Search and Destroy programme.

As the conflict escalated and the threat of using nuclear weapons grew, the anti-war movement began organising across the States and gaining new ground. It should be noted, however, that in 1965 the war in Vietnam had still overwhelming public support in the US – even though LBJ's landslide victory against Barry Goldwater in 1964 was driven, among other factors, by the president's embrace of peace-oriented rhetoric. On 24 March 1965, 3,000 students assembled for a teach-in at the University of Michigan in Ann Arbor. Similar rallies were soon held in campuses across the country. The first mass anti-war protest also broke out that March in Berkeley, California. The following month, the influential leftist student organisation, Students for a Democratic Society, organised its famous March on Washington, which drew nearly 20,000 people. Activists across the country were destroying draft cards (DeBenedetti and Chatfield 107–108), using blood, paint, or fire to do so. These symbolic protests soon became liturgical in form – they were performed in public to much ceremony and accompaniment of protest songs (Du Plessix Gray). Regardless of the growing anti-war impetus, Anne Morrison recounted that she and her husband both felt that their efforts in the cause of peace were ultimately futile.

A day after the Morrison's self-incineration, Anne received a letter from her husband, which he must have written before leaving for the Pentagon and mailed on the way there. The letter attempted to justify the decision to perform his final protest, emphasising that he had finally received guidance on what to do (Morrison Welsh 36). The message also included a newspaper clipping of an interview that a French reporter conducted with Father Currien in a Saigon hospital. In the interview, he described how after a skirmish with the Việt Cộng American forces bombed a village, killing at least seven civilians. This tragic event presumably served as the catalyst which prompted Morrison to finally take action.

His wife recounted (6–7) that after they ate lunch together that day, she headed out to pick up six-year-old Ben and five-year-old Tina from school. Norman, meanwhile, left for the Pentagon, with little Emily in tow. It is unclear how he went about the self-burning, because it seems that no footage or photographs of the incident exist. Witness testimony indicates that Morrison arrived at the entrances on the Potomac side of the Pentagon moments before Department of Defense employees began leaving for the day. Accompanied by his daughter, he was holding a large glass jar filled with petrol. A traffic policeman later testified to having seen a man, holding an infant, walking up and down the fence that ringed the garden outside the Pentagon, whereas passersby claimed that at one point Morrison climbed the fence's parapet and began addressing the slowly gathering crowd. Other witnesses recounted that the man, along with the baby, was instead pacing the rectangular garden fenced by a low brick wall. The security guard, who called the fire department from his booth after Morrison set himself alight, reported that the flames were at least 3 m high. Seeing the fire, two soldiers – lieutenant colonel Charles Johnson and staff sergeant Robert Bundt – leapt into the garden to snuff the flames out with their overcoats, suffering burns in the process. Then, Morrison collapsed into a shallow ditch and uttered his last words, which none of the witnesses could understand. When a doctor from the Pentagon finally reached him, the Quaker was already unresponsive, but still alive and desperately gasping for air. He died a couple of minutes later, in the ambulance en route to the hospital.

All these reports stand as proof that Morrison's protest was far from impulsive, and his cold calculation shines through in his choice of the highly symbolic venue and specific timing. The Quaker decided to perform self-immolation in the late afternoon, about the time when Pentagon staffers would be leaving the building, allowing Morrison to pull them in to witness his act without much effort.

Why Morrison took his infant daughter with him and what happened to her as he burned will perhaps forever remain a mystery. Some witnesses reported hearing someone yell for him to let Emily go. Others claimed that the Quaker set her down next him, and still others said that he handed the child off to one of the women in the crowd. The coroner's report said that

138   Selected contemporary ultimate protests by fire

Morrison dropped Emily and she fell into the nearby bushes, sustaining no injuries (Morrison Welsh 7). In her memoirs, his widow wrote: "What I believe is that Norman held our precious youngest child as long as he dared, then placed her on the ground and struck the match" (7). This version of events seems to be corroborated by the fact that the child was not bruised, scratched, or burned. Furthermore, Norman brought with him a supply of formula, nappies, and dummies. His intentions may be gleaned from his farewell letter to his wife: "At least I shall not plan to go without my child, as Abraham did" (qtd. in Morrison Welsh 36). Perhaps the Quaker presumed that, like the biblical patriarch before him, he too would be required to sacrifice his child, only for the divine to intervene in the last instance. His wife believed that Emily was there to represent the Vietnamese children – innocent casualties of war. Years later, Emily Morrison herself wrote that by taking her, her father may have been trying to ask his witnesses: "How would you feel if this child were burnt too?" and emphasised: "I believe I was there with Norman ultimately to be a symbol of truth and hope, treasure and horror all together. And I am fine with my role in it" (qtd. in Morrison Welsh 162). These conjectures notwithstanding, one thing is certain: the presence of the infant child – regardless of Morrison's initial intentions – is what ultimately drew massive public attention to the incident, as evinced by newspaper headlines, most of which highlighted the fact.

As I already mentioned, the Quaker was not the first American to sacrifice their life in fiery protest against the war in Vietnam. He was preceded by 82-year-old Alice Herz,[49] who burned herself on 16 March 1965 in Detroit, nearly eight months before him, an incident that the Morrisons were well aware of (Morrison Welsh 3). The woman was a fellow peace activist – she authored multiple anti-war essays and articles, and was active in a number of organisations, including Women for Peace, Women Strike for Peace, and Women's International League for Peace and Freedom. Her farewell appeal, addressed to the nations of the world, UN Secretary-General Sithu U Thant and President Johnson, was proof that she was not a desperate woman, but instead burned herself in the hopes that her sacrifice would change the course of US foreign policy in the Far East. Her death, however, went mostly unnoticed in the US, while those few headlines that did report her demise tended to call her mental health into question. Genuine public reaction, however, was sparked only by the death of the Quaker from Baltimore.[50]

We can only presume the reasons behind the two burnings' different receptions. Aside from Emily's presence, one factor that significantly impacted the optics of Morrison's sacrifice was its venue, a symbol of American military power; on top of that, Morrison burned himself (by accident, in all likelihood) right below secretary McNamara's window (which we will come back to later in the chapter). His social standing also affected the reception – as a young, white man, a Quaker, and a husband and father, he embodied the American middle-class ideal, which necessarily drew public attention. In this context, it would be prudent to bring up the rhetorical question asked by Cheyney Ryan with regard to Herz's act: "Might there be something particularly troubling about an act of self-immolation when performed by a *woman* that explains the resistance to speak of it?" (17).[51]

Furthermore, as convincingly demonstrated by Jon Coburn, it could be argued that Herz was simply ahead of her time. By mid-March 1965, public opinion still paid very little attention to Vietnam, while the anti-war movement, as I already pointed out above, was only beginning to gain steam. The situation was starkly different only six months later, as the escalation of the conflict was followed by a shift in public sentiment.

A few days before the Morrison incident, on 28 October 1965, New York was set to be the stage of a big anti-draft protest. Charles DeBenedetti and Charles Chatfield wrote that in October 1965 alone, 36,000 men were conscripted, the highest number since the war in Korea (128). Many Americans believed that the draft was inherently biased, as it primarily targeted young lower middle-class males, as well as workers and farmers. Therefore, it was not just the war itself that aroused the indignation of American leftists, but so did the social inequalities that conscription exacerbated. Liberal organisers from the Committee for Non-Violent Action planned to hold a draft card burning on Foley Square in Manhattan. It turned out, however, that the event would have to be postponed, because the four men who intended to burn the cards got lost in the crowd of protesters, photojournalists, and reporters. The protest was restaged on 6 November, soon after Morrison's death. The 1,500-strong gathering assembled on Union Square and began with a moment of silence in his honour. But right before the draft cards were to be burned, a counter-protester with a fire extinguisher appeared to prevent it from happening. War supporters began chanting: "Give us joy, bomb Hanoi" and – apparently in reference to the Quaker's self-incineration – "Burn yourself, not your cards" (qtd. in DeBenedetti and Chatfield 128–129). Around that time, the US military infamously launched six major bombing missions within a 48-hour timeframe, killing the highest number of Vietnamese since the beginning of the conflict. Responding to the general mood and reports of the missions' heavy civilian toll, Roger LaPorte performed a self-immolation on 9 November 1965. Following his death, a rumour began to circulate that peace activists signed a suicide pact that would result in one self-burning per week until the cessation of hostilities. All of this led to Morrison's death quickly becoming, to put it crudely, the talk of the town.[52]

Seeing as Morrison had not left behind any farewell letter for the public, had not carried any posters or banners, and had taken his daughter with him to Washington, there was a real chance that he would have been quickly labelled mentally unstable by public opinion. That ultimately did not come to pass, because Anne Morrison released a statement immediately after her husband's death, while still in the hospital (and yet unaware of the contents of his letter she would receive the following day), in which she called his act an anti-war protest (6). In the days, months, and years that followed, she continued her peace activism, aspiring, to quote Nicholas Patler, "to honor her husband and his sacrifice" (4). A week after Norman's death, Anne wrote in the newsletter of the Stony Run Friends Meeting, the Morrisons' spiritual community, that her husband believed ending the war was absolutely necessary, and saw the conflict, due to the passions and hatred it bred, as the greatest threat to both the Vietnamese and the American peoples. Furthermore, she got involved with the work of the nationwide American Friends Service Committee and soon joined its executive committee. Throughout the years, she maintained control over the narrative on her husband's death. His spiritual brethren supported the narrative as well, as evidenced by the 3 November 1965 statement released by the Stony Run Friends Meeting, in which the assembly emphasised how they "have come to appreciate the depths of his commitment to the way of peace" (qtd. in Morrison Welsh 40).

Despite clear explanations from his family and friends, some journalists continued to claim that Morrison's self-immolation stemmed from mental health issues. *Baltimore Evening Sun*'s Robin Frames, for example, wrote that "Beneath his deep convictions lay a form of paranoia," while *Life* columnist Loudon Wainwright called his death "truly pitiful," but later acknowledged that although some saw the sacrifice as "vain and insane," it would still force many to reevaluate the "condition of the American conscience in regard to Vietnam" (qtd. in Morrison Welsh 45). Harsh opinions like these are understandable, given how alien fiery self-sacrifice was to the Western cultural sphere. Dissenting voices appeared even among the Quaker community. Some Friends believed that self-directed violence was still violence, even if undertaken in pursuit of a noble goal. Others emphasised that Morrison may have wounded or even killed his infant daughter and, furthermore, acted without first consulting his congregation. With regard to the latter, Sallie King wrote: "the imperatives of God transcend the authority of the Church," so "even a devoted Friend like Norman Morrison" could ignore "the clear instruction of the faith to check his leading with the group" because he felt certain "that God has told him to act" (136).

Most Quakers believed, however, that Morrison acted in accordance with the best traditions of their movement, namely that he followed the Inner Light and pursued what he felt called to. Two days after his self-burning, a group of Friends from Baltimore held a two-hour vigil outside the Pentagon, during which they read from Gandhi, Camus, Buber, and Thoreau. Following the vigil, they released a statement: "We do not necessarily approve of persons burning themselves to death. ... But we are sympathetic to all expressions of concern about the suffering of humanity" (qtd. in Morrison Welsh 44). Similar sentiments were expressed at another vigil, held on 6 November 1965 at the Stony Run Meeting House.

It is difficult to establish with any degree of certainty whether Morrison's death spurred on the development of the anti-war movement in the US.[53]

Self-burning corresponded to Gandhi's principles of non-violence, which, in turn, informed the practice of civil disobedience preached and embraced around that same time by Martin Luther King, Jr. and his followers. It was a remarkable manifestation of *satyagraha* – the ultimate expression of conviction that did not resort to violence against others.[54] It was a practice encouraged (although not in such radical a form) by a key figure in the anti-war movement and King supporter,[55] Rabbi Abraham Heschel, who stressed that protesters had to be ready to sacrifice, even lay down their lives, for the cause. In one of his sermons, he condemned the "evil of indifference" and contended that

> Mere knowledge or belief is too feeble to be a cure for man's hostility to man, man's tendency to fratricide. The only remedy is *personal sacrifice*, to abandon, to reject what seems dear, even plausible, like prejudice, for the sake of a greater truth, to do more than I am ready to understand for the sake of God.
>
> (qtd. in Morrison Welsh 57)

However, the anti-war movement in the US was hesitant to embrace self-immolation, mostly due to the horror it spawned and self-directed violence it entailed. This was the reasoning of Dorothy Day, an influential Catholic thinker and peace activist. Her position on fiery self-sacrifice, outlined in the essay *A Brief Flame*, was ambivalent at best. As Cheyney Ryan pointed out: "She could not bring herself to *accept* such actions, in part because they contradicted her insistence that nonviolent commitment should be an essentially undramatic affair," characterised by "ordinariness," and, as such, devoid of any measure of "theatricality" (18). On the contrary, she argued, non-violent action should focus on the long term and reject, to quote Thomas Merton, "the fetishism of immediate visible results" (qtd. in Ryan 23), pursuing instead a strategy of persistence. As Day herself eloquently put it, it was not about the ability to "gallantly stand before a firing squad," but about rejecting the fear of losing "a job because of not taking a loyalty oath, or buying a war bond, or paying a tax" (qtd. in Ryan 21). Her position on the practice notwithstanding, Day still could not bring herself to denounce it in unambiguous terms, as she believed that it was not driven by despair, like suicide, and was compelled, instead, by the same logic as non-violence, one based on identifying with the victims. Ryan pointed out that when talking about self-burning in the American context, Day often spoke of identification rather than compassion or empathy. In her opinion, immolators were trying to experience the same suffering that was inflicted on other peoples by Americans. The activist did not believe that Alice Herz suffered "*for* the Vietnamese – a phrase that would suggest that her actions were animated primarily by a kind of compassion." Rather, she spoke of her as "*sharing* their suffering, so that their sufferings *are* her sufferings too" (26). Ryan also stressed the essential difference between sharing another's *suffering* and another's viewpoint or outlook (27), as immolators strove not to share in

142 Selected contemporary ultimate protests by fire

a sensual or cognitive experience, but sought a sense of oneness with another human being, produced through real-life, whole-body physical experience.

Perhaps this was why Morrison's death, reported nationwide by Vietnamese radio, proved so poignant to the Vietnamese. Here was someone from the opposing camp, so to speak, employing a language they understood – a language of suffering, rooted in Vietnamese tradition, rather than the language of imperialist oppression. They were further touched by the fact that he must have been so desperate that he ultimately chose to perform the self-burning in the presence of his child, a symbol of hope. This particularly emotional reception was quickly exploited for propaganda purposes. Five days after the Quaker's self-burning, Tố Hữu (Nguyễn Kim Thành), North Vietnamese revolutionary poet and member of the Central Committee of the Communist Party of Vietnam, wrote the propaganda poem *Emily, My Child* (qtd. in Morrison Welsh 102–105). The piece opens with a brief dialogue between Norman and his daughter,[56] in which the Quaker explains the reasons for his act and then denounces Johnson and McNamara as cruel and cowardly. The poem was part of the school curriculum in Vietnam until the mid-1980s, when Thành, by then Deputy Prime Minister, was blamed for the disastrous monetary reform and forced to resign his post.

On 18 November 1965, *The Vietnam Courier* – a Hanoi newspaper published in English – carried a column on Morrison, with a photo of the American attached. In typically "uplifting" tone, the author of the piece wrote:

> We knew that from the depth of America, proud of its tradition of freedom and democracy, one day a piercing voice would rise. ... Anne Morrison, mourn over your husband, but be proud of him; millions of Vietnamese women now take you to heart. Weep for your dad, Ben, Tina and Emily Morrison, but be aware that beyond the Pacific, millions of Vietnamese children have adopted you as their brother and sisters.
> (qtd. in Morrison Welsh 108–109)

Less than a month later, on 11 December, *The New York Times* published an interview with North Vietnamese Prime Minister, Phạm Văn Đồng, in which the official claimed that Morrison's sacrifice was such a shock to the Vietnamese that spontaneous demonstrations in his memory were still breaking out across the country, while Morrison himself was enshrined in the national pantheon (Morrison Welsh 109). In less than three weeks, the authorities in Hanoi managed to release a commemorative stamp, emblazoned with the flame-engulfed visage of the Quaker, misidentified as "Noman Morixon," above a crowd of American protesters holding anti-war signs. His likeness was used in mass-produced posters, where he was placed side by side with the "father of the nation," Hồ Chí Minh himself. The posters were plastered everywhere – on factory walls, truck windshields, bicycle frames, even rucksacks of soldiers marching south down the Hồ Chí Minh trail. Mass commemorative rallies were held for Morrison across North Vietnam, and he even had a street named after him in Hanoi. The Revolutionary Museum had pictures of Morrison and Herz on display, and the guides were well-prepared to talk of their sacrifices.[57]

Around a month after her husband's death, Anne Morrison received an official invitation to visit the Democratic Republic of Vietnam, but refused, because she knew the journey would be exploited for propaganda purposes. When she finally visited Vietnam in 1999 with her daughters and their husbands, she was received with the highest honours and deeply moved that many people across the country still remembered her husband's sacrifice and knew the Tố Hữu poem by heart (Morrison Welsh 140–157). Anne Morrison finally decided to travel to Vietnam only after receiving an invitation from the American Embassy there, a rare gesture of acknowledgement of her husband's self-sacrifice by Washington.[58] A similar gesture was extended to Morrison previously, from an even less expected direction, but was unofficial in nature.

The influence of the protest on Robert McNamara

As I already mentioned, Norman Morrison burned himself right outside the Pentagon window of Robert NcMamara, who at that point was such a fierce proponent of the conflict in Southeast Asia, that some took to calling it "Mr. McNamara's war" (Ellsberg 90). The self-burning, which took place less than 20 m from his third-floor office, made a profound impact on the government official.[59] He was later repeatedly reminded of the incident by the many vigils for Morrison that the Quaker community held at the site.

It was only decades later, in a *Newsweek* interview published 3 August 1992, that the former secretary of defence for Kennedy and Johnson revealed that the young Quaker was one of the key people who led him to doubt the American involvement in Vietnam. Following the interview, Anne Morrison wrote a letter to the official, in which she explained her husband's intentions, but McNamara never replied. However, in his 1995 memoirs, *In Retrospect: Tragedy and Lessons of Vietnam*, the official recounted how profoundly he had been affected by the event he had witnessed from his office window 30 years ago:

> I reacted to the horror of his action by bottling up my emotions and avoided talking about them with anyone – even with my family. I knew Marg and our three children shared many of Morrison's feelings about the war. ... And I believed I understood and shared some of his thoughts. ... The episode created tension at home that only deepened as dissent and criticism of the war continued to grow. (216)

In the Oscar-winning 2003 documentary *The Fog of War: Eleven Lessons from the Life of Robert McNamara*, directed by Errol Morris, when asked about Morrison and the meaning of his sacrifice, the former defence secretary replied that the period was a horrible time for his family and that he was not

144   Selected contemporary ultimate protests by fire

willing to talk about it.[60] Later, he added that his family was under so much stress in those days, that both his wife and his adolescent son developed stomach ulcers.

The ideological evolution that the official underwent at the time was further explored in Paul Hendrickson's 1996 book *The Living and the Dead*. The author brings up McNamara's deposition in the 1982 libel suit that General Westmoreland brought against the broadcaster CBS. Westmoreland, the commander of US forces in Vietnam in 1964–68, claimed the broadcaster baselessly accused him and his fellow officers of deliberately underreporting the strength of North Vietnamese forces in order to maintain troop morale and drum up public support for the war. When asked by the CBS counsel about the moment he realised the war could not be won, the former defence secretary replied that he may have surmised so already in late 1965. According to Hendrickson, declassified Department of Defense documents unambiguously indicate that McNamara began pressing on Johnson to halt the bombing campaigns against Vietnam already a month after Morrison's death. The journalist argued that memos and minutes from high-level government meetings evince that the self-immolation became a sort of emotional catalyst for the evolution that was taking place in McNamara's thinking, a shift which eventually led him to step down from the Pentagon position in February 1968.[61] Years later, the former secretary acknowledged that American policy in Vietnam was a mistake, one which he was, to a considerable extent, personally responsible for (Morrison Welsh 96–99).

After McNamara's memoirs were published, Anne Morrison – touched by the willingness of such a high-ranking official to publicly admit his mistake – wrote to him again, this time including a brief statement:

> To heal the wounds of that war, we must forgive ourselves and each other, and help the people of Vietnam to rebuild their country. I am grateful to Robert McNamara for his courageous and honest reappraisal of the Vietnam war and his involvement in it. I hope this book will contribute to the healing process.
>
> (qtd. in Morrison Welsh 99)

As McNamara's book met with a rather hostile reception, a vote of confidence from such a prominent voice was very welcome by the author. He phoned Morrison to say how grateful he was for her forgiveness and ask for permission to use her remarks in upcoming advertisements for his memoir that would soon be published in *The New York Times*. Reportedly, he also often brought them up during his public appearances. Anne Morrison recounted that:

> McNamara and I had a surprisingly relaxed and candid conversation. It was almost as if we knew each other, almost as if we hadn't been on

opposite sides of the chasm that had split our country apart three decades earlier. Norman's death is a wound that we've both carried. In an odd way, we came into a kind of communion with each other. (100)

Has McNamara managed to strike up an equally profound relationship with Nhất Hạnh, whom he received in the Pentagon in late 1967 to discuss the war in Vietnam? Nicholas Patler asserted that the American official may have seen in the monk a particular extension of Morrison's: "It seems unlikely that it would have ever crossed the secretary's mind to invite a Buddhist anti-war activist to his office before witnessing the Quaker's self-immolation" (18). Patler concluded that McNamara's inner journey had been long and full of suffering. It began with Buddhist monks and nuns, of whom the secretary may have heard only in passing, burning themselves to protest the war from afar, led through Morrison's self-burning outside his Pentagon window, which seemed to have awakened McNamara's conscience, and finally concluded with Hạnh's gentle presence in his office (18). With regard to the self-immolation of Thích Quảng Đức, McNamara's guest wrote that "Like the crucifixion of Jesus," it "expressed unconditional willingness to suffer for the awakening of others. Accepting the most extreme kind of pain, he lit a fire in the hearts of people around the world" (Nhat, *Love* 43).

A unique coda to the McNamara-Morrison relationship was drafted by Sean Devine, a Canadian playwright whose debut play *Re:Union*, put on in 2011 as a coproduction of the Pacific Theatre and the Horseshoes and Hand Grenades Theatre in Vancouver,[62] brought together the figures of the defence secretary, the Quaker, and his daughter Emily. The play jumps between 1965 and 2001 to portray Morrison's daughter's attempts to find her bearings in a post-9/11 world. A woman of 37, Emily is already older than her father on the day of his auto-cremation. To honour his memory and protest against the PATRIOT Act, signed into law on 26 October 2001, three days before the action of the play begins, and against George W. Bush's Global War on Terror, she decides to organise her own terrorist attack on the anniversary of her father's self-burning. To that end, she arranges a meeting with the former secretary of defence, at that point an 85-year-old man. In the play, McNamara calls Morrison's sacrifice an ineffective act performed by a committed egotist. The official, once convinced that cold, mathematical data analysis was sufficient to make decisions about killing,[63] seems unable to escape the trap of history. Emily accuses him that he once had the power to change the course of the conflict, but lacked the fortitude that such an act required. The play seems to imply that although the viewpoint held by Morrison may have seemed deranged, it was not more so than McNamara's calculating methods. The drama stood as an apt illustration of the well-known adage about history moving in circles because of people's inability to

146 Selected contemporary ultimate protests by fire

heed its lessons, a precept that would prove to be particularly ominous in the face of 9/11 and the run-up to the war in Iraq.

Impotent decency? On Peter Brook's theatre performance US and his semi-documentary Tell Me Lies

The doubts that shook Robert McNamara bring to mind the uncertainty-fraught questions about whether to give or abandon battle that the archetypal Hindu warrior, Arjuna, put to the god Krishna before the legendary clash between the Pandavas and their cousins the Kauravas. The conversation during which the god introduces the despairing archer to the *dharma*, the righteousness supposed to keep life in balance, makes up the best-known, central fragment of the classic Hindu epic, the *Mahābhārata*. It was during the war in Vietnam, when he was working on the performance *US*, an attempt at a diagnosis of British society in the light of the conflict raging in Indochina, that Peter Brook first heard of the famous epic (Brook 160).[64] When critics denounced his effort as merely a useless gesture, he asked them to consider what would happen if an American general commanding troops in the Pacific theatre of war asked himself the same question Arjuna had in *Bhagavad Gītā*: "Should I fight?" (Hunt and Reeves 96).

Self-burning, including the immolation of Norman Morrison, was a central theme in both the 1966 play *US* and the film *Tell Me Lies*, shot the following year and extensively alluding to the theatre piece.[65]

In late 1965, soon after the incident outside the Pentagon, the British director, along with his collaborators from the RSC, decided to tackle the subject of Vietnam, because – as Brook wrote in his text *U.S. Means You, U.S. Means Us* – it "was more powerful, more acute, more insistent a situation than any drama that already existed between covers" (61). As a result of the 15-week-long search held in the summer 1966, involving experimental explorations and rehearsals during which British performers had the opportunity to collaborate with remarkable theatre artists, such as Joseph Chaikin of New York City's Open Theatre, as well as Jerzy Grotowski and Ryszard Cieślak of Wrocław's Laboratory Theatre, the company produced *US*, a three-hour-long, two-part performance which premiered at London's Aldwych Theatre on 13 October 1966.

The play was supposed to make the audience aware that the tragedy of war reached far beyond Indochina, and its significance transcended the plain fact that US combat operations overseas burned people alive. The tragedy also lay in the eagerness of people in peaceful, Western democracies to drown that horror out. The director wished to puncture that purely documentary veneer, the facade of facts that the media outlets covering the first televised war were so keen to plaster the viewers with. Developing the means to penetrate the shell of the audience's indifference, to reach their consciences despite their individual sensibilities being numb from constant exposure to images of horror, was absolutely key here, all the more because, as argued by Grotowski – whom Brook deeply admired and eventually befriended – "The public does not like to be taxed by problems. It is much easier for the spectator to find in the play what he already knows" (241–242). In other words, the British director dreamed of a theatre that would allow both its performers and its audience to *confront* the horror of war, that would encourage them to determine their own personal standpoint on the issues at hand, hopefully followed by a more proactive attitude and greater political involvement. This was what Brook himself had done, when he joined renowned British artists such as John Arden, Jonathan Miller, Harold Pinter, or Vanessa Redgrave in supporting the anti-war *Angry Arts Week*, held at the London Roundhouse from 27 June to 2 July 1967, which included poetry readings, live music performances, film screenings, debates, and symposiums. Brook was not interested in theatre that would engage in political agitation or propaganda, but one that would foster civic attitudes, thus confirming its utility as an instrument of raising public awareness and – possibly – encouraging activism.

Before Brook, no one in English mainstream theatre had really tried to explore current political affairs so openly; neither had anybody tried to produce a performance in such a collective manner. The play was indeed a joint effort,[66] but the decision to make it so was not entirely voluntary – it was partially forced by the dearth of dramatic texts dealing with the war in Vietnam. Furthermore, Brook, as no other director at the time, was capable of injecting the experiences of European and American avant-garde theatre into the mainstream, availing himself of emerging artistic ideas and practices, such as happenings, in this endeavour.

In her analysis of the performance text, published in book form in 1968, Lena Petrović indicated that the play had two key themes, which were closely intertwined: one was flight – a metaphorical attempt to soar above one's own prejudices, thought patterns, and formulaic behaviours, while the other was self-immolation, conceived here as the ultimate, profoundly radical exemplification of involvement. The scholar noted that it was Brook's interrogation of the motives driving such a liminal act, as well as audience's capability to understand such a dramatic sacrifice that made fire and its symbolic uses a central theme of the performance – embodied here by napalm, the charred bodies of Vietnamese victims, the flames engulfing those who decided to burn themselves in protest, as well as "the inner burning of total involvement that Brook worked to ignite in his actors, the sparks hopefully catching the audience" (125). This is where the workshop Grotowski and Cieślak ran for the theatre company proved so crucial. After all, the motif of sacrifice played a key part in subsequent Laboratory Theatre productions, while both personal confrontation with edge experiences and the search for one's own answers to deeply existential questions stemming from the theme tackled by a given play were cornerstones of working with actors in Grotowski's poor theatre. This is also why the cast of *US* appeared on stage in everyday clothes

148   Selected contemporary ultimate protests by fire

and – in accordance with the countercultural spirit of the times – under their own names.

In the play, the subject of self-burning is brought up three times. First in the opening, when the story reenacts Thích Quảng Đức'a act and sets the tone for the performance. Secondly, the first part concludes with the reenactment of Norman Morrison's self-sacrifice. The final appearance of the theme is in the conversation of a young man intent on following Đức's and Morrison's examples with a radical who has lost her faith in the effectiveness of protest and called for revolution instead.

The scene in the first part features a huge effigy of a US marine with a rocket in his abdomen and dolls made up like Vietnamese children stuck in his eye sockets. Below him is a heap of junk, out of which one of the actors slowly pulls a piece of yellow fabric, while three others are rummaging through the clutter in search of petrol cans. Glenda Jackson brings in a wig and garments that are supposed to make her look like Madame Nhu. Then, Mike Pratt climbs onto the stage and the six actors freeze, as if in anticipation. Soon afterwards, the remaining performers join the six already on stage and together they begin quietly chanting a song about Icarus, the caterpillar who will never get to become a butterfly and soar if he continues to embrace pragmatism and seeks nothing beyond a comfortable life that does not demand any commitment. After the song, Mike declares: "Saigon is the only city in the world where the garbage stands uncollected on the street corners and they burn people," while Clifford (Rose) adds: "There have been so many assassinations that people are afraid. They do not raise their voices. They prefer to say nothing. When we burn ourselves, it is the only way we can speak" (qtd. in Hunt et al. 33). He then moves forward and sits down, while Henry (Woolf) mimes dousing him with kerosene. Upon seeing Clifford give a nod, Henry lights a match and the rest freezes in expectation. Then they all begin chanting another song, with the lyrics taken from Adrian Mitchell's *To Whom It May Concern*:

> I was run over by truth one day.
> Ever since the accident I've walked this way.
> So stick my legs in plaster
> Tell me lies about Vietnam. (qtd. in Potter)

Passages from the poem would appear throughout the play, providing an ironic commentary on further attempts to break the vicious circle of illusions. This opening sequence well illustrates the poetics that Brook chose, patching together a number of genres into a heterogeneous drama drawing on a variety of different media (including text, performance, song, and documentary materials), capable of switching moods in a heartbeat, like in a genuine revue. In accordance with Brechtian principles, individual sections of *US* were punctuated with ironic songs and other interludes that undermined the scenic illusion. The gallows humour, meanwhile, was supposed to help viewers sit through the play's more violent passages.

After the abridged and metaphorical lecture on Vietnamese history, the American use of torture, and the superpower's duplicitous policies in Indochina, the play segued mid-first act into a sequence which served to illustrate how protest, disobedience, and dissent all stand as testament to human determination and creativity, although few ultimately embrace these, as most fear going against the immense power of the state. The segment, *Moon over Minnesota*, drew on actual events that took place in early 1966 in Big Lake, where a 19-year-old draftee by the name of Barry Bondhus vandalised his local draft board office, for which he was sentenced to 18 months in jail and fined 2,500 USD. First, he defaced his draft forms by writing "Earth" and "Human" in the "Place of birth" and "Nationality" fields, and later broke into the office and poured two buckets of human faeces into a filing cabinet containing enlistment papers. Then he patiently waited to be arrested, and was promptly tried and sentenced. He left prison in March 1968. It is generally believed that his subversive act – jokingly referred to as a shit-in,[67] a reference to popular sit-ins and teach-ins – brought much needed public attention to similar acts of obstructing the draft. In Brook's drama, the story of the rebellious youngster played out primarily through song, eventually enshrining Bondhus among America's premier artists-outsiders, rebels, and thinkers, and putting him in league with the likes of Allen Ginsberg, James Baldwin, Mark Twain, or Walt Whitman (Hunt and Reeves 117).

It is with this lighthearted story that Morrison's self-burning was juxtaposed in Brook's performance. In the reenactment, Bob Lloyd goes out to the frontstage, then picks up a real petrol can to mime dousing himself with kerosene and setting himself aflame. He writhes and slowly collapses to the ground, with lips wide open and clasped hands raised up over his eyes. As he goes still, a pause ensues, followed by an announcement over the PA system about the man's immolation and death. Throughout, Bob remains motionless on the floor, while the rest of the cast sit in a semi-circle behind him. After another brief pause, the performers then begin quoting from Quakers who stood vigil for Morrison after his death, including from Anne Morrison. They paint a portrait of a man who was neither a fanatic nor an eccentric, but a happy husband and father, for whom love stood as the supreme value. "And although love has become a trite concept that grown men are embarrassed to speak about, it is a radical idea, perhaps the most truly radical idea of the human race" (qtd. in Hunt et al. 108).

This scene was later referred to in the second act, performed on a nearly empty stage, which revolved around the clash of two different standpoints. Mark (Jones) is preparing to perform a self-burning on the steps of the American Embassy in London, which he wants to carry out while holding a letter containing an appeal for peace. Dissuading him from his plans is Glenda (Jackson), who questions the validity of his protest, claiming that in such an indifferent, cynical world, his self-immolation would translate into nothing more than a couple of cheques sent to charities by people wishing to assuage their consciences. Then she goes on to argue that blocking the streets and throwing the city into chaos will be a much more efficient strategy. Mark, in turn, replies that "somewhere, someone" has to feel the same way he does, and claims that one has to transcend arguments rooted in reason and calculations, as the war in Vietnam is a "reasonable war," run by "statisticians, physicists, economists, historians, psychiatrists, mathematicians, experts on everything, theorists from everywhere," which means that "Even the atrocities" could be "justified by logic" (qtd. in Brook 209). Mark's disquisition suggested that in order to find a way out of the quagmire that the war in Vietnam had become, the world had to reject hedonistic egoism and instead seek out the suffering Other.

Glenda develops the diagnosis further and describes a reverse process which she sees in British adolescents, whose youthful love of Mahler and Dostoyevsky gradually is supplanted by typical pursuits of bourgeois leftist theatre lovers, afraid of expressing their own views (Petrović 130). The war, she goes on, is impossible to disentangle from, as many wish to see it continue, if not in Vietnam then maybe in "Thailand, Chile, Alabama." All they have to do is reach for the endless supplies of martial paraphernalia that seem to be commonly available. In order for true change to come, the girl argues, a revolution is necessary, a fire to cleanse the minds and transform the human consciousness, as new life can begin only in the ruins of our old homes and our old tongues. Glenda believes that only forcing people to face their own mortality could return them to their primordial vulnerability and existential qualities. In the finale, she cries that it is her dream for the war in Indochina to spill across the globe, for the fire to reach the shores of Britain and lay bare the true face of its hypocritical society. Brook, however, left it to the audience to decide which of the two positions (or both) should be considered ineffective and futile.

In the next scene, which was the finale, the play brought together – literally and figuratively – fire and flight, its two dominant themes. Holding a small table and a black box in his gloved hands, Bob Lloyd walks out onto the proscenium. Like a stage magician, he opens the box to release two butterflies, and then pulls out a lighter to set the wings of the third insect aflame (the last one was made of paper, a fact which the audience was unaware of). The remaining actors freeze and begin staring out at the audience, holding their gaze up until the theatre emptied out completely.

Geoffrey Reeves pointed out that throughout its six-month run, all 50 performances of the play put on in exactly the same form because any and all changes forced the authors to seek reauthorisation from the censors at the Lord Chamberlain's Office (censorship was abolished in the UK only in 1968) were fully sold out. Some performances ended with thunderous ovation, but most were met with scant applause, as they left the audiences in a state of silent reverie. In a handful of instances, some viewers stayed behind in the theatre and began openly discussing the war. One time, a middle-aged woman stormed the scene to prevent Lloyd from setting the butterfly on fire, saying that something could indeed be done. The same thing happened with two Quakers, who purchased front-row seats for their second viewing in order to prevent what they saw as another butterfly dying (Hunt and Reeves 112). Brook later admitted that the play would have been much more impactful had it been put on only once, and thus indeed become a happening. Some decidedly unfavourable reviews notwithstanding, the play seemed to have hit a nerve with what was at the time, it should be noted, a mostly middle-class audience (Sulik 206).

In Peter Whitehead's little known 1967 documentary *Benefit of the Doubt*, which featured footage from the performance itself, Brook can be found explaining his own motives and responding to what some saw as a thread of explicit anti-Americanism running through his play:

> For us to take the illusory position of saying: "We in England are not American, we have nothing to do with America therefore we can judge" to me is evasive and hopelessly naïve. We are in no position to dissociate ourselves ... from America, and turn America into *them* that we can then label and dismiss. That *them* is ourselves and it's from there that came this ambiguous, double-sided title *US*.

The notion was further elucidated in the performance, which clearly suggested that the US can by no means be a monolith if they gave birth to people such as Bondhus and Morrison.

This attitude was further emphasised by the pacifist film *Tell Me Lies*, which – according to its opening sequence – is a story "of London." Produced in summer 1967, the film featured numerous allusions to his play's ideological elements, included many of the songs by Adrian Mitchell and Richard Peaslee, and even boasted much of the same cast. As private and state production companies refused to underwrite his film for fear of financing a propaganda piece, the director himself managed to secure the necessary funding from 70 middle-class Americans who decided that the film should be produced (Trewin 161–162). The picture was released on 12 February 1968 in New York and later in London, but aside from a couple of scathing reviews it was mostly ignored by critics (Trewin 159–162). The only text to feature a more measured opinion was Bolesław Sulik's *Search for Commitment* published in *The Tribune*. The film fell victim to the circumstances of its release. It was supposed to be shown at the 1968 Cannes Film Festival, but the festival was called off in a gesture of solidarity with striking French workers and students. Following a screening at the Venice Film Festival in autumn 1968, the film disappeared. After the negatives were found years later in the British Film Institute's archives, the picture was digitally restored in 2012 – with Brook overseeing the process – and given a new lease on life, so to speak.

152 Selected contemporary ultimate protests by fire

As keenly pointed out by Scott MacKenzie in his insightful 2009 text *Atrocities at the Door* (published before Brook's fifth cinematic effort entered wide distribution), *Tell Me Lies* has lost very little relevancy over the years. The reasons are twofold. First, its use of vaguely Brechtian self-reflexive tropes that both push genre norms and suspend the scenic illusion situates the picture squarely alongside postmodernist aesthetics, typical of concepts such as pastiche, irony, and self-reference, crucial in contemporary strategies of representation. The second reason, the more important of the two in my opinion, is the fact that the film tackles a problem that we still deal with today – the rise of pervasive indifference, powerlessness, and cynicism, driven, among other factors, by the veritable flood of horrific imagery produced by the culture of voyeurism, of which Susan Sontag wrote in *Regarding the Pain of Others*, that it converts the news into entertainment (85). Soon after the premiere, Brook brought up the words of American journalist and political commentator Murray Kempton, who believed that the situation in Vietnam at the time was "more indecent than the concentration camps ... Because this time everyone sees it, everyone knows" (210). In his film, the director developed that diagnosis even further, touching upon the *pornographisation* of gaze, a concept which implies that the eagerness with which shocking, vile imagery of real–life warfare, distributed by the media and other official outlets, is consumed, is inversely proportional to the consumer's proximity towards said conflict.

The film is bookended by the picture of a Vietnamese mother holding a baby wrapped head to toe in bandages covering extensive napalm burns. In both appearances, the picture is shown by Mark (Jones) to his friend Bob (Lloyd), as the former ponders how long one can look at a picture like that with genuine interest. Early in the film, the photograph turns out to be a freeze-frame that suddenly "comes to life," lending further gravity to the situation, but moving images soon lose their power too, when endlessly recycled by television broadcasts. That is why, near the end of the film, Mark asks whether the reaction would have been any different had the figures in the picture entered the room in person. The frame then freezes on the door and slowly fades to white, an equivalent of the silence that enveloped the audience after the play ended, opening up a space in which individual choices of each viewer could be interrogated.

Between those bookends, the film examines what Bolesław Sulik called the "search for a meaningful commitment" (206). Faced with abhorrent facts and statistics, and even more horrifying imagery, young, left-leaning Brits – Mark, his partner Pauline (Munro), and their friend Bob – set out to find a role for themselves that would allow them to meaningfully react to the painful reality around them. Bob believes that the only difference they can make is by injecting Vietnam into people's lives in a way that would encourage them to read activist literature and listen to voices others than those pumped out by the mainstream. He even ponders engaging in a sabotage attempt that would insert a subliminal message – the word "Vietnam" in block letters – into TV broadcasts and cinema screenings.

As I already pointed out, *Tell Me Lies* described itself as a film about London – and rightly so, as the film is firmly embedded in the city, both in its ideology and in its production. Pauline and Mark roam the English capital, joining protest marches and rallies, seeing anti-war dramas in the theatre, listening to famous actors read poetry at the *Angry Arts Week*, engaging in meaningful debates. During a brief exchange between Mark and Paul Scofield on the meaning and the feasibility of protest, Brook's own King Lear launches into a polemic, rife with noble and righteous phrases, about putting pressure on the ruling powers. Compared against the sheer brutality of the war, however, the words ring hollow and Mark remains sceptical. Although he initially seems convinced by an activist (Glenda Jackson) speaking at Trafalgar Square, who quotes from Che Guevara on the necessity of waging international war against the forces of US imperialism, he quickly changes his mind and, seeing a protest outside the American embassy, finally reveals that mass movements terrify him. Brook offers ironic commentary on these typical Western quandaries by quoting from Chairman Mao, whose *Little Red Book* Glenda is reading aloud, with her mouth right next to the ear of the sleeping Mark: "The intellectuals often tend to be subjective and individualistic, impractical in their thinking and irresolute in action, until they throw themselves heart and soul into mass revolutionary struggles."

The protagonists then attempt, without much success, to deliver an anti-war petition to George Brown, the Foreign Secretary, and later try to phone him. In Brook's film, efforts like these – much like the earlier conversation with Scofield – occupy the intersection of documentary and feature film, abiding by the film's own internal logic, resulting in a genre that the film itself calls, in one of many self-referential sequences, a *semi-documentary*. The broad array of attitudes and ideologies presented by the picture, ranging from honest civic engagement with Guevara's and Mao's notions of revolution, is then rounded out with statements from Labour MPs: Thomas Driberg, Reginald Paget, Ivor Richard, as well as from novelist Kingsley Amis and deputy editor of *The Sunday Telegraph* Peregrine Worsthorne, recorded at an impromptu cocktail party arranged by Brook. It turns out, however, that Mark and Pauline's conversations with members of the political and cultural elites, filmed *cinéma vérité*-style, contain nothing but platitudes about the supposed threat of Communist invasion and the necessity of protecting the liberal world order. The politicians all seem convinced that American withdrawal from Vietnam would result in further bloodshed on an even larger scale and continue to bicker whether the UK should also send troops to Southeast Asia in order to buttress the credibility of the transatlantic alliance. They fail to show any interest in the moral aspect of the conflict and are unwilling to contemplate its underlying causes.

154 Selected contemporary ultimate protests by fire

Their comments are then juxtaposed with the voices of two American Black Power supporters, again shot *cinéma vérité*-style, astonishingly, at the same party. The remarks offered by Stokely Carmichael, one of the leaders of the Civil Rights Movement in the US, that "white violence has bred colored violence" and that peace can only be achieved through unconditional equality and freedom for the oppressed, seem too dogmatic to Mark, if otherwise correct. The voice of the young Vietnamese woman, Jacqueline (Porcher), also seems to evince the notion that there are simply no easy ways out of the quagmire and that wishing for peace alone seems facile and dangerously naïve.

After taking stock of all these positions, Brook then quotes the notorious fragment of the reenacted self-burning from *Mondo cane 2*. It is difficult to say whether the director knew the scene was an elaborate deception, but what ultimately matters is the profound impact the recording has on Mark and Pauline, and the realisation that their spectrum of possible reactions to the war in Vietnam lacked this one response – the most personal and radical of them all. After seeing the film, Mark visits the local Buddhist *sangha* and asks its head what his reaction would be if he were to sacrifice his life for the cause of the Vietnamese nation. Upon hearing the offer, the monk gently dissuades him from the idea, saying that he should seek other ways to help, and annihilate or set alight only his own greed, ill will, and illusions.

Yes, we seem to hear Mark think, but Norman Morrison has nevertheless sacrificed himself in a gesture of solidarity with the Vietnamese. Staged in a faux *cinéma vérité* aesthetic, the Quaker's meal with his family and subsequent self-burning on the steps of the Pentagon (the American Embassy in Grosvenor Square standing in for the Washington landmark) give cause for a closer look at the condition of the American society. The black-and-white Morrison flashback sequence, which cuts away just as he flicks on the lighter, is followed by another scene, filmed in full colour, in which a group of Americans discuss his act and whether it had any impact, and if so, what kind of impact and on what. Anne Morrison, her words uttered by Pauline, is the first to speak. The Quaker's widow recounts that it took her 18 months after her husband's death to find the strength to visit the Pentagon (accompanied by Emily and a friend and her two children). As they were leaving the building through the inner courtyard during lunch hour, Anne was struck by how bizarre it was to see smiling, happy people inside a building which issued orders to kill around the clock. Morrison's sacrifice, we hear a young man say, failed to change anything because the US government is unwilling to hear those who speak truth to power. The only thing that sways Americans, a young woman adds, is the death of their sons, husbands, and brothers. But even those deaths usually reaffirm them in their support for the war, because otherwise their loved ones would have died in vain. A middle-aged man then reveals that Morrison's death inspired him to reflect on American society in general and how Americans should accept that this notion of an America of great ideals is a thing of the past.

The film explores many different faces of the US: it combines authentic statements from American military and Senate Foreign Relations Committee officials pondering a nuclear strike on China, a quote from Malcolm Browne's *The New Face of War* on the use of torture by US troops, and an excerpt from a conversation with a helicopter pilot, whose job in the war is to ferry captured Việt Cộng, and who continues to emphasise the amount of good that America did for the Republic of Vietnam. Alongside the rather lighthearted tale of Barry Bondhus, the film also features a lively comedy sketch called *1,001 Ways to Beat the Draft*. Morrison's sacrifice, therefore, is but one possible position of many available within the breadth of American public life.

But to the young Brit, it must have been an object of morbid fascination or obsession, as later in the film we see Mark dreaming about himself setting fire to the American Embassy (with the catchy tune *Flame, Flame, God is Flame* playing in the background). Bolesław Sulik wrote that:

> The representation of true commitment is a horribly magnificent image of self-immolation of a Buddhist monk; Norman Morrison's imitative self sacrifice ... already appears to us a somewhat forced act, less real; an English attempt to follow seems pathetically irrelevant. (207)

The film also made short work of rebel attitudes by demonstrating that revolution rarely solves fundamental dilemmas, such as choosing how to take action or how to reconcile oneself with death and mortality. Brook himself did not offer any solutions. The film was bitter, laying bare people's general powerlessness and portraying middle-class decency "as impotent in the face of an issue like Vietnam" (Sulik 207). And indeed it was doubly bitter, as its many ironic, self-skewering interludes often exposed the manifold traps that lay in wait for the unwary politically involved artist. In one of these interludes, Marjie Lawrence introduced herself and spoke a little about the fun that the cast was having shooting the film.

When critics of *US* disputed whether theatre should ever tackle the subject of war since art was ultimately powerless to change its course, Brook replied that he himself harboured no illusions about that (208). Nevertheless, his work was a testament to his belief in the role of art as a space in which to hold individual and personal confrontations with uncomfortable and painful truths. When viewed decades after its initial release, Brook's film does not feel like an unearthed treasure of the past, but rather a meditation on some very contemporary problems, particularly relevant to viewers attuned to unearned suffering across the globe. It raises issues that artists continue to see as important, especially those who ponder whether using art as a primary means of assistance to victims of war, rather than relying on direct relief or financial help, is indeed the sensible choice in the light of the brutal realities of proxy wars, the Syrian conflict chief among them.

Notes

1 The word *thích* implies we are dealing with a monk. The term derives from *thích ca* or *thích già*, an honorific indicating that the bearer descends from the Shakya, the clan to which the founder of Buddhism, Shaykamuni (Siddhārtha Gautama), belonged. The phrase *thích nữ* implies the bearer is a Buddhist nun.

2 The picture is one of two images of self-burning that continue to dominate the collective imagination on the subject. Another photo of the immolation, depicting a later moment of the incident, was named 1963 World Press Photo of the Year. A year later, Browne received the Pulitzer Prize (jointly with *The New York Times* journalist David Halberstam) for his Vietnam reporting. The following year, Browne published *The New Face of War*, featuring the influential photo on the cover.

3 It bears noting that no Nobel Peace Prize was awarded in 1967, with the Nobel Committee claiming that King's letter, in which he named a potential candidate, was a violation of Academy protocol, and one of the reasons behind the Committee's decision.

4 The writer first unveiled the poem to the public in 1964, at an anti-nuclear demonstration in London, during which protesters clashed with police in Trafalgar Square. On 11 June 1964, he read his verses, to a standing ovation, at the International Poetry Incarnation, a famous gathering of Beatniks held at the Royal Albert Hall. The event, featuring appearances from poets from 20 countries – including Beat icon Allen Ginsberg – managed to draw an audience of 7,000 and emerged as a seminal moment in the history of British underground art. The event was filmed by Peter Whitehead (*Wholly Communion*, 1965), who later shot *Benefit of the Doubt* (1967), an hour long film documenting the creative process behind *US*. Mitchell kept updating his poem as years passed, adding new verses about further US military interventions.

5 A different take was offered by James Harding, to whom *US* "was a kind of aggrandized appropriation that subordinated Thích Quảng Đức's to the operative values of Western experimental theatre" (47).

6 Some press reports said that the monk was 73 at the time of the incident. However, the date of birth on the monument erected next to the site of the self-burning suggests that he was seven years younger.

7 Stanley Karnow recalled (297) that a student of Buddhism told him about another monk who offered to sacrifice his life, but Đức supposedly claimed that seniority gave him precedence.

8 The authorities initially planned to charge the two monks who assisted Quảng Đức in his preparations with murder, but abandoned the idea in fear of exacerbating already strained tensions (Keefer and Smith, no. 169).

9 Marjorie Hope met with the monks from the Từ Đàm Pagoda in Huế in Central Vietnam in November 1963, where 71-year-old Thích Tiêu Diêu had set himself alight only three months earlier. She recounted hearing that the Buddhist hierarchs "silently" consented to the elderly monk's sacrifice, but resisted when younger people wanted to follow his example (154).

10 There is extensive literature available on the subject. See, among others, Chanoff and Doan; Demery; Dommen; Jacobs; Joiner; Jones; Karnow; Miller, E.; Miller, W.; Shaw; Topmiller. Documents detailing American foreign policy in Vietnam in 1963 are available online (Keefer; Keefer and Smith).

11 Accounts of the event feature contradictory information as to the location from which the procession set out. My presumption that it launched from the Ấn Quang temple was informed by the signage seen above the car that brought Đức to the site. The car itself was preserved and converted into a museum exhibit and is currently on display at the Thien Mu Pagoda complex in Huế.

12 The journalists were aware that the monks were using them as additional cover for their own actions, as their presence was a guarantee that police brutality would be kept in check. As self-immolations continued across Vietnam, foreign correspondents grew more sympathetic in their depiction of the Buddhists, as evinced by the words of journalistic stalwart and Diệm sympathiser Marguerite Higgins: "What was President Ngô Đình Diệm doing to cause these Buddhists to choose such a horrible death as self-immolation? ... The fact that [this question] presumed *a priori* the guilt of Diệm bothered me not at all" (2–3).

13 The issue, as it pertained to Browne's photographs, was discussed by Susan Sontag in *On Photography*: "Photographing is essentially an act of non-intervention. ... To take a picture is to ... be in complicity with whatever makes a subject interesting, worth photographing – including, when that is the interest, another person's pain or misfortune" (11, 12).

14 Although Catholicism was introduced to Vietnam by missionaries in the 16th century, it was the French who helped it flourish.

15 The temple was built at the site of an apparition of the Virgin Mary which reportedly took place in 1798, a period of intense persecution of Catholics in Vietnam.

16 It bears noting that although the reform-minded Second Vatican Council (1962–65) was still in session at the time, no official position of the Catholic Church on Hinduism, Buddhism, Islam, and Judaism has yet been decreed. Rome's turn towards establishing dialogue with other faiths was finally codified in the *Nostra Aetate* (*In Our Time*) declaration, promulgated on 28 October 1965.

17 Aside from the more prominent figures, the clan also included Diệm's two younger brothers, Cẩn and Luyện (the eldest of the six, Khôi, was killed by Hồ Chí Minh's troops in 1945). Cẩn ruled over Annam as a dictator, while Luyện served as ambassador to Great Britain. A key role in the regime was also played by Nhu's wife, Catholic convert and descendant of North Vietnamese aristocracy, Trần Lệ Xuân, generally considered the Republic's first lady as Diệm died a bachelor. She was widely known for her uncompromising stance on Buddhists, and for her striking looks.

18 Some continue to speculate that the incident was instigated by the Communists or CIA agents, who wanted to precipitate the fall of Diệm and his unpopular regime by provoking the Buddhist community into entering the political arena.

19 The country was mired in nepotism and corruption, with the populace kept in check through widespread terror. As a result, a group of ARVN officers made two unsuccessful attempts on his life (in 1960 and 1962).

20 This particular interpretation is best illustrated by Peter Hopkins' 1964 satirical painting *Ambassador of Good Will*. In the foreground, the picture shows a Buddhist monk dousing himself with kerosene, overshadowed by foreign officials sitting in a rickshaw pulled by two exhausted coolies.

21 The subject was explored earlier – in 1960 – by remarkable French sinologist Jacques Gernet. It bears noting here that Vietnam has been a part of China's sphere of political and cultural influence for centuries.

22 History knows instances of children feeding slices of their own flesh to parents in times of famine (Yu 62–88).

23 It is possible that the monk was not invoking the efforts of his distant forerunners, but referring instead to events of a more recent past, as, to quote Hammer: "In 1948 in the Chinese city of Harbin, one bonze had resorted to self-immolation ... apparently to protest the treatment of Buddhists by the Chinese Communists" (146). Biggs contended that "Entering the monastery as a young boy early in the

158   Selected contemporary ultimate protests by fire

20th century, he [Đức] would also have known of monastic suicides by fire in French Indochina in the 1920s and 1930s" ("How" 416).

24   This point was stressed by Huế monks that Hope spoke with in late 1963, as well as Nhất Hạnh in his letter *In Search of the Enemy of Man*. Some monks, however, rejected self-immolation as they believed it to be a violation of their doctrine (Topmiller, "Struggling" 145). Buddhist Sallie King argued that the act was stuck in a strange limbo between being embraced and rejected, as it affirmed the immolators' will to help their fellow man, but could not be recommended to anyone in good faith (144).

25   These delays grew as tensions kept rising and were accompanied by increased scrutiny from law enforcement. Journalists routinely reported being followed and having their communications tapped, while some were even expelled from the country on Madame Nhu's orders.

26   Contrary to popular opinion, Browne's photos were not immediately published on the front pages of every newspaper across America. The 12 June 1963 edition of *The New York Times* ran a piece by David Halberstam, *Diem Asks Peace in Religion Crisis*, on page three, and accompanied it with a photograph of monks blocking a fire engine from moving down the street. *Life* magazine reported on the self-immolation with a three-paragraph piece illustrated with three photographs – but did so only on 21 June. As explained by Yang, "Resistance to such images came from some senior news editors in the United States who often 'altered or killed stories that criticized the establishment opinion'" (7). In the early days of American involvement in Southeast Asia, photo editors still shied away from using pictures that did not sanitise the horror of war, and the publication of Browne's photos of Thích Quảng Đức's act marked an important watershed moment.

27   In this context, it should be noted that the 27 June and 15 September 1963 editions of *The New York Times* included full-page advertisements sponsored by influential American ministers from the newly established Ministers' Vietnam Committee, in which they called on President Kennedy to reconsider his support for the South Vietnamese regime (Jones 295). The demands, capped with the headline "We, too, protest," were accompanied by the notorious photo of the burning monk – considered proof that widespread reports of the regime's brutality were true. The ad in the 15 September edition also claimed that 17,000 clergymen from across the US had joined the protest (Yang 17).

28   In her insightful study of the two most famous photographs, Yang pointed out the considerable differences between them. The first one depicts the monk's final moments before death, and its impact derives from the tension between (false) hope and what we know to be inevitable (13), whereas the other captures the moment when death becomes "palpable," which can, for some people, be an impulse prompting them to action (16).

29   Cẩn was tried by a military tribunal and executed on 9 May 1964. The coup was survived by Luyện and Archbishop Thục, who at the time was away in Rome, attending a session of the Second Vatican Council.

30   The 5 October self-immolation of 37-year-old Thích Quảng Hương was followed on 27 October by the self-incineration of 23-year-old Thích Thiện Mỹ, the latter performed in a highly symbolic location – the square outside a Roman Catholic cathedral.

31   This is also how the incident was portrayed in Philip Roth's 1997 novel, *American Pastoral*. Seen on TV, the self-immolation becomes a turning point in the life of the 11-year-old Merry. Ewan McGregor's 2016 film adaptation of the novel also borrows the Italian film's reenactment of the incident.

A lotus in a sea of fire   159

32 The self-immolation of Thích Quảng Hương was also captured on film, but the camera used to shoot the footage was quickly confiscated from the American journalist by the police (Biggs, "Self-Immolation" 147).

33 Furthermore, the police attempted to extinguish the flames engulfing Mỹ, as evinced by a handful of photos taken during the incident. The footage documenting this self-burning was featured in Ingmar Bergman's *Persona* (1966) and later appeared in a number of TV programmes and documentaries (including Clay Claiborne's suggestive 2007 piece *Vietnam: American Holocaust*). The CBS News special *Death of a Regime*, broadcast shortly after the coup that brought down Diệm, also featured a portion of the footage, but used a different fragment of it than *Persona*, showing the incident from another angle.

34 As rightly pointed out by Harding, "Whereas the image presented by Artaud is one of forcibly bringing heretics back to the mainstream of the Church, Thích Quảng Đức's self-immolation is apocryphal and unorthodox, breaking with and remaining outside of the mainstream of Buddhist practice" (44). Furthermore, Đức's composure stood in stark contrast to "signaling through the flames" (Harding 44).

35 Nora Alter pointed out ("Vietnamese" 10) that several 1960s plays included self-immolation as a key motif, including Armand Gatti's *V comme Vietnam* (*V for Vietnam*), André Benedetto's *Napalm* (both 1967), and Günter Grass' *Max* (1969). The Open Theatre's Off-Off Broadway production of *Viet Rock* (1966) alluded to it, while James Rado and Gerome Ragni lampooned self-burning in their Broadway musical *Hair* (1967) (Harding 46). Later on, the theme also appeared in *How I Got That Story* by Amlin Gray (1979).

36 If the shot showing the monk with burns on his face was to be used – as, for example, the Canadian band Delerium has on the cover of its 1999 album *Faces, Forms & Illusions* – designers or editors have usually used either only the silhouette of the burning figure or other means to alleviate the horror that the photograph exuded.

37 One of the photos of Quảng Hương taken during his self-incineration was also repeatedly reworked and used as a template by painters and graphic designers.

38 One featured a burning chimpanzee seated in a distinctive pensive pose, revealing a play on both words ("The Burning Monk(ey)") and the iconic image.

39 Later on, Banksy created his own original piece that drew on Browne's iconic photo. The piece includes the words "Made in China. Tibet," indicating that the artist wanted to draw public attention to the wave of protest self-burnings that swept the Roof of the World.

40 Marker co-wrote the screenplay with Jean-Luc Godard, wrote commentary, and edited the film, while the association he co-founded, Société pour le lancement des œuvres nouvelles S.L.O.N. (The Society for Launching New Works), co-produced the 115-minute-long collaborative piece.

41 Resnais' authorship was established by scholars rather than by the film itself, as individual sections of the picture – pursuant to the chief principle of collective expression – did not carry any credits.

42 In this case, authorship was easier to establish as the segment opens with a clapperboard featuring Godard's name in the frame.

43 It was indeed read as such in the 1960s by people on the right. It bears noting, however, that the film was pulled from distribution soon after release, in the wake of two cinema bombing attacks.

44 The incident took place exactly two years after the murder of Diệm and his brother Nhu. There is no indication, however, that Morrison made any plans for his self-burning to coincide with the anniversary.

45 That footage was shot probably in early spring 1967, over a year after Morrison's death.

46 The homages Anne Morrison mentions include a sculpture from a series on Vietnam created by Hungarian artist Farkas Aladár. She also brings up a number of poems written by Anglophone authors, including James Bond, Craig Chaffin, Amy Clampitt, David Ferguson, Alexander Laing, Adrian Mitchell, Hugh Ogden, and George Starbuck (85–94).

47 Morrison graduated from a Presbyterian seminary in Pittsburgh with a bachelor's degree in theology in 1959 and joined the Pittsburgh Friends Meeting with his wife. After moving to Baltimore in 1962, he took up the post of executive secretary of the Stony Run Friends Meeting.

48 Three days before his self-incineration, Morrison heard in a meeting that civilian casualties in Vietnam outnumbered military deaths three-to-one (Patler 2).

49 A German Jew, she fled to Switzerland with her daughter Helga after Hitler seized power. From there, they moved to France, where they were detained after the war broke out. In 1942, both left France for the US.

50 As demonstrated by Jon Coburn, Herz's self-burning received widespread attention outside the US, particularly in the Democratic Republic of Vietnam (36–38). The publication of *Phoenix* – a collected volume of Herz's letters and documents edited by Japanese pacifist Shingo Shibata – in Amsterdam (1976) further bolstered her international standing. The anthology also featured a reprint of the only domestic "informative appraisal of her death written by Hayes B. Jacobs for the July-August 1965 issue of *Fact Magazine*" (Coburn 33).

51 Coburn demonstrated that Herz's act challenged standards of acceptable female behaviour and norms of protests binding women activists. He concluded by asserting that her radical anti-imperialism did not suit the "historical perceptions of 1960s women's peace activism as the preserve of housewives and mothers," while "her transnationalism further stymied historical recognition for her protest" (41).

52 Coburn wrote that "Morrison's actions inspired further self-immolators and protest suicides" and listed the followers, including the 24-year-old Celene Jankowski, who set fire to herself on 11 November 1965 in her Indiana home after becoming "despondent over casualty reports from Vietnam" (46).

53 Certain cases reveal that Morrison's self-burning had tremendous potential to inspire change. Brian Willson first heard a song extolling Morrison in 1969, in the home of a local family he came across during his service in Vietnam. Only then did he realise how important the Quaker's sacrifice was for people across the Pacific. The realisation was so powerful, that it spurred him to begin organising protests inside army ranks. After graduating from law school, Willson spent years studying homelessness, suicide, and substance abuse among Vietnam veterans suffering from PTSD and chemical poisoning brought on by exposure to Agent Orange. In 1986, he went to Nicaragua, where he witnessed first-hand the crimes of the Contras, the right-wing rebels trained and supported by the Reagan administration. The experience inspired him to join the anti-war movement. He engaged in hunger strikes and acts of civil disobedience including the 1987 protest at the Concord Naval Weapons Station in California. Protesting arms shipments to Nicaragua and El Salvador, Willson and two other members of the Veterans Peace Action Team sat down on the train tracks to block the passage of a munitions train. As a result, he lost both legs below the knee, suffered a fractured skull and a number of other injuries. In 1992, he published his autobiography, *On Third World Legs*, which he dedicated to Morrison, whose sacrifice forever altered the course of his life (Morrison Welsh 81–84).

54 As explained by Simanti Lahiri, *satyagraha* can be translated as "truth force." The term was "coined by Gandhi during the nationalist movement to describe his particular brand of protest action. Practitioners in the west [sic] have also referred it to as civil disobedience or, less accurately, passive resistance" (Lahiri 285).
55 For example, he marched with King from Selma to Montgomery in March 1965.
56 The dialogue was obviously fiction, as at the time Emily was still an infant. It is possible that the Vietnamese believed her to be older.
57 This personality cult that has sprung up around Morrison in North Vietnam must have been quite robust, if Susan Sontag still found it important enough to mention after coming back from her June to July 1968 controversial trip to Hanoi (*Styles*).
58 People who burned themselves in protest against the war in Vietnam are not officially commemorated in the US. Only George Winne, a history student at the University of California in San Diego, who set himself alight on 10 May 1970, as anti-war sentiments among students were nearing an all-time high, had been given a memorial. It was erected in 2014, on the initiative of Niall Twohig, in Revelle Plaza on the UCSD campus, the site of Winne's self-incineration ("Memory"). Earlier, less than a year after his death, Winne was commemorated by UCSD visual arts professor Michael Todd, who planted an informal eucalyptus grove in his memory with the help of a handful of students. In 2000, a small plaque with information on Winne was installed there. In 1976, the Plaza became home to Virginia Maksymowicz's *Thirty Blocks*, a sculpture composed of bricks arranged to resemble a piece of sidewalk or a public square. On their surface, the slabs carry a burned imprint of a human body and a couple of small objects. Installed without permission, the sculpture was quickly associated with the radical sacrifice of the student even though the artist herself stressed that it was not her intention to illustrate his act ("History"). The sculpture was one of her 'fake fossils,' clay sculptures that Maksymowicz created in hard-to-reach locations across campus and intended to disintegrate over time. *Thirty Blocks* survived, however, and is often taken for a piece of the actual plaza on which the self-immolation took place.
59 This was also how it was portrayed in the 2002 biographical TV film *Path to War*, directed by John Frankenheimer, which featured Victor Slezak as Morrison and Alec Baldwin as McNamara. Available accounts seem to indicate, however, that McNamara had not witnessed the whole incident, but only its finale, including the arrival of the ambulance.
60 This segment appears in lesson number nine, *In Order to Do Good, You May Have to Engage in Evil.*
61 Historians believe that Johnson decided to dismiss McNamara after the secretary issued a series of memos on 1 November 1967, in which he called for an end to the bombing and negotiations with Hanoi (Patler 12). Aside from Morrison's self-immolation, McNamara could have also been swayed by mass anti-war protests in Washington, and the March on the Pentagon, a peace demonstration that drew nearly 50,000 people between 21 and 23 October 1967. The manifestation outside the Department of Defense headquarters was depicted in Chris Marker's 1968 documentary *La sixième face du pentagone* (*The Sixth Side of the Pentagon*). In *Fog of War*, McNamara also acknowledged that he knew he had to change his thinking on Vietnam after he had realised that very few American allies actually helped the US war effort in Vietnam – no assistance was rendered by Japan, West Germany, the UK, or France.
62 Devine's play, which premiered on 21 October 2011, was directed by John Lang. Morrison was played by Evan Frayne, Alexa Devine appeared as Emily, while

Andrew Wheeler portrayed McNamara. The performance used a number of multimedia screens which broadcast a live feed from the stage interspersed with archival footage. *Re:Union* was remounted in Ottawa in 2015, with the author stepping in as director. The play appeared in print in 2013 and was later amended after its revival (Dunn 21).

63 This was a reference to McNamara's work at the Office of Statistical Control during World War II, where he was tasked with evaluating the effectiveness of American bombing campaigns in Asia. The defence secretary was also widely known for using systems analysis in decision-making.

64 After nearly 20 years, Brook finally adapted it for the stage. He would later return to it a number of times, most recently in *Battlefield* (2016).

65 There is extensive literature available on the subject. See, among others, Brook (61–63, 206–211); Helfer and Loney (136–139, 141–144, 177–178); Hunt et al.; Hunt and Reeves (96–120); Kustow (159–171); Trewin (152–162); Williams (73–112).

66 The programme listed the involved artists: Brook oversaw the production and directed the play; Denis Cannan penned the script; Sally Jacobs handled costume design and set decoration; American Richard Peaslee composed the music; Adrian Mitchell wrote the lyrics; David Read managed lighting; Michael Kustow and Michael Scott adapted the documentary material, while Albert Hunt and Geoffrey Reeves served as production assistants. Richard Helfer and Glenn Loney compiled a comprehensive list of all the artists involved in creating both productions (136–137, 141–142).

67 Ben Zimmer wrote that in 1964, activist Saul Alinsky, the author of the seminal manual *Rules for Radicals*, planned to force the Chicago mayor to follow through on his promises to the city's poor by joining up with the Woodlawn Organization to stage mass *shit-ins* and *piss-ins* in Chicago's O'Hare Airport. The plan presumed that activists would occupy all the toilet stalls in the airport, while a rotating crew would keep all the available urinals busy. The protest was ultimately called off as the threat itself was enough to bring city hall officials to the negotiating table. The planned operation closely followed Alinsky's principles for community organisers that he would later compile into his book, including embracing unpredictability and wielding ridicule like a weapon.

References

The online resources identified below were consulted multiple times. All of them were active as of 1 December 2018.

Alinsky, Saul. *Rules for Radicals: A Practical Primer for Realistic Radicals.* Random House, 1971.

Allain, Paul, and Jen Harvie. *The Routledge Companion to Theatre and Performance.* 2nd edition. Routledge, 2014.

Alter, Nora. "Vietnamese Theatre of Resistance: Thich Nhat Hanh's Metaphysical Sortie on the Margins." *Imperialism and Theatre: Essays on World Theatre, Drama, and Performance,* edited by J. Ellen Gainor, Routledge, 1995, pp. 1–18.

———. *Vietnam Protest Theatre: The Television War on Stage.* Indiana UP, 1996.

Artaud, Antonin. *The Theatre and Its Double.* Translated by Mary Caroline Richards, Grove Press, 1958.

Battersby, Lucy. "Under the Influence: Rudd's Work Echoes Banksy." *The Age* [Melbourne], 23 May 2008. www.theage.com.au/entertainment/art-and-design/under-the-influence-rudds-work-echoes-banksy-20080523-ge73y9.html.

Benefit of the Doubt (fragment). Directed by Peter Whitehead, appearances from Peter Brook, Michael Kustow, Glenda Jackson, 1967. *YouTube.* 23 Feb. 2011. www.youtube.com/watch?v=XuDiZPNryW4.

Benn, James. *Burning for the Buddha: Self-Immolation in Chinese Buddhism*, University of Hawai'i Press, 2007.

———. "Multiple Meanings of Buddhist Self-Immolation in China: A Historical Perspective." *Revue d'Etudes Tibétaines*, no. 25, 2012, pp. 203–212.

———. "Where Text Meets Flesh: Burning the Body as an Apocryphal Practice in Chinese Buddhism." *History of Religions*, vol. 37, no. 4, 1998, pp. 295–322.

———. "Written in Flames: Self-Immolation in Sixth Century Sichuan." *T'oung Pao* [Leiden], vol. 92, Fasc. 4–5, 2006, pp. 410–465.

Biggs, Michael. "Dying Without Killing: Self-Immolations, 1963–2002." *Making Sense of Suicide Missions*, edited by Diego Gambetta, Oxford UP, 2005, pp. 173–208.

———. "How Repertories Evolve: The Diffusion of Suicide Protest in the Twentieth Century." *Mobilization: An International Quarterly*, vol. 18, no. 4, 2013, pp. 407–428.

———. "Self-Immolation in Context: 1963-2012." *Revue d'Etudes Tibétaines*, no. 25, 2012, pp. 143–150.

Brook, Peter. *The Shifting Point: Forty Years of Theatrical Exploration, 1946–1987.* Methuen, 1989.

Browne, Malcolm W. *Muddy Boots and Red Socks: A Reporter's Life.* Times Books, 1993.

———. "The Buddhist Protests of 1963." www.pbs.org/weta/reportingamericaatwar/reporters/browne/protests.html. Accessed on 25. Feb. 2019.

———. *The New Face of War.* Bobbs-Merrill, 1965.

———. "The Story Behind the Burning Monk." Interview by Patrick Witty. *Time.* 28 Aug. 2012. time.com/3791176/malcolm-browne-the-story-behind-the-burning-monk/#end.

———. "Viet Nam Reporting: Three Years of Crisis." *Columbia Journalism Review.* 2 Dec. 2012. archives.cjr.org/fiftieth_anniversary/viet_nam_reporting_three_years.php?page=all#DUC.

Chân, Không. *Learning True Love: How I Learned and Practiced Social Change in Vietnam.* Parallax Press, 1993.

Chanoff, David, and Van Toai Doan. *Vietnam: A Portrait of Its People at War.* I.B. Tauris, 2009.

Coburn, Jon. "'I Have Chosen the Flaming Death': The Forgotten Self-Immolation of Alice Herz." *Peace & Change: A Journal of Peace Research*, vol. 43, no. 1, 2018, pp. 32–60.

"Cronkite Interview of JFK." *YouTube.* 8 Nov. 2009. www.youtube.com/watch?v=UM3uaXp8DAk.

DeBenedetti, Charles, and Charles Chatfield. *An American Ordeal: The Antiwar Movement of the Vietnam Era*, Syracuse UP, 1990.

Demery, Monique. *Finding the Dragon Lady: The Mystery of Vietnam's 'Madame Nhu.'* Public Affairs, 2013.

Dommen, Arthur. *The Indochinese Experience of the French and the Americans: Nationalism and Communism in Cambodia, Laos, and Vietnam.* Indiana UP, 2001.

Du Plessix Gray, Francine. "The Ultra-Resistance." *The New York Review of Books*, 25 Sep. 1969. www.nybooks.com/articles/1969/09/25/the-ultra-resistance/. Accessed on 25. Feb. 2019.

Dunn, Katrina. "Andrew Wheeler's Governing Body." *Canadian Theatre Review*, vol. 166, 2016, pp. 21–27.

Ellsberg, Daniel. *Secrets: A Memoir of Vietnam and the Pentagon Papers*. Penguin Books, 2002.

Fierke, Karin. *Political Self-Sacrifice: Agency, Body and Emotion in International Relations*. Cambridge UP, 2013.

Fisher, David. *Albion's Seed: Four British Folkways in America*. Oxford UP, 1989.

Forest, Jim. *Love is the Measure: A Biography of Dorothy Day*. Orbis Books, 1994.

Gernet, Jacques. *Le suicide par le feu chez les bouddhistes chinois du Ve au Xe siècle*. Collège de France, 1960.

Grotowski, Jerzy. *Towards a Poor Theatre*, edited by Eugenio Barba, Routledge, 2002.

Halberstam, David. *The Making of a Quagmire: America and Vietnam during the Kennedy Era*. Revised edition. Rowman and Littlefield, 2008.

Hammer, Ellen. *A Death in November*. E.P. Dutton, 1987.

Harding, James M. "Incendiary Acts and Apocryphal Avant-Gardes: Thích Quảng Đức, Self-Immolation, and Buddhist Spiritual Vanguardism." *Performing Arts Journal*, vol. 38, no. 3, 2016, pp. 31–50.

Hariman, Robert, and John Lucaites. "Dissent and Emotional Management in a Liberal-Democratic Society: The Kent State Iconic Photograph." *Rhetoric Society Quarterly*, vol. 31, no. 3, 2001, pp. 4–31.

Helfer, Richard, and Glenn Loney, editors. *Peter Brook: Oxford to Orghast*. Harwood Academic Publishers, 1998.

Hendrickson, Paul. *The Living and the Dead: Robert McNamara and Five Lives of a Lost War*. Alfred A. Knopf, 1996.

Higgins, Marguerite. *Our Vietnam Nightmare*. Harper and Row, 1965.

"History Set in 'Thirty Blocks' of Clay." *Guardian UCSD*, 28 May 2013. ucsdguardian.org/2013/05/28/history-set-in-%E2%80%9Cthirty-blocks%E2%80%9D-of-clay/.

Hope, Marjorie. "The Reluctant Way: Self-Immolation in Vietnam." *Antioch Review*, vol. 27, no. 2, 1967, pp. 149–163.

Hunt, Albert, and Geoffrey Reeves. *Peter Brook*. Cambridge UP, 1995.

Hunt, Albert et al., editors. *US*. Calder and Boyars, 1968.

Jacobs, Seth. *Cold War Mandarin: Ngo Dinh Diem and the Origins of America's War in Vietnam, 1950–1963*. Rowman and Littlefield, 2006.

Jan, Yün-hua. "Buddhist Self-Immolation in Medieval China." *History of Religions*, vol. 4, no. 2, 1965, pp. 243–268.

Joiner, Charles. "South Vietnam's Buddhist Crisis: Organization for Charity, Dissidence, and Unity." *Asian Survey*, vol. 4, no. 7, 1964, pp. 915–928.

Jones, Howard. *Death of a Generation: How the Assassinations of Diem and JFK Prolonged the Vietnam War*. Oxford UP, 2003.

Karnow, Stanley. *Vietnam: A History*. Revised and updated edition, Viking Penguin, 1991.

Keefer, Edward C., editor. *Foreign Relations of the United States, 1961–1963*, vol. IV, Vietnam, August–December 1963, United States Government Printing Office, 1991.

Keefer, Edward C., and Louis S. Smith, editors. *Foreign Relations of the United States, 1961–1963*, vol. III, Vietnam, January-August 1963, United States Government Printing Office, 1991. No. 146. Telegram from the Embassy in Vietnam to the Department of State. Saigon, 9 Jun. 1963. history.state.gov/historical-documents/frus1961-63v03/d146. No. 169. Telegram from the Embassy in Vietnam to the Department of State. Saigon, 12 Jun. 1963. history.state.gov/historicaldocuments/frus1961-63v03/d169.

King, Martin Luther, Jr. "Nomination of Thich Nhat Hanh for the Nobel Peace Prize." 25 Jan. 1967. www.hartford-hwp.com/archives/45a/025.html.

King, Sallie B. "They Who Burned Themselves for Peace: Quaker and Buddhist Self-Immolators During the Vietnam War." *Buddhist-Christian Studies*, vol. 20, 2000, pp. 127–150.

Kolankiewicz, Leszek. *Święty Artaud* [Saint Artaud]. 2nd edition. Słowo/obraz terytoria, 2001.

Kustow, Michael. *Peter Brook: A Biography*. St. Martin's Press, 2005.

Lahiri, Simanti. *Suicide Protest in South Asia: Consumed by Commitment*. Routledge, 2014.

Loin du Vietnam. Realised by artistic collective: Jean-Luc Godard, Joris Ivens, William Klein, Claude Lelouch, Chris Marker, Alain Resnais, and Agnès Varda, produced by S.L.O.N. and La SOFRA SAS, 1967. *YouTube*. www.youtube.com/watch?v=SBe9CDDbvCo.

MacKenzie, Scott. "Atrocities at the Door: Peter Brook's 'Tell Me Lies,' Images of Terror and Brechtian Aesthetics." *Cineaction*, no. 76, 2009. www.questia.com/library/journal/1G1-194486567/atrocities-at-the-door-peter-brook-s-tell-me-lies.

"Madame Nhu's Response to Thich Quang Duc." *YouTube*. 13 Sep. 2006. www.youtube.com/watch?v=d_PWM9gWR5E.

McCutcheon, Russell. *Manufacturing Religion: The Discourse on Sui Generis Religion and the Politics of Nostalgia*. Oxford UP, 1997.

McNamara, Robert, and Brian VanDeMark. *In Retrospect: The Tragedy and Lessons of Vietnam*. Times Books, 1995.

"Memory Against Forgetting: The May 1970 Peace Memorial at UCSD." *San Diego Free Press*. 17 May 2014. sandiegofreepress.org/2014/05/memory-against-forgetting-the-may-1970-peace-memorial-at-ucsd/#.W9cCDjGNx2E.

Merton, Thomas. "Nhat Hanh Is My Brother." www.buddhistdoor.net/features/nhat-hanh-is-my-brother.

Miller, Edward. *Misalliance: Ngo Dinh Diem, the United States, and the Fate of South Vietnam*. Harvard UP, 2013.

Miller, William. *Henry Cabot Lodge: A Biography*. James H. Heineman, 1967.

Mondo cane 2. Directed by Gualteiro Jacopetti and Franco Prosperi, 1963. www.dailymotion.com/video/x2dlezi_mondo-cane-2-1964-feature_shortfilms.

Morrison Welsh, Anne. *Held in the Light: Norman Morrison's Sacrifice for Peace and His Family's Journey of Healing*. With Joyce Hollyday, Orbis Books, 2008.

"Nation: In the Lion's Cage." *Time*, 18 Oct. 1963. content.time.com/time/magazine/article/0,9171,873743,00.html.

"Nguy Tạo Va Xuyen Tạc." 18 Nov. 2011. thuvienhoasen.org/a13530/nguy-tao-va-xuyen-tac.

Nhat Hanh, Thich. "Letter to Martin Luther King." www.aavw.org/special_features/letters_thich_abstract02.html.

———. *Love in Action: Writings on Nonviolent Social Change*. Parallax Press, 1993.

———. *Peaceful Action, Open Heart: Lessons from the Lotus Sutra*. Parallax Press, 2008.

———. *Vietnam: Lotus in a Sea of Fire*. Hill and Wang, 1967.

Nhat Hanh, Thich, and Daniel Berrigan. *The Raft is Not a Shore: Conversations Towards a Buddhist/Christian Awareness*. Beacon Press, 1975.

Patler, Nicholas. "Norman's Triumph: The Transcendent Language of Self-Immolation." *Quaker History and Literature*, vol. 104, no. 2, 2015, pp. 1–23.

Petrović, Lena. "Drama's Moment of Truth: 'Death and the Maiden' and 'US / Tell Me Lies about Vietnam'." *Facta Universitatis* [Niš], vol. 13, no. 2, 2015, pp. 117–134.

Potter, Terry. "Adrian Mitchell's Poetry and Protest: 'To Whom It May Concern (Tell Me Lies about Vietnam)'". www.letterpressproject.co.uk/inspiring-older-readers/2018-07-15/adrian-mitchells-poetry-and-protest-to-whom-it-may-concern-tell-me-lies-about-vietnam.

Ryan, Cheyney. "The One Who Burns Herself for Peace." *Bringing Peace Home: Feminism, Violence, and Nature*, edited by Karen J. Warren and Duane L. Cady, Indiana UP, 1996, pp. 16–32.

Shaw, Geoffrey. *The Lost Mandate of Heaven: The American Betrayal of Ngo Dinh Diem, President of Vietnam*. Ignatius Press, 2015.

Shibata, Shingo, editor. *Phoenix. Letters and Documents of Alice Herz: The Thought and Practice of a Modern-Day Martyr*. Grüner, 1976.

Sienkiewicz, Karol. "'Lego Concentration Camp' – Zbigniew Libera." 2010. culture.pl/en/work/lego-concentration-camp-zbigniew-libera.

Skow, Lisa, and George Dionisopoulos. "A Struggle to Contextualize Photographic Images: American Print Media and the 'Burning Monk'." *Communication Quarterly*, vol. 45, no. 4, 1997, pp. 393–409.

Sontag, Susan. *On Photography*. Anchor Books, 1990.

———. *Regarding the Pain of Others*. Picador, 2003.

———. *Styles of Radical Will*. Anchor Books, 1991.

———. *Under the Sign of Saturn*. Vintage Books, 1981.

Staples, Amy J., and Charles Kilgore. "An Interview with Dr. Mondo." *American Anthropologist*, vol. 97, no. 1, 1995, pp. 110–125.

Sulik, Bolesław. "Search for Commitment." *US*, edited by Albert Hunt et al., Calder and Boyars, 1968, pp. 206–207.

Tell Me Lies. Producer-Director Peter Brook, performances by Mark Jones, Pauline Munro, and Robert Lloyd, Continental (A Ronorus Film), 1968; Brook Productions, 2013.

Topmiller, Robert. "Struggling for Peace: The Unrecognized Sacrifices of Buddhist Women during the Vietnam War." *Journal of Women's History*, vol. 17, no. 3, 2005, pp. 133–157.

———. *The Lotus Unleashed: The Buddhist Peace Movement in South Vietnam, 1964–1966*. UP of Kentucky, 2002.

Trewin, John C. *Peter Brook: A Biography*. Macdonald, 1971.

Vågnes, Øyvind. "Lessons from the Life of an Image: Malcolm Browne's Photograph of Thích Quang Duc's Self-Immolation." *On Not Looking: The Paradox of Contemporary Visual Culture*, edited by Frances Guerin, Routledge, 2015, pp. 251–264.

Van Thanh, Rudd. "What Are They Saying about My Art?" van-t-rudd.net/what-are-they-saying.html.

Williams, David, editor. *Peter Brook: A Theatrical Casebook*. Methuen, 1988.

Willson, Brian. *On Third World Legs*. Charles H. Kerr, 1992.

Yang, Michelle Murray. "Still Burning: Self-Immolation as Photographic Protest." *Quarterly Journal of Speech*, vol. 97, no. 1, 2011, pp. 1–25.

Yu, Jimmy. *Sanctity and Self-Inflicted Violence in Chinese Religions, 1500–1700*. Oxford UP, 2012.

Zaroulis, Nancy, and Gerald Sullivan. *Who Spoke Up? American Protest against the War in Vietnam, 1963–1975*. Doubleday, 1984.

Zi, Jun Toong. "Overthrown by the Press: The US Media's Role in the Fall of Diem." *Australasian Journal of American Studies*, vol. 27, no. 1, 2008, pp. 56–72.

Zimmer, Ben. "Remembering the Shit-in." stronglang.wordpress.com/2014/12/16/remembering-the-shit-in-2/.

Chapter 2

Confronting defeat

On two protest self-incinerations performed after the Warsaw Pact invasion of Czechoslovakia

Figure PIII.2 Kevin Maginnis *Self-Immolation* (2013).

168 Selected contemporary ultimate protests by fire

The protest self-burning of Ryszard Siwiec, a philosopher and accountant from Przemyśl, took place at Warsaw's Decennial Stadium on 8 September 1968, during the annual harvest festival attended by high-ranking members of the Polish United Workers' Party and regime officials, including First Secretary Władysław Gomułka himself. It differed from other, more prominent self-immolation incidents, which were performed across the Eastern Bloc in protest against Communist oppression. The incident was not a "sudden, adolescent gesture of despair and protest, but a profoundly deliberate act, premeditated, and carried out with terrifying meticulousness that drove the idea from its inception to shocking execution" (Werner 6).

Siwiec was old enough to be the father of 20-year-old Czech student Jan Palach, who in all likelihood had not heard of the Warsaw incident when, inspired by the anti-war self-burnings in Vietnam, he doused himself with petrol and set himself alight in Prague's Wenceslas Square four months after the Pole. Siwiec, nearly 60 years old, was married with five children; the eldest, Innocenta, was two years Palach's senior, while her sister Elżbieta was his age. He set out for the capital wearing a pale blue suit, a distinctive beret with a stem on top, and holding an attaché case – looking the very model of *homo sovieticus*, unassuming and long reconciled to the system. His death failed to make him a symbol of resistance or enshrine him in the national pantheon, whereas Palach was openly mourned by thousands of his compatriots. Also unlike the Czech student, Siwiec and his protest were summarily ignored – despite the fact that the self-immolation unfolded in a stadium filled with people and was the first contemporary incident of this sort in this part of the world.

The two protests, however, were not entirely dissimilar. Both men protested alone and pursued a fiery end in the face of defeat, addressing their ultimate acts to browbeaten and apathetic countrymen and women. And both were driven to self-sacrifice by an intrinsic imperative, a sense that someone had to cry out in defence of fundamental values such as dignity, truth, and liberty. And finally, as diagnosed by filmmaker Agnieszka Holland, "Neither could in any way be considered fanatical or irrational. They were deliberate and meticulous about their sacrifice, and fully aware of the pain it would cause them and their loved ones" ("Ogień").

In the wake of the suppression of student protests and the regime's anti-Semitic campaign in March 1968, as well as the invasion of Czechoslovakia by Warsaw Pact forces on the night of 21 August 1968, the Poles found themselves mired in apathy and gripped by a fear which Małgorzata Szpakowska argued was driven by fresh memories of the terror of post-war Stalinism. The Polish cultural anthropologist asserted that people were still predominantly mistrustful and, as such, "may have grumbled and griped, but kept any anti-regime views and opinions strictly to themselves" (Szpakowska 289–290). Palach's protest took place during the period of the so-called "normalisation" (which in fact meant re-Stalinisation) immediately following the

Warsaw Pact crackdown, when the Czechoslovak regime quickly moved to undo the achievements of the Prague Spring, leaving the people disheartened by the reestablishment of censorship, the curtailing of freedom of assembly, and the purging of anyone who dared to speak out against the authoritarian party line that Moscow sought to reintroduce. Both protests, therefore, were desperate cries that aimed to penetrate the consciences of the immolators' compatriots. In Siwiec's case, the appeal was also quite literal, as in the final part of his taped manifesto we hear the older man, his voice raised but breaking, delivers his desperate plea:

> People! People! Come to your senses! You, young people, the future of the nation, do not let yourselves be led to the slaughter every twenty years in order that one schism or another might dominate over the world. Do not let yourselves be slaughtered so that one group or another might gain total power. Those of you who have not yet forgotten the most beautiful word on earth – "mother"! Those of you who still harbour inside you a spark of humanity, of human feelings, come to your senses! Hear my cry, the cry of an ordinary, gray man, the son of a nation that has come to love its own and others' freedom above all else, above its own life – come to your senses! It is still not too late!
>
> (qtd. in Blažek, *Ryszard* 199)

The title of the subchapter dedicated to Siwiec, who himself was (erroneously) called the "Polish Palach" (Karcz 5), is a reference to the two minutes of silence – bucking the customary minute of silence for the dead – that close Maciej Drygas' critically acclaimed documentary *Usłyszcie mój krzyk* (*Hear My Cry*). Produced after the regime's 1989 collapse in Poland, the film introduced Siwiec into the public discourse, both at home and abroad (McKelvey B26). The title, however, can also be viewed in a more metaphorical manner, as a reference to the silence that his sacrifice was met with both in People's Poland and, following the 1989 transformation, in the Third Republic, as it would take some years before state authorities would either recognise or appropriately honour his act.

Siwiec's self-burning was a profound tragedy to his immediate family, which left them to fend for themselves against the challenges of everyday life and the stigma they had to bear. A contemplation of their plight formed the narrative through-line of Drygas' *Testament* (1992), a radio drama that rather unfairly remains eclipsed by its author's moving documentary.

Even though released nearly 30 years ago, Drygas' achievements continue to stand as the most compelling works of art (although documentary in nature, their artistic value is beyond dispute) to have dealt with the figure of Siwiec. Although the man himself would later be explored in a handful of Polish plays,[1] none of these subsequent efforts ever matched Drygas' ability to take on mankind's immanent struggle to liberate itself from earthly limitations and totalising discourses. The particular value of his works also derives from their suggestion of a narrative that transcends simple heroics – while ennobling both Siwiec and his sacrifice (particularly the film), they simultaneously encourage the audience to interrogate the very act of self-immolation.

Although the self-sacrifice of the Czech student was a genuine shock to the Czechoslovaks, the public ultimately embraced it and viewed it not through the lens of "individual categories, but rather as a figurative model of resistance" (Kulmiński 180). Palach grew to express the collective emotions of the people – emotions which were running particularly intense in the light of the events of 1968 and the country's uncertain future, the latter made further worse by society's misgivings about its potential direction. Palach's protest, however, captured public attention worldwide and is to this day considered one of the most prominent examples of altruistic self-burning in history.

At the time, Czechoslovakia was very much the subject of international attention, first due to the events of the Prague Spring and efforts to democratise the regime, and later in the light of the crackdown of "fraternal" socialist republics and its consequences. The international community was deeply sympathetic to the Czech and Slovak struggles for self-determination, and, during the turmoil of the late 1960s, saw attempts at reform in the Eastern Bloc a symptom of the emergence of a new economic and political model, one that would transcend the Cold War-driven capitalism–communism binary.

Both local and foreign reporters portrayed the self-sacrifice of the Czech student as the first incident of its kind in modern European history, a detail which further excited the public's imagination. However, they were either unaware or unwilling to mention the earlier protest self-burnings of Siwiec and Vasyl Makukh: the latter was a Ukrainian citizen who set himself alight in Kyiv on 5 November 1968 to take a stand against Soviet rule in Ukraine and the Warsaw Pact invasion of Czechoslovakia. His auto-cremation was covered up by state security.

Due to its earlier use in Asia, self-immolation was seen in Czechoslovakia (and Poland as well)[2] as culturally foreign and mostly associated with Buddhism, a view further reinforced by the Eastern Bloc's eager publicising of instances of anti-war self-burnings in Vietnam for anti-imperialist propaganda purposes. This, in turn, meant that the student's protest had to be filtered through the local, indigenous system of values and beliefs. Hence, many narratives about Palach often invoked in this particular context the fiery martyrdom of Jan Hus, the Czech national hero, religious reformer, and martyr, who refused to recant his beliefs, though attacked by the Catholic Church as heretical, and was eventually burned at the stake at the Council of Constance in 1415. Palach himself identified with Hus, thus becoming "the other Jan" in the eyes of the Czechs. The comparison was widely employed at the time, including by novelist and essayist Milan Kundera, who claimed that while embracing the choice made by Hus seemed reasonable, following in the footsteps of Palach seemed unthinkable (Sabatos 204). This time, however, Kundera, the author of *The Book of Laughter and Forgetting* (a novel that perfectly encapsulated the spirit of post-1968 "normalisation"), turned out to be patently wrong. Palach's sacrifice and its impact on fellow Czechs appeared to have been so profound that the student was soon followed by many other immolators, among them another Jan.

On 25 February 1969, exactly a month after Palach's memorable funeral, Jan Zajíc, an 18-year-old student at the Šumperk technical college, set himself on fire in an archway off Wenceslas Square in Prague, an act that referenced Palach and his self-burning both literally and symbolically. Zajíc's sacrifice, however, failed to stir the nation. Not only because the self-immolation itself came to nothing – despite meticulous preparation, the young man got turned around and instead of running out onto Václavské námesti, he went up a nearby stairway where he eventually died. But also because this time the authorities aggressively moved to restrict the spread of news about the event, leaving it significantly underreported, and later refused Zajíc's wish to be buried in Prague. Quickly labelled a copycat, he would forever remain the "other."[3]

Agnieszka Holland – a contemporary of Palach who may well have passed him in the streets of Prague, where she studied at the local film school – directed a three-part TV series, *The Burning Bush* (2013), which portrayed both of the immolations. Her series is one of two key works that invoke and interrogate the actions of "Torch no. 1"; the other major achievement is, in my opinion, a pair of architectural structures, *The House of the Suicide* and *The House of the Mother of the Suicide*, designed by John Hejduk (1929–2000), an architectural theorist, educator, and poet born in the US to Czech immigrants. The structures were erected in Prague's Jan Palach Square in January 2016 – on the 47th anniversary of the Charles University student's self-immolation. Both the series and the installations naturally revise the memory of his protest and do so on a rather large scale, given their character. But that is not what makes them so crucial. I have selected them from a sprawling collection of artworks that draw on the figure of Palach and his violent end (a comprehensive analysis of which would warrant another book), because in my opinion they, like Drygas' remarkable efforts, transcend the flat, one-dimensional heroic narrative that seems to prevail in the field. I believe that both artists managed to accomplish that feat by emphasising the terrible price that such a violent sacrifice exacts not only from those who lay down their lives, but also from their loved ones.

Two minutes of silence: the self-immolation of Ryszard Siwiec (Poland, 1968)

The performer, his act, and the aftermath

Thanks to the work of several individuals and institutions,[4] today we have a detailed picture of what happened that fateful September 1968 at Warsaw's

172   Selected contemporary ultimate protests by fire

representative sporting arena.[5] As I already mentioned, although Siwiec self-immolated in front of tens of thousands of onlookers, news of his protest went mostly unreported and did not reach the general public, neither then nor later. Although Radio Free Europe (RFE) revealed his death in an April 1969 report and, in 1981, Siwiec's eldest son Wit, himself involved with the dissident movement since the end of the 1970s, published an anniversary pamphlet through the underground press entitled *Żywa pochodnia na stadionie X-lecia* (*The Living Torch at the Decennial Stadium*), the incident remained mostly unknown to the broader audience.[6] It was only Maciej Drygas' black-and-white documentary *Hear My Cry*, released in 1991 (after the former regime's censorship authority was disbanded), to widespread critical acclaim and a European Film Award, and his follow-up radio play *Testament*, premiered in 1992 and recognised with the prestigious Prix Italia, that broke the silence on Siwiec and began the gradual process of installing his sacrifice in collective consciousness.

Drygas interviewed members of Siwiec's family – his widow, Maria Siwiec, and all five of his children, as well as his cousin and a handful of his friends from Przemyśl. The director also managed to gain access to previously un-released militia files from the investigation. Using newspaper and television advertisements, he managed to reach a handful of eyewitnesses whom he eventually interviewed on camera in the decaying remains of the Decennial Stadium. Preparing the film, Drygas also spoke with medical personnel who tended to Siwiec in the municipal hospital in Warsaw's Praga district where he was brought by state security immediately after the incident. The director even managed to locate a seven-second-long piece of footage in the Warsaw Documentary Film Studio archives, shot by Polish Newsreel camera oper-ator Zbigniew Skoczek, which showed Siwiec in the act of self-immolation (Drygas, "Było"). Both Drygas' documentary and his radio drama feature fragments of a recording that Siwiec taped probably a couple of days prior to his journey to Warsaw. Both works also contain passages from his will, drafted in April 1968.

The gravity of Drygas' works and the fact that he was able to reconstruct the eeriness of the situation from the depths of oblivion seem to have im-bued the 1968 incident with additional impact. His works focused not just on the protagonist or the motivations and reactions of his immediate family, but keenly emphasised the degree to which his self-sacrifice was summarily ignored by the public. Years later, in the introduction of the Polish album *Ryszard Siwiec, 1909–1968*, the director wrote: "To this day I cannot explain with any certainty why Siwiec's dramatic protest was so futile. Many hypoth-eses have been put forward, but none that will stand when confronted with the documentary material" (qtd. in Blažek, *Ryszard* 10). I will attempt to ex-amine these presumptions more closely, a feat made considerably easier by the materials Drygas compiled, some of which were released first in the *Kwartalnik Filmowy* quarterly (1993) and later in the *Karta* journal (2005), although both sources relied on a slightly different selection (Kaliski, "Płomień"). The process will also rely heavily on Blažek's aforementioned album, which features Siwiec's last will in its entirety, and records produced by the state security apparatus in the wake of the incident. A recording found in 2001 in the archives of the Office for State Protection (UOP), compiled from footage shot by two separate cameras and featured in Piotr Morawski's 2002 documentary programme *Tajne taśmy SB* (*The Secret Tapes of State Security*), will also be of considerable use. Additionally, my sources will include the 2013 testimony of nurse Ewa Biały, who found herself in the same section of the stadium's terracing at the time of the incident.

The violent protest was the product of a lengthy internal process that Siwiec underwent in response to recent social and political developments at home and abroad. Siwiec (born 1909) can ultimately be considered a representative of the pre-war intelligentsia, whose cardinal values included honour and service to God and to the country. With a degree in philosophy from the Jan Kazimierz University in Lviv (Skolarczyk 323), Siwiec came from rare stock – according to estimates, university graduates who survived the war made up only around 1% of Polish society (Duch-Dyngosz). After completing his education, he found work at the Lviv tax authority and continued in a clerical capacity after moving to Przemyśl in 1936, where he later met his future wife. After the outbreak of World War II, he worked as a city groundskeeper (rumour has it that he wanted to avoid serving as a tax collector for the occupying forces) and then as director of a local produce purchase centre. In all likelihood, he was involved to some extent with the covert structures of the Home Army, but no documents that would corroborate his participation have been found (Skolarczyk 324). After the end of the war, he refused a job teaching history as, according to his family, he did not want to participate in the indoctrination of schoolchildren (Strasz 282). To support himself and his growing family, he approached a partner to set up a small winery that would also produce mead, where he later served as accountant and developed new recipes – staying on even after the plant was nationalised by the regime in 1952 (Blažek, *Ryszard* 13). As many of his fellow countrymen and women in People's Poland, he worked hard to make ends meet, eventually setting up a small poultry and flower farm.

After the futile victory over Nazi Germany, Siwiec must have felt alienated from his new, unsovereign homeland. So he undertook what scholars of totalitarianism call *internal emigration* – in his room, under a portrait of the First Marshal of Poland, Józef Piłsudski, he listened to RFE broadcasts, read from his sweeping book collection, and typed out critiques of the new regime, sometimes in pamphlet form, signing them with his *nom de plume* "Jan Polak" (John Pole). His cousin, Tadeusz Kamiński, mentioned that for many years Siwiec was a reserved, stern, and taciturn man. Allegedly, it was only in 1960 that he suddenly began "sharing his thoughts" in bouts which resembled "the eruption of a volcano that stays calm for years, silently gathering steam, and

174   Selected contemporary ultimate protests by fire

then suddenly explodes" (qtd. in Drygas, "Usłyszcie" 45). It is possible that he saw the events of 1956 and the "thaw" across the Eastern Bloc as a sham and ultimately rejected and repudiated the new regime. As a resident of a small, provincial town, he was somewhat forced into isolation. That is probably why he tried to involve his eldest daughter in his political ruminations. Since he associated with academic circles, it is likely that he was profoundly troubled by the regime's 1968 crackdown against them. He tried reaching out to protest leaders and asked his daughter Elżbieta to mail letters to key figures in the movement (Kaliski, "Płomień" 79). His critical appraisal of the events of 1968 can also be found in the aforementioned recording he taped a few days before his death. Aside from the critique, the tape also held an appeal to his compatriots to speak out "in defence of those who are being taught socialism by means of police truncheons" (Blažek, *Ryszard* 187). Elsewhere in the recording, he can be heard fulminating about the anti-Semitic campaign the regime whipped up in order to resolve a power struggle inside the Communist party (Skolarczyk 328).

It was probably under the influence of these traumatic events that he decided to draft his last will and testament on 20 April 1968, which included his decision to carry out the protest "against the tyranny of evil, hatred, and lies that is overwhelming the world" (qtd. in Blažek, *Ryszard* 167). His will, which his immediate family received in the mail after his death, bequeathed nearly all of his belongings to his wife, while his children were to receive select books from his collection, with symbolic dedications, as well as patriotic memorabilia. In the document, he suggested his children embrace "unity of thoughts, words, and deeds" as the basis of all their future efforts (qtd. in Blažek, *Ryszard* 168). The date the will was drafted makes it apparent that he decided to sacrifice his life in protest long before the crushing of the Prague Spring, although the intervention indubitably made an impact on him. He brought up the incursion multiple times in his taped appeal and in the anti-regime pamphlets that law enforcement found inside his attaché case at the stadium.

It is hard to say when Siwiec chose the sports stadium as the venue for his protest. The account provided by the head of the Przemyśl district delegation to the harvest festival seems to indicate that the decision was made just prior to the event. However, it is also known that Siwiec undertook meticulous and extensive preparations for the protest. His daughter Elżbieta mentioned that his notes included a concise plan of action outlined in bullet points. "The list said, one: entry into stadium – finally cleared. Two: who is the protest for? Three: what slogans? Four: clothing. Five: petrol, matches. Six: location at the stadium. Seven: timing. Eight: second and final confession" (Drygas, "Usłyszcie" 74).

Before leaving for Warsaw, Siwiec recorded his appeal at the Casimir Castle in Przemyśl, using equipment he borrowed from the Fredreum Theatre, conveniently located on the castle premises, as recording devices were far beyond the reach of ordinary citizens at the time. "Ryszard flicked the tape

Confronting defeat 175

recorder on and began reading his typewritten disquisition straight off the pages. He amended some of the passages on the fly, and rounded out others with additional phrasing. His voice was breaking here and there, and tears were streaming down his cheeks," recounted his friend, Władysław Mazur (qtd. in Kaliski, "Płomień" 81). Why did he decide to record his thoughts, which presciently foreshadowed the collapse of communism at a time when no one in Poland actually dared believe it? He could have just as well compiled them into a farewell letter, arranged in neat typescript. The passages from the speech that Drygas used in both the documentary and the radio drama may fail to give us an accurate idea of its length. Reading the speech out loud in its entirety took Siwiec 45 minutes. Throughout the disquisition, he often addresses both his fellow countrymen and women, as well as the members of the Soviet Politburo, calling on both to embrace a genuine, progressive socialism, to strive for dignity and democratisation. It is likely then that the tape was his attempt at crafting a response to the flowery rhetoric of Gomułka, whom Siwiec considered "the greatest ignoramus ever to sit on the Polish throne" (qtd. in Blažek, *Ryszard* 126).

As his train neared Warsaw, Siwiec penned a brief letter to his wife and children, which he then gave to an acquaintance en route to the stadium, asking the man to deliver it to his family upon return to Przemyśl. Finding no one home, the messenger's wife then stuck the letter into the doorframe. The note was quickly picked up by state security and added to the case file as evidence, where it remained for the next 23 years, until Drygas returned it to the addressee. At the stadium, Siwiec deliberately switched seats in order to find himself almost directly across the parade stand.

In People's Poland, the regime used the annual harvest festival as a propaganda vehicle, celebrated with requisite pomp and usually held in major sporting arenas. The objective of the grand event was to appease the farming peasantry, recognised by party ideology as one of the leading powers in the state, second only to the workers. During the official celebrations, representatives from villages across the country appeared one after another to report to their local party secretaries the successful completion of the summer harvest. The celebrations in Warsaw were particularly festive and appealed to wide swaths of urban and rural Poles. In 1968, the Sunday of the celebrations was a beautiful day and the festivities began promptly at 10 am. After Gomułka's opening speech, in which he spent considerable time justifying his decision to send troops to Czechoslovakia with the Soviets, the festival commenced in earnest – folk bands and folk dancers, over 2,000 people in total, began a series of live performances. In a gesture designed to appease the youth, the musical acts included the popular big-beat band No To Co. Reports from the event were broadcast by radio, while camera crews roamed the stadium grounds to capture footage for the Polish Newsreel. Public order in the arena was maintained by uniformed militia patrols and a number of plainclothes state security officers equipped with photo and video cameras.

This Potemkinist facade, the kitschy, carefree (un)reality, was then brutally disrupted by Ryszard Siwiec and his violent protest against the existing order. To borrow the phraseology devised by Maria Janion, renowned Polish literary scholar, his act was intended to "interrupt the spectacle" of power (126). This notion of competing spectacles was also explored by Polish theatre director Lech Raczak who, referencing the fact that Siwiec's self-burning was ignored by the onlookers while the song and dance part of the celebrations went on uninterrupted, posed a rhetorical question: "Was this the day when spectacle ultimately triumphed over reality?" (111).

Siwiec doused himself with solvent and set himself alight just as the gifts ceremony began. The footage featured in *The Secret Tapes* clearly shows Siwiec yelling, flailing to drive away the militia officers trying to put out the flames, and then fleeing. The whole event unfolds in front of bystanders, looking on from a couple of metres away. One shot portrays Siwiec in a close-up, as he stands, the flames already extinguished, amidst a crowd of onlookers, and is then led away to a car. The footage clearly indicates that he neither distributed the pamphlets nor unfurled the Polish flag, as Wit Siwiec had suggested in his brochure. The footage also implies that the people around him definitely heard the protest slogans he was bellowing.

It is also quite clear that the incident was brief, not much longer than 10–15 minutes from start to finish, including the militia leading Siwiec out, and that the bystanders became passive onlookers almost at once, as law enforcement immediately intervened to put out the fire and remove the burned man from public view, his appearance horrifying, repulsive even. The shock was amplified by the surprise – the incident hit the unsuspecting witnesses like a bolt from the blue. Ewa Biały recounted that the purplish–yellowish–red flame that shot out before her in broad daylight was wholly irrational under the circumstances (135). The reactions of the assembled crowd included screams, fainting, aggressive behaviour, and attempts at rationalisation. All around the self-immolator, people were screaming in terror and calling Siwiec a lunatic, psychopath, or a drunk who spilled his booze and set himself on fire by accident.

It is rather unlikely that his self-burning remained unnoticed by people further away, as a pillar of black smoke immediately rose above the stadium and an uneasy murmur ran across the stands. Those closer to Siwiec did not react, unwilling to step out of line, afraid of the fire or potential blowback from state security. This seems to be corroborated by the account of Stanisława Kańska, a dance instructor who at the time found herself in a stadium tunnel rehearsing her routines with her group: "We didn't pay any attention to it, because we were already so focused on our business, right? And that, we just thought – an incident, that's it, gone in a blink" (qtd. in Drygas, "Usłyszcie" 52). It would seem that 20-plus years of Communist indoctrination, effectively implanting self-censorship within the people, had paid off handsomely.

Siwiec expected the world to hear about his protest – that, however, did not come to pass, at least not at the time. Although his self-immolation was the talk of the town in Warsaw over the next couple of days, most of it was just gossip (Kisielewski 98; Eisler 751; Dębska and Kaliski 34).[7] Neither the press nor the radio, foreign or domestic, carried any reports of the incident. No photos were published. It seemed as if the media conspired to erase the shocking event.

Suffering from extensive burns, Siwiec was transported straight to the hospital, where the staff put him in isolation. Select medical personnel were informed about the incident and ordered to keep silent. Remarkably, Siwiec remained conscious and openly discussed the reasons behind his act with his caretakers. Only his wife was allowed visitation, and other attempts at unsanctioned visits (of which there weren't any) were to be reported to law enforcement by the nursing staff.

Certain that her husband was in Tarnobrzeg, Maria Siwiec received a telegram on the night of 8 September, informing her that her husband was in a Warsaw hospital (Skolarczyk 334). Arriving in the capital the following day, she only learned about the incident at the clinic, and was forced to promise to the militia that she would not reveal her husband's self-immolation to anybody, not even her children. With her youngest daughter and three sons still at home, she knew full well that running further afoul of the regime at that point would only worsen her situation. Years later, Wit Siwiec revealed that he had no idea of the real circumstances of his father's death – like his younger brothers, he was sure their dad had perished in an accident. Only after one of the boy's teachers said that his father had died as a hero did he start to doubt the story he had internalised (Kaliski, "Płomień" 94–95).

Siwiec died on 12 September and was buried in the Catholic cemetery in Przemyśl three days later, with large crowds in attendance. The funeral ceremony was closely watched by militia and plainclothes state security operatives, so no one dared to give a speech (Kaliski, "Płomień" 94). Maria Siwiec recounted that friends began pulling away from the family soon after. Everything seems to indicate that private chatter on the Siwiec incident died down rather quickly, allowing state security to close the investigation already on 16 October 1968. Somewhat shocked, Drygas noted that state security did not have to undertake any special cover-up efforts: spreading denigrating gossip and enforcing a media blackout was enough to silence any public outcry ("Usłyszcie" 66). Militia officers involved in extinguishing Siwiec were put up for commendation, told that the immolator was nothing but a lunatic, and implicitly instructed to keep their mouths shut (Drygas, "Usłyszcie" 53).

Above, I already identified Communist indoctrination and indifference fostered by the regime as two key factors that significantly contributed to the fact that Siwiec's protest was so overwhelmingly ignored. Drygas, on the other hand, believed the mass denial stemmed from the immolator being ahead of his time ("Usłyszcie" 65). Indeed, prior to 1976, when the Workers'

178 Selected contemporary ultimate protests by fire

Defence Committee (KOR) was established, covert dissident circles were too disorganised and too weak to give a proper signal boost to Siwiec's protest. This is probably what Father Józef Tischner had in mind when he suggested that society would not have been able to turn a blind eye to Siwiec's sacrifice had it happened only a few years later (42). In other words, browbeaten and facing an entrenched regime at the peak of its power, Polish society was simply not ready to speak out against the system. Moreover, Siwiec mistargeted his protest. Instead of appealing to politically conscious students outside academic premises, he chose a compliant, tractable audience whose interest in being witness to violent political statements was marginal (Kaliski, "Płomień" 94).

A wholly different take on Siwiec's failure to reach his audience was offered by Zbigniew Wojciechowski, a Polish Radio journalist who had reported on the festival live from the stadium. The reporter saw it as "negligence" on Siwiec's part and suggested that had the self-immolation happened during Gomułka's speech, it probably would not have been overshadowed by the entertainers and may very well have been able to interrupt the First Secretary's address or at least force him to acknowledge the reason for the disturbance (Drygas, "Usłyszcie" 55).

Still other explanations emphasised how culturally alien Siwiec's fiery protest must have seemed to most of the public, particularly given the persistent taboo surrounding suicide in Catholicism (Skolarczyk 338–339). Although the Catholic Church "attempts, in certain cases, to either seek out or develop arguments that could minimise the suicides' moral responsibility for their actions or even absolve them entirely" (Strzałka 71), we need to remember that prior to John Paul II's promulgation of the 1983 Code of Canon Law, the Church's stance on suicide was informed by Benedict XV's 1917 Code, which unequivocally condemned suicide as a mortal sin. In the key document drafted by the Second Vatican Council, the 1965 Pastoral Constitution *Gaudium et Spes* (*Joy and Hope*), the Church reiterated the position that suicide was a dishonour to the Creator. The orthodoxy's unyielding stance on the matter turned out to be one of the key factors in shaping the public perception of Siwiec and his protest.

In all likelihood, Siwiec patterned his act after the anti-war self-burnings in Vietnam which were initially met in Poland with apprehension, later replaced by compassion, as the public grew to see the sacrifices as heroic. In such a context, Father Tischner argued that martyrdom had long traditions in Poland, exemplified by the universally endorsed and praised sacrifice of Father Maksymilian Kolbe in 1941. He pointed out, however, that although the Franciscan friar voluntarily laid down his life for another man in Auschwitz, his death was not a suicide but a murder. Hence, Tischner concluded, the bold choice to sacrifice one's life for a higher cause is at best praiseworthy or commendable, but cannot in any way be acknowledged as a heroic stance worthy of imitation (41).

Wishing to explain the reasons behind people's "dismissal" of Siwiec's protest, Polish cultural scholar Iwona Kurz examined the public discourse and the underlying mechanisms that may have so effectively facilitated the denial (26). Attempting to reconstruct the state of the collective consciousness at the time, she pointed out that it was underpinned by the struggle for the soul of the people that unfolded within the national paradigm between the regime and the Catholic Church, particularly evident around the 1966 celebrations of the millennial of King Mieszko I's baptism, traditionally considered the beginning of Polish statehood. Kurz wisely asserted that in the light of the country's general mood, steeped in nationalist pretence, xenophobia, and eruptions of anti-Semitism, Siwiec's protest "had to remain a glitch, an inconvenience to both the regime and the society, an interference to be purged" (40). She also suggested that the dismissal could have been a defence mechanism against what was seen as too morally demanding. In conclusion, Kurz emphasised that Siwiec's sacrifice, perceived as obscene, had to be erased as hailing from "beyond the official register of language, and beyond irony and the grotesque remaining polemically inclined against it" (40). Irony and the grotesque, it should be noted, which were omnipresent in highly popular Sławomir Mrożek's *oeuvre*, that consisted of absurdist commentary on loathsome, ugly reality.

Here, I would like to bring up one more detail which appears in both the eyewitness account of Biały and in Drygas' reflections. When the nurse ran up to the burning Siwiec, he looked as if "it" (fire?, pain?) "did not apply to him. He seemed beside the whole fiery affair, as if he wasn't the one burning" (Biały 135). The director also emphasised that when he finally saw Siwiec's face on the screen, he realised, to his considerable astonishment, that his "was not the face of a man suffering," while "his gaze was triumphant" ("Analiza" 156). It is my belief that in some people, sheer contact with the nearly inhuman or superhuman determination, such as that which allowed Siwiec to persist against the genius of death throughout this fascinating and terrifying "liturgy," could have triggered a range of defence mechanisms that ultimately resulted in the denial and dismissal of his sacrifice.

The memory discourse on self-immolation

In the memory discourse and contemporary media narratives, Siwiec's act is viewed primarily through the lens of the Warsaw Pact invasion of Czechoslovakia, and thus treated chiefly as an expression of solidarity with the pro-independence aspirations of Czechs and Slovaks (Kulmiński 66–68; Stach). However, a closer reading of his message and the words he uttered on his death bed, recorded covertly by state security (Kaliski, "Płomień" 97), reveals that his ruminations were suffused with notions of morality, and that the question of the Polish armed forces' participation in the invasion of neighbouring Czechoslovakia was only part of a much larger whole. Shortly before his death, Siwiec said that for truth, liberty, humanity, democracy, and love to flourish, lies, hatred, and terror have to be stamped out. He also emphasised that his life and the life of his family "are irrelevant compared to the threat of annihilation that mankind labours under every day" (Kaliski, "Płomień" 97). It may bear reminding here that in Siwiec's attaché case, the militia officers found a copy of the Polish, abridged edition of Toyofumi Ogura's *Letters from the End of the World*, a first-hand account of the Hiroshima bombing, which Siwiec apparently packed to busy his mind on the overnight train ride. The following morning, possibly influenced by the reading, he wrote to his wife: "It is to keep the truth, humanity, and freedom from disappearing that I die – a lesser evil than that death of millions" (qtd. in Błażek, *Ryszard* 10). Naturally, the invasion of Czechoslovakia may have been the proverbial straw that broke the camel's back and ultimately drove Siwiec to self-immolation, but the man intended his protest to shock his compatriots first and foremost, and wanted his fiery death to serve as a denouncement of the Communist system as a whole, particularly the imperialist policies of the Soviet Union, whose government he accused of escalating international tensions, stoking the arms race, and leading the world to the very brink of nuclear annihilation.

That his protest was (and continues to be) portrayed primarily through the lens of his opposition to the Polish armed forces' involvement in the crushing of the Prague Spring is ultimately the product of a number of separate factors, with two of them playing a key role in the process. The first is related to the fact that his altruistic gesture was noticed only in retrospect, after the widely reported self-immolation of Jan Palach, thus affecting the public perception of the earlier protest in Warsaw. The second involved the incorporation of Siwiec and his self-burning into the greater effort to restore good relations between Poles and Czechs, and Poles and Slovaks, which dissident circles undertook in the wake of the collapse of Communism across the Eastern Bloc.

After Palach's fiery protest, rumours of Siwiec's sacrifice were finally being regarded as true. On 27 January 1969, two days after the student's funeral, the French weekly *Le Nouvel Observateur* became the first international news source to report the tragedy that played out at the harvest festival in Warsaw. On 7 February, the story was reprinted by the British *New Statesman*, but it still rang false to some people, given that one letter to the editor questioned whether the suicide protest in Poland actually happened, arguing that if it were true, the whole of Warsaw would have heard about it within a couple of hours and RFE definitely would have reported it soon afterwards (Eisler 752). Years later, Jan Nowak-Jeziorański, long-term head of RFE's Polish desk, explained that, indeed, shortly after the incident, a party-affiliated journalist relayed the story to the RFE staff, but it seemed so outlandish that the radio decided not to run it (Kaliski, "Płomień" 95). Only after receiving an anonymous letter in 1969, which outlined in detail what had happened, did the producers finally decide to broadcast a brief report on the tragedy, but ultimately ran it in mid-April.[8] The letter was mailed by Władysław Mazur who, after seeing the international reaction to Palach's self-burning, decided to remind the world of a prior sacrifice that took place in Poland.

> Mazur had initially attempted to unsuccessfully deliver the letter to the British Embassy in Warsaw. When he realised that the British diplomats had taken him for a provocateur, he decided to send the letter via regular mail. He addressed it to a furniture manufacturer in Stockholm; the manufacturer, in turn, sent it to Radio Free Europe…

wrote Blažek on the matter (*Ryszard* 48–49). It could be argued, with considerable confidence, that Siwiec's self-immolation would have continued to linger in oblivion if it were not for Palach and the powerful reaction his death elicited.

Up until the release of Drygas' documentary, the death of Siwiec remained a mere sidenote and one entirely linked with the opposition to the invasion of Czechoslovakia. We should note here that the 450,000-strong Warsaw Pact force was roughly the same size as the Allied force amassed to storm Normandy in June 1944. This made the incursion the largest military operation launched on European soil since World War II (Kwapis 247). Although the core of the invasion force was made up of Soviet troops, the Polish People's Army provided the second-largest contingent, with three motorised divisions (Eisler 744–745). The invasion inevitably cast a long shadow over Polish-Czechoslovak relations. The country found itself unable to forgive Poles for Gomułka "proposing publicly to other high-ranking Communist leaders that the Czechoslovak situation be resolved by force. … Naturally, the decision to crush the Prague Spring had long been made in Moscow. But in the eyes of the Czechs, it was Gomułka who wronged them the most" (Eisler 747).

The Poles, on the other hand, reacted to the intervention with indifference, resignation, and fear, and even the smallest gesture of protest or solidarity with the Czechs required considerable courage. Although chances of repression ran high, some people nevertheless decided to protest openly, particularly representatives of the intelligentsia. Some ostentatiously renounced their membership in the Party, others distributed illegal pamphlets, scrawled anti-Soviet slogans on walls, and brought bouquets of white and red flowers adorned with blue ribbons to the Czechoslovak Cultural Centre in Warsaw; some writers and artists, including Jerzy Andrzejewski and Zygmunt Mycielski (in Poland) or Jan Lebenstein and Sławomir Mrożek (abroad), openly spoke of their solidarity in a number of letters. Although it is beyond doubt that many Poles sympathised with the Czechoslovak efforts to liberalise their system of government, and felt ashamed of their own country's participation in the armed crushing of these efforts, open protests were rare and their reach limited.[9] Small wonder, then, that Siwiec's spectacular and tragic act (which incidentally happened only a day after a Polish soldier drunkenly shot two Czechoslovak people to death) became highly symbolic to Czechs and Slovaks, as

182 Selected contemporary ultimate protests by fire

well as those Poles who struggled to wash away the shame of Polish political and military assistance in the invasion.

This is why the memorial plaque devoted to Siwiec's sacrifice, embedded in the Decennial Stadium on the initiative of the weekly journal *Tygodnik Solidarność* on 8 September 1990, in the early days of the regime change period, emphasised that particular aspect. In spite of Drygas' work and its emphasis on painting a broader, more complex picture of the event, this oversimplified narrative prevailed in the majority of commemorative practices to such an extent that it began to affect other locations that shaped the public memory discourse of the self-burning. Claims affiliated with that narrative appeared on the memorial plaque embedded in 2008 in the walls of his former Przemyśl home; on the plaque installed in 2009, on his 100th birthday, on the wall of the primary school in Dębica which he attended; and even on the black obelisk dedicated to his memory that was erected in 2012 next to the newly built National Stadium. Significantly, his headstone, straddling the intersection of public and private, stands as an exception to the rule. The pages of the book carved out of stone speak of a protest "against the subjugation of man," and mention the Order of Tomáš Garrigue Masaryk that Czech President Václav Havel bestowed upon Siwiec posthumously for his "struggles in defence of democracy and human rights" (qtd. in Blažek, *Ryszard* 159).

Indeed, the Czechs were the first to grant him state honours. The Polish government followed suit only two years later, when President Aleksander Kwaśniewski posthumously awarded Siwiec the Commander's Cross of the Order of Polonia Restituta on 19 August 2003. Maria Siwiec, however, refused to accept it, arguing that the recognition came much too late and was granted only to "prop up the reputation of this thoroughly discredited government," which at the time included a number of former Communist functionaries in high-level positions. She later added that she hoped to soon accept the award from "more worthy hands" (qtd. in Zambrowski 10). Her wish was eventually granted on 11 November 2007, after Kwaśniewski was replaced by Lech Kaczyński.[10] Her bitterness is perfectly understandable: almost universally ignored after it happened, her husband's sacrifice then failed to capture the attention of either the authorities or the public for nearly two decades after the collapse of communism, even despite Drygas' successes. Although the city of Przemyśl named one of its new bridges after Siwiec in 1991, all subsequent gestures of honouring his memory were mere imitations of prior efforts undertaken by the Czechs, including the publication of a commemorative album, naming streets after him, or erecting obelisks in his memory. It should also be noted that most domestic efforts to honour Siwiec's memory or promote his legacy were joint Polish-Czech-Slovak initiatives and/or organised with support from Czech and Slovak organisations or institutions.

This may be considered proof of some resistance against recognising Siwiec's sacrifice and enshrining the man himself in the national pantheon, which is what Tischner postulated, claiming him worthy of being mentioned in the same breath as other celebrated Poles, such as military leaders Tadeusz Kościuszko (1746–1817) and Józef Poniatowski (1763–1813), the soldiers of the 1944 Warsaw Uprising, and Father Kolbe. This reluctance might be explained in a number of different ways. Firstly, Siwiec's solitary death subverted the Romantic trope of individual sacrifice, which glorified armed martyrdom.[11] Tischner argued bitterly that had Siwiec thrown a live grenade into the unsuspecting stands or at least used himself as a living torch to burn high-ranking regime officials, his chances of being consecrated into the holy rolls of nationally revered martyrs would have been much higher. Secondly, "it is difficult to become a hero to one nation by laying down one's life in the interest of another" (Kulmiński 70), and that, as I already mentioned, was the prevailing reading of Siwiec's self-burning. Thirdly, self-immolation violated the religious taboos surrounding suicide. In other words, it is likely that had the Catholic Church embraced Siwiec as a hero, the nation would have followed suit, either before the fall of Communism or after. Catholic doctrine, however, obviously precluded the Church from doing so.

Hence, the domestic heroic discourse mentions Siwiec's protest only occasionally. Since the lower house of Polish parliament passed a bill on 6 March 2009, the eve of his 100th birthday, officially commemorating his protest and fiery death, Siwiec himself has been resurfacing in public discourse annually, mostly around the September anniversary (chiefly the round ones) of his act.

These problems are well-illustrated by the story behind the efforts to name after Siwiec the new national sporting arena which replaced the Decennial Stadium. The idea was first put forward by the Polish Commissioner for Human Rights, Janusz Kochanowski, in September 2008. The issue kept reappearing in the media as the 2012 UEFA European Championship, co-hosted by Poland, drew nearer – especially seeing that both the opening ceremony and the inaugural match between Poland and Greece were to be held at the newly constructed venue. In August 2012, the Polish parliament unanimously passed a bill to name the new stadium after legendary football coach Kazimierz Górski, who led the Polish national team to third place in the 1974 FIFA World Cup. The final decision, however, rested with the company managing the stadium, which subsequently suggested a competition be held to decide on the naming rights sponsor.

But before auctioning the rights, the KARTA Centre held a heavily symbolic event on 8 September 2013 – part celebration of the anniversary of Siwiec's protest and part effort to convince the ruling powers to name the sports arena after him. The event included a screening of excerpts from Drygas' documentary on the Jumbotron hanging above the pitch. And so, on the same day and at the same location where 45 years earlier his message fell on deaf ears, Siwiec's memorable words would now flow with full force through the PA system. Ironically, the event played out against empty stands, the vacant seats in post-Communist Poland standing as a peculiar inversion of the crowds that packed the terraces in People's Poland. In the event,

184 Selected contemporary ultimate protests by fire

we witnessed the convergence of Siwiec's long absence from public consciousness, the question of doing him and his sacrifice justice, and the future reception of his protest and his message. The performance of memory, assisted by cutting-edge technology, at a venue symbolising the rapid modernisation that Poland underwent following the 1989 regime change and its entry into the European Union, eventually ended in failure. In 2015, the naming rights were sold to PGE, a state-owned utilities company, and the arena was rechristened the PGE National Stadium.

It is beyond doubt that had the venue been named after Siwiec, the message behind his protest could have resonated better with contemporary society, particularly the youth. Meanwhile, broader reception of his sacrifice is still rather limited, notwithstanding the success of Drygas' film and the remediation it has been subjected to in recent years.[12] This particular state of affairs may soon change, however, as Siwiec's protest has resurfaced in public discourse after the public self-immolation of Piotr Szczęsny in 2017, whose sacrifice was often compared to Siwiec's, if only because Szczęsny's farewell letter contained numerous references to the message of his predecessor. However, many supporters of the ruling party Szczęsny targeted saw the comparison between the self-sacrifice carried out in a democratic country with the earlier self-immolation, performed under an autocratic system, drawn at the time by many columnists, commentators, and Internet users, as needlessly exploitative (Płużański).

A duet on self-sacrifice: on Maciej Drygas' documentary film Hear My Cry and his radio drama Testament

In his directing debut, Drygas (born 1956) seemed to have repeated the gesture of celebrated Polish theatre director Tadeusz Kantor who, like Charon, invoked and ferried the dead across the River Styx in his Theatre of Death. Offering the audience insight into the motivations driving the self-immolator, Drygas also gave a voice to Siwiec's family and the people who witnessed his drastic sacrifice. As the filmmaker himself remarked, he did not intend the film to be in any way educational or serve as commentary, but still felt a huge moral responsibility bearing down on him. He was also quite aware of the fact that his vision could possibly "drive the ensuing perception of Siwiec's act, as well as its historical and emotional interpretation" (Drygas, "Analiza" 151).

The months he spent mining relevant archives, a process that nearly became his own private investigation (the director is known for meticulous background research for his documentaries), yielded a trove of unique materials and reshaped the structure and the bearing of the resultant documentary and radio drama, each one running a little over 45 minutes long. Both works put front and centre the pursuit of truth consigned to oblivion and the discovery of what drove a man to lay down his life for noble ideas. Both feature archival footage and draw on official and private records, as well as interviews conducted with the family. Moreover, the staged reenactments which appear in both the film and the radio drama allowed them to transcend their purely documentary character. Finally, both pieces preserve the anonymity of the interviewees and embrace understatement by shunning all author commentary. In her interpretation of the film, Polish film scholar Bronisława Stolarska argued that the latter strategy translated into "heightened audience engagement and involvement in the reenactment of the events," but ultimately aims much higher, to "disrupt the viewers' cognitive confidence and awaken in them a sense of responsibility for their own consciousness" (309).

The narratives of both pieces were designed to postpone, for as long as possible, the moment in which the circumstances of Siwiec's death are revealed. In the opening of the film, an archivist admits that the Siwiec investigation case files were destroyed in 1985, while a priest reveals that parish records list "accident" as the cause of death. Later on in the film, his acquaintances paint a portrait of Siwiec and the values he espoused and tried to instil in his children, while his family takes turns reading from his will. The shots are interspersed with images of the harvest festival, implying that the tragic event had taken place at the joyous celebration. While his widow says it was suicide, Siwiec's son argues instead that his father had died a hero after accomplishing something remarkable. The 15-minute-long opening portion of the film ends with the camera pulling back from a table topped with brilliantly white linens, on which sit keepsakes and mementos of Siwiec, including his *last tape*, labelled "FATHER." Stolarska accurately noted that the scene:

> marks the passage onto a higher plane of reflection. The suggestion implicit in the image, which allows us to see an altar in a white cloth-covered table, is clear but not ostentatious. It tugs at the viewers' more or less conscious emotions stemming from a sense of belonging to a world of common values, but also inspires a sense of respect for mystery, further reinforced by the withdrawal of the camera. (312)

The mystery Stolarska mentions is familial, but it is also the mystery of death, the passage into an unknown ontic dimension.

The sense of communing with the sacred is further reinforced by the manner in which the priest (Tischner, unnamed like the others) is filmed. Looking directly into the lens, the minister speaks of the self-immolation of a Buddhist monk, intent on making his suffering communicate an important truth. He is filmed against a sparse, unfinished wall, illuminated with muted lighting and stripped of any religious symbols. The cinematographer for the film, Stanisław Śliskowski, said that in this abstract interior, the preacher's words did not "register as a sermon, but felt more like philosophy" (qtd. in Dondzik 92). The staged testimony of the priest – the only figure without any direct connection to Siwiec – bridges the first and second acts of the documentary. Within the structure of the film, it plays a part similar to that performed by the chorus in Greek tragedies, universalising the underlying message (Drygas, "Analiza" 157). In this capacity, the shot will reappear later to mark the film's other turning point and reinforce its solemn tone.

Similar devices appear in the second act, comprising sequences reenacting the events at the stadium, as well as testimony and self-appraisals from witnesses. To portray the harvest festival, Drygas used unreleased panoramic footage shot for a propaganda documentary showcasing Poland in 1968. He ultimately decided against cropping the footage to a more classic aspect ratio, which, in turn, gave the celebrations a slightly unreal feel. We see a procession of unnaturally elongated figures, led by the mistress of ceremonies holding a huge loaf of bread, heading straight towards the camera. In the background, we hear Paweł Szymański's *Partita III*, its notes infusing the scene in which the mistress raises the loaf up to the heavens with a peculiar sense of drama. Playing up the motif of the offering, an essential theme in the actual event, the director transformed a joyous celebration of fecundity into a ritual veering eerily close to a funeral.

The testimonies of the witnesses (radio reporter, militia officer, a woman who found herself at the stadium by accident, and a dance instructor), filmed at the now-decrepit stadium, reveal the course of the incident. To further accentuate the tragedy of the episode, the scenes showing the men carrying the huge festival wreath, accompanied by women moving along in a polonaise-like gait, play out in slow motion against a funereal score. The elongated figures carry onwards, as if marching in a procession. Moments later, we see the mouth of the tunnel in the distance, implying either the cortège nearing the stadium exit or impending death, the proverbial walking towards the light. In the background, we hear a drone accompanied by chiming bells, both of which continue into the next shot, which features the drawn out faces of girls, frozen still, solemn, attentively gazing at one single point. The music slows down, suggesting time itself had stopped – as if everything ground to a halt, as if some sort of calamity had just transpired, fixing everything and everyone in place. This metaphorical scene conjures up images of crowds observing minutes of silence for the dead, and brings to mind the early breath-catching moments after witnessing a tragedy.

The cameraman, photojournalist, and radio reporter all try to justify themselves and explain why they had not reacted to the sight of a man engulfed in flames. Each man speaks on his own behalf, but all hold attributes of their professions: a video camera, a photo camera, and a microphone, leading them to abandon some of their individuality in exchange for becoming a token representative of their profession. Then we cut back to the past again, with the drawn out figures of girls and boys, wearing traditional folk garb and dancing the polonaise down the pitch, lending credibility to the claim that "everything went back to normal" and that "the tunnel spat out a crowd of youths who ... began dancing" (qtd. in Drygas, "Usłyszcie" 53). But because the score continues along vaguely funereal lines, theirs is not a playful procession, but seems more like the motion of a tragic chorus.

We are first exposed to the image of Siwiec ablaze in a seven-second-long slow-motion sequence following the testimonies of the doctor, the nurse, the militiaman, and the fireman. We still do not get to see the main character, only the events around him. "People in the stands get up. Tensely gaze in the same direction. A woman puts her hand over her mouth, as if to silence a scream. A man next to her grabs his head in despair. Another peeks over his shoulder and freezes in disbelief" (Drygas, "Usłyszcie" 53–54). "We continue to witness a drama the epicentre of which remains outside the frame," the director wrote ("Analiza" 158), after explaining how that was possible:

> First we took every tenth frame, blew them up, and developed them into photographs. Then, the DP and I ... pored over the photos to reconstruct the course of the incident. This produced a precise script comprising a couple dozen shots. Then we used a stop-motion camera, sitting on a mount fitted with a micrometre head, to film the picture put out onto a huge screen by a stop-motion projector. Such a setup allowed us to shoot precise panoramas, both horizontal and vertical. (155–156)

This treatment fleshed out details that previously went unseen, "for example, someone in the crowd was fleeing while holding their shoes, someone else snagged their head on an umbrella that bent as a result, while someone else still was apparently so overwhelmed by the scene they buried their face in their hands" (Drygas, "Analiza" 156). Their reactions, gleaned through technical means, are surprisingly consistent with the self-justifications of witnesses from earlier. The aforementioned comments from the unnamed priest effectively serve as a caesura for this part of the film. The clergyman stresses the significance of conscience in individual human choice, while his statements stand as a warning against hasty judgments. Why? This we learn in the final portion of the documentary focused on Ryszard Siwiec's message, with the self-immolator himself making his first appearance.

The slow-motion footage, focused on the frantic action and the hysterical reaction of people surrounding Siwiec (who continues to remain out of sight), is contrasted here with his methodical disquisition addressed to the Soviet authorities and his passionate appeal to his fellow Poles to come to their senses. The sequence is followed with appraisals and interpretations of his protest, which are then capped off with the epilogue; in this coda, we finally get to see the performer, engulfed in flame. Caught in freeze-frame, it is his face – in which Drygas saw jubilation and triumph (over death?, pain?, his own reservations about seeing the act through?) – that we are left with as the film ends. Szymański's clear, fast-paced score suddenly cuts out, and then the screen silently fades out to white.

188 Selected contemporary ultimate protests by fire

In an apt turn of phrase, Polish writer and reporter Krzysztof Kąkolewski likened the 168-frame-long piece of footage that Drygas located to a "shard of an amphora from which the shape of the original vessel is meticulously reconstructed" (5). Using this "shard," the director attempted to recreate the consciousness of the deeply indoctrinated society. And that particular shot greatly influenced the structure of the film, effectively organising its course. The dramatic framework of the picture was designed deliberately to postpone the introduction of this brief sequence, which the authors considered absolutely pivotal.

In the analysis above, I focused on those means of expression that drew on expressionist poetics, in order to highlight how they contribute to the film's particular sort of tension and help us examine its artistic aspect. They were juxtaposed with passages telling of his wife making him sandwiches to take on the trip and her cleaning his suit. In the film, however, these household duties and the words of Siwiec's family and friends were ultimately eclipsed by the portrayal of his gesture and the focus on the overabundance of meaning it generated. In no way does that imply, however, that Drygas ever cast any judgement on his protagonist, moral or otherwise – above all, he tried to understand him and show that his actions were driven by noble intentions and carried no trace of insanity.

Where Drygas' film was primarily an examination of society and its willingness to submit to a power structure and ignore the sacrifice of a man who wanted to tear that façade down and preserve his own subjectivity, the radio drama focused chiefly on the tragedy of his family. If the film was a psychodrama session for the witnesses, then the play was one for Siwiec's loved ones. The impact of Drygas' documentary was rooted in formal rigour (Dondzik 92). Stripped of any genre elements and following a highly rigid structure, the picture was partitioned into three nearly equal parts, separated by segments featuring the priest. It opened with a staged prologue which featured a reenactment of the burning of files and records by state security operatives, and was capped off with a corresponding epilogue showing Siwiec engulfed in flames. The director focused solely on two timelines (the dramatic past and 1990, when the witness testimonies were recorded) and skilfully jumped between the two. He also cut down the number of locations to a necessary minimum – even the doctor and the nurse were interviewed at the stadium rather than the hospital. However, despite the sparseness, the film still feels almost baroque when compared to the radio play.

The austerity of the radio drama is evinced by the significantly reduced cast and number of story settings. Very few segments deal with something other than the Siwiec household, and these are inserted primarily to help the listeners immerse themselves in the events of 1968. The prologue, featuring testimony from the Siwiec family, is followed by, and seemingly juxtaposed with, a series of audio segments from official state records: crowds chanting Gomułka's pseudonym, "Wiesław, Wiesław," an excerpt from one of the First

Secretary's speeches, a Czech radio report on Warsaw Pact forces crossing the Czechoslovak border, automatic rifle fire, a roaring crowd against an ambulance siren, and a passage from the Czechoslovak national anthem. Then, the play takes us forward in time, and another radio broadcast, with folk music and song and an excerpt from the Polish national anthem, informs us that we are now at the harvest festival in Warsaw. Aside from that, the play includes Siwiec's wife and five of his children reading his testament, passages from his manifesto, four excerpts from declassified state security files, as well as the rustle of paper sheets and dispassionate testimonies from family members. The play does not feature appearances from the archival records clerk, the priest from Przemyśl, friends nor more distant relatives. Neither does it include incident witness testimony or commentary from the unnamed priest.

Drygas' two works, however, share a correspondingly expressive, profoundly dramatic, solemn, almost funereal score, composed by Paweł Szymański; the only difference is that he was commissioned to score the drama, whereas the film resorted to one of his existing pieces. By design, the play gives much of the airtime over to the Siwiec family. It also features longer passages from his manifesto, played back here as they are in the film, with crackling and static in the background, suggesting the recording was made decades earlier. Their special status is further emphasised by the soundtrack – only a portion of the finale is devoid of the background music, to make the ending even more impactful. The music gravitates towards extremes, as dynamic, dramatic passages are contrasted with gentler, slower phrases written in a minor key.

As I already mentioned, the narrative here unfolds slowly, gradually. The death of the family patriarch is first brought up by Innocenta, against a mournful score, and then explored further by her brothers who discuss the role of their father in their lives. From the very first moments, it is clear that we are dealing with a difficult subject. The Siwiec children talk freely – although clearly still in some pain, their words carry not even a trace of undue sentimentality. A thread of sorrow runs through their words, a longing for the absent father who was so loved and so needed. Each of the family members speaks only on their own behalf, there is no interfamily dialogue at the dinner table,[13] and, thus, no familial "we" to speak of. In the face of tragedy and loss, only the "I" remains, the solitary individual.

The play also borrowed from the film the segment with Siwiec's will being read aloud by the family member that the given passage pertains to, with some parts delivered by many voices simultaneously. And like the film, the play is stripped of genre elements, such as the sounds of typical household bustle, implying that the family no longer has a home, a common safe space to return to, and remains a collection of individuals saddled with a burden they are struggling to bear. Their testimonies unfold in silence (only the prologue is scored), so that all of the audience's attention stays on the sentiments of the Siwiec family. Because his immediate family is given most of the airtime, we can now glean more insight into Siwiec himself and his habits;

190 Selected contemporary ultimate protests by fire

still, the family mostly talks about the incident, rather than discuss happy or private memories of the man.[14] Although each testimony teems with barely concealed emotions, they seem devoid of any warmth – as if the wound the incident opened still has not healed 20 years later, the trauma still fresh and unprocessed.

In the radio drama, Siwiec's name comes up even later than in the film – uttered by his son Wit, as he begins reading from his father's will. We learn of his self-immolation not from eyewitnesses but from a state security officer, perfunctorily reading an official report on the incident while a harvest festival polonaise plays in the background. The biggest difference between Drygas' two works, however, is the way they treat the relationship between the husband and wife and the father and his children, as well as their reactions to his death.

The former is explored and emphasised by an extended segment dealing with Maria Siwiec's stay in the hospital. In the course of the intimate, moving confessions, the wife, her voice breaking, gives us a glimpse of her husband's final moments and the emotions she was dealing with at the time. She brings up his first words upon seeing her in the hospital (in jest, and making light of his situation, he said: "Allow me to pay my respects, m'lady") and mentions that he also inquired after the children and whether they knew the truth. Maria also reveals how terribly powerless she felt, disoriented, torn between the hospital and the family home: "There are these gaps in me, cracks through which my memories slip. Where I was, where I went... I know I went to the station, picked up a ticket and then returned it, because I thought 'why buy the ticket if he's staying here,' and then I thought: 'I left my children at home'" (qtd. in Drygas, "Testament" 79).

The key moment in her account, however, revolves around a moment Maria has never publicly discussed before. Just before he lost consciousness, Maria believes her husband tried to tell her something, confess, apologise perhaps, but she quickly changed the subject, a decision she would later come to regret. In another profoundly moving moment, Maria recounts tenderly declaring: "Ryszard dear, what you did... you are a hero" (qtd. in Drygas, "Testament" 80), so that he would know she bore him no ill will. So attuned was she to the suffering of her husband that she swore that at the moment of his death she could hear him calling, pulling her awake. Maria's poignant and painful account stands as testament to her perfect love and devotion to her husband.

The impact of the widow's testimony (and confession) is further amplified by being woven together with the words of the eldest son Wit, 16 years old in 1968, tearfully sharing his memories of seeking authority figures in his teens and slowly realising that only his father could have played that role for him. This, in turn, led him to join the ranks of the dissidents, a decision that his loved ones had trouble accepting, as the family had already sacrificed more than enough. He, however, was ready – as he later revealed to his wife – to follow his father's example and immolate himself, further testifying to the boy's need for approval from the absent parent, a need that was utterly pressing, but ultimately doomed to unfulfilment.

A fitting counterpoint to the mother-son testimony could be found in a later segment, comprising an excerpt from Siwiec's recording ending with the words: "There is no price too steep for preventing this inhuman system from taking over the world" (qtd. in Drygas, "Usłyszcie" 55), and a passage from a state security report, noting that Siwiec had never been under psychiatric care and was considered of sound mind. Before we hear Siwiec's last words, prophesying the collapse of the Soviet Union and calling on his compatriots to awaken from their torpor, we once again hear from his wife and children, their words running the gamut of emotions. The youngest, Mariusz, barely 12 at the time of the incident, recounts how he could not stop himself from crying at the funeral. Adam, two years his elder, begrudged his father for abandoning those who needed him most. Wit, on the other hand, believed that he himself failed and was still guilt-ridden at the time of recording. In Innocenta, the resentment she felt towards Siwiec for saddling her mother with a burden she was almost unable to bear eventually gave way to regret at not being able to help her father – a feeling she would have a hard time dealing with later in life. Elżbieta, on the other hand, sought to understand what compelled her father to abandon his wife and children.

This family psychodrama session is capped off with an appearance from Siwiec's wife, her words another testament to her compassion and sensitivity, where she admits that she always thinks about her husband's suffering, first, and ponders his motivations and the futility of his gesture, second. The radio play closes with a final passage from the Siwiec recording – the one in which he declares the word "mother" to be the most beautiful in the whole world and pleads with his audience, his voice trembling, to heed his call, this cry of an ordinary man.

Retreading the path he followed with the documentary, Drygas also decided against having the radio play push any sort of interpretations onto the audience. Instead, he offered them access to the reactions of the Siwiec family and allowed them to confront the family's pain, their emotional turmoil, and the challenges they faced. As in the documentary, he distilled the message by focusing on just two points in time. This approach, however, precluded him from exploring the adversities the family had to face later on, leaving the audience to take up that task on their own.[15] Like the viewers before them, the listeners of the radio drama would have to judge the consequences of Siwiec's actions in their own hearts, and on their own decide whether the price he paid for his convictions was worth it. The director mentioned that during post-screening Q&A sessions, viewers often felt the "need to share their own experiences of facing situations that demanded of them a more involved stance" (Drygas, "Analiza" 159). In my opinion, the play – although valuable in and of itself – perfectly complements its better-known cinematic counterpart. Together, the two function as a duet on self-sacrifice, with the

192 Selected contemporary ultimate protests by fire

radio play placing a much bigger emphasis on the familial aspect of the tragedy. Although the family perspective is explored in the documentary, I believe the play painted a much fuller picture of the profound impact that the decision to undertake such an act in public may have on the private sphere.

The other Jan: the fiery self-sacrifice of Jan Palach (Czechoslovakia, 1969)

Liminal time as an essential context of Jan Palach's self-immolation

Jaroslava Moserová, a burn treatment specialist, translator, writer, politician, diplomat, future Czech presidential candidate, and one of the last people to see Jan Palach alive, said that the time she spent with the student in the hospital was forever seared into her memory – just like the days immediately following his death.

> I wasn't with him when he was being taken upstairs to the intensive care unit, but one of the nurses that was with him said that he kept repeating: "Please tell everyone why I did it. Please tell everyone." I spoke with him for quite a long time, because he was able to speak right after the admission – later on he started having great difficulties breathing – so he not only could talk, but the reason why he did it was quite clear. It was not so much in opposition to the Soviet occupation, but the demoralization which was setting in, that people were not only giving up, but giving in.
>
> (Moserová, "Remembering")

It is these experiences that Moserová examined in her 1993 dramatic monologue *A Letter to Wollongong*, which she wrote in Australia (where she was serving as ambassador) to commemorate the 25th anniversary of the Prague Spring. Initially written for the radio, the piece was later adapted for the theatre and staged across the globe. The play tells a story of Prague burn unit nurse, recruited by state security, who pens her émigré brother an account of everything that has been happening since the Warsaw Pact invasion. Moserová's drama delves into issues like resistance and subservience to autocratic regimes, and explores dealing with a burdensome past. In the letter, the nurse explains that Czechs were vanquished not when the Soviets crossed the border, but when they, as a nation, started to give up (Sabatos 211).

In an interview she sat for in 2006, a year before her death, the author admitted that instead of speaking openly about Palach, she preferred to describe the gloomy, despondent atmosphere that pervaded the country:

> In fact, what the regime did to our way of thinking and our attitude was the greatest crime that the regime committed. It forced us into hypocrisy

Confronting defeat   193

and forced us to teach our children to be hypocritical. Truth was suppressed to an unbelievable degree. During the totalitarian regime, people thought ambitiousness was irreconcilable with decency because if you had any ambition and tried to build a career you had to make concessions to the regime.

(Moserová, "From")

Moserová argued that these attitudes, exhibited nationwide, were all the more unacceptable because unlike in the 1950s, when resistance could mean death, living under the Communist regime in the late 1960s and the early 1970s did not require collaborating with the secret police or joining the Party ranks.

The post-invasion conditions in the country, as portrayed by Moserová, were indeed miserable, but the truth is that in January 1969 the situation was not all that bad. At the time, the policy of the so-called "normalisation," implemented gradually under pressure from the Soviet Union, had not yet reached the momentum it eventually accumulated after Alexander Dubček was replaced as First Secretary of the Central Committee of the Communist Party of Czechoslovakia by reform sceptic Gustáv Husák at the Party session on 17 April 1969.

This launched a decisive turn in the course of events in Czechoslovakia. The dismissal marked the end of the period of reform and renewal, and heralded, in a rather spectacular manner, the coming "consolidation and normalisation" in both the party and in society.

(Kwapis 305)

Seeing the situation in the country taking a turn for the worse, on 9 August 1969, Václav Havel penned his famous letter to Dubček, who by then was the President of the Federal Assembly. In the letter, Havel called on Dubček to reembrace rather than deny his past efforts to reform the regime, and implored him to refrain from self-critiquing his own prior opposition to the 1968 invasion.

Your act would thus become a moral mirror, its reflection condemning us as clearly as Jan Palach's death had – but with much more enduring consequences. Many of your compatriots would treat it as a yardstick against which to measure oneself, a signal that a meaningful future was still within reach, a promise of sustenance, both political and personal.

(Havel, *Síla* 49)

The once-leading figure of the Prague Spring, however, was at the time already thoroughly marginalised in politics and had no power over social attitudes.

On 21 August 1969, the first anniversary of the invasion, the Czechs were still bold enough to stage numerous protests across the country, during which "five protesters were killed, dozens were seriously hurt, and hundreds

194 Selected contemporary ultimate protests by fire

suffered minor injuries" in skirmishes with Czechoslovak troops, deployed for the first time against their own compatriots (Kwapis 308–309). However, in response to the unrest, the Party, dominated by hardline conservatives from spring 1969 onwards, decided to clamp down on dissident tendencies. The party leadership "directed its propaganda machine to knock the nation into a mindless stupor and took measures to intimidate potential trouble-makers" (Kwapis 310). The media and key state institutions were purged of all those who were insufficiently ardent in their support of the new order. Cowed into submission, powerless and resigned, many Czechs withdrew into their private lives.

The situation in January 1969 was a little different, because the country was still in transition – the dangerous, liminal time *in-between*, marked by an uncertainty about the future.

Initially, the "normalisation" moved rather slowly, as the occupying forces left the implementation of Moscow's directives to the local cadres. At that point, that was the more prudent and effective approach, as Czech officials still enjoyed popular support; the nation, roused by the events of the Prague Spring, exhibited much valour and maturity in the early days following the invasion, but, embittered and ravaged by a sense of betrayal, later turned to passive resistance. The situation gradually worsened, reaching a low point on 16 October 1968, when the regime signed a treaty on the "temporary" presence of Soviet forces, retroactively sanctioning the invasion. The decision sapped the public's trust in the Communist Party leadership and was met with fierce opposition from students who held a mass demonstration just before the treaty was ratified by the Federal Assembly two days later.

Despite the regime's crackdown, civil society continued to flourish, while the task of defending democratising reforms was taken up primarily by student and trade associations. The former eventually organised a nationwide strike in November 1968. The students' postulates went unheeded (to the dismay of Palach, who participated in the protest), but popular support for their dissent testified to the solidarity between social classes. When the higher echelons of the regime were once again rocked by conflict, with the conservatives lining up to oust Josef Smrkovský, a key reformer and candidate for president of the federal parliament (Czechoslovakia was federalised on 27 October 1968), an unlikely coalition of intellectuals, journalists, student associations, and factory workers threatening further strikes came to his defence. The presidential seat was ultimately taken by Peter Colotka, a politician widely seen as progressive, while Smrkovský became the head of one of the parliament's houses. All of these events unfolded between 16 and 18 January 1969, coinciding with Palach's self-burning. The student's timing seemed impeccable, as he managed to tap into the public mood at a time when "the Czech youth was swept with an atmosphere of idealism and pro-independence exaltation" (Holland, "Tak"). He chose to act when people were on the brink of surrender, but not yet ready to give in completely.

To recapitulate, if Palach had protested a couple of months later, after all civil liberties had been curtailed, the censors had tightened their grip on the flow of information, and Husák had consolidated his position and that of his inner circle, it is possible that the cowed populace would have been afraid to openly manifest its devotion to democratic values, of which Palach became a symbolic defender. Furthermore, it is possible that news of his protest would have been suppressed and would never have reached the public, the incident itself would have been covered up, while Palach would have been framed as mentally unstable or a degenerate, which was par for the course for similar cases in the Soviet Bloc.

The student, his protest, death, funeral, and the aftermath

There is a multitude of sources on Palach. First among them is *Živé pochodně* (*Live Torches*), a collection of poetry, reflections, and memoirs edited by Josef Sádecký and published in 1980 in Zurich by Czech émigrés. The volume was followed two years later by *Jan Palach. Ein biografischer bericht* (*Jan Palach: A Biographical Report*), a non-fictional account of Palach's life, also published in Zurich and penned by Czech journalist and essayist Jiří Lederer. The book appeared in the original Czech only after the fall of the Eastern Bloc, in 1990, seven years after the author's death, and eventually became the foundation of the majority of press and academic discourses around "Torch no. 1" (Kulmiński 79). The following year, students from Charles University's Department of Philosophy compiled a collection of writing and photographs under the title *Ve jménu života Vašeho...* (*In the Name of Your Life*).[16] In 1994, Miroslav Slach, a writer who was Palach's history teacher at the elementary school, published a collection of reminiscences entitled *Světlo v soumraku* (*The Light in the Darkness*).

The first exhaustive academic publication on Palach, however, the voluminous collection *Jan Palach '69*, edited by historians Peter Blažek and Jakub Jareš, journalist Patrik Eichler, and featuring a meticulously detailed account of Palach's act (Blažek et al. 39–89), was published only on the 40th anniversary of the immolation of the self-styled "first torch." Work on the publication was preceded by the development of the janpalach.cz website, launched in 2007 on the initiative of the Student Council of the Charles University's Department of Philosophy, which featured comprehensive information on the student from Prague (available in eight languages), numerous photographs, illustrations, archival documents, as well as films, radio broadcasts, and basic biographical information about the 14 other people who burned themselves for political reasons in Czechoslovakia and elsewhere.[17]

The year 2009 also marked the publication of *Poslední dny Jana Palacha* (*The Last Days of Jan Palach*), a book authored by psychiatrist Zdenka Kmuníčková, who wrote the medical examiner's report on Palach, as well as the premiere of

196   Selected contemporary ultimate protests by fire

Kristina Vlachová's TV documentary *Poselství Jana Palacha* (*Jan Palach's Message*), which featured archival footage, and contemporary interviews with Palach's brother Jiří, his friends, and people who either knew him or had contact with him following the incident in Wenceslas Square.[18] In 2013, Agnieszka Holland's TV mini-series *The Burning Bush* was released alongside a promotional website,[19] faithfuliremain.com, which featured information about the series, interviews with the cast and crew (in English, Czech, Hungarian, and Polish), as well as testimony from people who lived in Czechoslovakia in the 1960s, including Palach's friends. Together, the aforementioned sources offer a comprehensive biographical and factual record of Palach and his protest.[20]

Jan Palach was born in Prague on 11 August 1948, which made him part of the first post-war generation to be brought up under the Communist regime that took power in the February 1948 coup. He was born into a middle-class family that belonged to the Czechoslovak Hussite Church and owned a confectionery shop in a small town of Všetaty near the capital, operated by his father Josef, a member of the Czech National Social Party.[21] Josef's wife, Libuše (née Kostomlatská), was a stay-at-home mother who took care of the couple's two sons – Jiří (born 1941) and Jan. The Palachs tried to bring their children up in the patriotic traditions of the First Republic. In the early 1950s, Josef Palach, like most small-business owners in the Stalinist era, was forced to close his store down and find employment as a labourer. To make ends meet, Libuše Palachová got a job as a saleslady at the rail station canteen in Všetaty. In 1957, she joined the Communist Party to make sure that her sons would have no trouble enrolling in college. Following Josef's fatal heart attack, which he suffered when Jan was barely 14 years old, his brother dropped out of medical school and moved away to find work in a factory, leaving Jan alone at home with his mother.

In his rather idealised portrait, Slach claimed that the boy was an avid reader of historical and adventure novels (Karl May's work chief among them), and a fine chess player and athlete. Jan's sweeping reading list allegedly included the writings of 17th-century Czech thinker and reformist John Amos Comenius, and the father of the independent Czechoslovakia, Tomáš Garrigue Masaryk.

After graduating from the Mělník high school, Palach wanted to study history, but failed to get a seat at the Department of Philosophy despite passing the entrance exams. Eventually, he enrolled at the Prague School of Economics and switched schools two years later, finally securing a place in the history programme. In college, he joined the voluntary student work brigades, which were shipped off to the Soviet Union to perform manual labour, a decision driven perhaps by the fact that he was a self-admitted Russophile; like the majority of the Czechoslovak populace, he was thankful to the Soviets for liberating his homeland from Nazi occupation.[22]

Blažek contends that Palach definitely had an interest in politics. Before the Prague Spring erupted, he reportedly distributed typewritten pamphlets to his friends, which included a reprint of a letter authored by Aleksandr

Solzhenitsyn, copies of speeches delivered at writer conventions, as well as columns penned by writer and journalist Ludvík Vaculík, noted author of *The Two Thousand Words* – a manifesto signed by key figures of Czechoslovakia's public and cultural life, published in support of reforms in four national newspapers on 27 June 1968. It is also known that Palach visited Masaryk's grave in Lány on 28 October 1968. In his biography, Lederer asserts that it is difficult to gauge the intensity of Palach's political interests due to the dearth of relevant sources. His friends mentioned that he was interested in the work of the Czech and Moravian Students' Union, but never actually joined its ranks. In this particular context, it also bears noting that 1968 marked Palach's first trip to the West. On 1 October 1968, already after the Warsaw Pact invasion, he left for France, where he spent three weeks helping with the grape harvest.

It is hard to say, without any ambiguity, when exactly Palach decided to self-immolate. On Christmas Eve, he went to the midnight mass in the Roman Catholic church in Všetaty, and attended the service at the Evangelical Church of Czech Brethren in Libiš the following day. Years later, Pastor Jakub Schwarz Trojan reminisced about a brief conversation with Palach after the service, during which the student asked him what can be done to shock the nation out of its stupor. Perhaps he made the decision after he failed to receive a reply from Lubomír Holeček, a leader in the student movement, to whom Palach wrote on 6 January 1969 to suggest storming the building of a Czechoslovak radio station and using it to broadcast a call to a general strike.

Palach began preparing his final performance at the very last minute. The day before, he attended the funeral of his uncle in Libiš and later took the morning train to Prague. It seems that he wrote the first draft of his open letter, which he planned to distribute in the square, upon returning to his university dorm at 8 am. Then he rewrote it in four slightly different versions (Blažek et al. 360–363). We can surmise that he prepared neither a banner nor pamphlets, as he expected that his protest would be publicised by the Czechoslovak Writers Union, Holeček, and his friend from his *alma mater*, Ladislav Žižka, to all of whom he sent letters (the fourth he took with him in an attaché case). The letters were signed "Torch no. 1," and the author styled himself one of a group of volunteers who decided to lay their lives down for the cause of liberty. He emphasised that he drew the opening spot, and thus the right to write the first letter and be the first torch of many, by way of a lottery. The letter also listed the alleged group's postulates, including abolishing censorship; banning *Zprávy*, a Czech-language newspaper published by the occupying force, which often carried brutal attacks on the Prague Spring and its leaders; and launching an open-ended general strike in support of these demands. Palach considered them reasonable and requested they be met by 21 January 1969,[23] warning that further "living torches" would burn if they weren't. In the postscript, he wrote that he hoped "no more fire would be necessary," while the letter sent to the writers union said: "January 1968

198 Selected contemporary ultimate protests by fire

began from the top, so January 1969 would have to move from the bottom," a reference to the fact that the 1968 reforms began with the removal of Antonín Novotny from the post of First Secretary on 5 January 1968, whereas now it would fall to the Czechoslovak people to take matters into their own hands.

If the student really had invented the group of self-professed torches (and given that no such group has ever been identified, it seems that he had indeed plucked it from thin air), then his gambit worked. Not only did it put pressure on the authorities, it also left the public accordingly shocked, because essentially anyone could be a fellow torch, ready to burn themselves when their time came. For his part, Palach was interested primarily in reaching workers from major industrial facilities, like the ČKD, whom he brought up in the letter to Holeček. The effectiveness of the strategy was later confirmed by Holland:

> we swallowed it hook, line, and sinker, all of us: the authorities, the police, state security, president Ludvík Svoboda, people on the streets, other students. The youth were swept with so intense an exaltation at the time, and the memory of the November general university strike was still so powerful, that it was indeed strange that such an organisation of torches had not in fact existed.
>
> ("Siła" 28)

Blažek determined that Palach left his dormitory around 11 am and mailed the above-mentioned letters on his way to Wenceslas Square. He also sent a postcard to a friend with whom he used to organise student trips to the USSR. Below a brief message of greeting, the card was signed: "Your Hus," an indication of Palach's self-identification with the Czech national hero, a fact I already touched upon. In the account of his first visit with Palach's mother after the boy's death, Slach mentioned that he found numerous press clippings on Buddhist self-burnings in Vietnam in his room. We can surmise, therefore, that his chosen form of protest was driven by more than just illustrious Czech history, a notion seemingly corroborated by the testimony of the nurses assigned to him, who reported that the young man repeatedly claimed that he was by no means a suicide and that he "set himself alight in protest, like the Buddhists in Vietnam" (*Poselství*), where – in his view – that course of action produced tangible results.

After purchasing two plastic containers he filled with kerosene, Palach probably went straight to the National Museum, where he arrived around 2.30 pm. He intentionally selected a spot with a heavy footfall around the clock, but the potent symbolism of the setting probably played a significant part in his choice, too. Robert Kulmiński explained:

> Many pivotal events in the history of Czechoslovakia and later the Czech Republic took place in or around that spot – from the declaration of independence, the celebrations of the 1,000-year anniversary of Czech statehood, through Nazi parades, the proclamation of nationalisation,

Warsaw Pact parades, up to the Velvet Revolution. Wenceslas Square was the stage on which the spectacle of national history played itself out. (47–48)

Furthermore, Palach may still have had fresh memories of the riots that broke out in the square on the first day of the invasion, and the brutal suppression of an anti-Soviet protest held here on 7 November 1968 (the anniversary of the Bolshevik Revolution), which he attended.

The young man's act was witnessed by many, and their testimonies have been preserved in police investigation files, allowing us to create a detailed reenactment of the incident. Blažek determined that:

> Palach hung his jacket over the railing next to the fountain, then pulled a bottle labelled "ether" from his case and put it to his face. Later, next to the fountain, he doused himself with kerosene and set himself alight. He jumped over the railing and ran between the parked cars towards the St. Wenceslas monument.
>
> ("Protest")

On the way there, he was nearly struck by a passing tram, which was what probably caused him to turn towards the delicatessen, although he was originally heading down the square. As he collapsed by the store, a public transit despatcher and a handful of bystanders attempted to snuff out the flames with their coats. On Palach's request, they also opened the attaché case he left by the fountain and read the letter he stuck inside. Minutes later, a Ministry of the Interior ambulance, which by sheer coincidence was passing nearby, pulled into the square. Before Palach was admitted, conscious but in a hopeless condition, to the Plastic Surgery Clinic at 61 Legerova Street in Prague on 2.45 pm, the paramedics attempted to bring him to the nearest hospital, right off Charles Square – indicating that the young man was removed from the site of the incident very quickly, within 20 minutes at most. The very act of protest and its immediate results were not captured by photo nor video cameras. A sizeable crowd gathered at the site of Palach's self-immolation and soon, police and firemen arrived as well, to interrogate the first batch of witnesses, take photographs for the records, and pick up the student's personal belongings – including the letter, the singed canister (the other melted from the heat), and the glass shards from the ether bottle.

The Czech News Agency (ČTK) reported on the self-immolation barely two hours after the incident, initially mentioning only the student's initials. Later that evening, a follow-up report was aired. Meanwhile, journalists began arriving at the clinic shortly after the incident to inquire after the student's condition, despite the hospital administration's decision to release any reports only through the ČTK. Although the regime tried to suppress and manipulate the flow of information about Palach (Kulmiński 75), over the following days news outlets across the country continued to run stories on

200 Selected contemporary ultimate protests by fire

the drastic episode. Palach's self-burning was also reported abroad, thanks to foreign journalists on the ground in Czechoslovakia (over a dozen of whom would soon be expelled). Within hours of the incident, the Czech and Moravian Students' Union sat for an emergency meeting and released a statement calling the self-burning a political protest. The following day, just before noon, the Union held a public reading of Palach's farewell note in the assembly hall of the Charles University's Department of Philosophy. This confirms that news of his deed and its character quickly reached the public, which, in turn, greatly influenced the course of events.

Immediately following Palach's self-burning, the nation was gripped by growing tension, released in random acts of support for his demands. One of the first of such acts was a protest hunger strike launched on 17 January by two students on the site of the immolation, outside the National Museum. They were soon joined by a dozen or so young people, workers, and high school students, including the then little-known Jan Zajíc (Kwapis 298). The strikers persevered through freezing temperatures for a few days, staying in tents or wrapped in blankets. At the time, similar protests were held in Brno, České Budějovice, Bratislava, and a handful of other locations.

On 17 January, Palach was visited by his mother and his brother, both in a state of shock. Aside from the medical staff, no one else was allowed to see him. Even police investigators, who wanted to question Palach about the group he was allegedly a part of, were refused access by the head of the burns unit. Many on staff recounted later that Palach insisted the group was real, one such confession was even recorded by Doctor Kmuníčková on tape. The student was also reportedly very interested in the public's reactions to his act.

The following day, the first spontaneous demonstration broke out in Prague, with around 1,000 mostly young people in attendance, who called for Palach's demands to be met and chanted disparaging remarks aimed at Soviet Union leader Leonid Brezhnev and at Husák. In the light of the civil unrest, some high-ranking members of the Central Committee feared Soviet retribution and further deterioration of Czech-Soviet relations, maybe even a takeover by the occupying force stationed in the country. After a conference call with the Czechoslovak Communist Party leadership, Brezhnev ordered Soviet forces to withdraw from Czech streets (Kwapis 297), but on 23 January issued a letter, co-signed by Soviet Premier Alexei Kosygin, in which the two ordered the Czechoslovak leaders to bring their people to heel. So admonished, the regime immediately moved to bring the situation, and the upset nation, back under control. Already on the day of the incident, newly elected Prime Minister Stanislav Rázl and Education Minister Vilibald Bezdíček met with university students to explain the complexity of the situation they were facing.

In the eyes of the authorities, a strike (especially an open-ended one) that the radicals called for, supposed to throw popular support behind Palach's demands, could only upset the fragile economic situation, kick off an inflation spiral, and eventually trigger a political crisis that could prove deeply disruptive to the reformers and their plans. Abolishing censorship was out of the question, especially given that it was already seen as too lenient and too liberal by Moscow and the local hardliners. Pulling *Zpravý* out of circulation was also beyond the realm of reason, as the Party leadership held (not incorrectly) that the printing and distribution of the newspaper was wholly out of their hands.

(Kwapis 297)

Ultimately, the government refused to accede to the demands, but to relieve the pent-up tension, the Party granted the students permission to hold a memorial march for Palach – provided they guarantee that the public order would not be disturbed. Just in case, however, military and police units were put on alert nationwide on 19 January.

Meanwhile, one of the doctors brought Eva Bednáriková, Palach's friend from his dorm, to the hospital, allegedly at his own request, and she later claimed that he urged her to bring Lubomír Holeček, too. The immolator supposedly asked the two visitors to pass on to the other "torches" to desist from further self-burnings. Blažek argued that the whole thing may have been a set-up organised by state security to prevent further suicide protests. After the two visitors left, Palach's condition deteriorated, until the doctors finally pronounced him deceased around 3.30 pm. His body was then moved to the Pathology Department of the University Hospital on Studničkova Street, where sculptor Olbram Zoubek clandestinely took his death mask, thus beginning the posthumous life of his body.[24]

Most high-ranking politicians (with Husák being one of the few exceptions) expressed their regret at the death of young man, while simultaneously condemning the form of protest he chose.[25] On 19 January, Dubček, President Svoboda, Czechoslovak Prime Minister Oldřich Černík, and Smrkovský all sent their condolences to Palach's mother, each stressing the purity of her son's intentions and his fervent love for his homeland, and highlighting that his sacrifice was a tragic misstep in their journey towards a better, socialist future for all. All of these notions were later repeated in the official media discourse surrounding the incident. Palach's protest was mostly portrayed as a result of an individual's misunderstanding of the vagaries of politics, as "his wishes aligned with the aspirations of the authorities" (Kulmiński 95). The media also denounced his chosen form of protest as too drastic and incompatible with European culture. Some went so far as to claim that the act further exacerbated the already dire political situation, and "if similar protests were to continue, chances were the Warsaw Pact would stage another intervention for stability reasons" (Kulmiński 88).

The next day, thousands marched down the streets of Prague in the student-organised "silent march"[26] – from Wenceslas Square to the Department of Philosophy building, where the clocks were stopped at the exact time of Palach's death. Protesters at the head of the march carried funeral and state flags,

202 Selected contemporary ultimate protests by fire

along with a portrait of the deceased student and banners bearing the Czech coat of arms. The protest concluded with a handful of speeches which invoked the leading figures from the national pantheon, and Professor Josef Charvát compared Palach's protest with the historical intransigence of Hus. That same day, unknown perpetrators renamed the plaza outside the Department of Philosophy from Red Army to Jan Palach Square, but the enamel plaques bearing the new name that went up a couple of days later were soon taken down.

The authorities attempted to influence the alleged group of "torches" by airing an appeal on 20 January, in which a group of renowned intellectuals and figures respected by the Czechoslovak youth (including chess grandmaster Luděk Pachman, poet Jaroslav Seifert, and Lederer), together with President Svoboda (Kwapis 297), called on them to refrain from further self-immolations and encouraged the purported conspirators to come out of hiding. The plea of the president was particularly emotional, as he learned during the broadcast that another self-burning had just taken place in Plzeň, leaving 25-year-old worker Josef Hlavatý with severe injuries.

The regime, which allowed the students to shape the narrative following the first auto-cremation, would not make the same "mistake" again. Already the next day, the daily *Rudé Právo* ran headlines that depicted Hlavatý as an alcoholic with family problems, a portrait later echoed by TV and radio outlets, and framed the incident as a suicide attempt brought on by personal issues, dismissing any link between him and the clandestine suicide group. Hlavatý died five days later (on the day of Palach's funeral), but because the intentions behind his act were denigrated, his own funeral went mostly unreported. Similar disinformation tactics were employed following two subsequent self-burning attempts – of 23-year-old construction worker Miroslav Malinka, who set himself alight on the night of 21 January in Brno, and 16-year-old student Jan Béreš, who self-immolated on 26 January in Cheb. Thanks to immediate help from passersby, who quickly extinguished them, neither man suffered significant injuries.

Although it is somewhat surprising how easily the public accepted the regime's claims that the three incidents were not politically motivated, Czech historians later determined that neither case was as clear-cut as previously thought. Indeed, Hlavatý's motivations were most likely of a personal nature, as investigators discovered that his self-burning came less than two weeks after the court granted his wife a divorce and full custody of their two children. The site of his protest, however, was symbolically charged: he burned himself in Dukla Square, where before the war there had stood a memorial to the Czech National Revival. Hlavatý also had a history of actively opposing the Soviet occupation – he painted anti-Soviet graffiti on walls and pulled road signage down to confuse foreign troops. Even if suicide was his primary goal, he was ultimately inspired by Palach to choosing what specific form it would take. The remaining cases were also influenced by Palach's fiery sacrifice. Before setting himself alight, Malinka visited the student's memorial site in

Liberty Square in Brno, while Béreš attended Palach's funeral in Prague, and later wrote four farewell letters in which he laid out his political demands and invoked the "Torch no. 1."

These later incidents illustrate the emotionally charged atmosphere that gripped the nation. With state security showing restraint, student unions organised mourning marches in cities across the country, similar to the one held in Prague. Columns of pilgrims journeyed on foot to the capital to visit Wenceslas Square, where the monument of the Czech patron saint – plastered with pamphlets, portraits of Palach, and decorated with candles and flowers – soon became an impromptu shrine. In front of the monument stood a makeshift honour guard flying the national flag, a clear indication of the national-hero status that the populace was according to Palach. On the fountain outside the National Museum, someone installed a reproduction of the student's death mask.

> Over the next couple of days, mass student rallies were held in every single academic facility in the country, with students, even those who stood by Palach's demands, speaking out against embracing similarly drastic measures. The idea of a general strike was also ultimately dismissed.[27]
>
> (Kwapis 298)

Was Hlavatý's self-immolation scrubbed so easily from the public consciousness because he left no note and the regime media swiftly convinced the nation that he was a failure? Or maybe the country found itself governed by a peculiar economy of grief, where the people – focused on mourning Palach and preparing for his funeral – were unable to emotionally cope with another extreme event? Regardless of the nation's emotional capacity, the preparations for Palach's burial continued. Set for 25 January, the ceremony was organised by the Czech and Moravian Students' Union, which also managed to secure a permit for the procession to march through the centre of Prague, mostly because the earlier "silent march" proceeded without incident. Student representatives also made efforts to have Palach interred in Slavín in the Vyšehrad Cemetery, with other prominent figures of Czech culture, science, art, and technology, but government officials ultimately refused their request. In the light of that, it was decided that Palach would be buried in the oldest necropolis in Prague, the Olšany Cemeteries.

The Palach funeral was given a very formal setting – it was a genuine *pompa funebris*, which, according to all the rules that governed such an event, "forced all the attendees into a frame drawing on national history and national culture, marked them with a stamp of empathetic participation" (Ratajczakowa 147). To seniors, the funeral bore a resemblance to the similarly solemn ceremony for Masaryk 30 years earlier.

The day before the burial, the coffin was laid out in the courtyard of Karolinum, the historic side of Charles University, with an honour guard standing watch. Tens of thousands of people, waiting in kilometre-long lines, turned out to pay their respects throughout the day, bringing flowers and funeral

204 Selected contemporary ultimate protests by fire

wreaths. Later that evening, a mass was held in Všetaty, with most of the townspeople in attendance. Next day the celebrations continued in the capital, starting with an early afternoon event in the Karolinum courtyard, which included a performance of the national anthem and speeches from prominent academics. Also in attendance were government officials – Education Minister Bezdíček and Minister of Sports Emanuel Bosák, both of whom were relatively unknown to the public (as both took office less than three weeks before), which, in turn, made the absence of high-ranking regime functionaries that much more noticeable (Blažek, "Funeral").

After the service, the coffin was placed inside the hearse, behind which a funeral procession formed. Its passage through the centre of Prague was watched by dozens, possibly even hundreds of thousands of onlookers, many of whom travelled to the capital from all across the country. According to many participants, the nation seemed swept with numbness and misery, but nevertheless still gripped by a peculiar exaltation and a sense of solidarity (Kwapis 298). The final farewell at the Olšany Cemeteries was attended only by Palach's immediate family, invited guests, and selected reporters, while the eulogy was delivered by Pastor Trojan.

The solemn, reflective mood brought on by the funeral did not last long. Already the next day, a spontaneous demonstration broke out near the Statue of St. Wenceslas and quickly spread across the city, leading to riots that were soon suppressed by police. Nearly 200 people were arrested, most of them youths. The next evening, around 2,000 people protested in Wenceslas Square, the last such gathering to take place there. To prevent further assembly, the regime ordered the spot turned into a green area.

Naturally, Palach's gravesite quickly became a symbolically charged site; thanks to a public fundraising effort, on 1 June 1969 the grave was covered with a large bronze plate, cast by Zoubek, featuring a depiction of human remains on the top. The tomb saw many visitors, with Czechs, Slovaks, foreign diplomats, reporters, and tourists coming in to pay their respects, leave flowers, candles, and notes, sometimes even poems.

In many cities across Europe (e.g., in Amsterdam, Florence, Milan, Rome, and Vienna), people poured into the streets in a gesture of solidarity with the Czechoslovak people. Some Western TV stations even ran a live video feed from Palach's funeral. Blažek wrote:

> UN Secretary General, U Thant, expressed his condolences over the death of Jan Palach. Italian PM, Mariano Rumor, paid his respects to him as well, and Indian PM, Indira Gandhi, said that he joined the gallery of world sufferers, alongside Mahatma Gandhi. Even Pope Paul VI paid tribute to Jan Palach's memory in his message of 26 January 1969 when he stated: "We can uphold the values that put self-sacrifice above others to the supreme test, but we cannot approve the tragic form taken on behalf of their aims."
>
> ("Foreign")

Appraisals of the self-immolation and its long-lasting influence

The world ultimately saw Palach not as a suicide, but – as he wished all along – as a man capable of altruistic self-sacrifice, deserving of the utmost compassion and appreciation.[28] This was due to a number of reasons. Firstly, his message was simple, facilitating widespread uptake. His demands also seemed realistic, as he did not focus on unattainable objectives, such as the removal of the regime or taking up arms against the Soviets. The specific media framing of the event also played a significant part in shaping its reception. In an editorial published soon after the incident in *Reportér*, Lederer called it "an appeal to consciences" and a "summons to acts that could restore the nation to a life of dignity in a free country" (qtd. in Kaliski, "Przed" 48–49).

Furthermore, the eager acceptance of a heretofore unknown young man into the national pantheon testified to the mythmaking potential of self-immolation as a borderline act. Because – as Kundera pointed out in his 1973 novel *Life is Elsewhere* – "the act of dying has its own semantics, and it matters how a man dies, and in what element" (293). According to the writer:

> Jan Hus and Giordano Bruno could not have died by the rope or by the sword; they could have died only at the stake. Their lives thus became the incandescence of a signal light, the beam of a lighthouse, a torch shining far into the space of time. For the body is ephemeral and thought is eternal, and the flicker of fire is the image of thought. Jan Palach ... would have been less likely to succeed in making his cry ring out to the nation's consciousness as a man who had drowned. (293–294)

The key piece of the puzzle, however, seemed to be the need that gripped the Czechoslovak people at the time – a time of moral exaltation and tribulation; the yearning for cultural heroes, individuals ready to sacrifice, even lay down their lives for their convictions. First, the people saw such a hero in Dubček, particularly after his famous radio address, delivered upon his return from Moscow, where he was shipped off to by the Soviets immediately after the invasion. In the speech, the First Secretary called for unity, order, and loyalty to socialism and the Party leadership, arguing that such assistance from the public would speed up reform. The unscripted address, which the clearly emotional Dubček delivered holding back tears, made a profound impression on the nation. Some believed that their leader was ready to defend reforms against adverse circumstances (Kwapis 254). But others saw the emotional frame of his speech as evidence that the cause was already lost (Holland, *Magia* 42–43).

Jan Palach offered a rejoinder to the deficit of heroism that pervaded the nation as "normalisation" crept on, subverting the stereotype that labelled Czechs as restrained.[29] Leaders of student organisations and some columnists "cast" him as the protagonist of a peculiar morality play, a notion evinced at the very least by his death mask being treated as a relic and put on display not only at the site of the incident, but also during the funeral service, and later at his *alma mater* (where it replaced a bust of Lenin), all to the unquestioning assent of the public. His young age and gender also played a significant role. A young, handsome man, whose student ID pictures were the key point of reference as regarded his looks, was, in the eyes of the still predominantly patriarchal Czech people, a much better candidate for a national hero than any other woman, regardless of the highly ambivalent character of the heroics of self-immolation. On the one hand, fiery self-sacrifice requires boundless courage; on the other, however, it is a passive, defensive form of protest that can be – stereotypically – associated with women. That particular notion needs little in the way of evidence – the paltry number of people who, outside historian and Bohemist circles, remember Blanka Nacházelová is proof enough. (Nacházelová was a student who poisoned herself with gas in her family home in Jihlava on 22 January 1969, in a gesture of solidarity with Palach and his demands.)

This is by no means an indication that Palach's protest was embraced without criticism or reservations. Naturally, I do not mean here the denouncements of Party hardliners, such as the conservative politician Vilém Nový, who claimed that the naïve student fell prey to ruthless manipulations of right-wing provocateurs and fed the public conspiracy theories about "cold fire," which Palach allegedly used, believing the liquid he was dousing himself with would erupt in flame but leave him unburned. Some voices rejected self-burning purely on ethical grounds, seeing it as a course that cannot be ultimately recommended to anyone. The moral ambiguity of self-immolation was soon laid bare by the wave of burnings triggered by Palach's example.[30] One such voice was Petr Uhl, a dissident and co-founder of the illegal Trotskyist Revolutionary Youth Movement, who criticised the demobilising impact of Palach's spectacular protest, which could neither be advocated nor encouraged.[31] These sentiments were echoed by Josef Mašín, a member of the resistance movement against the Communist regime in Czechoslovakia in 1951–53. Basing his rejection on logic similar to Uhl's, he ultimately used a military analogy to support his argument, claiming that in a battlefield scenario, ordering one's own forces to maim or kill themselves in confrontation with the enemy would be patently absurd.

The Church's official position on Palach's protest corresponded to views espoused by the Vatican – although the pope appreciated the student's capacity for self-sacrifice, he took issue with its ultimate form. In an address aired by the Vatican Radio not long before his death in 1969, Josef Beran, the Archbishop of Prague, said: "I bow to his heroic courage, although I cannot admire his desperate deed" (qtd. in Stach 305).

The potent social energy generated at the time eventually fizzled out without transcending the sphere of the symbolic, yielding no tangible political gains. From this perspective, Palach's protest ultimately proved ineffective, as the regime refused to meet any of his demands. As Polish historian Robert Kwapis aptly pointed out: "Most people simply decided to wait out the confusion, becoming passive and apathetic in the process. Furthermore, contrary to Palach's intentions, the incident also broadened the internal rifts in the reformer camp" (299).

In this context, it bears repeating that both Czechs and Slovaks were moved at the time by another event of a radically different nature – the Czechoslovak hockey team's two-time victory over the Soviet team (2-0 in the first match, 4-3 in the second) at the 1969 World Ice Hockey Championships in Sweden. Broadcast live, the matches on 21 and 28 March "were watched by nearly everyone in the country. After the victories, elation swept the nation. Within its grievously wounded consciousness, these athletic triumphs ascended to symbolic status, becoming a token redress for the plight of the occupation" (Kwapis 301). Following the second match, 150,000 people poured into Wenceslas Square where, after a provocation by undercover state security officers, they wrecked and later set fire to the offices of the Soviet national carrier Aeroflot.

Sabine Stach emphatically argued that later on, "some dissidents openly criticised the mythologisation of Palach, arguing that in the long run it had not revived, but rather ended, the resistance against the occupation in Czechoslovakia" (305). It was as if people were suddenly struck by the prospect that they would have to sacrifice everything, even their lives, to defend the democratisation process and their own fundamental values. It felt as if they were truly horrified by their own reflection in Havel's moral mirror, the idea that they would never be able to adopt the heroic comportment that Palach called them to with his borderline act. Ludvík Vaculík touched upon that in his 1983 autobiographical novel *Český snář* (*The Czech Dream Book*), which Havel called a grand story of "the heroism and tragedy of a man ... seeking to rediscover his fading integrity" (*Síla* 161):

> Unattainable examples make the depression of the others worse. Someone has to give millions of people absolution because they did not burn themselves like Jan Palach, because they did not strike, because they went to the election, because they did not sign the Charter 77, and because they may not be able to withstand various violent measures.
>
> (qtd. in Stach 306)

Although Palach's protest proved futile in terms of immediate and short-term political gains, and the mythology that grew around his outlook may have had a demobilising and petrifying effect, the expressive power of his act, as well as the memory of the communal experience that it engendered, continued to manifest themselves in later years. To quote a passage from Havel, we could say that they were "the virus of truth as it slowly spread through the tissue of the life of lies, gradually causing it to disintegrate" (Havel et al. 24).

208 Selected contemporary ultimate protests by fire

After all, Palach's protest was a "symbol around which dissent could be rallied" (Holland, "Siła" 28).

That issue was also discussed by Eva Kantůrková, author, screenwriter, and Charter 77 signatory, in a *samizdat* essay exploring the moral dimension of Palach's protest, wherein she wrote that his voluntary death expressed his desire to preserve his own dignity and restore it to his fellow man, while its luminous impeccability stood as an antithesis to the misery that mired those to whom the Prague student addressed his desperate plea. Kantůrková saw his act as an ethical memento whose power was founded solely upon a single individual decision, which evinced his opposition to being stripped of agency with regard to his own life.

This particular theme was also explored by Lara Weibgen, who argued that Palach offered to others not his own life as much as a vision of his death – "the haunting and indelible apparition of a human body on fire" (59). Kundera admitted that it was Palach's burning body, rather than witnessing a world war, the horror of the death camps, or experiencing Stalinist terror, that gave him the clearest sense of an impending apocalypse (Sabatos 204). The imagined depictions of the dramatic moment and its consequences were bound to make a profound impression on the Czechoslovaks' collective imagination. By asserting that he alone had the right to make decisions about his own flesh, he simultaneously denied the repressive regime that same right, and declared his unwillingness to be just another docile body, meek, compliant, and carried by the current of events (Weibgen 59).

The fact that it withstood numerous attempts to expunge the student and any memory of him from the collective imagination seems a testament to the sheer power of that vision and the legend that accompanied Palach. The media rarely, if ever, discussed him after his funeral. The regime also rejected all public petitions to erect a monument to the student, and instructed state security to take a closer look at the people responsible for them. As the first anniversary of Palach's death drew nearer, his name went mostly unmentioned in public. Six months later, in July 1970, the half-ton bronze plate covering his grave was removed and melted down. Palach's family were subject to a long campaign of intimidation, intended to persuade them to agree to exhuming and cremating his body, which finally took place on 22 October 1973, in the small hours of the morning to minimise public scrutiny. Palach's tomb was replaced with a new headstone bearing the name Maria Jedličková.[32] Petr Blažek wrote: "The urn was collected by Libuše Palachová. She was able to deposit it at the Všetaty municipal cemetery only in late March 1974" ("Operation").

Members of the Czechoslovak diaspora, which grew considerably during the "normalisation" period, tried to preserve Palach's memory by publishing books on the student and erecting memorials. But it would not be these efforts that would ultimately drive Palach's name, with tremendous force, back into the Czechoslovak public sphere.

The aforementioned power of the vision and the myth resurfaced on 9 January 1989, a week before the 20th anniversary of the self-immolation, which was to be marked with an unsanctioned memorial event on Wenceslas Square, organised jointly by five dissident groups. Around that time, Havel received an anonymous letter, in which the author announced their intention to self-burn on the eve of the anniversary in protest against political oppression. Havel implored state television to allow him to appeal to the would-be immolator and dissuade them from following through with the plan, but was ultimately refused, leading the dissident to appear on RFE, which the regime had stopped jamming the month before. A similar plea was voiced by Dana Němcová, the then-spokeswoman of Charter 77. Both were soon charged with inciting sedition and interfering with state affairs, and Havel was ultimately sentenced to nine months in prison.

Regardless, people still streamed into the square and demonstrations continued for the next couple of days. However, as Blažek pointed out, most were violently suppressed, with law enforcement deploying water cannons and special riot troops against the protesters ("Jan"). In Czech historiography, the demonstrations that broke out during the so-called "Jan Palach Week" and led to the arrest of over 1,400 civilians are widely considered the beginning of the end of the Communist regime, and a harbinger of the Velvet Revolution which began on 18 November 1989.[33]

Thus, years later, it became apparent that one of the slogans featured prominently during the January 1969 riots – "We shall remain faithful" – was actualised on a mass scale. Another thing that has since become clear is that Palach's act laid the foundation for widespread dissent without which "the collapse of Communism in Czechoslovakia would remain a mere reflection of external processes, no more than a ricochet of the perestroika" (Holland, "Siła" 28).

Between the dead and the living: on John Hejduk's architectural structures The House of the Suicide and The House of the Mother of the Suicide, and Agnieszka Holland's TV mini-series The Burning Bush

The Prague student ended up inspiring artists not just in Czechoslovakia and the former Soviet Bloc, but also across the globe, becoming an icon of resistance against oppression (he also ended up having other ideas projected onto him; more on that later). This influence persisted beyond the immediate aftermath of the Wenceslas Square incident and beyond the observance of the anniversaries of his death, although these events generated a plethora of commemoration practices, some of which were official,[34] others informal,[35] and still others illegal.[36] We would be hard pressed to find a field in either culture or the arts on which his protest had not left a mark. Echoes of his sacrifice can be found in literature (mostly in poetry, but also in prose

210 Selected contemporary ultimate protests by fire

and drama), opera, classical music, performance art, dance theatre, sculpture, painting, poster art, filmmaking, and other areas of popular culture, such as pop music or comic books.[37] Palach's visage has been afforded the status of symbol and – like the omnipresent stylised portrait of Che Guevara, killed in Bolivia less than six months before the student's protest – now adorns postage stamps, commemorative coins, memorial medals, and T-shirts, and has even been used as a template for tattoos.

Charles Sabatos pointed out that in literature, Palach's burning or charred flesh has been replaced with an "imaginary body," a metaphor of his heroic sacrifice (194). This particular image, along with the mythologising narrative and representations teeming with pathos, has been a central point around which the Prague student's presence in culture have converged. On the other end of the spectrum are those pieces that tend to strip the gilding off and demythologise his figure, simultaneously humanising him.[38]

Many commemorative practices and other cultural activities also brought about semantic shifts with regard to the reasons and meaning of his protest. For example, Palach has been embraced by Italian nationalists, who venerated him as a symbol of the struggle against communism,[39] whereas the student was a self-professed supporter of the reforms introduced by the Czechoslovak Communists. This particular paradox was brought up by left-leaning film artist Pier Paolo Pasolini, who soon after Palach's death wrote that the student's protest was not a manifestation of his anti-communist stance. On the contrary, it clearly demonstrated "to what level of idealism a young Communist, born and raised in a Communist world, could be driven. An idealism which allowed him to commit an act worthy of an ancient age; of a modern Vietnamese saint" (Sabatos 195). Such a frame, however, also seems a self-serving misrepresentation, as Palach was by no means a young Party cadre or even a member.[40]

As I already mentioned, two of the most important works that reawakened dormant memories and interest in Palach (and not just in the Czech Republic) – John Hejduk's *The House of the Suicide* and *The House of the Mother of the Suicide*,[41] and Agnieszka Holland's *The Burning Bush*[42] – also transcend the simplistic heroic narrative, but do so without subverting or distorting the meaning of his sacrifice.

It was allegedly seeing Paul Cézanne's *La maison du pendu* (*The House of the Hanged Man*, ca. 1873), and its simple, geometrised interpretation of the depicted buildings and the landscape, that first gave Hejduk the idea of paying homage to Palach's sacrifice. Another key inspiration was *The Funeral of Jan Palach*, a poem by Hejduk's friend,[43] New York poet, critic, and art historian David Shapiro. Composed in 1969 and published two years later in *A Man Holding an Acoustic Panel*,[44] the poem accentuated the relationship between mother and son. The verses portray a lyrical subject (Palach) who finds himself no longer bound by gravity, signifying, on the one hand, his transition onto a different plane of existence, and on the other, his transcendence of earthly bonds, a feat which only cultural heroes (or mystics) are capable of. An element of pathos surfaces in the final verse, which discusses weeping, seemingly immobilised astronauts (itself an allusion to riveting news of the American moon landing). The mother is given an equal standing with her son. The verses paint her as strong enough to gaze into the open grave and, if we were to read the final line literally ("And it was alright I was dead"), forgive her son. But her pain and despair are so raw and so penetrating that they seem to nearly offset the heroic nature of her child's fiery sacrifice.[45]

Hejduk first created a series of drawings which looked like sketches of buildings and corresponded with the poet's verses. These drafts later became "figures" that were supposed to illustrate his theoretical concepts on reinvigorating public spaces, which he outlined in his *Lancaster/Hanover Masque* (Hejduk, "Theater"), itself drawing on 16th-century English court masque. In 1986, together with students from the Georgia Institute of Technology in Atlanta and in collaboration with Hejduk, James Williamson launched an effort to bring the two structures to life, despite the fact that they were initially expected to remain solely on paper. The project was concluded four years later, with the completed cedar cuboids, approximately 2.7 m wide, 2.7 m long, and 3.6 m tall, and their top face stuck with 49 4-m-long spikes, making both structures over 7 m tall in total. In 1990, they were exhibited temporary at the Georgia Institute of Technology's College of Architecture and were later disassembled for storage on GIT premises. Three years after Hejduk's death, they were reassembled for *Sanctuaries: The Last Works of John Hejduk* (2003), an exhibition held at the Whitney Museum of American Art in New York, and then finally turned over to the Canadian Centre for Architecture in Montreal which holds most of the artist's writings, papers, illustrations, and designs.

In 1991, after the collapse of the Soviet Bloc, Hejduk installed a second version of the structures in the Royal Garden of Prague Castle, dedicating them to the people of Czechoslovakia and President Havel. There, they stayed on display for nearly a decade, until they were finally taken down due to extensive water damage. Hejduk's daughter, Renata, recounted that the idea to reinstall the structures was first floated just before her father's death (Zeiger). However, due to adverse circumstances, the idea became reality only 15 years later. Made out of metal, the structures were installed at the Alšovo embankment near the Academy of Arts, Architecture & Design in January 2016, next to a metal plaque bearing Shapiro's poem written in Czech and English.[46]

Hejduk's structures resemble buildings but are much smaller in size; on the other hand, it is difficult to see them as sculptures. They seem provisional (as they are relatively easy to disassemble and install in another location) but aspire to monumentalism, resembling miniature mausolea. Their form invites anthropomorphisation and reading the two as a mother-son pair, an interpretation further facilitated by the spikes, which resemble human hair and help our imaginations register the cuboids as human heads. Although arranged at an angle to one another and set around 5 m apart, they have to be seen as a single whole. Only then do they reveal the full extent of their import and acquire additional meanings.

Although identical in volume, the two carry some distinctive features. The spikes of the "Mother" are vertical, resembling hair standing on end in response to terrible news or a horrifying sight, whereas atop the "Son," the spikes are slanted at an angle, suggesting an explosion. *The House of the Suicide* is covered with polished stainless-steel panels, and when the sun is out, the structure gleams with metallic luminescence. *The House of the Mother of the Suicide*, meanwhile, is covered with tiles of weathering steel, which has a much higher tolerance for adverse weather conditions – exposure to air and rain causes a protective rust-like film to appear on its surface. Its subdued colour scheme brings up associations with mourning, pain, destruction, or collapse.

Other differences between the two are less pronounced. *The House of the Suicide* is a self-enclosed space, with no doors or windows. We can only imagine how it would feel to be trapped inside that – supposedly – claustrophobic, dark, tiny space, like in a peculiar mausoleum or prison cell. At the base of the other structure's rear wall (looking from the "Son"), there is a small door that allows passage inside. Standing in the cramped "room," which evokes the female womb, we can climb up on a small platform and gaze through a crack out onto the adjacent structure. Thus, the "Mother" keeps constant watch over her "Son," and the vision of her "burning" or "luminous" child will forever haunt her. Ultimately, it is up to us to decide whether that gaze will be regretful, compassionate, or simply impatient.

Despite their pronouncedly geometric design, commonly associated with urban fabric, the two structures nevertheless seem strange, an alien presence disrupting the cityscape. They look like bizarre hairbrushes, discarded toys of giant children, surrealist dice, or deformed, unusable Rubik's cubes. No other sculpture honouring the memory of Jan Palach, not even the bronze plate over his grave or the death mask, installed across the square near the main entrance to the Department of Philosophy building, has embraced such bold expressiveness before. Hejduk's work stands apart, especially when compared to the monument erected next to the site of Palach's self-immolation, unveiled in 2001. The latter is formed by paving stones arranged in two circular burial mounds, joined by a bronze cross, oriented to reflect the position of Palach's body following his collapse. On its left arm, the cross bears the names of Palach and Zajíc, along with the dates of their births and deaths. Given the low profile and horizontal configuration, the memorial is fairly inconspicuous. The prostrate cross conjures up images of Christ falling under the weight of human sin, unambiguously situating both "Torches" squarely within the tradition of Christian martyrdom. Hejduk's piece, on the other hand, examines the relationship between a mother and her child, giving equal weight to both the martyr and those left behind to grieve and mourn him. Although the installation could also be read as drawing on Christian tradition, offering a reinterpretation of the *Mater dolorosa* theme, the underlying metaphor in its case is much less unambiguous.

That inquiry into the relationship between the living and the dead is what Hejduk's piece and Holland's mini-series have in common. The latter, too, explores the lives of those who have to deal with the aftermath of the drastic, hair-raising incident, attributing perhaps more significance to their recovery than to the heroic act of self-sacrifice that will forever stand as an indelible mark on their lives. Such treatment does not imply a disavowal of the act itself, but rather a willingness to examine other aspects of the self-sacrifice.

In the wake of the 1989 regime change, the Czechs have pursued a number of gestures seeking to redress prior efforts to denigrate Palach's memory,[47] but he nevertheless began gradually fading from public discourse not long after the Velvet Revolution. Commemorative narratives naturally resurfaced around relevant anniversaries (the 40th was celebrated with particular pomp), but when in 2008 French Prime Minister Nicolas Sarkozy offered to turn Hungarian sculptor András Beck's piece *In Honour of Jan Palach* over to the Czech Republic, Prague officials, in a particularly revealing development, refused, and the sculpture ultimately ended up in the provincial town of Mělník (Sabatos 213).

The story behind the development of *The Burning Bush* seems to confirm the notion that Palach has been somewhat marginalised since 1989. In 2009, three Czechs – screenwriter Štěpán Hulík, still in college at the time, and two producers, Tomáš Hrubý and Pavla Kubečková, both Hulik's junior – approached Czech public television with the idea of developing a film based on the Palach incident, but were promptly turned down. Author of *Kinematografie zapomnění* (*Forgotten Cinematography*, 2011), a study of Czech filmmaking in the "normalisation" period, and fervent enthusiast of the Polish cinema of moral disquiet, Hulík saw the rejection as motivated not by the gradual erasure of Palach and his protest from the collective memory, but by how vexing these past events still were to older Czechs. The screenwriter explained:

> People who lived through 40 years of Communism are ashamed of not behaving as courageously as they would have liked. They shun the past and do not seek to understand what really happened. A new generation had to come in to give the normalisation period a fresh, less biased look.

The project was eventually picked up by HBO, which then approached Holland to direct. The choice was motivated by a handful of factors. Firstly, she knew the context well – in 1966, not even 18 years old at the time, she enrolled at the Film and TV School of the Academy of Performing Arts in Prague (FAMU),[48] which she graduated from in 1971. Thus, she had first-hand experience of the Prague Spring, the invasion, and ensuing "normalisation." Holland emphasised that these experiences – alongside the political trial which landed her in jail for a month for allegedly assisting the infiltration of illegal literature into Poland – ultimately shaped her as an artist and person (Holland, "Katechizm" 41–47; *Magia* 106–122).[49] Secondly, the years she spent in Czechoslovakia immersed her in the language (Holland would go on to translate Kundera and Havel) and the culture of the country, which were particularly flourishing at the time. Moreover, early in her filmmaking career, she explored similar themes as one of the foremost representatives of the moral disquiet genre. In later years, the question of ethical responsibility in complicated socio-historical situations would continue to play an important role in her work. Consequently, with Holland in the director's chair, it was guaranteed that the mini-series would be imparted with appropriate gravity rather than becoming another typically Czech tragi-farce, mining the absurdities of communism for laughs. Her prior work on highly acclaimed series like *The Wire*, *Treme*, or *Ekipa* (*The Prime Minister*) also played a part in her selection.

Holland would later acknowledge in an interview ("Dwie" 10) that in the past she had often been tempted to take a stab at the Prague Spring, but lacked the proper key to do so. Hulík's script, of which she spoke very highly, finally allowed her to bring that idea to life. Blending truth and fiction,[50] the young screenwriter focused not on the figure of Palach himself (even the name of the actor who played him was not in any way highlighted in the end credits), but on the consequences of his act on those closest to him and others.

The film revolves around the defamation suit brought by Libuše Palachová against Vilém Nový, a member of the Communist Party, soon after her son's death. Hulík created a meticulous reenactment of the factual record, as detailed as Holland's efforts to reflect the general mood of the late 1960s.[51] However, the screenwriter focused on Palach's family, ignoring the remaining actual plaintiffs in the suit. It bears noting here that Party hardliners wanted to exploit the self-immolation of the Prague student to purge the party ranks of reformists. Nový had first peddled his absurd "cold fire" theory already in an interview with Agence France Press in late January 1969. Three weeks later, he repeated it at a meeting in Česká Lípa (his power base) and added the names of the alleged "culprits," whom he believed to have inspired the protest. The list included two writers and alleged Prague Spring supporters Vladimír Škutina and Pavel Kohout, student activist Holeček, legendary long-distance runner and Olympic champion Emil Zátopek, and chess master Pachman. After these baseless accusations, all five decided to sue and in March 1969 brought a civil defamation suit against Nový. Libuše Palachová also sought legal recourse and asked lawyer Dagmar Burešová to represent her in court.

For a few weeks, the official sought to delay and obstruct the proceedings by failing to pick up his court summons, then attempted to use his parliamentary immunity and deflect the charges by claiming that the suit was merely an attempt to smear a public servant devoted to the socialist cause. Furthermore, Nový petitioned the court for change of venue, so that the case would be tried in Česká Lípa rather than in Prague. The petition, however, was dismissed, and the trial began in the capital on 20 May 1969. Because a tape recording of Nový was discovered, the public expected a quick resolution to the case. However, the presiding judge proved a loyal party servant and dismissed it, ordered the plaintiffs to pay the court fees, and labelled them enemies of socialism (Blažek, "Trial").

The mini-series cuts down the number of plaintiffs to two – Palach's mother and the fictional student leader Ondřej Trávníček, a decision which might be interpreted as an attempt to reduce the number of narrative avenues to explore in the show. But the pruning also meant that the series would now focus on two women – Palach's mother (played by Jaroslava Pokorná) and a young attorney (Tatiana Pauhofová).[52] The former is agonising over her son's death and the fact that he left her without a word of goodbye, despite writing letters to others, while the latter's indomitable attitude illustrated a strain of heroism so different from Palach's. This is by no means to say that the film is a staunchly feminist title, although the series definitely touches on the erasure of women from the official narratives of the dissident movement. The girls active in student organisations are shown as responsible for taking calls and making coffee – the real decisions are always made by their male colleagues. Even the judge presiding over the defamation trial is treated by Nový's counsel like a waitress, and by no means is he merely disrespecting her professional conduct.

Although the series was addressed to a broad audience, it shunned facile, black-and-white interpretations. Defending her child's good name is an obvious course of action to Palachová, but a part of her pursues it for her own sake, because if Jan's protest was rendered senseless, she would have been stripped of that remnant of solace provided her by the thought that his sacrifice was not in vain. The lawyer, on the other hand, is torn over the case, which she feels is hopeless, and tries to shift the decision as to whether to actually take it onto her husband. It is only after she considers the future of her two daughters, in whom she strives to instil the values she holds dear, that she decides to take a stand. Even Nový (Martin Huba) is far from being a one-dimensional villain, as the series takes care to reveal, albeit indirectly, that his earlier work abroad landed him in a Stalinist prison.

Alas, the staunch determination of the two women comes at a price. Palachová is hounded by the secret police, and harassed with calls and visits in the dead of night, as well as with pictures showing close-ups of her son's burned flesh.[53] Burešová's husband, a brilliant doctor with a promising career, is forced to give up his plum hospital job and seek employment in a second-rate clinic, while state security puts their home under round-the-clock surveillance. Holland uses the two women to show that individual choices dictated by common decency may in time prove as heroic, although maybe

216 Selected contemporary ultimate protests by fire

not as spectacular, as Palach's fiery sacrifice. In contrast to separate, isolated acts, however, their particular strain of everyday heroism required undaunted, consistent commitment.

The four-hour-long mini-series, situated somewhere between court drama, conspiracy thriller, and docudrama, was the first full-feature production to take up the story of the student from Prague. Palach himself, however, remains a background character throughout the first episode. The camera almost always pictures him from afar, precluding the audience from seeing his face (Holland, "Nasz"). One particular example of this camera direction can be found in the self-immolation sequence that opens the series, reenacted with meticulous attention to detail.[54] The student is observed from far off by the public transit despatcher – the same one who will later extinguish the flames. Then, the image briefly cuts to a young man wearing a white shirt, but shows us only his torso and the hands holding the matches. Later on, as he runs down the square engulfed in flames, we mostly see his back intercut with footage of passerby reactions. This infuses the scene with a certain dynamism and allows it to avoid outright voyeurism. To eschew gratuitous use of graphic imagery and communicate to the audience that despite his semi-mythical status Palach himself remains an elusive figure, his face continues to sit just outside the frame for the remainder of the first episode.

In this context, the contrast between the framing of the Palach's final act and that of Jan Zajíc is particularly significant. The second chapter opens with a close-up on Zajíc, standing in the toilet in a building near Wenceslas Square and spreading floor polish over his body, then dousing himself with flammable liquid, and finally ingesting poison. So prepared, he sets out for the square, but ultimately sets himself aflame in the passageway, behind a windowpane, the flames engulfing him just out of view.

The docudrama explores the profound impact of heroic symbolism by drawing clear Christological references, an example of which can be found in a brief scene near the end, set in the cemetery following Palach's exhumation and cremation. Seeing another name over the grave where her son was buried, the disconsolate mother wails: "Where is my son?!" Palach, the director seems to say, lives on in the people, like Jesus before him, a notion seemingly confirmed by the unyielding, indomitable spirits of Burešová[55] and the 1989 protesters, shown taking to the streets in the epilogue. However, as aptly pointed out by Polish film critic Tadeusz Sobolewski, in Holland's hands, the mysterious transfiguration of Palach's face into a vaguely Christlike icon unfolds "without sweeping religious, patriotic, nor symbolic exaltation." This may be result of the drama's focus on the human aspect of the incidents, the suffering of the immolators' families, and the reactions of individuals, rather than on the broad and impersonal public response they drew. The artistic choices of the director were ultimately driven by her belief that borderline events touch us on a deeply individual level, making blanket judgements and generalisations not only unwarranted, but potentially misleading. Holland put it in simpler terms: "We lack tools that would give us insight into the conscience of the nation" ("Siła" 28).

The series meaningful portrayal of "normalisation," stripped of undue irony and stylisation, earned critical and popular acclaim in the Czech Republic. While cathartic to elder Czechs, *The Burning Bush* helped the younger generations shape their own identities and attitudes (Holland, "Tak").

Notes

1 These include Jan Panas' 2008 play *Komandos* (*The Commando*), Magda Fertacz's *Nie gaście* (*Don't Put Out the Flame*, 2012–13), and Krzysztof Szekalski's 2013 drama *Samospalenie* (*The Self-Immolation*).

2 Bohdan Urbankowski, author of the 1969 commemorative poem *Pamięci Jana Palacha* (*In Memory of Jan Palach*), recounted that upon hearing the news from Prague reported by Radio Free Europe, Polish students were plunged into "incredulous debates and bizarre ethical confusion. It seemed so 'strange,' 'un-European' even, hearing about Buddhists burning themselves was nothing new, but to see it here, in the heart of Europe, was really odd" (32).

3 After the regime change in Czechoslovakia, his family's grave in Vítkovo near Opava was fitted with a replica of Olbram Zoubek's bronze plate that sat on Palach's grave in Prague's Olšany Cemeteries. The memorial plaque installed on the school he attended in Šumperk is nearly identical to the one hanging by the Department of Philosophy entrance – the only difference being the death masks adorning the plaques, both of which were taken by Zoubek. The monument to Palach and Zajíc unveiled in 2001 in Prague also sits on the site of the former's self-immolation. A short educational film on Zajíc, *Jan Zajíc – pochodeň č. 2* (*Jan Zajíc: Torch no. 2*), was released in 2012.

4 Among them Maciej Drygas, Petr Blažek (a Czech historian specialising in the history of the Communist regimes in Czechoslovakia and Poland), Jerzy Eisler (a historian from the Polish Academy of Sciences and the Institute of National Remembrance), and the KARTA Centre (a Polish NGO working to document and publicise the contemporary history of Poland and Central and Eastern Europe).

5 As one of the biggest arenas of its kind in Europe, it was host to numerous sporting events, such as international football matches or the final stages of the highly popular annual bicycle Peace Race, but also the regime's venue of choice for cultural and propaganda events.

6 For example, in *A Minor Apocalypse*, Tadeusz Konwicki's 1979 novel, which revolves around a political self-burning, the author fails to make even a single mention of Siwiec, despite bringing up several other people who voluntarily "walked themselves to the stake": "a Buddhist monk," "a certain Czech," and "a Lithuanian" (Konwicki 226), alluding to Thích Quảng Đức, Palach, and Romas Kalanta. Also quite tellingly, Maciej Bieniasz's series *Płonący* (*The Burning One/s*), which the painter created in 1966 in response to the wave of self-immolations sweeping Vietnam, was used in the late 1960s to discuss Palach's death but not Siwiec's (Gryglewicz 70). This was also true for *Western* (1969), a story authored by Józef Hen, a Polish writer and essayist of Jewish descent, in response to the political and social unrest that swept Poland and Czechoslovakia in 1968. The narrative opens with a self-burning, but in all likelihood Palach's rather than Siwiec's, particularly given subsequent allusions to events in Czechoslovakia. Furthermore, a handful of Polish artists dedicated to Palach the pieces they created soon after his death in Prague. These included Kazimierz Wierzyński, who on

218 Selected contemporary ultimate protests by fire

the day of Palach's funeral wrote the commemorative poem *Na śmierć Jana Palacha* (*For the Death of Jan Palach*), and Bohdan Mazurek, composer, sound engineer, and teacher associated with Polish Radio's Experimental Studio, who composed and recorded two versions of *Epitafium na śmierć Jana Palacha* (*Epitaph for Jan Palach*) soon after the burial. Before 1989, the piece was known as just *Epitafium* and only the composer's closest friends were aware of the meaning behind it. A similar fate befell Barbara Zbrożyna's sculpture *Sarkofag pamięci Jana Palacha* (*A Sarcophagus in Memory of Jan Palach*, 1969), whose form was developed around the shape of a hospital stretcher. Fearing harassment by the regime, the piece was displayed under the titles *Sarkofag I* (*Sarcophagus I*) or *Pamięci JP* (*In Memory of JP*). Neither is there any indication to suggest that Józef Dolak and Walenty Badylak, two other Poles to self-immolate in the Polish People's Republic (the former in 1972, the latter in 1980), were in any way inspired by Siwiec or even familiar with him.

7 It is possible that these rumours inspired Jerzy Ryszard Zieliński, a legendary figure in the Warsaw's bohemian circles in the 1960s and 1970s, to paint his September 1968 picture *Gorący* (*The Hot One*). To quote Luiza Nader: "Against the smooth, blue backdrop, blood-red, explosive forms come together into an outline of the face of a man engulfed in flame, the fire seemingly unceasing. The blues and reds stand in stark contrast to each other; fluid, billowing, intense forms of red are set against the smooth, steady background" (30).

8 Prior to that, the 30 March 1969 edition of *Na Antenie* (*On the Air*), Radio Free Europe's official paper, carried a brief report on Siwiec's protest and a note explaining why the report had not been published earlier.

9 In her 1969 poem *W świetle Jana Palacha* (*In the Light of Jan Palach*), author Anna Pogonowska reproached her compatriots: "Even this flame / the pulse of a fellow people / failed to flush our cheeks / our paleness reeks of rot" (79).

10 Official recognition of Siwiec's death came even earlier from the Slovaks – on 4 September 2006, the Slovakian ambassador presented Wit Siwiec with the country's highest order given to foreign citizens.

11 Naturally, Siwiec situated himself, at least to some extent, within the Romantic tradition of rebellion, which often involved laying down one's life for the cause. His protest can be read as a reference (although it is unclear whether intentional or not) to the death of Karol Levittoux, the leader of a conspiracy against the Russians, who in 1841 set his prison cot on fire and perished in the flames to avoid divulging the identities of his co-conspirators under torture (Zeler).

12 In their play *Fuck... Sceny buntu* (*Fuck... Scenes of Revolt*), produced in Krakow in 2017, Marcin Liber and Krzysztof Szekalski quoted entire passages from Drygas' film, which were projected onto a horizon in the background. Jadwiga Rodowicz-Czechowska's *Polish-Japanese Dziady/Soreisai/*祖霊際, produced in Warsaw the following year, also featured footage from *Hear My Cry*. The performance, which drew on Adam Mickiewicz's Romantic drama *Dziady* (*Forefathers' Eve*) and its adaptations developed by the Laboratory Theatre (1961) and the Centre for Theatre Practices 'Gardzienice' (1981), dedicated a memorable scene to a handful of 20th-century self-immolators, including Siwiec and Piotr Szczęsny.

13 The recordings were captured in Poland, as well as in Canada and the US, where Innocenta Siwiec and her three brothers eventually emigrated to.

14 In a 2009 conversation with Katarzyna Skolarczyk (330), Siwiec's daughter Elżbieta and his son Wit recounted that their mother used to say their father liked to go out with friends "for a small beer or two."

15 One such omitted incident involved Maria Siwiec writing a letter to the regional police commandant in Rzeszów, asking him to authorise the release of a typewriter that investigators seized from the Siwiec home, so that she could "seek additional income by writing" (qtd. in Blažek, *Ryszard* 220). Neither did Drygas mention

whether the Archdiocese of Przemyśl continued to render financial assistance to the Siwiec family, on account of them being a multi-child household, after Ryszard's demise. The harassment of Maria Siwiec is public knowledge – "she has had her wages withheld, so, without any means of support, she was forced to sell, among other paraphernalia ... her husband's books and his collection of pipes" (Strasz 283).

16 The book, whose title is a quote from Zajíc's poem written in tribute to Palach, was dedicated to the first two "Torches" and to Evžen Plocek, who also sacrificed his life in defence of democratic values in Czechoslovakia. A worker, an ideologically committed member of the Party, and a proponent of reform, Plocek set himself on fire in Jihlava on 4 April 1969 during a festival. At first, attendees believed the fiery figure was just another carnival attraction and did not rush in to help. Two pamphlets were found by his side – one said: "Truth is revolutionary, wrote Antonio Gramsci," while the other: "I endorse the human face, I detest lack of compassion – Evžen." Plocek died five days later, leaving behind a wife and an adolescent son. His funeral in Staré Hory sparked a mass demonstration, but the media were soon barred from reporting on his death and the case quickly faded into oblivion (Blažek et al. 95–102).

17 The project staff also managed to organise a three-day international academic conference and an exhibition held at the Karolinum and at the National Museum in Bratislava.

18 The 40th anniversary of Palach's death also coincided with the release of a book by Salesian friar Jindřich Šrajer, *Suicidium, sebeobětování, nebo mučednictví? (Suicide, Self-Sacrifice or Martyrdom?)*, in which he attempted to interpret Palach's behaviour from a Christian ethics standpoint.

19 The series was released alongside the rap track *Gorejący krzew (The Burning Bush)*, featuring vocals from Eldo (Leszek Kaźmierczak) and Pelson (Tomasz Szczepanek), and an online music video for the song. In 2012, Lukáš Kokeš released his documentary on the making of the HBO series.

20 Agnieszka Holland pointed out that some spots in Palach's biographical record remain rather vague ("Siła" 28). For example, the only thing known about his love life is that he had a disabled friend who he had been taking care of since they were children. After his self-immolation, she claimed to have been his fiancée, probably in an attempt to increase her own stature.

21 Despite the similarities in name, the party, established in 1898, had nothing to do with Nazism. During World War II, most of its members were involved with the resistance movement. After 1945, the Czech National Social Party became a part of the National Front and was eventually renamed the Czechoslovak Socialist Party in the wake of the Communist *coup d'état*. In the Stalinist period, its members were persecuted by state security for allegedly aiding the fascists.

22 Besides, as argued by Holland, the Czechs have never suffered at the hands of the Russians as the Poles have. Furthermore, they saw the 1938 Munich Agreement as an unpardonable betrayal and have since treated the West with habitual mistrust (Holland, "Tak").

23 In an early version, he called for dismissal of a handful of pro-Soviet politicians from office but ultimately scrapped these demands.

24 The sculptor cast a handful of replicas of the mask, one of which he gave to Palach's mother and another to the Department of Philosophy's student union (Kulmiński 145).

25 In Slovakia, however, the regime unanimously condemned the protest. In a statement released on 20 January 1969, the government of the Slovak Socialist Republic denounced the alleged group of volunteer martyrs as inspired by right-wing extremists who exploited the students' zeal to further their agenda.

220 Selected contemporary ultimate protests by fire

26 Upon witnessing the event, Bohdan Mikulášek composed the song *Ticho* (*Silence*), which was later used in Milan Peer's 1969 short documentary under the same title. Along with Stanislav Milota's short *Jan 69* (which was considered lost for years) and Vladimír Kubenko's documentary *Tryzna* (*Funeral Ceremony*), both likewise shot and edited in the immediate aftermath of the incident, the film is considered iconic.

27 The reactions to Palach's protest were much more subdued in Slovakia and mostly limited to academic circles, the exception being a memorial service for Palach held in Bratislava on the day of his funeral, which ended up drawing at least 2,000 people. This was the result of the measures undertaken by the Slovakian government, which refused to grant permits for any marches, manifestations, or religious services for the deceased student. In this context, it bears remembering that resistance to re-Stalinisation was generally much weaker in Slovakia. This may have been the result of the Soviets "bribing" the country by granting Slovakia the status of a separate republic on 1 January 1969. It should be noted here that Palach still has no monument in Slovakia, and no street bears his name there.

28 The answer of an unnamed 50-year-old mother, responding to a survey that was printed on 24 January 1969 by a newspaper published by Charles University to gauge the public mood concerning the self-immolation, exemplified the prevailing sentiments. The woman claimed that if her son decided to pursue a similar protest, she would have been proud of him (Blažek, "Public").

29 It was Kundera who wrote in the early 1980s that the revolting image of Palach engulfed in flames went against the very nature of his fellow Czechs, whom, prior to the Prague Spring, the writer considered devoid of heroism and often labelled cowardly and mediocre (Sabatos 204).

30 Estimates say that up to the end of September 1969 as many as 30 people tried to kill themselves by setting themselves on fire (seven of whom succeeded), although the political motivations of most of them were flimsy at best. One of the last of the 30 was the 19-year-old Jan Polásek, who set himself alight in Brno on 21 August 1969, on the first anniversary of the Soviet invasion.

31 In this particular context, we ought to take another look at a passage from Havel's seminal 1978 essay *The Power of the Powerless*, in which the author goes over legitimate forms of protesting an authoritarian government: "anything from a letter by intellectuals to a workers' strike, from a rock concert to a student demonstration, from refusing to vote in the farcical elections, to making an open speech at some official congress, or even a hunger strike" (23). Noticeably, the list did not include self-immolation, despite the fact that Havel considered Palach's protest to be profoundly significant, as evinced by his television appearance on 21 January 1969, during which he pleaded with the regime to fulfil the student's demands (*Poselství*).

32 The removal of Palach's remains is the subject of Dobroslav Zborník's 1996 documentary *Příběh Palachova hrobu* (*The Story of Palach's Grave*).

33 The Palach myth resurfaced 14 years later, when the Czech Republic was rocked by a wave of self-immolations in March and April 2003, during which one of the victims, Zdeněk Adamec, overtly referenced the death of "Torch no. 1."

34 Many towns across Europe named their streets and squares after Palach. Czech astronomer Luboš Kohoutek gave the asteroid he discovered in August 1969 the name 1834 Palach. Memorials and monuments to Palach have been erected in Všetaty, Mělník, Prague, as well as in Rome, London, Brussels, and Vevey in Switzerland.

35 For example, the oldest rock club in Croatia, located in Rijeka, is called Palach.

36 One such illegal effort was *38 Nails for Josef Toufar and Jan Palach*, held by Czech designer Otakar Dušek on 19 January 2014, the anniversary of Palach's death. With a handful of friends, Dušek nailed black-and-white likenesses of Palach

and Toufar to the façade of the building on Legerova Street, which once housed the Plastic Surgery Clinic. Toufar, a Catholic priest and victim of Communist repressions, died in the same building on 25 February 1950. Nailed below the likenesses of the two men were their names and dates of their deaths.

37 The third section of the *Jan Palach '69* anthology (Blažek et al.) features three essays on the presence of Palach and his protest in Czech documentaries, literature, and classical music. Veronika Jáchimová wrote her entire thesis on the subject. Key sources on that particular topic include the janpalach.cz website (particularly the "Memorial Places" section, which carries detailed information on sculptures and relevant photographs) and Kulmiński's book. The broadest and most exhaustive inquiry into Palach's presence in literature has been compiled by Sabatos. The poems the student inspired or was featured in could easily fill out a separate, dedicated anthology. As far as prose is concerned, the most prominent example has to be Lenka Procházková's *Slunce v úplňku* (*The Full Sun*, 2008), the first Czech novel to take on the subject (Sabatos 212–213). The list of plays he inspired includes *Palach* (1970) by Alan Burns and Charles Marowitz, *Jan Palach* (1971) by Erwin Sylvanus, the radio monologue *Letter to Wollongong* (1993) by Moserová, and *Torch No. 1* (2009) by David Pownall. In 1985, Sylvanus' play inspired Luna Alcalay to write a libretto for an opera. Allusions to Palach also feature in Pier Paolo Pasolini's final play, *Bestia da stile* (1966–74). Palach appears as one of the Torches in Magda Fertacz's *Don't Put Out the Flame* (2012–13). With regard to performance art, Lara Weibgen convincingly demonstrated that Palach's protest became the key reference point for efforts of underground radical body artists active in Czechoslovakia in the second half of the 1970s. Other examples can be found in the work of Polish performance artists Krzysztof Jung and Wiktor Szostało. The former's *Całopalenie. IV epitafium uliczne pamięci Jana Palacha* (*Self-Immolation IV: A Street Epitaph in Memory of Jan Palach*, 1979) saw Jung burning a web made of sewing threads, while the latter's *Performance for Freedom* (1983), which carried a number references to Palach, was the first piece Szostało created after leaving Poland for the US in the wake of martial law being declared at home. An example of Palach's influence on dance theatre can be found in *JAN*, the 2013 piece by the Czech group ProART dedicated to Palach, Pasolini, and the Czech dissident Milada Horáková, who was sentenced to death in a show trial and executed in 1950. Popular music was particularly attuned to these cultural echoes, and artists running the entire gamut of genres were either inspired by Palach's protest, dedicated their songs to him, or referenced him and his act in their lyrics. Examples include ballads by the Prague Spring bard Karel Kryl and the influential Polish protest singer Jacek Kaczmarski, as well as songs from pop performers Karel Gott and Michal Hrůza, rappers (Ciph Barker), folk rockers (Epydemye), alternative rock musicians (Kasabian), hard rockers (Zippo Band and Lina ci Rovina), punks (Protestant), and even heavy metal bands (Lamb of God). This list is by no means complete and is provided merely to demonstrate how widely the Palach incident echoed across culture.

38 That other end of the spectrum is where we would find Petr Vyoral's 2009 black-and-white graphic novel *Poslední Čech* (*The Last Czech*), portraying an alternate version of history, in which Palach dismissed the idea of self-immolation on account of his future wife and children. Sitting at a bar with a friend 40 years later, he wonders how he and the rest of the "Torches" would have been perceived today. "The comic book ends with excerpts from the comments section posted under a piece published on the website www.aktualne.cz. Predictably, most of the comments are negative, hostile, and quite vile, with one poster going so far as to claim that 'He was an idiot and now they're making him out to be a hero'" (Kulmiński 179).

39 As evidenced by *Jan Palach*, a song written in 1974 by Fabio Ragno and performed by the right-wing group Gruppo Padovano di Protesta Nazionale.

40 Another example illustrating how curious some of the cultural echoes of Palach's protest may be can be found in the 2012 short horror film *The Spirit of Jan Palach*, directed by Will Thomas Freeman. In the film, Palach (or his embodied spirit, to be more precise, its face charred black) plays the role of feminist saviour, presiding over the emancipation of a young woman, dominated and harassed by her father – a despotic priest whose actions in no way reflect his own principles and beliefs. Inspired by Palach's spirit, the woman finds deep inside herself the courage and the power to take a stand against her brute father, and extricate herself from both the toxic relationship and her dependence on a religion responsible for further entrenching the patriarchal power structure.

41 Czechs have also been using abbreviated versions of the names: *Dům syna* (*The House of the Son*) and *Dům matky* (*The House of the Mother*).

42 The mini-series premiered on 27 January 2013. An abridged version intended for cinemas was released in the Czech Republic on 12 September 2013.

43 Hejduk met Shapiro at the private arts school Cooper Union for the Advancement of Science and Art in New York, where he helped establish the School of Architecture, of which he was later dean for many years.

44 The poem was later reprinted in Hejduk's *Lines: No Fire Could Burn* (123). Later on, it also inspired a short opera piece created by Connie Beckley for the American Opera Projects in New York (1990).

45 The poem quotes the words of Libuše Palachová, recorded by state security during her son's burial.

46 Over a year later, a replica of the piece called *The Jan Palach Memorial* was installed in the square outside the Cooper Union in New York. Its temporary presence was linked with an exhibition exploring the story behind the piece and other accomplishments by Hejduk. The structures were erected by students and alumni of the school, a move which neatly corresponded with the architect's communitarian ideas and views.

47 Aside from the aforementioned publications, these efforts included the following: renaming the plaza outside the Department of Philosophy building to Palach Square (1989); reinterring Palach's ashes in his original tomb at the Olšany Cemeteries and renovating it (1990); and installing a memorial plaque on the façade of the Department of Philosophy building (1991) and President Havel's decision to bestow upon Palach the Order of Tomáš Garrigue Masaryk, in recognition of the student's contribution to the struggle for democracy and human rights (1991).

48 FAMU was open to students with just a high school diploma, whereas Polish film schools required candidates to have a master's degree.

49 See the 2013 Polish-Czech documentary *Powrót Agnieszki H.* (*The Return of Agnieszka H.*), directed by Krystyna Krauze and Jacek Petrycki.

50 In a TV interview ("I Know"), Holland said that the series is 80% truth and 20% fiction. And indeed, the docudrama features a number of fictional characters, including the police major Jireš. However, the storyline, which sees the officer attempt to leave the country with his family, but their car breaks down near the border and he has to push it over into Austria, was based on real-life events (Sobolewski).

51 For example, some footage was shot on location in the real-life Palach household in Všetaty, which was renovated for that express purpose (Holland, "Temat"). The visuals in the series are so convincing that it is hard to separate archival footage from footage shot on set.

Confronting defeat 223

52 In the film, Burešová is younger than her real-life counterpart, who was 40 at the beginning of the trial.
53 Libuše Palachová died in 1980, aged 63. Her death at a relatively young age may very well have been brought on by the tragic death of her son, on the one hand, and the regime's continued campaign of harassment, on the other. Her elder son was also targeted by the authorities – he was sacked from his job and his daughters had trouble enrolling in university.
54 This is thanks to Petr Blažek who served as a consultant on the film.
55 Following the collapse of the Communist regime, the lawyer served as Minister of Justice and Chairwoman of the Czech National Council.

References

The online resources identified below were consulted multiple times. All of them were active as of 1 December 2018.

Biały, Ewa. "Byliśmy znieczuleni" [We Were Callous]. *Karta* [Warsaw], no. 77, 2013, pp. 134–136.

Blažek, Petr. "Foreign Response." www.janpalach.cz/en/default/jan-palach/zahranici.

———. "Funeral." www.janpalach.cz/en/default/jan-palach/pohreb.

———. "Jan Palach Week." www.janpalach.cz/en/default/jan-palach/palachuvtyden.

———. "Operation 'Grave'." www.janpalach.cz/en/default/jan-palach/akcehrob.

———. "Protest." www.janpalach.cz/en/default/jan-palach/protest.

———. "Public Response." www.janpalach.cz/en/default/jan-palach/spolecnost.

———. *Ryszard Siwiec 1909–1968*. English translation Dominika Ferens, Instytut Pamięci Narodowej, 2010.

———. "Trial." www.janpalach.cz/en/default/jan-palach/proces.

Blažek, Petr et al., editors. *Jan Palach '69*. Univerzita Karlova, Togga, Ústav pro studium totalitních režimů, 2009.

Dębska, Agnieszka, and Bartosz Kaliski, editors. *Całopalny: Protest Ryszarda Siwca* [The Self-Immolated: Ryszard Siwiec's Protest]. Ośrodek Karta, 2013.

Dondzik, Michał. "'Powołuję do życia pewien świat' – Macieja Drygasa dokumentalna tetralogia o PRL-u" ['I Am Bringing a Certain World to Life: Maciej Drygas' Documentary Tetralogy on the Polish People's Republic]. *Pogranicza dokumentu* [The Limits of the Document], edited by Mikołaj Jazdon et al., Centrum Kultury Zamek, 2012, pp. 89–100.

Drygas, Maciej. "Było wtedy ostre słońce… Jak powstawał film o Siwcu" [The Sun Was So Bright Then…: On Making the Film about Siwiec]. *Kwartalnik Filmowy* [Warsaw], no. 1 (61), 1993, pp. 63–67.

———. "Testament (słuchowisko dokumentalne)" [Testament (Documentary Radio Drama)]. *Kwartalnik Filmowy* [Warsaw], no. 1 (61), 1993, pp. 69–83.

———. "Usłyszcie mój krzyk (lista montażowa)" [Hear My Cry (Montage List)]. *Kwartalnik Filmowy* [Warsaw], no. 1 (61), 1993, pp. 44–59.

———. "Analiza warsztatowa filmu dokumentalnego 'Usłyszcie mój krzyk'" [A Workshop Analysis of the Documentary 'Hear My Cry']. *Images* [Poznań], vol. 16, no. 25, 2015, pp. 147–160.

Duch-Dyngosz, Marta. "Jesteśmy potomkami chłopów" [We Have Descended from Peasants]. Interview with Jacek Wasilewski, *Znak* [Krakow], no. 5 (684), 2012. www.miesiecznik.znak.com.pl/6842012z-prof-jackiem-wasilewskim-o-genealogii-polskiego-spoleczenstwa-rozmawia-marta-duch-dyngoszjestesmy-potomkami-chlopow/.

Eisler, Jerzy. *Polski rok 1968* [The Year 1968 in Poland]. Instytut Pamięci Narodowej, 2006.

224 Selected contemporary ultimate protests by fire

Gryglewicz, Tomasz. "Bunt studencki marca 1968 w Krakowie i jego konsekwencje artystyczne" [The Krakow Student Rebellion of March 1968 and Its Consequences in Art]. *Quart* [Wrocław], no. 3 (70), 2011, pp. 64–71.

Havel, Václav. *Siła bezsilnych i inne eseje* [The Power of the Powerless and Other Essays]. Translated by Agnieszka Holland et al., Agora, 2011.

Havel, Václav et al. *The Power of the Powerless: Citizens Against the State in Central-Eastern Europe*. Routledge, 2009.

Hejduk, John. *Lines: No Fire Could Burn*. Monacelli Press, 1999.

Holland, Agnieszka. "Dwie rewolucje" [Two Revolutions]. Interview by Agnieszka Wiśniewska. *Holland*, Wydawnictwo Krytyki Politycznej, 2012.

———. "'I Know How Fragile Freedom Is'." Interview by Bohdan Zachary. *YouTube*, 12 Jan. 2015. www.youtube.com/watch?v=_XPZ8JQWyn0.

———. "Katechizm salonowej rewolucjonistki" [The Catechism of the Courteous Revolutionary]. Interview by Cezary Michalski. *Holland*, Wydawnictwo Krytyki Politycznej, 2012.

———. *Magia i pieniądze* [The Magic and the Money]. Interviews by Maria Kornatowska. Znak, 2012.

———. "Nasz kolega Jan Palach" [Our Colleague Jan Palach]. Interview by Tadeusz Sobolewski. *Gazeta Wyborcza* [Warsaw], no. 52, 2 Mar. 2013, pp. 34–35.

———. "Ogień niszczy, ale też oświetla. Jak gniew" [Fire Destroys, but Also Illuminates. Like Anger]. *OKO.press*, 21 Oct. 2017. oko.press/agnieszka-holland-o-samospaleniu-piotra-ogien-niszczy-tez-oswietla-gniew/.

———. "Siła bezsilnych. 'Gorejący krzew' – serial o sensie ofiary" [The Power of the Powerless: 'Burning bush' – A Series About the Sense of Sacrifice]. Interview by Marek Zając, *Tygodnik Powszechny* [Krakow], no. 11, 17 Mar. 2013, pp. 28–29.

———. "Tak się robi kino historyczne" [How Historical Cinema Is Made]. Interview by Ewa Gajewska and Łukasz Grzesiczak, *Przegląd* [Warsaw], no. 10, 7 Mar. 2013. www.tygodnikprzeglad.pl/tak-sie-robi-kino-historyczne-rozmowa-agnieszka-holland/.

———. "Temat leżał na ulicy, aż przyszłam i go wzięłam" [The Subject Was Out There, I Just Had to Come and Pick It Up]. Interview by Monika Żmijewska, *Gazeta Wyborcza* [Warsaw], 11 Mar. 2013. wyborcza.pl/1,75410,13537689,Agnieszka_Holland__Temat_lezal_na_ulicy__az_przyszlam.html.

Hulík, Štěpán. "Holland opowiada o Palachu" [Holland Speaking on Palach]. Interview by Tadeusz Sobolewski, *Gazeta Wyborcza* [Warsaw], 27 Feb. 2013. wyborcza.pl/1,75410,13467152,Holland_opowiada_o_Palachu.html.

Janion, Maria. *Czas formy otwartej. Tematy i media romantyczne* [The Time of Open Form: The Topics and Mediums of Romanticism]. Państwowy Instytut Wydawniczy, 1984.

Kąkolewski, Krzysztof. "'Szczytami i dnem' jak mówił Wańkowicz" ['On Peaks and Bottoms,' as Wańkowicz Used to Say]. *Kino* [Warsaw], no. 12, 1991, pp. 2–5.

Kaliski, Bartosz, editor. "Płomień Ryszarda Siwca" [Ryszard Siwiec's Flame]. *Karta* [Warsaw], no. 44, 2005, pp. 78–97.

———. editor. "Przed Kartą 77" [Before Charter 77]. *Karta* [Warsaw], no. 77, 2013, pp. 36–57.

Kantůrková, Eva. "On the Ethics of Palach's Deed." *Good-bye, Samizdat: Twenty Years of Czechoslovak Underground Writing*, edited by Marketa Goetz-Stankiewicz, Northwestern UP, 1992, pp. 175–180.

Karcz, Zygmunt. "Polski Palach" [The Polish Palach]. *Tygodnik Solidarność* [Warsaw], no. 18 (55), 1989, p. 5.

Kisielewski Stefan. *Dzienniki* [Diaries]. Iskry, 1998.

Konwicki, Tadeusz. *A Minor Apocalypse*. Translated from the Polish by Richard Lourie, Farrar, Straus, Giroux, 1983.

Kulmiński, Robert. *'Tu pali się ktoś...' Ryszard Siwiec, Jan Palach, Zdeněk Adamec* ['Here Is Someone Burning...']. Libron, 2016.

Kundera, Milan. *Life is Elsewhere.* Translated from the French by Aaron Asher, HarperPerennial, 2000.

Kurz, Iwona. "Między chrztem a samospaleniem. 'Teatra polskie' drugiej połowy lat 60." [Between Baptism and Self-Immolation: 'Polish Performances' in the Second Half of the 1960s]. *1968/PRL/Teatr,* edited by Agata Adamiecka-Sitek et al., Instytut Teatralny im. Zbigniewa Raszewskiego, 2016, pp. 23–41.

Kwapis, Robert. *Praska Wiosna* [The Prague Spring]. Wydawnictwo Adam Marszałek, 2003.

McKelvey, Tara. "A Fiery Death Comes Back to Haunt Poland." *New York Times,* 26 Apr. 1992, p. B26.

Moserová, Jaroslava. "From Dick Francis to Wollongong." 2005. www.radio.cz/en/section/books/jaroslava-moserova-from-dick-francis-to-wollongong.

———. "Remembering Jan Palach." 2003. www.radio.cz/en/section/witness/jaroslava-moserova-remembering-jan-palach.

Nader, Luiza. "Afektywna historia sztuki" [The Affective History of Art]. *Teksty Drugie* [Warsaw], no. 1, 2014, pp. 14–39.

Płużański, Tadeusz. "O tym, jak media 'głównego nurtu' wykorzystały antykomunistyczny protest Ryszarda Siwca" [How the 'Mainstream' Media Used Ryszard Siwiec's Anti-Communist Protest]. Stowarzyszenie Dziennikarzy Polskich, 2018. www.sdp.pl/analizy/15704,uslyszcie-moj-krzyk-tadeusz-pluzanski-o-tym-jak-media-glownego-nurtu-wykorzystaly-antykomunistyczny-protest-ryszarda-siwca,1537776454.

Pogonowska, Anna. *Kluczgc za prawdą* [Seeking the Truth]. private ed., 1991.

Poselství Jana Palacha [Jan Palach's Message]. Directed by Kristina Vlachová, Čzeská Televize, 2009. *Youtube.* 16 Jan. 2013. www.youtube.com/watch?v=Qm80YRIAB4Q.

Raczak, Lech. *Szaleństwo i metoda. 48 tekstów o teatrze* [Madness and Method: 48 Texts on Theatre]. Wydawnictwo Miejskie Posnania, 2012.

Ratajczakowa, Dobrochna. *Galeria gatunków widowiskowych, teatralnych i dramatycznych* [The Gallery of Performative, Dramatic, and Theatrical Genres]. Wydawnictwo Naukowe UAM, 2015.

Sabatos, Charles. "The 'Burning Body' as an Icon of Resistance: Literary Representations of Jan Palach." *Gender and Sexuality in 1968: Transformative Politics in the Cultural Imagination,* edited by Lessie Jo Frazier and Deborah Cohen, Palgrave Macmillan, 2009, pp. 193–217.

Shapiro, David. *A Man Holding an Acoustic Panel.* Dutton, 1971.

Siwiec, Wit, editor. *8 września 1968. Żywa pochodnia na stadionie X-lecia. W trzynastą rocznicę śmierci Ryszarda Siwca wszystkim miłującym prawdę* [8 September 1968: A Living Torch at the Decennial Stadium: An Appeal to All Those Who Love the Truth on the Thirteenth Anniversary of Ryszard Siwiec's Death]. Młodzieżowa Oficyna Wydawnicza Mowa, 1981.

Skolarczyk, Katarzyna. "Polski Palach czy czeski Siwiec. Uwagi do biografii Ryszarda Siwca" [Polish Palach or the Czech Siwiec: Remarks on the Biography of Ryszard Siwiec]. *Wschodni Rocznik Humanistyczny* [Radzyń Podlaski], vol. 7, 2010–11, pp. 321–339.

Sobolewski, Tadeusz. "Jan Palach i odwaga na co dzień" [Jan Palach and Everyday Courage]. *Gazeta Wyborcza* [Warsaw], no. 17, 21 Jan. 2013, p. 12. wyborcza.pl/1,75410,13266655,Jan_Palach_i_odwaga_na_co_dzien.html.

Stach, Sabine. "An Ordinary Man, a National Hero, a Polish Palach? Some Thoughts on the Memorialization of Ryszard Siwiec in the Czech-Polish Context." *Acta Poloniae Historica* [Warsaw], vol. 113, 2016, pp. 295–313.

226 Selected contemporary ultimate protests by fire

Stolarska, Bronisława. "Usłyszcie mój krzyk… O filmie Macieja Drygasa" [Hear My Cry… On Maciej Drygas' Film]. *Między słowem a obrazem* [Between Word and Image], edited by Małgorzata Jakubowska et al., Rabid, 2005, pp. 303–320.

Strasz, Małgorzata. "Ryszard Siwiec." *Opozycja w PRL. Słownik biograficzny, 1956–1989* [Opposition in the Polish People's Republic: Biographical Dictionary, 1956–89], edited by Jan Skórzyński et al., vol. 2, Ośrodek Karta, 2002, pp. 282–283.

Strzałka, Jan. "Dramat wyboru Ryszarda Siwca: Refleksja teologiczno-moralna" [Ryszard Siwiec's Drama of Choice: Theological and Moral Reflection]. *Ryszard Siwiec Pro Memoria*, edited by Ryszard Brzostowski and Mariusz Zemło, Polskie Towarzystwo Historyczne Oddział w Tarnowie, 2015, pp. 57–71.

Szpakowska, Małgorzata. "Po Marcu 1968: teatr studencki" [After March 1968: The Student Theatre]. *1968/PRL/Teatr*, edited by Agata Adamiecka-Sitek et al., Instytut Teatralny im. Zbigniewa Raszewskiego, 2016.

Tajne taśmy SB [The Secret Tapes of State Security]. Directed by Piotr Morawski, produced by Media Kontakt, TVP SA Program 1, 2002. *YouTube*. 16 May 2015. www.youtube.com/watch?v=Lxbeppfmseo.

Tischner, Józef. "Myśmy tej śmierci nie przemyśleli" [We Didn't Think This Death Over]. *Kwartalnik Filmowy* [Warsaw], no. 1 (61), 1993, pp. 41–43.

The Burning Bush. Directed by Agnieszka Holland, performances by Tatiana Pauhofová, Jaroslava Pokorná, Martin Huba, HBO, 2013.

Urbankowski, Bohdan. "Czas płonących pochodni" [The Time of Burning Torches]. *Gazeta Polska* [Warsaw], no. 11, 18 Mar. 2015, pp. 32–33.

Weibgen, Lara. "Performance as 'Ethical Memento': Art and Self-Sacrifice in Communist Czechoslovakia." *Third Text*, vol. 23, no. 1, 2009, pp. 55–64.

Werner, Andrzej. "Nikt nie usłyszał" [Nobody Heard]. *Kino* [Warsaw], no. 12, 1991, pp. 6–7.

Zambrowski, Antoni. "Ryszard Siwiec dotąd nieodznaczony" [Ryszard Siwiec Still Not Decorated]. *Gazeta Polska* [Warsaw], no. 34, 20 Aug. 2008, p. 10.

Zeiger, Mimi. "John Hejduk's 'The House of the Suicide' Structures Get New Life in Prague." *The Architect's Newspaper*, 2016. archpaper.com/2016/01/hejduks-house-suicide-structures-get-new-life-prague/.

Zeler, Bogdan. "Śmierć spiskowca: Karol Levittoux w liryce polskiej" [The Death of the Plotter: Karol Levittoux in Polish Poetry]. *Znajomym gościńcem* [Along a Familiar Road], edited by Tadeusz Sławek, Uniwersytet Śląski, 1993, pp. 67–74.

Chapter 3
Sparks
On two self-burnings protesting the exploitation of subalterns

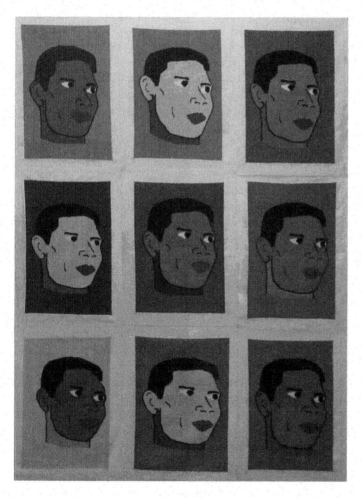

Figure PIII.3 Majd Abdelhamid *Bouazizi* (2012).

228   Selected contemporary ultimate protests by fire

Chun Tae-il (Chŏn or Jeon Tae-il), the 20-year-old Korean labourer and contemporary of Jan Palach, set himself on fire on 13 November 1970 at Pyeonghwa Sijang (Peace Market) in Seoul's Dongdaemun district, following police efforts to quash civil unrest spurred by the financial hardships, stagnating wages, and lack of prospects faced by workers on the lower rungs of the economic ladder. The protests were a stand against inhuman working conditions that were widespread in the Korean textile industry during its rapid modernisation and industrialisation. The President, Park Chung-hee, tasked his compatriots to secure a lead in the economic race against their neighbours (and ideological adversaries) to the north, and later catch up with other developed nations – Japan chief among them. In the pursuit of that goal, no cost was too great, and so rampant exploitation, low wages, and appalling working conditions in South Korean sweatshops were simply presented to the public by the Park regime as an inconvenient side effect of a necessary policy. In a way, Chun's self-incineration can be read as an act of a subaltern intent on proving that he can speak (Spivak). Although the grammar and phrasing of this pronouncement were particularly hard to repeat, under the dictatorial regimes of Chun Doo-hwan (1980–88) and Roh Tae-woo (1988–93), others soon followed his example, burning themselves to show up the government's authoritarian grip on power and civil rights violations.

These self-burners also pressured the dictators to reveal the truth about the 1980 Gwangju massacre, which took place during an uprising against Chun Doo-hwan soon after he took power in a *coup d'état*. In the lead up to the first Olympic Games held in the former colony, another wave of unrest swept the country in June 1987, ultimately forcing Chun Doo-hwan to step down and the regime to introduce broad reforms. Later that year, the country held its first direct elections since 1971, with the president picked by the people rather than MPs, as was the case in the Fourth (1972–80) and the Fifth Republics (1981–87). It is estimated that over the course of nearly three decades of right-wing authoritarian rule (1961–93), around 100 people performed suicide protests for political reasons, with the majority of them choosing fire to do so (Park 80).[1] As pointed out by Kim Hyojoung, "Suicide protesters seem to have willingly and voluntarily sacrificed their lives in an effort to spawn and invigorate movement activism among half-hearted activists and apathetic bystanders and instigate further protest activities" (549).

The self-incineration of Chun Tae-il sparked a wave of civil unrest and revived the South Korean labour movement, while his act, and the way it was reported in the press, drew much attention to the situation of the marginalised masses denied the economic windfall of the Miracle on the Han River. Thus, the sacrifice of the young fabric cutter from Seoul became the *spark* that awakened the consciousness of Korean workers and society at large. This specific metaphor was later used by Tae-il's biographer, Cho Young-rae, as well as the filmmaker Park Kwang-su, who directed a film based on the life of the young worker. In English, both works bear the same title, *A Single Spark*. Both will be discussed in the subchapter *A drop of dew*, a reference to the sobriquet Chun chose for himself, writing in his journal about his intention to become the *dew* that will ease the hardships of those who toiled beside him and whose suffering affected him deeply.

Both the spark and the dew drop, polar opposites as far as natural elements go, are minute phenomena that hold a promise of something greater, a potential hidden in the specific and singular. After all, a spark can ignite an explosion, while a single drop can make the cup run over, drowning a nation in the bitterness of those cast aside. It is this particular notion that will underpin this chapter, juxtaposing two separate self-burnings, 40 years and half a globe apart.

On 17 December 2010, the 26-year-old street fruit vendor, Mohamed Bouazizi (Tarek al-Tayyib Muhammad ibn Bu'azizi), set himself alight outside the magistrate's office in Sidi Bouzid, to draw public attention to the injustice he suffered at the hands of the local officials and law enforcement. Reports of his act, first spread mostly by his family, friends, and online, were almost instantly picked up by Qatari news outlet Al Jazeera, sparking a wave of protests that ended the 23-year-long reign of Tunisian President Zine El Abidine Ben Ali, who fled the country on 14 January 2011.[2] These events are widely considered to have triggered the Arab Spring, a series of protests and uprisings that swept the MENA (Middle East and North Africa) region from 2011 to 2013.

And so a local incident in a provincial town in central Tunisia became a spark that engulfed almost the entire region in flame, spreading unrest from Mauritania to Syria. But such an intense reaction was possible only because the spark fell upon a powder keg of civil discontent, widespread poverty, lack of prospects, massive unemployment (particularly among the younger segments of the population), as well as nepotism, authoritarian tendencies, and the arrogance of the ruling regimes and their officials. Tahar Ben Jelloun, a Moroccan author writing primarily in French, used the above metaphors of *droplet* and *spark* speaking in one of his interviews:

> It's really the drop that makes the water overflow. ... After so much humiliation, after years of suppression and oppression, comes the time when too much is too much and you have someone like that young Tunisian, Mohamed Bouazizi, who set himself on fire and suddenly became the spark that ignited the whole revolt.
>
> ("Democracy")

There is nothing to suggest that Bouazizi was, like Chun Tae-il, driven by altruism and the common good. In all likelihood, he merely intended to publicly blame the local officials for the injustices he suffered. In other words, in his case the self-burning was supposed to publicise individual iniquity, and the *hogra*, an Algerian Arabic term for the humiliation felt by those held in habitual contempt by arrogant, abusive rulers and decision-makers. But because that indignity was all too familiar to many across the region, Bouazizi inadvertently became a symbolic figure, representing the fates of the forgotten masses, while the ensuing course of political events subsequently transformed him into a champion of the popular *intifada* (uprising). His life as a small vendor, skirting the grey edges of illegality, was familiar to millions of Tunisians and others across the region (Jallad). Given his background, protesters found it easier to identify with him than, for example, Tunisian army general Rachid Ammar, whose courageous refusal of Ben Ali's order to shoot the protesters proved a turning point in the popular rebellion (Schraeder and Redissi 13). Although the Tunisian uprising had many heroes, Bouazizi became the definitive icon of the unrest, an ironic twist given that his own protest lacked a specific political stripe – which is not to say that it lacked a political dimension in general. As Banu Bargu keenly observed:

> His fatal act, as a solitary and spontaneous performance of self-destructive violence, points to the emergence of a new repertoire of radical political action that has served as an injunction for the masses to take action in order to reclaim a dignified life before the fatalism of the present. (34)

As a symbol and a media celebrity, a status conferred upon him posthumously, Bouazizi was stripped of his own subjectivity within the public sphere, becoming a *totem* for the protesters or a *logo* of the revolution (Jacobson 19). For reporting purposes, he was positioned as the *face* of the revolt, because no other figure could claim similar recognisability in its earliest stages. Many academics pointed out the need to deconstruct the strange discursive accretion that grew around the figure of Bouazizi, who was seen not only as a symbol of resistance against the injustice of the local regime, but also (by Occupy Wall Street activists, for example) as an ally in the struggle against the nefarious alliance between government officials in Washington and America's corporate elites (De Soto). One attempt to restore a measure of individuality to Bouazizi was undertaken by Ben Jelloun. His novella *Par le feu. Récit* (*By Fire: A Story*) painted a portrait of someone who decides to embrace the most radical form of protest and subsequently becomes "a vehicle for expressing collective pain" (Jallad).

Both young men – Chun and Bouazizi – were soon enshrined by their respective cultural circles as heroic figures who spoke for the dispossessed. Due to the sheer scope of events in the MENA region and their repercussions, Bouazizi is naturally the more recognisable of the two, while Chun is still known mostly inside Korea. Conversely, whereas Chun's story served as the basis for a 1995 Korean drama, no filmmaker has to this day decided to take on the life of Bouazizi, despite his ostensibly greater recognisability and some preliminary announcements from Tarak Ben Ammar, a Tunisian-born film producer with major Hollywood connections. As for Bouazizi, Ben Jelloun's novella remains the most important cultural echo of his self-burning, singular in its attempt to transcend the symbolic dimension of the act, itself embraced primarily by homages hailing from the visual arts, and to interrogate the human experience of someone who rather inadvertently became a folk hero.

A drop of dew: the self-immolation of Chun Tae-il (The Republic of Korea, 1970)

Chun Tae-il's life and death

Cho Young-rae's biography of Chun Tae-il, written in 1974–77, remains the definitive source of information on the life of the young textile worker. First published in 1983, the book was released anonymously, as the author was a known lawyer whose defence of dissidents in Korean courts has earned him the ire of the Park Chung-hee and Chun Doo-hwan regimes. The subject's name was also stripped from the title, and the book was ultimately printed as *The Life and Death of a Young Worker*. The South Korean Ministry of Culture and Information quickly banned it, while the police raided a promotional reading, sealing off the exits and placing people involved with the publication and Chun's mother, Lee So-sun (Yi So-seon), under house arrest. The book, however, continued to circulate away from the prying eyes of the authorities, and the future course of events in South Korea demonstrated that the regime's concerns about the title were not unfounded. Only after public life underwent a gradual liberalisation in the 1990s could the volume be re-released under its original title, *The Beautiful Life of Chun Tae-il* (1991). The author, however, died a few months before the second edition went to press and never lived to see his name in print. The edition included passages taken out or changed in 1983 for fear of reprisals from the regime. It also became the cornerstone of all future discourses of the figure of Chun and his self-immolation, on which the authors of some 20 books published in Korean and Japanese extensively drew (Cho, Y-r. 54).[3] The book was also developed into the screenplay of Park Kwang-su's 1995 drama *Areumdaun cheongnyeon Jeon Tae-il* (literally *Beautiful Youth Chun Tae-il*; *A Single Spark*).

Eight years later and with considerable support from the Korea Democracy Foundation, the Seoul imprint Dolbegae published the English translation under the same title as the film. The translation was drafted by Chun's younger sister, Chun Soon-ok, who along with her mother, had become involved in the Korean textile industry labour movement in the 1970s. In 2003, after graduating from the University of Warwick with a PhD in sociology, she published a book on the movement and put the phrase, "They are not machines," some of the last words her brother cried out as flames engulfed him, in the title.[4]

Cho Young-rae based his biography of Chun primarily on the writings in the young man's journal (1966–70),[5] and the accounts provided by his family and friends. I will draw on the book to paint a portrait of the turning points in Chun's life, making sure to emphasise the specific context in which the biography was written and which, presumably, transformed it from a purely factual account into something of a hagiography.

232 Selected contemporary ultimate protests by fire

Cho established that Chun Tae-il was born in Daegu on 26 August 1948, less than two weeks after the Republic of Korea was established in the southern portion of the Korean Peninsula. Following four decades of occupation (1905–45) and exploitation at the hands of Japan, the country was one of the poorest in Asia. After the occupying force capitulated, and Soviet and American forces took up positions in, respectively, the north and south of the Peninsula, a demarcation line was drawn along the 38th parallel, splitting the country into administrative zones under Russian and US control. Although the partition was initially temporary, it became entrenched as the Cold War set in, and continues even today. On 9 September 1948, soon after Rhee Syngman was inaugurated president in the south, Kim Il-sung proclaimed the Democratic People's Republic of Korea in the north. Chun Tae-il was born into a divided Korea, soon to be stage to a bloody fratricidal war (1950–53).

Chun was the first child of Chun Sang-soo, a poor tailor working in a garment factory, who would later go on to open his own shop, and Lee So-sun, the daughter of a resistance fighter slain by the Japanese when she was only three. During World War II, Lee was conscripted into forced labour for the colonisers. Married and destitute, she became a pedlar but was soon forced into begging. When the Korean War broke out, the family fled the approaching Communist forces for Pusan, and later moved to Seoul to look for employment and better prospects after the Armistice Agreement was signed in Panmunjom. Although they spent their first months in the Korean capital living under a bridge, their situation improved after Chun Sang-soo opened his own shop, soon becoming stable enough for the parents to send young Chun to school.

> Paradoxically, the family's moderate success was undermined by the 1960 students' revolution which overthrew Syngman Rhee's regime. Just before the mass uprising of the Seoul students, Chun Tae-il's father secured a large and seemingly profitable order: he was supposed to produce a large number of school uniforms. He borrowed money to buy the cloth and other necessary items, only to discover that the order was cancelled due to the revolution. The family was again broken and saddled with a large debt.
> (Lankov)

Due to the dire financial straits the family found itself in, Chun was forced to drop out of school barely two years later, while his father began sinking into alcoholism following a series of poor business decisions. He went bankrupt a number of times, selling all of his assets and starting from scratch to provide for his family, which had since grown to include four children. At the time, Chun and the rest of his family were suffering from extreme poverty. As a teenager, he sold newspapers and umbrellas on the street and shined shoes to help his starving family make ends meet. He also ran away from home multiple times. In May 1963, he finally managed to recommence his education – enrolling in middle school in Daegu, where the Chuns moved to, unable to afford life in the capital. Unfortunately, less than a year later his father pulled him out of school so he could help at home.

In 1964, Chun's parents split up and his mother left for Seoul, intending to find work as a housekeeper, a decision which at the time signalled a significant decline in social status, perhaps comparable only to seeking employment in prostitution. Barely 16 years old, Chun Tae-il resolved to follow her and fled home once again, this time taking his youngest sister with him. Soon realising they could not manage, Chun was forced to leave his sister in an orphanage. In the meantime, his mother's health deteriorated significantly and she had to sell her hair to a wigmaker, a particularly humiliating ordeal for a woman in Korea at the time. Ultimately, despite misfortunes along the way, mother and son managed to reunite in Seoul.

As mentioned above, in the 1950s and 1960s Korea underwent rapid modernisation and industrialisation, which only accelerated after Park Chung-hee came to power in a *coup d'état* on 16 May 1961. The hardline president, known for his casual disregard of civil rights, formulated and implemented a five-year economic plan (1962–66) which laid the infrastructural foundation for the country's subsequent economic development. At the time, the Korean economy was developing at breakneck speed, growing at a rate of nearly 4%, and catapulting the country from a backwards, agrarian state, worn down by colonial exploitation and fratricidal war, into a stable partner for the US in the region. The subsequent five-year plan, emphasising the development of heavy machinery and petrochemical industries, further reinforced that upward trajectory, in effect lifting considerable portions of the Korean populace out of poverty. The economic growth also enabled a national school-building effort, which almost eliminated illiteracy.

Although these achievements painted a very favourable portrait of South Korea on the international stage, for many ordinary citizens, hailing, as Chun Tae-il did, from the lower classes (*minjung*), everyday reality was far from pretty. In private textile and garment factories, workers were subject to predatory exploitation, especially prevalent in early stages of Western-style capitalism. Owners had no regard for employees' health and kept the wages low. Claiming, therefore, that the country owed its economic success to efficient and consistent economic policy, maintained by successive governments, would be misleading at best, as the Miracle on the Han River was founded upon the rampant exploitation of tens of thousands of workers, a notion well-illustrated by the fortunes of Chun Tae-il himself.

In spring 1964, 16-year-old Chun found work at the Peace Market in Seoul, the heart of Korea's garment industry – although the term would be an overstatement, as in the early 1960s it comprised a chain of manufactories, where the majority of the work was done by hand, with only the sewing performed with machines imported from Japan. In 1961, the Cheonggyecheon district of

234 Selected contemporary ultimate protests by fire

Seoul, home to a sprawling slum neighbourhood and countless smalltime textile shops as late as the 1950s, was finally redeveloped and modernised. The city razed the old wooden shops and replaced them with a three-story brick-and-mortar building with 25,000 m^2 of commercial space, with the ground floor intended for retail outlets and the upper stories for manufacturing facilities. In 1968, the area also saw the construction of the five-story, slightly smaller Donghwa Market, and the four-story Tong-il retail centre. Building management was entrusted to private corporations, which also handled all security and safety arrangements in the area they came to call Samdong. The corporations were also responsible for maintenance and cleaning, as well as all contacts with the authorities regarding tax and labour matters. Over time, these corporations became mouthpieces for private business owners, and worked to protect their interests, often at the expense of the workforce in their employ.

Chun Tae-il discovered in 1970 that the area held around 900 textile shops, which employed over 25,000 workers in total. The mills, clustered in a relatively small area, covered nearly 70% of the domestic demand for garments, and the shops serviced both wholesale and retail customers. The hired hands working in the shops included cutters (mostly men), machinists (mostly women), and an assistant and a helper contingents (mostly young girls aged 12–16). Women accounted for over 80% of the workforce. New workers were trained on the job – after a few years, a helper could rise through the ranks to become a machinist. Given the terrible working conditions and low wages, however, staff turnover was consistently very high, particularly among the helpers.

In most of the small manufacturing facilities, 25-m^2 rooms typically held around ten sewing machines, cutting tables, and ironing boards. Each shop usually had a staff of 25, giving each person a tiny workspace. The owners tried to increase floor space by cramming mezzanines into 3-m-tall shops, creating the infamous attic rooms where ceilings hung so low that the machinists were unable to stand up straight. The shops were cramped, windowless, and lacked adequate ventilation and lighting fixtures. There were not enough available toilets, and access to running water was limited (Cho, Y-r. 277).

The shops ran on a flexible schedule, usually opening at 8 am and closing after 10 pm (with a 30- or 60-minute lunch break). But when the owners received a large enough order, working hours were significantly extended and the employees were given pills or amphetamine shots to keep them awake. It was quite common for workers to stay inside their shops for days at a time, labouring almost around the clock. On the other hand, in the summer months, when orders usually dropped off, employees were forced into unpaid leave or had to take up menial custodial jobs. Workers had only two Sundays off per month, despite the fact that many owners were self-declared Christians (Catholics or Protestants).

Wages depended on the line of work. Cutters were paid best, as they also served in administrative roles in many of the smaller shops, overseeing the staff and managing work logs. Experienced machinists were a rung below them. The two groups could expect wages from 5 to 15 times higher than the helpers, at the time earning around 1,500 wons per month, the equivalent of 6 USD in 1965. Very few workers were hired on a permanent basis (only experienced cutters and machinists were offered fixed-term employment), the rest worked on temporary contracts. Wages were paid irregularly, often behind schedule, and workers repeatedly fell prey to overtime pay theft or were otherwise swindled out of their earnings.

In the cramped, airless spaces of the shops, suffused with the din of machinery, the odour of perspiration and textile colourant, and often left unheated in the winter, the workers spent as many as 12 or more hours every day. It is no wonder, then, that the majority of them suffered from a variety of ills. Machinists reported losing feeling in the tips of their fingers from pressing on the fabric, which often took away their ability to use chopsticks. Cho writes (121) that female workers took to saying that after three years in those conditions, the chances of finding a husband dropped significantly. Although the labour code required employers to arrange periodic medical checkups for workers, most either ignored the injunction or sent only a portion of their staffs to the doctors. Because the checkups were also handled by the corporations managing the Samdong area, the exams were often perfunctory, and many of the lung X-rays were faked. Whenever an employee was rendered unable to work, they were unceremoniously let go.

As previously mentioned, Chun Tae-il found work there in spring 1964, the move marking a significant step up in social status for the young man. In 1966, at the time barely 18 years old, he was promoted to seamster-machinist, but ultimately decided to retrain as a cutter, so that he would be able to better help the exploited female helper staff. At the time, he often walked back home after work (which, in turn, meant frequent police stops as the country was still under curfew) to save money on public transport and use the savings to buy food for the starving helpers. Chun's journal entries reveal that he was very attuned to the suffering of the people around him. In winter 1969, he wrote: "I hate this era where people have become commodities, where a person's individuality and basic aspirations are scorned, where the branches of hope are lopped off: I hate humanity that chooses to degrade itself into a commodity in return for existence" (qtd. in Cho, Y-r. 140).

His journal also reveals that Chun was fully aware of his creeping, gradual transformation into, in his own words, "a machine," "a mechanised puppet," or "a living corpse." Chun's biographer emphasised: "What is indeed astonishing is that Tae-il, who had not even completed middle school, could overcome the slave mentality and be able to see through to the reality of the social conditions" (Cho, Y-r. 153). The boy was particularly affected by his interactions with a young female helper diagnosed with severe tuberculosis. Although Chun raised money from his fellow workers to help the girl, she was fired as soon as she returned from hospital. The young man realised that she was discarded like a broken object, because the cost of treatment far exceeded the combined total of her wages.

In 1968, Chun learned from his father, who himself was active in the labour movement following the liberation of Korea, that Korean business owners were bound by the provisions of the labour code, which also permitted union organising. But rather than encourage the boy, Chun's father advised him against pursuing activism, given the prevailing social climate of the time. Efforts to organise labour could end up with him being marked a troublemaker and blacklisted from future jobs. In the light of the ideological struggle between North and South Korea, independent activism and grassroots organising were in danger of being seen in the pro-US Republic of Korea as evidence of Communist sympathies. Unions were not outlawed, but were officially subordinate to the government, itself widely considered a puppet of the US, and not just by the Communists in the north. Given his experience, Chun was aware that owners of the garment shops were openly flouting the provisions of the labour code, even though it stipulated severe fines for inspectors who failed to report code violations, up to dismissal and even time in jail. Realising all this finally inspired Chun in 1968 to set up an organisation that would protect workers' rights.

Despite some initial hurdles, Chun and a friend managed to band together a group of ten and form an organisation in late June 1969, soon after the death of Chun's father, and the first meetings were held at his house. Chun Tae-il initially suggested they call themselves Baabohye (The Society of Fools), saying that he and his fellow workers were indeed fools, unaware of their own rights. That is also what they were called by an older worker that Chun tried to recruit. Cho Young-rae wrote (174–175) that a label like that was likely to have come from someone who had experienced the colonial rule of the Japanese, the political upheaval in the wake of the liberation in 1945 and the Korean War, as well as the military rule that followed it, and was thus naturally inclined to gravitate towards accommodation, obedience, discipline, and loyalty. Chun's group, meanwhile, ridiculed the "normality" rooted in conservatism and tractable compliance, and instead focused on mastering the intricacies of Korean labour law and championing employees' rights.

The group decided to start with a worker survey, while Chun pooled his monthly wages and purchased a labour law handbook, which ultimately proved too complex for an average labourer with no formal education or training in law. Chun and his fellow workers also tried to expand their numbers and sought the backing of philanthropists interested in opening a model shop to demonstrate that running a law-abiding business could be profitable. Unfortunately, their noble efforts were cut short, as Chun was quickly sacked and marked as a troublemaker, preventing him from finding new employment, while a handful of other members were conscripted into the armed forces. The rest of the group, also fired from their jobs, were successfully intimidated and stopped coming to meetings. By winter 1969, the group was on the verge of disintegration.

Out of the nearly 100 surveys distributed to workers, only 30 were returned to Chun Tae-il, with most of the rest intercepted by worried employers. This failure further confirmed what Chun knew from first-hand experience, but it also inspired him to visit the labour inspectorate in the local magistrate's office and to submit a petition to the Ministry of Labour. At the former, local officials dismissed him out of hand, while at the latter his pleas were met with non-committal, bland responses. The experience was a jolt to the young activist. The realisation that city and state officials were in collusion with private business owners to preserve the status quo quickly snuffed out whatever remained of his enthusiasm. Probably it also drove him to depression, as the first traces of Chun's suicidal intentions appeared as early as 30 September 1969, in a letter he sent to a friend.

In mid-October 1969, Chun Tae-il began a two-month stint in construction, his most physically demanding job yet. His journal entries from that period are a testament to his alienation and solitude, painting a picture of a man marginalised and powerless. The extent of his desperation is revealed by the blueprint for the model law-abiding business he sketched out in March 1970. In order to boost his own credibility in the eyes of philanthropists he wanted to ask for start-up money, he decided to donate his cornea. The business plan he drafted proved how well he knew the garment industry and suggested that he wanted his model company to serve as an incubator where new, just forms of labour and employment could be developed (Cho, Y-r. 241).

Chun's attempts to improve the situation of other workers were unsuccessful – his survey, his spur-of-the-moment worker rights organisation, and his petition all came to nothing. All he had left were his dreams of his fair labour company and direct action, such as protests and strikes. At the time, Korea was rocked by a series of student protests, sparked by attempts to revise the constitution and reform term limits. Up until that point, electoral law allowed a president to be elected to the highest office for a maximum of two terms. As General Park neared the end of his second term, he moved to change the law and stay in power. The attempt was met with fierce resistance from the students, and the protests must have made quite an impression on Chun, who may have witnessed some of the clashes between the demonstrators and the riot police.

Cho Young-rae contended that Chun began seriously contemplating suicide protest towards the end of 1969. There is no way, however, to trace the origin of his idea to do so by means of self-immolation. Chun may have heard about Huh Jik, an opposition politician who set himself alight on 25 July 1965 on the steps of the National Assembly in Seoul to protest against the treaty reestablishing relations between Korea and Japan. Press reports on Buddhist self-immolations across Vietnam also may have influenced his decision.

Chun's biographer suggests that spring 1970 marked a period of intense internal strife for the young worker. He withdrew from his social circle and stopped writing his diary. Creditors who lent him money when he was out of work and busy setting up the Society of Fools now hounded him for repayment. To make matters worse, city authorities had municipal constructions crews raze his family's makeshift home, which had been built on city property without proper permits. Defying officials, Chun rebuilt the home with his mother, only for the city to raze it again. This tug of war continued for months. Around that time, he moved to a Christian retreat in northern Seoul to join a construction crew building a new church – a job he landed thanks to his mother and her connections in the local Protestant community. This time of reflection helped him arrive at the decision to return to the Peace Market in order to – as he wrote down in his diary on 9 August 1970 – "become the dew for countless withering innocent lives" (qtd. in Cho, Y-r. 254).

Chun began setting up a labour union almost immediately after getting a job back at the Peace Market. Before long, he banded together a handful of cutters, including a couple of his friends from the Society of Fools, into what they came to call the Samdong Friendship Association. Revising its earlier approach, the group intended to develop contacts in the media in order to drum up publicity and support for the worker cause. Ahead of the 1971 presidential election, the beleaguered regime, under sustained attack from opposition candidate Kim Dae-jung, future Nobel Peace Prize laureate (2000) and President of the Republic of Korea (1998–2003), sought to bolster its image with the people. Suddenly, the media became much more receptive to stories highlighting the plight of blue-collar workers. Chun had approached the editor of *Kyunghyang Sinmun*, one of the largest national dailies, who promised to run an investigative piece on the realities of Samdong, on condition that Chun and his group bring him credible data. So the Association organised a detailed worker survey, this time taking measures to keep the forms away from the prying eyes of their employers. A report compiled from 120 surveys was brought to the editor and forwarded to the Korean Ministry of Labour on 6 October 1970, along with a petition signed by over 100 people that called on the government to intervene and put a stop to exploitation. The newspaper ran an in-depth piece on the subject the following day. The Association bought 300 copies and distributed them in Samdong, giving an immense boost to the nascent organisation's credibility with the local workforce.

On the heels of the *Kyunghyang Sinmun* piece, Chun and his associates began negotiating with the Ministry inspector and officials from the corporation managing the Samdong area. But as it became apparent that the talks were simply a delaying tactic, the group decided to hold a demonstration outside the Ministry of Labour on 20 October, the day the parliament was set to receive its annual briefing from Ministry officials, assuming that the authorities would be reluctant to use force against civilians so close to the elections. Regime officials, however, smothered the inexperienced negotiators with assurances to compel them to abandon their plans (Cho, Y.C. 77).

Although the most favourable timeframe had passed, Chun and his friends began planning another protest, set for 13 November, during which Chun would read passages from the Labour Standards Law and then ceremonially burn it, to emphasise how little it had been enforced. The gesture was particularly symbolic for Chun himself, because of his earlier intense belief in the code as source of change. The protesters prepared a number of banners and placards, saying: "Give us sunshine once a week," "We are not slaves," and "We are not machines" (Cho, Y-r. 297). As the organisation was under surveillance by the Korean Central Intelligence Agency, the regime quickly moved to disrupt the protest. Security personnel and police cut off access to the avenue in the Peace Market where the organisation planned to hold a demonstration. Business owners were warned about the rally by city officials and tried to prevent their staff from joining, but despite these efforts the protest still drew around 500 people.

The crowd, along with the security forces assembled to disperse it, would later bear witness to Chun Tae-il's self-immolation, which took place soon after the police arrested a handful of Chun's fellow members and destroyed the group's placards. "With the planned protest on the brink of cancellation due to interference, Chun poured a can of flammable paint thinner prepared for the event all over his body and was set on fire by an unsuspecting friend" (Kim, H. 544), so the act probably cannot be considered an auto-cremation *sensu stricto*. According to multiple eyewitness accounts, engulfed in flame, the young man ran towards the crowd, calling on the assembled to continue the fight for better conditions for the workers and imploring them not to let his death be in vain. Then he collapsed and the fire continued to consume him for a couple of minutes, as the people around him were in a state of shock and nobody tried to put out the flames (Cho, Y-r. 315). Only later did someone finally throw a jacket over his charred body. After an ambulance arrived around 30 minutes later, Chun was taken to a nearby medical centre and then to St. Mary's Hospital, where he died around 10 pm. Cho Young-rae wrote (319) that before dying, Chun managed to pass a word to his mother, pleading with her to continue his struggle.

A worker demonstration broke out at the site of his self-immolation around 2.30 pm. The protesters replaced the confiscated placards with makeshift banners on which they wrote their demands with their own blood. The strikers also clashed with riot police who soon moved in to disperse the furious crowds.

The aftermath of the act, its impact on social life in South Korea, and commemorative practices

Although at the time hundreds of workers were dying from overwork or were toiling away in extremely adverse conditions (miner deaths were particularly frequent), the suicide protest of Chun Tae-il, whom the people

240 Selected contemporary ultimate protests by fire

quickly began calling a martyr (*yeolsa*), genuinely shocked the public. Korean historiographers (Doucette) believe that his desperate act helped break the silence about the widespread exploitation of workers and rampant labour law violations. The incident drew responses from labour circles, student and academic organisations, even religious associations. This broad consensus brought together disparate social groups and helped draw attention to issues ignored by the mainstream media, transforming them into matters of public concern. Thus, Chun's self-sacrifice was not just one of the most important events in the history of the South Korean labour movement, but also a pivotal event in the contemporary history of the country in general (Cho, Y.C. 55). Editors of the influential Korean magazine *Dong-A Ilbo* anticipated these developments and wrote already in 1971 that as the Korean War was the symbol of the 1950s and the April 19 Revolution which toppled the Rhee regime was widely considered the icon of the 1960s, so would Chun Tae-il's self-burning one day come to define the decade (Cho, Y-r. 36).

Three days after the incident, a group of around 100 law students from Seoul National University (SNU) set up a committee tasked with forming an alliance for the protection of civil rights. The committee proposed a public funeral be held for Chun, and the suggestion was welcomed by his mother. It bears noting that Lee So-sun already refused a similar proposal from regime officials who, bent on sweeping the incident under the carpet, promised to cover all funeral costs and offered her considerable recompense.

Civil unrest soon gripped the nation. Rallies, hunger strikes, and memorial services for Chun Tae-il were held at campuses across the country, and students were soon joined by religious activists. Protests invariably turned to riots, which often ended in violent clashes with the police. On 21 November, protesters held an overnight sit-in at the SNU, during which one student attempted to take his life by jumping into the Han River. Later that night, the police arrested a student from the humanities department carrying a petrol can, who admitted that he was planning to follow Chun's example. On 25 November, during a joint Catholic-Protestant memorial service for the worker, Pastor Kim Jae-joon delivered a rather self-critical eulogy: "We Christians have come together not so much to grieve Chun Tae-il's death, but to lament over the apathy and hypocrisy of the churches of Korea" (qtd. in Cho, Y-r. 34). Chun's biographer wrote that widespread protests in the wake of the self-burning bolstered the opposition against the Park regime and reinvigorated the withered independent labour movement. Protests were breaking out on an unprecedented scale, with demonstrators levelling sharp criticism against the Federation of Korean Trade Unions, financed and controlled by the regime, and individuals warning of more self-burnings.[6]

The unrest continued over the following months. On 21 December 1970, Chun's friends from the Association, joined by his mother, climbed to the roof of the Peace Market and began a protest against police efforts to disrupt the Cheonggye garment workers union that the Association founded exactly two weeks after Chun's death. They also threatened to jump off the roof to their deaths should the police continue to harass them.

As the self-immolation took place in the lead up to the election, Kim Dae-jung, presidential candidate from the New Democratic Party, took to the stage on 21 November 1970 to express his profound regret at the death of Chun Tae-il, later promising to make Chun's demands a key part of his programme. In response, the incumbent President, General Park, highlighted the need to improve working conditions and strengthen social security. Ahead of the fast approaching election in late 1970, the workers' cause championed by the young protester was widely commented on in the media and became a permanent fixture of any election debate.

As noted by Cho Young-rae,

> Some people sent money anonymously to Tae-il's family. Several labour organisations collected funds with the aim of erecting Tae-il's statue and memorial. Some philanthropists offered to build a Chun Tae-il memorial centre. Young people held memorial services for Chun Tae-il, printed his diary and distributed it to other labourers. (39)

But all these efforts ceased on 17 October 1972, when General Park (who won the April 1971 election by a narrow margin) declared a nationwide martial law. The amended *Yusin* ("renewal") constitution granted the president sweeping executive power, allowing him to use decrees to suspend civil liberties guaranteed by basic law, and transformed the presidency into legalised dictatorship. The amendments also extended the length of the presidential term to six years and made deep changes to the country's electoral system – the president would be elected by the MPs, and only two-thirds of parliamentary seats would be subject to popular elections, with the rest going to presidential appointees. With the introduction of martial law, the regime also moved to suppress students and workers, and protests were usually dispersed by force. The authorities also banned a number of student organisations, severely curtailed the freedom of the press and religious assembly, and imposed restrictions on the Korean Federation of Textile Workers Union that the Cheonggye chapter belonged to.

Thanks to Lee So-sun's tireless efforts (Kim, H-s.), the self-sacrifice of her son did not fade into oblivion following the authoritarian turn of President Park, who was himself later murdered in a 1979 *coup d'état*. The memory of Chun's death was also meticulously preserved under the authoritarian governments of Generals Chun Doo-hwan and Roh Tae-woo. The Chun Tae-il Foundation, established to support workers who found themselves in dire personal and financial straits, was created in 1981. Using the money it raised, the Foundation opened the Chun Tae-il Memorial Hall in 1985. Because Chun left behind three unfinished novels, three years later the keepers of his memory decided to fund a literary prize in his name, to be awarded annually for outstanding literary works either written by workers or focused on working class issues.

As the country liberalised, the memory of Chun and his death slowly filtered back into public discourse. The unabridged version of his biography was finally published aboveground in the early 1990s and was soon followed by the release of the film *A Single Spark*, while in 1996 Seoul authorities named a street after him not far from his last place of employment. Efforts to preserve his memory were crowned in September 2005, when the Foundation erected a memorial on the Beodeuldari Bridge spanning the Cheonggyecheon Stream in the centre of Seoul, depicting the young worker emerging from the pavement.

Chun Tae-il's mother took up his cause and continued his work. For 40 years, Lee So-sun served as the leading figure in a number of initiatives established to improve the lives of workers and protect their rights. She organised protest marches, demonstrations, and rallies; she also headed an association that rendered assistance to the widows of men who had laid down their lives for the cause of democracy in South Korea. Her tireless public service earned her the nicknames "The Mother of Workers" and "The Mother of the Powerless." Unfortunately, the woman did not live to see the activists prevail and the city authorities name a Seoul bridge after her son on 1 November 2012 ("Jeon"). She died on 3 September 2011. Her two final years, as well as the marches held in her memory, were the subject of *Eo-meo-ni (Mother)*, a documentary by Korean director Tae Jun-seek.

The hero in the making: on Park Kwang-su's film A Single Spark

A Single Spark was released on 13 November 1995,[7] 25 years to the day after the events at the Peace Market. At the time, Korea was already two years into the administration of Kim Young-sam, the first non-military President to take the office in three decades, who himself was barred from pursuing political activity back under the Chun Doo-hwan regime. In 1987, Kim lost the first direct presidential elections held in post-war Korea, defeated by Chun Doo-hwan's successor, Roh Tae-woo, because the opposition put forward two candidates – Young-sam and Kim Dae-jung – who ended up splitting the vote. After taking over the office in 1993, he declared an amnesty for thousands of political prisoners, and then significantly broadened the scope of democratic reforms launched by his predecessor under pressure from the public and the international community, the latter taking an active interest in Korea ahead of the 1988 Summer Olympics which the country was slated to host. Film scholar Kim Kyung Hyun reported that the premiere of Park Kwang-su's drama coincided with the arrest of both Chun Doo-hwan and Roh Tae-woo on a bevy of charges, including corruption, defrauding the public purse, treason, and seditious intent (111).

The TV mini-series *Morae Sigye* (*Hourglass*), released in early 1995 to wide-spread acclaim, could be said to have prepared the ground for the impending trial of the generals.[8] The plot of the series features two men on opposite sides of the conflict. One, a law student, is conscripted into the army and sent to Gwangju to suppress a nascent popular revolt, while the other is involved in the struggle for more civil rights and liberties. The show proved very popular and was watched by over 70% of Koreans with access to TVs. The issues underpinning the plot were later developed in the non-commercial 1996 title *Kkotnip* (*A Petal*), directed by Chang Song-u. Both pictures – *A Single Spark* and *A Petal* – were indicative of a shift in Korean filmmaking, towards films reckoning with and trying to make sense of the country's traumatic past. Naturally, given the political situation in Korea, it is hard to imagine similar works being produced before 1993.[9]

The other issue that comprised the contextual backdrop of the film was the financing of non-commercial film projects. At the time, there were no institutions in Korea that would offer public funding for ambitious filmmaking efforts. This meant that directors lived and died by their box office returns, and had to rely on deals with *chaebols*, Korea's large industrial conglomerates, for financing. What is particularly significant about *A Single Spark* is that the film was produced primarily with money raised from small donors – donations from over 7,000 people, totalling around 500,000 USD, covered around half of the picture's budget. Ironically, the remaining costs were covered by Daewoo, a conglomerate widely known for its repressive union policies. A number of factors contributed to the success of the donation drive – the most prominent two being the film's subject matter and the reputation of the director, widely considered the leading figure of the New Korean Cinema, whose past credits included four very well-received feature films.

After graduating from the SNU, Park Kwang-su (born 1955) founded and headed Seoul Yŏnghwa Chiptan (The Seoul Film Collective), a movement aspiring to reinvigorate Korean filmmaking, which at the time focused primarily on commercially viable entertainment. The director was also active in the student movement protesting against the military dictatorship in Korea. According to Kim Kyung Hyun (96), his 1988 debut – *Ch'ilsu wa Mansu* (*Chilsu and Mansu*) – was considered a major step towards freedom of expression and freedom to take on important issues. The picture told the story of three marginalised workers who tried to hide their blue-collar backgrounds. Hyun also wrote that Park's follow-up efforts, including *Kŭ dŭl do uri ch'ŏrŏm* (*The Black Republic*, 1990), *Perŭlrin rip'ot'ŭ* (*The Berlin Report*, 1991), and *Kŭ sŏm-e kago sipta* (*To the Starry Island*, 1993), all took on pressing social issues, often tied to the country's political past. All three featured protagonists hailing from the intelligentsia – in *The Black Republic*, a young student activist is living and working in a small mining town to hide from the regime, while the protagonist of *To the Starry Island* tries to bury his father on his native island, but his efforts are met with fierce resistance

244 Selected contemporary ultimate protests by fire

from the locals, most of whom were blackmailed by the dead father during the Korean War ("Korean"). Kim Kyung Hyun argued that Park's work "helped lead Korean cinema out of the 1980s, when quasi-pornographic films and melodramas featuring dysfunctional males proliferated" (98), as his characters were rational, consistent, and – last but not least – portrayed in interactions with the *minjung*.

In *A Single Spark*, however, the scepticism as to the possibility of reconciliation between disparate social classes that characterised Park's earlier efforts is replaced with hope. The protagonist, a young dissident by the name of Kim Yeong-su (played by Moon Sung-keun),[10] is romantically linked with Kim Jung-soon (Kim Bo-kyeong), a female worker active in the labour movement, and attempts to draft an account of the life and death of Chun Tae-il (Hong Kyoung-in). This means that rather than go for simple reenactment, the film juxtaposes the story of the young worker with the experiences of people persecuted by the regime five years after his self-immolation. Thus, the screenplay directly references the fortunes of Chun's biographer. In hiding from state security and intent on writing the definitive account of the events of 1970, Kim pays a visit to the Peace Market, where he realises that not much has changed since Chun's death, then speaks with Chun's mother and throws himself into the job of writing the biography of a figure who seemed so important to activists fighting against the Park regime. This was the director's way of stressing the fact that the book about the young worker was supposed to keep up dissident morale in the face of the regime crackdown, and implying that Chun was wrenched from oblivion and made into a heroic figure because it was precisely what the people slowly losing all hope in the possibility of change in the political landscape needed.[11]

Aside from the film's prologue and epilogue, both set in the early 1990s, the storyline takes place in two separate timeframes – 1970 and 1975 – with the former shot in black and white and the latter in colour. The monochrome footage gives us snapshots from Chun Tae-il's life – as imagined by the writer, of course. In the first, he is a teenager selling umbrellas on the rainy streets of Seoul; then, we see him working in the garment industry and in construction. He is the iconic, idealised hero, static, with a fixed character and worldview. Moreover, he seems attuned to the suffering of others and determined to help. He finds unceasing support in his mother, while his father reveals to him the existence of the labour code. Although awkward in his first steps as an organiser, he quickly brings together a group of young hotheads. These snapshots are interspersed with scenes from the other timeframe, giving us a glimpse of the life of the writer and his pregnant wife and showing their harassment by state security.

Here and there, that structure breaks down – one particular example can be found near the end, when Kim, working as a stoker at the time, has a vision of Chun visiting him in the boiler room and taking him on a trip out of town, leading him down the road into the unknown. That snapshot emphasises how engrossed Kim had become in the story with which he was grappling, to the point where he had started identifying with his own protagonist, whom Kim had begun seeing as a tangible part of his coloured reality rather than a detail from the monochrome past. The other breakdown can be found in the finale, in the self-immolation scene.

The act is foreshadowed already in the scene immediately following the opening, in which we see the peaceful street march from the early 1990s, the assembly finally permitted following initial democratic reforms. Moments later, we see a nearly 30-second-long black-and-white close-up of a young man, sopping wet, who pulls out a lighter and sets the book he is holding aflame. The film then cuts to the writer's small room. The sequence with the book reappears in the finale, but this time continues. It turns out that the young man sets not only the volume, but also himself on fire, then runs out onto the street and calls for improved working conditions. The picture suggests that he chooses immolation to mobilise those still on the sidelines, afraid of getting involved. As he runs, he clips a bicycle and falls. The camera shows shocked protesters running up to him, the scene unfolding in slow motion, but we cannot hear what they are saying as the sound is muted – only a gentle piano score can be heard. The crowd of witnesses is joined by women from the garment shops who, intimidated by their employers, were afraid of participating in the protest. Snapping back to colour, the film cuts to the writer again, showing his figure leaning over the manuscript, then raising his eyes and listening to cries coming from somewhere far away, seemingly from the depths of the past: "We are not machines" and "Observe the labour law!" Then, the film shows Chun, still engulfed in flames and in colour, approaching the camera in slow motion, his mouth open in cries of silent protest (the piano score continues from the previous scene), until his face, twisted in a grimace of overwhelming pain, fills the entire frame.

This twofold portrayal of the self-immolation is key to the picture's underlying message. The first rendition shows Chun from the back and the side, hiding his visage from view. The sequence is brief, and the entire event – although still horrifying – becomes almost mundane, an impression reinforced still by the somewhat comical collision with the bicycle. The second rendition, representing the writer's highly idealised picture of the self-immolation, makes a radically different impression, especially given the writer's earlier admissions that he had started interpreting the worker's sacrifice in religious terms. As a result, Chun, portrayed with his arms spread out, can seem in his final moments nearly a Christ-like saviour figure.

The dramatic finale leads into the epilogue. We see the writer strolling down the street next to the Peace Market. It is a bright, peaceful day, with faint noises of the city coming from the background. The author takes a seat on a small bench and notices a young man holding his book, with Chun's photo on the cover. This implies we are back in the 1990s, the flash-forward bookending the picture. The nameless man passes Kim by and walks away, finally turning around. We realise then that it is Chun himself. The picture freezes, and the credits roll over the freeze-frame. Here is the young worker, "resurrected" through his biography, realising his dream of a better life for the Korean people, the director seems to say. Thus, the film may be interpreted as an illustration of the writer's creative process, as he crafts his character thinking about the future of his unborn child. In one of the closing sequences, Kim desperately wants to see his wife, even though the woman, in the care of his parents, is under close state security surveillance. The sight of his pregnant beloved is supposed to help him reconcile himself with Chun's own sacrifice, and push him over the edge to write the final chapter of Chun's biography.

Slow-paced and suffused with melancholy, the film does not show graphic events in an explicit manner. We do not see brutal clashes with the police, only their consequences – like in the scene, where the writer, at the behest of his wife, assists a beaten female worker whom the police had shipped off to a poverty-stricken suburb to intimidate and break her. Although the oppressive reality is teeming with harassment, the only violence we ultimately witness is Chun's self-incineration. The picture seems rooted in the characteristically Korean sentiment of *han*, a blend of sadness and hope, a sense of longing for bygone happiness, and a dreadful lack of fulfilment. This doleful mood can also be the product of the times in which the film was produced. Kim Kyung Hyun wrote that:

> in the mid-1990s, the prevailing cultural attitudes were defined by terms like nihilism, disillusionment, and ennui. Although the people elected President Kim Young-sam, who was inaugurated in 1993, it was uncertain whether the government was the one for which people had literally given their lives only a few years earlier. With close alliances between big corporations and the Korean government maintained, the exploitation of the *minjung* continued, making it extremely difficult for the masses to generate resistance against the newly formed hegemonic power, which, unlike previous regimes, was not visibly exploitative. (99)

Hence, the portrayal of the worker hero – or, more precisely, portraying him through the eyes of an intellectual constructing his very image – may have been especially important to the audience. The film paid homage to a historical figure and was thus an apologia for the struggle for civil rights and dignity. It aroused class consciousness and enveloped events from the past in a pleasant aura of nostalgia. All this, however, was just its surface layer.

A more penetrating read reveals that oppressive realities compel us to create heroes and craft mythologies around them, to have them serve as reference points and inspiration to those losing hope. Kim Kyung Hyun rightly noted (100) that with his film, the director interrogated the circumstances in which ordinary people are put on a pedestal to be elevated above their brethren, and examined the reasons that drove the writer to resurrect Chun five years after his fiery death. By having the film reflect the process of crafting

Chun's heroic biography, Park Kwang-su could present the idealised image of the young worker, while simultaneously shunning responsibility for the hagiographic tone of the film itself. Perhaps the director realised that in the newly liberal reality, still uncertain and frail, deconstructing the legend would be ill-advised. This led him to unambiguously link the sacrifice, an act forever emblazoned in Korea's collective consciousness, with the political transformation brought on by widespread protest and opposition against the regime, and do so already in the prologue. Such a framing seems to imply that the young worker is indeed the father of that incredible success, with his act laying the foundation for those processes the culmination of which we observe in the film's opening sequence.

The drop that made the cup overflow: the protest self-burning of Mohamed Bouazizi (Tunisia, 2010)

The real and the iconic Bouazizi in social, historical, and economic contexts

As the whole world seemed to be watching the events in Tunisia in late 2010 and early 2011, the figure of Mohamed Bouazizi ended up drawing unprecedented international attention, with newspapers and press agencies publishing hundreds of reports about the man himself and the course of the 17 December 2010 incident (Abouzeid; Davies; Ryan, "How", "The Tragic"). Naturally, written in near real time, these reports were bound to include some inaccuracies and mistakes. These, however, can be rectified using sources written since the event.

Alec Jacobson's *Duality in Bouazizi*, published soon after the scholar's visit to Tunisia in spring 2011, is among the most important sources of information on Bouazizi and his fiery act. The author spoke with the immolator's family, who moved to El Marsa near the capital after his death, and interviewed Tunisians critical of Bouazizi, who saw his self-incineration as an egotistic protest rather than an act of heroism intended to alleviate the misery of his fellow countrymen. Jacobson rightly noted (2) that although the young man has never given an interview, never written anything, nor organised a dissident movement, he has been elevated in the collective consciousness to something of a celebrity. As I mentioned before, this conceptual Bouazizi became a symbol of the revolt (quite literally so, as protesters often put his blown-up visage on banners and placards) and a staple of media reports on the events in Tunisia. Jacobson was one of the first to make the effort to study the real Bouazizi, not filtered through media narratives. A similar task was taken on by Peruvian economist Hernando De Soto and his associates from the Lima-based think tank Instituto Libertad y Democracia, who decided to seek out first-hand information about the man. They set out for Tunisia, to get a feel for the real Sidi Bouzid. The results of their efforts were compiled into

The Real Mohamed Bouazizi. The biographical portion of this chapter will draw primarily on these two sources.

Mohamed Bouazizi was born on 29 March 1984 in Sidi Bouzid to a family of limited means. His father, a construction worker pursuing contracts primarily in neighbouring Libya, died when Mohamed was almost four, and his mother, Mannoubia, remarried some time later, wedding her brother-in-law. His stepfather's health issues prevented him from finding employment, forcing Mohamed, then still a teenager, to seek odd jobs to help his large family[12] make ends meet. This, in turn, led him to drop out of high school before graduation and – contrary to most media reports – prevented him from enrolling in college. Bouazizi resided with his family in a modest domicile, the legal status of which, according to De Soto, was murky.

Peter Schraeder and Hamadi Redissi reported that the unemployment rate among the 15–24 demographic in Tunisia was as high as 30%. Recent university graduates were hit the worst, leaving nearly half of them consistently jobless. The numbers, however, fail to reflect the gravity of the situation in a small provincial town, far from any industrial base or areas with heavy tourist traffic. Writing about the causes of Ben Ali's downfall, Dominique Lagarde pointed out (247) that by favouring the privileged elites, the president created a system that left ever-growing groups of young people without prospects, a course of action that led the disenfranchised to pour out onto the streets to protest and occupy government buildings at least a handful of times in the second half of the 2000s. Although the regime faked the officially published data, the president must have realised the true extent of the unemployment because in a speech delivered in early 2010, he declared the year "the year of Tunisian youth," a label that seems particularly ironic in hindsight (Lynch 74).

Poverty was also widespread and affected a growing number of Tunisians. In the context of Bouazizi's self-burning, Nana Bemma Nti from the Kofi Annan International Peacekeeping Training Centre in Ghana wrote (80) that there are many definitions of poverty in use – some utilise income criteria, while others are based on subjective sentiments, such as experiencing shame while out in public. Over the years, economists have attempted to devise more objective metrics by which to define poverty, for example, referring to basic living costs. In 2008, the average Tunisian family spent over 36% of its household budget on basic foodstuff. In 2010, however, over a million people (around 10% of the population) declared that their financial situation has worsened since 2008, with multiple factors driving the slump, including the global financial crisis and its distant echoes: decrease of tourism revenues and slashed wages for Tunisian expats working abroad, resulting in tightened access to hard currency (Schraeder and Redissi 8). In the economically backward portion of the country, which included Sidi Bouzid, all of these disadvantages were particularly pronounced.

The situation was made even worse by fear, as at the time Tunisia was effectively a police state, with the president in command of a 100,000-strong state security force, including a special tourism police and university police detachments, as well as the Presidential Security and National Guard, all of which were established to protect the president's interests (Schraeder and Redissi 6). The media pointed out that together these security forces had more manpower than the army, which was underpaid and used mostly for border guard duty. After Ben Ali took power in a bloodless coup on 7 November 1987, deposing Habib Bourguiba,[13] the first President of independent Tunisia (by claiming him no longer fit for office due to health reasons), his compatriots had high hopes for him, as he promised them rule of law, democracy, and freedom of the press and assembly. At first, it seemed he was intent on keeping those promises, especially after he released political prisoners, forbade torture, and abolished the office of president for life. But this period of progressive politics did not last long.

> The 1989 elections bring the first changes. Prevented by law from having their own party, the Islamists begin openly denouncing the regime, leaving it somewhat intimidated. In 1990–91, the police begin rounding people up, particularly on university campuses … human rights advocates protesting against torture and the abuse of police powers quickly find themselves in the regime's crosshairs. Proponents of a more open Tunisia gathered around the president eventually give up and resign, leaving the sycophants to take their place.
>
> (Lagarde 246)

Up until 2009, Ben Ali won presidential elections five times, a feat possible only after he abolished the three-term limit in a 2002 referendum. Schraeder and Redissi wrote (8) that with each victory, the Tunisian regime became more repressive and less inclined to deal with socio-economic issues plaguing the populace. Admitting these problems ran the risk of damaging Tunisia's image as the most progressive of Arab countries, an image that has been carefully maintained by many Western politicians who perceived Ben Ali as their protégé. They believed him an efficient politician, who waged a ruthless war against the Islamists (although one that was not exactly all that effective, as evinced by the 2002 Al-Qaeda attack on a synagogue on the island of Djerba) and guaranteed internal stability, allowing business to continue unfettered and tourists to pour in after Tunisia became an attractive holiday destination.

To add insult to injury, not only were the Tunisians at the mercy of the tightening grip of the authoritarian regime, softened, for the sake of the West, by the pretence of "free" elections, they also had to reckon with the regime's corruption and nepotism. In 1992, Ben Ali remarried, and his betrothed, Layla Trabelsi, brought with her, to borrow from Lagarde, "a particularly troublesome dowry, including a dozen brothers-in-law and about the same

250 Selected contemporary ultimate protests by fire

number of sisters-in-law" (246). The families of the president and his universally despised wife began taking over ever larger sectors of the economy, carving out their own empires, where corruption and skirting the law were commonplace. According to the Central Bank of Tunisia, relatives of the president and the first lady owned at least 180 state enterprises. The privileged clan also came into possession of sprawling estates, tracts of land, and construction plots, often illicitly. The worsening corruption was reflected in Tunisia's Transparency International ranking – whereas in 2005 it was placed 43 out of 178 monitored countries, five years later it was already down in 59th place (Schraeder and Redissi 9). Polish journalist Marcin Pazurek wrote:

> in the early days of the Ben Ali regime, corruption was a problem only for business people, investors, people up the chain. … Slowly at first, it crept downwards, until it finally reached ordinary people and you could not register a car or get your kid a job without paying someone. As the regime drew closer to collapse, more or less everyone had some dirt under their fingernails, so to speak. (24)

It is in this deeply corrupt, authoritarian, and kleptocratic country that Mohamed Bouazizi tried to keep himself, his mother, his uncle, and siblings above the poverty line. According to Mannoubia Bouazizi, her son even undertook an abortive attempt to join the armed forces, but ultimately all his efforts to find stable employment failed. To secure some sort of income, he took up selling fruit on the street, "almost certainly without a permit" (Jacobson 8). Without a fixed stall or booth, he trudged around hauling a cart. Finding spots where he could quickly push enough volume of his goods was a part of the job, as was being street-smart enough to evade policemen whom vendors had to pay off to get away with selling goods without a permit. De Soto wrote that in 2010 Mohamed graduated to a fixed spot outside the governor's office, for which he had to pay protection money to local officials to the tune of 3 dinars per day, around 2 USD at the time. Do Soto estimated that Bouazizi's weekly income was about 73 USD, which means that the payoffs devoured a fifth of his earnings. The young man did not run his business as a legal entity with a fixed address or an office, and without proper documents, earning prospects for street vendors were limited at best, while the vendors themselves lived in constant fear of further harassment from city officials or law enforcement. Do Soto noted that nearly half of all the Tunisian workforce was employed by extralegal businesses, with the total number of people forced into similar arrangements in the region as high as 100 million. Niall Ferguson, historian of politics and economics, argued that the prevalence of these informal labour relationships continues to be one of the chief hurdles in the development of many weaker economies across the globe. Framed like this, the scholar wrote, the Arab Spring may be read primarily as "a revolt by frustrated would-be entrepreneurs against corrupt, rent-seeking regimes that preyed on their efforts to accumulate capital" (31).

De Soto reported that the young Tunisian strove to pool enough money to buy or lease a used pick-up truck to source his goods with farmers rather than middlemen and wholesalers, which would allow him to boost profits. He also sought to secure a fixed stall at the local fruit and vegetable market, as it offered a semblance of financial stability. Mohamed's friends believed he was the opposite of an activist, and his mother confirmed that he had no interest in politics and barely watched the news. Acquaintances from the market saw him as a practical man, a trustworthy worker they sometimes hired to do their books and handle their bills. Bouazizi "had worked his entire life to establish a small place in the local market economy – and lost it in a matter of minutes" (De Soto).

Jacobson wrote that it is unlikely that we will ever learn the exact course of that fateful day. What we do know is that on the morning of 17 December 2010, around 10.30 am, Bouazizi had a row with a municipal officers, probably over his lack of permits and their attempt to force a bribe out of him. The officers, including Faida Hamdi, tried to confiscate Bouazizi's scales, leading to a scuffle during which the woman, according to Bouazizi's family, slapped the vendor, spat on him, turned his cart over, and disrespected his late father. Ultimately, the guards confiscated "two crates of pears, a crate of bananas, three crates of apples," all of which he bought on credit, "and a second-hand electronic weight scale worth $179" (Ferguson 31). It is not clear whether they beat the vendor or took his cart as well, as some media outlets suggested. Desperate and furious, Bouazizi went to the municipal administration building to make an official complaint and retrieve his property. The city official, however, declined to see him and refused to reverse the decision even after the young man threatened to set himself on fire (Fierke 220). Scorned and powerless, he went to purchase flammable liquid and returned to the administration building, where, around 11.30 am, he walked out into traffic and set himself alight, yelling: "How do you expect me to make a living?!" (qtd. in Jallad 153).

We have no way of knowing whether Bouazizi had any contact with his family, or in any way warned them of his intentions, between his failure to retrieve his property and the self-immolation. It bears noting, however, that both his cousin Ali and his stepfather found themselves at the site of the incident.[14] The stepfather later recounted that as flames engulfed Mohamed, onlookers panicked – someone tried to put out the fire, while others took out their phones to snap pictures or record a video of the incident. With burns covering nearly 90% of his body, the young man was taken to a local first aid station, but was quickly transferred to a bigger hospital in the coastal town of Sfax due to the gravity of his condition. After his self-burning sparked a wave of protests and drew the attention of the regime, Bouazizi was again transferred, this time to the specialist burns unit in Ben Arous on the outskirts of Tunis.

252 Selected contemporary ultimate protests by fire

De Soto rightly noted that the idea that losing 225 USD in property would warrant a horrifying death in flames may seem absolutely ludicrous to most Europeans and Americans, but many in Tunisia and across the greater region knew perfectly well the desperation that pushed Bouazizi to do the unthinkable. "In their eyes, Bouazizi had not been just the victim of corruption or even public humiliation, as horrible as they are; he had been deprived of the only thing that stood between him and starvation – the loss of his place in the only economy available to poor Arabs" (De Soto). With his equipment and capital taken away, he found himself facing a dead end. With his final act, however, he demonstrated that although the marginalised may seem stripped of agency, they are still capable of choice, even if that choice entails something as severe as deciding between life and death. The savagery of these measures also elevates their visibility in the eyes of authorities and other people (Jallad 161). In short, with his final act, Bouazizi seemed to have asserted: "I burn, therefore I am" (Burhani 83).

The role of framing and hybrid media networks in transforming a street vendor into a symbol of the revolution

The findings of both De Soto and his team and Jacobson bring up many legitimate arguments. But the issues they delve into do not provide an exhaustive enough explanation for Bouazizi's rise from street vendor to national hero – particularly given how easy it was to discredit his motivations by, for example, accusing him of mental instability. Before setting himself ablaze, Bouazizi had not prepared any banners or placards, and had not written any pamphlets or farewell notes, which made the message underpinning his protest even more vulnerable to manipulation by the regime-controlled mass media. Furthermore, contrary to many media reports, Bouazizi's was not the first self-burning to take place in contemporary Tunisia, and it was not its novelty, its radicalism, nor its spectacular character that ultimately decided the future course of events in the country, leading to the unprecedented flight of the disgraced, once all-powerful Ben Ali.

According to Merlyna Lim's findings, included in her illuminating text *Framing Bouazizi*, which I will draw on in this portion of the chapter, on 3 March 2010, nine months earlier, a similar self-incineration took place in Monastir, a port city on the eastern coast of Tunisia, claiming the life of 30-year-old street vendor Abdesslem Trimech. Moreover, less than a month before the Sidi Bouzid incident, on 20 November 2010, Chams Eddine Heni set himself alight in Métlaoui in western Tunisia. Aside from these two incidents, seven more self-incinerations took place in the country over the months preceding Bouazizi's fiery act. None of them, however, elicited a similar reaction despite sharing similarities in background, motivation, and, in Trimech's case, a nearly identical course of events. The incidents sparked only a handful of protests, all of which went mostly unreported and were quickly dispersed by the police.[15] Ben Ali's state security forces were very adept at this sort of work, honing their crowd control skills during a six-month-long revolt in the phosphate works in the central Tunisian town of Gafsa in 2008, put down with a combination of force and media blackout. In pro-regime media, the protesters were portrayed as subversives and extremists in the service of terrorist organisations.

In the case of the Sidi Bouzid incident, however, similar efforts to quash the nascent revolt proved unsuccessful. Seeking to explain the different outcomes, we need to focus primarily on the role that social media played in the incidents. Lim pointed out, however, that by no means such a focus should be taken to imply that the Jasmine Revolution was a "Facebook-driven revolt," a notion readily embraced by many writers and academics. The media scholar believed that social media was simply one more tool in the protesters' arsenal, and that it was their determination and ingenuity that played a key role in the success of the revolution.

The use of different avenues to mobilise social resistance against the regime in the wake of Bouazizi's self-burning was, to some extent, motivated by the fact that in Tunisia, anti-regime efforts were the domain of two separate groups. On the one hand, there were workers and labour union representatives, online rarely or not at all; on the other hand, there were online activists, most of whom were younger people hailing from more well-off classes and larger urban centres.

Lim reported (3) that Tunisia was the first Arab country to be connected to the Internet (1991). When online access was offered to the general public five years later, the authorities created a special agency (L'Agence Tunisienne d'Internet) to monitor the content appearing on Tunisian websites and curtail access to sites promoting human rights, political parties, and selected news portals. Rigorous censorship of online content, however, did little to discourage activists from using the web for political purposes. The first Tunisian digital think tank, Takriz, was launched in 1998, while the websites for Perspectives Tunisiennes and TuneZine debuted online in 2000 and 2001, respectively. 2004 marked the emergence of the very first Tunisian blogs and the founding of Nawaat.org,[16] an independent collective blog that doubled as a thought exchange platform for regime critics. Prior to 2010, however, all efforts to translate Tunisian online political activism into real-world settings failed, likely because at the time, 70% of the population still lacked access to the Web. Lim also emphasised that Tunisian online protesters "seldom raised issues that resonated with working-class activists" (4), and *vice versa*, as evinced by the lack of online traction received by privately taken videos of the Gafsa riots. At the time, Tunisia was still pronouncedly split, economically and socially, into the poorer interior and the wealthier coast, and the Gafsa case clearly demonstrates that in 2008, regime critics on- and offline were still fighting separate battles. Typically, the working-class activists sought improvement of working conditions and higher wages, whereas the middle-class activists focused on civil rights. Only the Bouazizi incident caused them to rise above their divisions and begin building genuine social solidarity, a process which required that the incident itself be properly framed and interpreted.

Lim found that Mohamed's distant cousin with a history of anti-regime activity, Ali Bouazizi, played a significant part in the process, as he appeared outside the magistrate building moments before the suicide protest and later recorded footage of the incident with his phone. Then, he collected photos of Mohamed engulfed in flames from other witnesses and packaged them for online distribution. He was perfectly aware of the power of this particular medium, believing, in his own words, that "images are like weapons, they can help topple a regime" (qtd. in Lim 6). Later that day, a friend helped him put together a video, which Ali then uploaded to Facebook just before 7 pm, along with a handful of pictures of his cousin's dreadful actions. Significantly, unlike other social media networks, Facebook was not banned in Tunisia, and the images, as is typical of that particular medium, spread online like wildfire. They were designed to shock their intended audience, appeal to their sense of righteous justice, and elicit an intense emotional reaction, such as compassion or outrage. It is beyond doubt that if Ali had drafted a text-only account of the incident, it would never have produced a response as powerful as that elicited by the visuals. As in the case of Thích Quảng Đức, the appeal of a local incident was amplified manifold by images thereof. However, as evinced by the protests in Gafsa, graphic images alone (in this case laying bare the brutality of the regime forces) are not enough to generate a broader response or mobilisation that would translate into real-life efforts aimed against the regime. A proper narrative is needed to channel the audience towards a specific interpretation aligned with one's own objectives.

Lim demonstrated that Trimech's self-burning, of which probably no pictures or footage exist, had been portrayed mostly as an act of a mentally deranged person, the "village fool," or an uneducated simpleton pushed to the edge. Meanwhile, the frame that Ali Bouazizi developed for the self-incineration of his cousin included two fundamental misrepresentations. Firstly, Ali portrayed Mohamed as an unemployed university graduate, even though the young vendor had not even graduated from secondary school. This change in Mohamed's biography immediately situated the protest in a political context, as it recast the vendor as a member of a class whose rights were under threat from the ineffectual and corrupt system – a group, we should add, that was highly active online and rich in Facebook users. Therefore, as Lim accurately contended: "Mohamed Bouazizi no longer represented the uneducated poor who struggle to provide food on the table, but represented all young people of Tunisia whose rights and freedom were denied" (7).

The other embellishment in Ali's story was the part about officer Faida Hamdi slapping Mohammed, a claim that was presented as fact even though there was not much in the way of evidence that would lend it any credibility. The policewoman later repeatedly denied that version of events. On the order of President Ben Ali, who wanted the whole incident swept under the carpet, Hamdi was arrested and jailed, although a subsequent trial exonerated her of all charges of wrongdoing (Davies). The Bouazizi family also dropped all charges against her by April 2011.[17] Regardless of the fact that, thanks to emancipatory reforms introduced by President Bourguiba, Tunisian women enjoyed a much greater degree of liberty than their counterparts in other countries of the region, and that the country itself was considered progressive,[18] the deliberate reframing that suggested a woman humiliated a man powerless to oppose her was a calculated decision aimed at eliciting a powerful reaction, particularly among Tunisian conservatives.[19]

These changes helped recast Bouazizi's suicide protest from being a desperate outburst of a man whose very survival was soullessly threatened into a catalyst in the struggle for civil liberties, freedom, and dignity, which enabled to equate him in the public's eyes with the well-educated youth burdened with poor economic prospects. The detail of the slapping, on the other hand, was supposed to rile the country's traditionalist base.

Lim argued that the course of events and the upswell of mass resistance against the authoritarian regime were definitely facilitated by the speed with which information about Bouazizi's protest and the demonstrations outside the Sidi Bouzid magistrates, which broke out in its immediate wake, spread across multiple channels. As mentioned before, a key role in that process was played by Facebook, which at the time had about a million active users in Tunisia, a huge increase from 2008, when the number barely exceeded 28,000. It bears noting, however, that most of these users were clustered in Tunis and other major urban centres along the coast, while in most smaller cities and towns in the central and western portions of Tunisia, reliable Internet access was basically non-existent, and even mobile coverage could be patchy. Furthermore, social networks in these areas had limited reach in 2010, because 95% of operational mobile phones in Tunisia were not used for data transfer due to exorbitant carrier rates, while smartphones represented a mere 2% of the total number of phones sold. Therefore, as Lim convincingly demonstrated, it was only the emergence of a hybrid media network, comprising social networks, the Qatari satellite network Al Jazeera, and distribution channels based on memory cards or telephone conversations, that allowed the news of Bouazizi's self-incineration to spread so far so quickly.

Lim found (9) that following the incident outside the magistrates, witnesses immediately began calling friends and relatives to inform them about what had happened. Among those contacted by Mohamed's uncle was journalist Zouhayr Makhlouf, who promptly left for Sidi Bouzid to learn more about the incident and write a piece about it. Because his phone was tapped by state security, the man was immediately apprehended outside his home, beaten, and had his camera taken away. But he still managed to spread news about

256 Selected contemporary ultimate protests by fire

the self-incineration using Facebook and e-mail, and also got in touch with Al Jazeera reporters.

Although officially barred from operating in Tunisia, Al Jazeera journalists continued to source footage and pictures from citizen journalists using the website sharek.aljazeera.net, developed for that exact purpose in November 2008, in the wake of a recent flare-up of the Israeli-Palestinian conflict in the Gaza Strip. Denizens of Sidi Bouzid also contacted a number of other journalists, while activists from SBZone, a small radio station, launched a full-scale information effort and shared the news with their regional correspondents and independent journalists from national media outlets. Scouring the Web for information about the Sidi Bouzid incidents, Al Jazeera reporters came across the Ali Bouazizi video and broadcast the footage later that day, alongside an interview with Ali, on Al Jazeera Mubasher, the network's all-Arabic channel airing mostly live coverage. A copy of the broadcast soon made its way onto Facebook. As a result, mere hours after the incident, news of the self-burning and the protests that followed it reached the majority of Arab countries in the region. Al Jazeera later stayed in touch with Ali and his friend Mehdi Horchani, who kept its staff up-to-date on the developments on the ground. Thus, the Qatari network, which, according to Tahar Ben Jelloun, "revolutionised the flow of information and communication in the Arab world" by refusing to shy away from graphic footage, holding "unflinchingly frank and aggressive discussions," and cross-examining witnesses with staggering efficacy (*Co to* 179), became the chief source of information on the dynamically shifting situation in the country.

This situation developed at a breakneck speed, as the protests in Sidi Bouzid continued and intensified, despite a visit from the Tunisian Minister of Development and the promise of earmarking 10 million USD for a jobs programme in the governorship. Two days later, Sidi Bouzid was rocked by more suicides (claiming the life of Lahseen Naji and Houcine Falhi, who climbed a transmission tower and touched the overhead power line), committed in protest against poverty and rampant unemployment, while civil unrest continued to spread, reaching as far as Menzel Bouzaiane, south of the provincial capital, and eventually spilling out to most towns in the area. On 24 December, major protests broke out in Thala, Kasserine, Meknassy, and Regueb. Later that day, police in Menzel Bouzaiane shot two people – one of the victims (Mohamed Ammari) succumbed to his wounds shortly after the shooting, while the other (Chawki Belhoussine El Hadri) held on to life for six more days. News about these incidents continued to spread across a variety of channels and media.

According to Lim (10), the #Sidibouzid hashtag appeared on Twitter on 18 December, and later that day Reuters published the first English-language report about the incident in the Tunisian city. The next day, Lina Ben Mhenni published the blog post about the incident, in which she repeated the untrue claim about Mohamed's university education, adding that he allegedly graduated from the University of Monastir. Later that same day, the French news channel France24 aired the first Western TV news report about the incident, which was later uploaded to YouTube. On 20 December, Al Jazeera aired the first English-language broadcast about the situation, rounding it off with viewer-submitted footage. Before the week was out, reports on the situation in Tunisia were published or aired by *Financial Times*, *Los Angeles Times*, CNN, the Swiss radio station RTS, Radio Netherlands, and the BBC. Alongside major news outlets, Internet users and bloggers continued to source updated information and post them across unofficial channels.

This picture perfectly illustrates how difficult it was to stem the flow of information across this networked, hybrid system – a reversal of the situation observed just two years before in Gafsa. Even extreme measures such as cutting off entire areas of the country from the Internet or even electricity, a course of action the Tunisian government pursued from 31 December 2010 to 2 January 2011, failed to put a stop to the spread of images and words, as the locals simply charged their phones in their cars. During the blackouts, Tunisians used their phones not only for calls and text messages, but also as makeshift radio transmitters to broadcast live audio feeds from protests and incidents. Some of these broadcasts, along with some text messages, were later converted into digital files and uploaded onto websites and social media profiles. Even after knocking out one or more avenues of distribution (by arresting bloggers, hacking websites, or using phishing attacks), the regime still found itself powerless to disrupt the spread of news, as they always seemed to reach the intended audience one way or another. Thanks to its decentralised nature (in this case, the lack of a single command centre vulnerable to attack), this web proved immune to traditional information warfare methods pursued by the regime.

The Tunisians' ingenuity and determination with respect to finding ways to continue distributing information seemed to know no bounds. This resourcefulness was well illustrated by the events in Thala and Kasserine, near the Algerian border, where Internet coverage was known to be patchy. When protests broke out in the two cities, police quickly cordoned them off and began brutally suppressing the outpouring of discontent. People used their phones to record police brutality and then passed the footage to activists, who transferred it to memory cards, which they then smuggled across the border into Algeria in their shoes. From there, the cards made their way to Tunis, where their contents were uploaded onto Facebook and picked up by Al Jazeera, which, in turn, recycled the intercepted footage and rebroadcast it via satellite.

The first protests in the capital broke out ten days after the events in Sidi Bouzid, with 300 lawyers demonstrating out on the street – a clear indication that the discontent was beginning to spread to the privileged, urban middle-class elites. The following day, 28 December, in an effort to alleviate the unrest, Ben Ali decided to visit Bouazizi in the hospital in Ben Arous for what was supposed to be a photo op for the president. Distributed by

258 Selected contemporary ultimate protests by fire

pro-government outlets, the picture seriously backfired on the regime. It was shared across Facebook and Twitter, with people adding sarcastic captions mocking its clearly propagandist character and the fact that the visit came much too late. Commenters also pointed out that the president and his entourage were not wearing masks, a requirement in the sterile environment of the burns unit. The photograph of the confrontation further reinforced the prevailing frame of the young vendor's protest, which painted his self-burning as an act of opposition against authoritarian rule. I was not able to establish whether Bouazizi was conscious during the visit or reacted in any way to what was happening around him, but his bandaged body was a symbol of his – and his compatriots' – powerlessness against the regime and his inability to resist its manipulations (Jacobson 28). Such a reading of the photograph may have further reinforced the protesters' resolve.

Around that time, Ben Ali received the Bouazizi family in his office and announced that they would be paid redress, while Mohamed would be sent to France for treatment, a promise which, to the bitter dismay of Mannoubia Bouazizi, would not be kept (Ryan, "The Tragic").

Later that day, the president appeared in a televised address, the first of three he would give before fleeing the country. In the speech, he accused the protesters of ruining the economy and warned that he would ultimately deal with them and do so with unwavering resolve. In the address delivered on 10 January, he added that the protests were organised by extremists and terrorists, but pronouncements like these no longer held any sway – neither domestically nor internationally. Ben Ali was no longer portrayed by the international news media as the sole guarantor of safety and stability in the region; instead, most outlets painted him as a ruthless authoritarian, eager to crush protesters despite his crackdowns leaving dozens dead (the brutal suppression of the 8–9 January riots in Kasserine being a prime example) (Schraeder and Redissi 11).[20]

In the wake of the death of Mohamed Bouazizi on 4 January 2011, and his funeral the following day, the protests intensified further. Lim reported that Al Jazeera, anticipating such a turn of events, shipped a large number of smartphones to Sidi Bouzid. The regime was prepping for action on the information front, too – it cordoned off the city and instituted a media blackout. On 5 January, Bouazizi was laid to rest in his hometown, with his funeral drawing a crowd of 5,000. Jacobson rightly noted (26) that the number included mourners, people who were drawn to Bouazizi's newfound status, as well as those who felt appearing at the funeral would signal their disavowal of the regime's brutal ways. Thanks to Al Jazeera, footage from the funeral procession, as well as the protests that broke out immediately after the ceremony, quickly made the news around the globe, proving that with support from new technologies, the resolve of the dispossessed could easily stand against government propaganda and authoritarian methods of restricting the flow of information.

Naturally, the events involving Bouazizi – the self-incineration, the presidential visit in the burns unit, and his death and funeral – were only a handful of cogs in the greater machine of protest and dissent that was picking up speed across the country. The fury of the populace was further exacerbated by a series of associated events: the 24 December arrest of popular rapper Hamada Ben Amor, performing under the stage name El Général[21] and widely known for his politically themed songs; the use of tear gas and brutal beatings to suppress a number of protests; and the use of live rounds by riot police. Ben Ali stayed in power as long as he was able to control the military and the flow of information. As soon as the Al Jazeera-supported citizen journalist network, active in Tunisia and abroad, emerged as an alternative source of information, the president's credibility and position were immediately threatened. And when the military switched sides and threw their support behind the protesters, the president's legitimacy was undermined beyond repair.

The act's religious context

On 22 April 2011, in a piece for the German weekly *Die Zeit* which would be included in the latest edition of his 2002 book *L'islam expliqué aux enfants (et à leur parents)* (*Islam Explained to Children (and their Parents)*),[22] Tahar Ben Jelloun wrote that "the act of self-immolation is wholly alien to Arab culture and tradition, and taboo to Muslims, as Islam, like other monotheist religions, forbids suicide and considers it an insult to the will of God" (*Co to* 213–214).[23] The fact that Mohamed Bouazizi violated a fundamental taboo of his religion to incinerate himself is no less intriguing than the general lack of objection to his burial despite this violation and the public's subsequent embrace of him as a martyr who ought to be commemorated by his people (Burhani 70). Given the context, we should note that the term "martyr" is reserved in Islamic tradition for those whose death is a testament of their faith (*shaheed*) or who sacrifice themselves in defence of faith (*fida'i*) (Ben Jelloun, *Co to* 97), never for suicides who take their lives for personal, egotistic reasons (*intihar*) (Fierke 198).[24]

Islam considers self-murder *haram* (forbidden and vile) but that does not mean that Muslims do not commit suicide.[25] Neither is self-burning exactly uncommon; committed primarily by women in the Middle East and Central and South Asia, in countries with both Sunni and Shia majorities, it is a way for them to protest against domestic violence and social injustice stemming from patriarchal cultural patterns, which consider gender-based discrimination valid (Rasool and Payton; Khosrokhavar; Aziz; Othman).[26] It is possible, however, that in many of these cases, the objective is to elicit guilt, in spouses or family members, rather than kill oneself; similar attempts are often labelled "parasuicides," according to the typology developed by American suicidologist Edwin Shneidman (225). As this type of self-burning is often performed in the presence of a husband or other relatives, the flames are usually extinguished quite quickly, leading to injuries but not loss of life. It is also hard to gauge the exact extent of the phenomenon as, given its inherent violation of religious taboo and the shame it brings, the families whose issues are aired in such a public manner rarely decide to report it to the relevant authorities or even appear at the hospital, and if they do, they claim that the burns are the result of an unfortunate accident (Jacobson 10). It is also possible that some of these incidents are the products of the so-called "honour killings," wherein a male representing the interests of the family douses a woman, who allegedly dishonoured her relatives in some way, with a flammable liquid and sets her on fire, purportedly to burn off the "shame" she brought upon her kin. Victims of honour killings also include women or girls who refuse to enter into marriages arranged by either a father or brother. Farhad Khosrokhavar reported that "in Iraq, after the fall of Saddam Hussein in 2003 … honour killings increased, in part due to the lack of state authority. In a single month, December 2007, 130 unclaimed bodies of women were found in the Baghdad morgue" (170).

In the wake of the highly publicised death of Bouazizi, whose deed involved actions similar to those undertaken by female domestic violence victims, and following the reworking of his act into a heroic gesture of resistance, self-incineration has been given a new lease on life in the Arab world, so to speak.[27] At least a couple of hundred people in the MENA region decided to follow the vendor's example, either dying engulfed in flames or sustaining grievous injuries in order to draw public attention to their suffering. These acts were not performed for religious reasons, which was a *sine qua non* in Islamic tradition for the mantle of "martyr." This marked a significant shift in the model of resistance, which up until that point had involved primarily violence directed outward, against others, whereas self-sacrifice was traditionally performed with arms in hand, and seen as a manifestation of the moral superiority of the person ready to perish in an uneven fight against a more powerful opponent.[28] Although this is by no means to imply that self-burning has completely replaced armed *jihad* (struggle), it has, at least for a time, provided a feasible alternative, and redefined the terms "martyrdom" and "self-immolation" to link them with actions lacking religious motives. The new model was based on "putting oneself to death in a manner that can leave no one indifferent, self-suppression being accomplished to denounce the illegitimacy of the political order," as rightly noted by Khosrokhavar (172). Ahmad Okasha, President of the Arab Federation of Psychiatrists, pointed out that these self-burnings had nothing to do with "martyrdom fantasies" and were simply "a cry for help, a plea against powerlessness, desperation and frustration" (qtd. in Fierke 219).

People setting themselves alight in MENA countries in 2011–12 – most of whom were men – patterned their acts after someone who was widely seen as a national hero and repeatedly glorified in popular narratives.[29] Importantly, these immolators decided to burn themselves regardless of the fact that their actions were unanimously denounced by Islamic clerics and scholars. Soon after the self-burning of 50-year-old Abdou Abdel-Moneim Jaafar outside the Egyptian parliament on 17 January 2011, scholars from the influential Sunni orthodox Al-Azhar University in Cairo issued a *fatwā* (legal opinion) condemning the act and others like it, and warned that auto-cremation was suicide and should be treated the same as murder. Thus, the faithful were forbidden from washing the body of a suicide (a requisite element of Muslim burial), and from offering prayers for and burying them.[30] A similar position on the matter was offered by Othman Battikh, the Grand Mufti of Tunisia, and Abdul-Aziz ibn Abdullah Al ash-Sheikh, the Grand Mufti of Saudi Arabia, both of whom called self-incineration an act of suicide rather than martyrdom, and emphasised that even the most extreme circumstances could not justify self-murder. They also declared that the deaths of Bouazizi or those who followed his example could not justifiably be called acts of martyrdom as neither was preceded by a call to *jihad* against the infidels or oppressive governments.

The only Islamic theologian to express a dissenting opinion was Yusuf al-Qaradawi of Qatar, Chairman of the International Union of Muslim Scholars. In his highly popular Al Jazeera show *Sharia and Life*, with an estimated audience in the millions, he not only refused to condemn Bouazizi, but asserted that he would ask Allah to forgive the young man the mortal sin he had committed, and pleaded with his viewers to offer similar prayers. A couple of days later, under pressure from the public who believed his declaration still too conservative, he further moderated his position, and asserted that Bouazizi's self-burning was justified, as it was a protest against humiliation and misery, and as such could not be considered a sin (Khosrokhavar 173). However, in the light of the growing number of self-incinerations across Arab countries, al-Qaradawi refrained from labelling Bouazizi a martyr, not to inspire anyone to follow his example. In this context, it bears bringing up that the cleric also went to great lengths to justify Palestinian suicide terror attacks against Israel, calling them acts of sacrifice and saying that for lightly armed Palestinian guerrillas, attacks like these were the only recourse that could bring change in the oppressive situations they found themselves in. In this particular case, however, as pointed out by Indonesian scholar Ahmad Najib Burhani, the suicide attacks were aimed against followers of a different faith (71).

Tahar Ben Jelloun believed that the fact that Muslims continued to follow Bouazizi's example, violating the commands of Allah, spelled the death throes of religious fundamentalism. In his view, orthodox rhetoric had finally lost its magnetic pull, as evinced by "hundreds of thousands of people pouring into the streets to protest corrupt and dictatorial regimes, without nary a mention of Islam or Allah" (*Co to* 214). It is undoubtedly symbolic that the protest self-burning which triggered a wave of similar acts took place in Tunisia, the country widely considered to be the most secular in the region. Also scholars such as Burhani or Khosrokhavar believed that Bouazizi's self-incineration and the burnings modelled after the vendor's could ultimately be considered a symptom of the gradual secularisation of Arab societies. Khosrokhavar underlined that "the people who committed self-cremation were not atheists or against Islam. They simply were secularised enough to restrict the realm of religion to their spiritual needs, leaving the social sphere to the freedom of human volition" (178–179).

And indeed, although the majority of Islamic theologians saw Bouazizi's act as a violation of the Koran's holy precepts, the public, as I mentioned above, instead read it as an act of heroism, acknowledging that the young man had full right to protest in this particular way against the injustice he suffered. At his funeral, the crowds chanted: "Farewell, Mohamed, we will avenge you. We weep for you today, we will make those who caused your death weep" (qtd. in Bady 137). Later on, Bouazizi was repeatedly recognised in a more official capacity, a testament to his posthumous elevation to glory and prestige. The new Tunisian government issued a commemorative stamp featuring his likeness, and renamed one of the main thoroughfares in Tunis after him. On the first anniversary of the incident, on 17 December 2011, city officials unveiled a new memorial to Bouazizi in Sidi Bouzid and announced that the city's main boulevard would now bear his name. At the unveiling, Moncef Marzouki, the newly elected Tunisian president said: "Thank you to this land, which has been marginalised for centuries, for bringing dignity to the entire Tunisian people" (qtd. in Khosrokhavar 174). Also present at the ceremony were representatives of the Tunisian National Dialogue Quartet, the four organisations that had played a key role in Tunisia's transition towards a pluralistic democracy and had jointly received the 2015 Nobel Peace Prize. Bouazizi's grave was draped with a Tunisian flag, confirming that he was seen as a national hero and would be treated accordingly.[31] However – as rightly pointed out by Bargu – the adulation accorded Bouazizi cannot be read solely as an expression of widespread desire for identification with acclaimed figures, but also as a symptom of "the need to forge a link between individual agency and history" (29).

The particular model of protest redefined by Bouazizi's act was ultimately undermined by the future course of political events in the MENA countries. The popular revolts, just like the 1979 Iranian Revolution, were eventually hijacked by Islamic fundamentalists, and the bloody civil wars that broke out in their wake in Libya, Syria, and Yemen cast a long shadow over the viability of that form of protest and its long-term effects. Following the Arab Spring, the region was subject to a series of seismic shifts, including civil wars; the reimposition of authoritarian rule; the entrenchment of religious fundamentalism, mass migration, and economic collapse; and the deaths and suffering of hundreds of thousands.

These developments were not without impact on the reception of Bouazizi's immolation. De Soto and Jacobson demonstrated that already in 2011, people disappointed with the scope and speed of reforms began focusing their discontent on Bouazizi's family. Although his relatives were initially treated with due reverence, they were soon accused of being the only ones who benefited in any measurable way from Mohamed's death, particularly after they moved from the impoverished province to a bigger home near the capital. Jacobson wrote: "Mass media and public presentations of the story consistently paint extraordinary pictures, but private discourse reveals an outright contradiction" (2), which boils down to the assertion that Bouazizi's role in the revolution was exaggerated, while his act was the result of him choosing to run away from his problems, choosing "the easier" way out. Although in 2014 the new government managed to amend and adopt a new constitution, the most liberal in the whole Arab world, the Tunisian economy suffered a near-collapse following the 2015 terror attacks in Tunis and Sousse carried out by fighters of the Islamic State. And as the country's internal problems grew worse, the voices that called for a reappraisal of Bouazizi's role grew louder, but ultimately failed to overturn the dominant hagiographic narrative, at least in the media discourse.

Reaching out towards the individual human experience: on Tahar Ben Jelloun's novella By Fire

The multitude of artistic works, created using a variety of techniques (from collage to embroidery),[32] focused on Bouazizi's face.[33] They have since turned it into a peculiar icon or a symbol. One particular piece that attempted to look beyond the superficial was Tahar Ben Jelloun's 2011 novella *Par le feu. Récit*.[34] In an interview with Deborah Treisman for *The New Yorker*, which published English translation of the novella on 16 September 2013, the Moroccan writer, considered one of the leading figures of Francophone literature in the Maghreb, explained that he wrote the story during a weeklong stay in the hospital in March 2011, in the midst of the *intifada*. First inspired to write the story after seeing the picture of President Ben Ali visiting the burns unit in Ben Arous, Ben Jelloun explained that he was motivated primarily by the desire to get through to a specific human experience and restore to Bouazizi, to borrow the author's words, a measure of "his humanity" (qtd. in Thomas).

Around the time of the interview, Ben Jelloun had published a book on the Arab popular revolts, a compilation of his columns, essays, and socio-political analyses and commentary on the course of events in the MENA countries. The portion on Tunisia and Bouazizi's protest, collected under the title *L'étincelle (Spark)*, was later reprinted together with the novella in 2016.[35] This is by no means to imply the liberally minded writer was pursuing some political agenda. In the aforementioned interview, Ben Jelloun described himself as an ordinary citizen with a modest interest in politics, who is, first and foremost, a storyteller and novelist whose remit involves primarily playing with words and stimulating the imagination.

264 Selected contemporary ultimate protests by fire

Ben Jelloun's politics and civic attitude were first shaped in 1966, when freshly out of higher education (he studied psychiatry and philosophy) and teaching in a university he was sentenced to a brief stay in a military penal camp for participating in a student protest against police brutality under the king of Morocco Hassan II. It was at the camp that he made the decision to try and make it as a writer. Since emigrating to France in 1971 (he left his homeland in protest against the Arabisation of philosophy, which he taught in French at the University of Rabat), he has written over 35 books, including novels, collections of poetry and short stories, dramas, non-fiction books on social and political issues, as well as a collection of essays and studies of current events, including his columns published in *La Repubblica*, *La Vanguardia*, and *Le Monde*. His works have been translated into over 40 languages, while the author himself has received a number of awards and honours, including the prestigious Prix Goncourt (1984) and the IMPAC International Dublin Literary Award (2004).

In the introduction she penned for her translation of *By Fire*, Rita Nezami pointed out that Ben Jelloun has taken on a broad range of subjects, including corruption, exploitation, gender- and race-based discrimination, as well as violence and authoritarianism in Arab countries. A humanist at his core, he has written about people who have found themselves on the rough edges of society, lending a voice to the unheard, the dispossessed, and the marginalised. Ben Jelloun believes that it is the duty of a writer to take notice of human suffering, to be humble and open to others, and to know how to package facts in a literary work in order to communicate better the excruciating experiences of the oppressed and the excluded. In a conversation with Ruth Schneider, Ben Jelloun detailed this approach as follows: "A novel can record the events that shake the world but there is no way it can explain it. It can give clues" ("Democracy"). Hence, rather than create art yielding potential political or social solutions, Ben Jelloun is more interested in writing which moves the readers, encourages them to identify with the characters, and inspires them to learn more about a given subject.

This particular attitude is likely what drove him to fictionalise the testimony of one of the few surviving prisoners of the Tazmamart, a secret Moroccan prison, where soldiers who took part in the failed 1971 coup against Hassan II were kept indefinitely and without trial, in horrifying conditions and total darkness. Ben Jelloun's 2001 book *Cette aveuglante absence de lumière* (*This Blinding Absence of Light*) was the shocking story of prisoners locked in cells only little bigger than a coffin and their struggle to preserve their sanity and humanity in these inhumane conditions. Both the book's real-life background and its focus on the struggle for dignity encourage us to treat the account of life in Tazmamart as a spiritual forerunner of *Par le feu*, published ten years later. At structural and stylistic levels, however, the later novella differs considerably from his earlier novel, which had laid bare human baseness and magnanimity alike. *This Blinding Absence of Light* is rich in metaphor and sophisticated phrasing, whereas the language and imagery of *By Fire* are much more sparse, even austere. The author decided that in the story exploring the experiences of Mohamed Bouazizi, "the style had to be simple, direct, dry," because "the subject didn't allow for adjectives and flowers!" Naturally, following that argument to its logical conclusion, we might say that Tazmamart as a subject also does not exactly lend itself to stylistic flourish, but it seems that ten years earlier the writer held different views. In Ben Jelloun's own words, while writing *By Fire*, he wanted the narrative to achieve the same "dryness" and "pared-down quality" which appears in the Vittorio De Sica's 1948 cult classic *Bicycle Thieves* ("This Week").

I deliberately wrote "the story exploring the experiences of Mohamed Bouazizi" rather than "the story of Mohamed Bouazizi," because the novella – although based on facts – does not explicitly confirm that Bouazizi is indeed its protagonist. The main character is introduced by first name only, Mohamed, while the story itself makes no mention of Tunisia. In two places the local currency is brought up, but instead of the Tunisian dinar, the narrative talks of rials, a name used for currency by Iran, Oman, and Yemen. Furthermore, the country in the story has been under authoritarian rule for 30 years (like Egypt under Hosni Mubarak), rather than 23 (like Tunisia under Ben Ali). The setting is further confused by a passing remark about singer Umm Kulthum, who hailed from Egypt but was popular across the entire region. Only near the end of its 24 scenes do we finally learn when the novella is set – from explicit dates of Mohamed Bouazizi's self-burning and death, both of them reflecting his real-life self-burning. All of these literary devices are supposed to imply that although the story itself is unique, it might as well have happened in any of the MENA countries, where similar problems are par for the course. Such framing allowed Ben Jelloun to universalise the particular experience of the young vendor.

But it also narrows the experience down. His Mohamed is not yet a historical figure – the "hero," "martyr," and "father" of the revolution into whom he will be remade by the media and the public. Above all, however, he is an individual man – a son, a brother, a young man in love, burdened with taking care of his diabetic mother and his siblings, and dreaming of a life together with Zineb, a receptionist in a local doctor's office, whom he has been in love with for the past two years. But as he realises that those dreams will never come true, he grows disappointed and despondent.

The novella begins soon after the funeral of Mohamed's father. In an early scene (and the work's first departure from factual events), the young man (30 years old in the story) burns the university diploma he received upon graduation from a history programme, as it is clear that the higher education he worked so hard for would not help him secure employment. As he watches the flames devour the document, he notices that the fire has somehow spared his name and date of birth, foreshadowing the events of the finale. The beginning also includes another suggestive image – of a

266 Selected contemporary ultimate protests by fire

column of ants that the protagonist observes while smoking cigarettes he had to buy singly, because he could not afford the whole pack. Laden with precious cargo, the insects represent the duties of the sole provider of the family – a role Mohamed did not want but was saddled with following his father's death. Unlike the real Mohamed, his fictional counterpart was only taking his first steps in his street vendor "career." Thus, the author shifts the emphasis (deliberately or otherwise) from the desperation of a young man forced to endure the toil of smalltime retail in support of his family towards the frustration of someone who has to bid farewell to their dreams of living a life better than their father's.

Fortune, however, finally smiles upon the fictional Mohamed, and he wins an airline ticket to Mecca in a university raffle. But cruel fate soon strips him of even that small inkling of luck, forcing him to sell the ticket at a loss to pool enough money to launch his street vending operation. Soon after, he is also forced to sell his precious books, including an original, leather-bound edition of *Moby Dick*, which he received for best marks in his senior year English class, to alleviate the family's dire financial situation and to purchase medication for his mother.

Ben Jelloun idealises his protagonist. His Mohamed is benevolent – he will not arrange a marriage between his sister and wholesaler Bouchaïb, a fraud, a boor, and Mohamed's supplier, even though it might have helped their finances as both men could have then gone into business together. He is caring – he believes the girl has a right to pursue dreams of education, and is willing to support her in the endeavour. He is honourable – he does not want to move in with Zineb to live with her parents, who are very fond of him, as he wants to show them that he would be able to provide for his future family. He is noble and proud – he cannot imagine himself becoming a police informant, even though that would guarantee at least some freedom from police harassment. He is attuned to the suffering of others – he is shaken by the injustice and brutality that the police exhibit towards his fellow street vendors. He is a capable businessman – barely a month into his operation, he is already able to buy from wholesalers with cash rather than on credit. He also makes plans to buy out his sick neighbour in the market, whose technologically minded children have no intention of taking the business over. He is undeterred by adversity even when he falls prey to harassment or extortion.

After a scuffle with the police, he dreams of his father, clad in white, beckoning to his son, foreshadowing Mohamed's death. Another ill omen appears when he comes across the funeral procession for a poor beggar who, in all probability, was beaten to death by the secret police. As was the case with his real-life counterpart, the fictional Mohamed decides to incinerate himself after his goods and equipment are confiscated by the police, leaving him humiliated and powerless in the face of city officials intent on teaching the young vendor an object lesson in compliance. In the novella, however, the events unfold at a much slower pace. After the scuffle with the officers and having been dismissed by city officials, Mohamed meets with Zineb, who advises him to go to the police and file a formal complaint. He agrees and they go together, but when the officer on duty asks for a copy of Mohamed's identification papers, they retreat, distrustful. The following day, Mohamed decides to burn himself in protest.

He prays for the first time since his father's death and then clothes himself in white and leaves, kissing the forehead of his sleeping mother goodbye and checking in on his siblings one last time. Borrowing his brother's moped, he visits a filling station where he pours petrol into a plastic bottle. The preparations complete, he sets off for the magistrates building, where he is once again rebuffed by sneering and soulless officials. Returning to the site of his scuffle with the police, he is again detained and humiliated – the female officer slaps him and spits in his face for daring to interrupt their breakfast. Disheartened, he returns to the magistrates, but is once again laughed out of the building. Only then does he make his final decision to self-incinerate in protest.

Ben Jelloun uses a stream of consciousness-like style to portray the violent turmoil that sweeps Mohamad's thoughts moments before he douses himself with petrol and strikes the match. He sees the faces of his loved ones, his beloved Zineb, a series of snapshots from the past and figments of his imagination. The latter includes the DVD box for Stanley Kubrick's Academy Award-winning *Spartacus*, which he saw earlier being crushed under the wheels of a police van destroying bootleg copies of films confiscated from street vendors. Using this particular film choice, Ben Jelloun implies the fate that awaits Mohamed in the end, the mantle of the hero of the revolution. Like the ancient gladiator, so will the young vendor rise up to lead the revolt, although in his case the leadership will remain strictly symbolic. Another reference can be gleaned in the author's descriptions of the protagonist's charred body, "entirely black, like a grilled lamb" (*By Fire*), the figure of the sacrificial lamb conjuring up obvious associations with Christ.

The final two portions of the novella offer a brief account, written in short, concise phrases, of what happened next: the president's visit to the immolator in hospital; the downfall of the autocrat; and Mohamed's rise to international hero-status, illustrated by a renowned film producer's attempts to purchase the rights to Mohamed's life's story from his family. At first, Mohamed's mother is unable to grasp the man's intentions, but her daughters quickly explain to her the truth of his schemes. After all, Ben Jelloun writes, Mohamed's story belongs to no one.

By changing key facts in the narrative, particularly those dealing with the circumstances of the self-burning, Ben Jelloun undermined the credibility of the incident itself. The protagonist bounces back and forth between the officers and the magistrates, and is given a lot more time (all night, basically) to ponder his choices and make his final decision. In this

268 Selected contemporary ultimate protests by fire

interpretation, however, he is also given more to lose: first and foremost his beloved, who understands his plight and supports him however she can. Regardless, Ben Jelloun accomplishes the chief objective he set for himself – in his retelling, the emblematic figure is given back at least a semblance of humanity, while small allusions manage to preserve the heroic dimension of the figure's act.

Written in near-real time, in the midst of political upheaval and the perversely celebratory mood it generated, Ben Jelloun's novella was the first literary attempt to examine the popular *intifada*. Perhaps this is what drove the seemingly inevitable idealisation of the protagonist and why the author ultimately failed take a more serious look at the questions which seem to come to mind when discussing the self-burning of a street vendor with a family to support. What did his self-incineration mean to his mother and his immediate family? What did it mean to the woman whom he loved, and who loved him back? Was it cowardice, a retreat from mounting responsibility, or was it quite the opposite – an act of courage? In Ben Jelloun's interpretation, Mohamed was undoubtedly under pressure, but by no means was he stuck in a trap from which there was no other way out.

Notes

1 Kim Hyojoung offers a total of 107 protesters who died by suicide protest between 1970 and 2004, and specifies that self-immolation was the predominant form, chosen by 78 of them (549). The dates above also indicate that protest self-burnings continued to occur following the democratisation of South Korea.
2 The president eventually reached Saudi Arabia, where he was promised asylum provided he renounced further political activity and contacts with the media.
3 See www.chuntaeil.org.
4 In later years, Chun Soon-ok was involved in academic work and founded a charity to support female workers, eventually becoming a parliamentarian from the New Politics Alliance for Democracy in 2012.
5 As mentioned by Cho Young Cheon, "While some of the journals were stolen or lost, five notebooks in which he kept his journal as well as some letters and essays he wrote were collected in the book *Don't Let My Death Be in Vain*" (55–56), published in South Korea in 1988.
6 On 2 February 1971, Kim Cha-ho, a young worker from a restaurant in the centre of Seoul, tried to perform a protest self-burning. In the presence of about 50 people, he first negotiated with the police for two hours and then set himself alight but was quickly extinguished. He later claimed he wanted to protest low wages and 18-hour workdays, and hoped his act would draw public attention to the poor working conditions in the food service industry, just as Chun's had for garment workers (Cho, Y-r. 35–36).
7 The film received the South Korean Blue Dragon Film Award for Best Movie in 1995; the following year, it was nominated for Best Picture at the 1996 Berlin International Film Festival.
8 In April 1997, Chun Doo-hwan was sentenced to death, while Roh Tae-woo received a 22.5-year prison term, but on appeal both sentences were reduced to life in prison and 17 years, respectively. Eventually, in 1997, outgoing President Kim Young-sam and President-elect Kim Dae-jung set both men free.

Sparks 269

9 Prior to that, all politically themed films were produced and distributed underground, away from the eyes of the regime.

10 Born in 1953, the actor was the son of widely known dissident and poet, Pastor Moon Ik-hwan, an associate of Kim Dae-jung in the struggle against the Park regime in the 1970s. Moon Sung-keun began his acting career in the mid-1980s and later teamed up with Park Kwang-su, starring in all his films. In 2009, he got involved with politics and three years later took over as leader of the social liberal Minjudang party.

11 In a conversation in the film, a character remarks that the dissidents had no way to put pressure on Park other than getting religious organisations involved, as they were the only ones with any influence over the Americans – benefactors and protectors of the regime.

12 Aside from his mother and stepfather, Mohamed also had to support his five siblings (three sisters and two brothers, the eldest of whom soon grew self-sufficient and left the family home for Sfax) (Ryan, "The Tragic").

13 Bourguiba was a veteran of the Tunisian struggle for independence from French colonial rule, and was elected president by the parliament in 1957, a year after Tunisia regained its sovereignty. In 1975, the country's constitution was amended to make him president for life.

14 Naturally, it is conceivable that the desperate Bouazizi tried to get in touch with his relatives to have them come and witness his act, the radicalism of which was supposed to prove the officer's guilt. If it were so, it would mean that he was capable of rationalising his actions despite the emotional turmoil he was in. However, we can only speculate whether he indeed wanted to ensure that news of his protest would spread by having a specific person or persons witness it.

15 Joachim Ben Yakoub indicated that protests following Trimech's self-incineration "only lasted one day" (256).

16 On 28 November 2010, Nawaat.org launched TuniLeaks, which featured those secret cables released by WikiLeaks that came from the American Embassy in Tunisia. The cables confirmed what most people already suspected or knew, namely that the families of Ben Ali and his wife were mired in scandals and misconduct (Ben Hassine 216).

17 To some extent it is perfectly understandable that Bouazizi's family tried to shift the emphasis towards the humiliation he suffered, rather than have the public focus on the family's poverty as the main reason for his self-incineration, as it allowed them to preserve some dignity. In doing so, however, they made a scapegoat of the police officer.

18 The first president of Tunisia strove to secularise the country following the Turkish template and expand women's rights. Thanks to his efforts, Tunisia outlawed polygamy, abrogated unilateral divorces (which gave the power to dissolve the marriage solely to the husband), legalised abortion, introduced equal inheritance rights, and allowed the option of not fasting during Ramadan.

19 One of the cartoons lampooning Ben Ali's downfall pointed to the alleged slap dealt by Hamdi (rather than Bouazizi's self-burning) as the moment that launched the regime's undoing. See Caricature.

20 In the third address, the president promised an end to violence and assured that he would not be seeking reelection in the upcoming 2014 presidential vote, while the regime would move towards liberalisation.

21 Incidentally, two weeks after Ben Ali's toppling, in an atmosphere of festive, elated anticipation, the rapper performed a show for a crowd of thousands. During the performance, Bouazizi's mother was brought on stage, confirming the special status the immolator enjoyed with the Tunisian public.

22 See English edition *Islam Explained.*

270 Selected contemporary ultimate protests by fire

23 *The Noble Qur'an* includes rather unambiguous passages on suicide: "And it is not [possible] for one to die except by permission of Allah at a decree determined" (3, 145); "And do not kill yourselves" (4, 29); and "do not throw [yourselves] with your [own] hands into destruction" (2, 195).

24 For the sake of accuracy, however, we should note that in the past Islamic jurisprudence differentiated between martyrs who died in the field of battle and those who perished in other circumstances. In other words, it was possible to be considered a martyr after dying in a car crash or due to complications from childbirth (Burhani 65). That does not change the fact, however, that in Arab countries martyrdom was generally associated with death in defence of the faith.

25 However, as highlighted by Polish suicidologist Brunon Hołyst: "All research seems to indicate that suicide is much less common in Islamic societies than in other religious communities" (117).

26 Self-burning was also pursued, albeit on a limited scale, by Kurds fighting the Turkish government for their right to self-determination, whose strategy was known to include suicide terror attacks and hunger strikes to death. In this case, however, we are dealing with a secular populace with leftist political views (Grojean 159–168).

27 It bears noting, however, that already in 2006 the Tunisian documentary filmmaker Sami Tlili "envisioned self-immolation as an ultimate act of resistance, albeit in a fictional way in his short film *Sans plomb* (*Unleaded*) captured the general mood of everyday desperation that caught the youth in the 2000s" (Yakoub 256).

28 Joachim Yakoub quoted a fragment of a letter by renowned Tunisian poet Abu al-Qasim Al-Shabbi (1909–34) to his friend: "Mad is the person who burns himself like incense for the sake of this foolish and ignorant people and, my friend, I am that mad person" (255). In the scholar's opinion, it confirmed that "self-immolation was already commonly propagated as an honorable albeit poetic act of political resistance during the struggle for national liberation" (256).

29 One example includes a homemade film uploaded to YouTube ("Mohamed Bouazizi"). In the video, Bouazizi's face is overlaid with an image of flames, while in the background, a man sings in Tunisian Arabic against a doleful guitar as the lyrics, translated into French, appear on the screen. The video portrays the young fruit vendor as a national hero, "the founder of democracy" and "the eagle who carries fire, the benefactor of humanity, the bird whose omen is happiness!" (qtd. in Khosrokhavar 177).

30 Incidentally, the proscription drew a harsh response online, with one user writing: "How hypocritical of Islamic clerics to declare suicide 'forbidden' under Sharia law when they refuse to publicly condemn bombers who kill themselves and innocent others in the name of Allah. Perhaps they don't consider it suicide if they are also killing the infidel" (qtd. in Fierke 219).

31 Bouazizi was recognised abroad, as well. On 8 February 2011, Bertrand Delanoë, the mayor of Paris at the time, named one of the squares in the capital after the Tunisian vendor. As one of five recipients, he was also posthumously awarded the 2011 Sakharov Prize, established by the European Parliament in 1988 to honour outstanding achievement in the struggle for equality and human rights, while *The Times* named him 2011 Person of the Year.

32 Two pieces from 2012 could be seen as excellent examples. One had eight women from a West Bank village collaborate with Palestinian artist Majd Abdelhamid on embroidering a nine-piece pop art portrait of the Tunisian vendor. The other saw Nepalese artist Sadish Dhakal feature the face of Bouazizi, tinted red, in his collage *Jamaraa Narahalaa*, which juxtaposed a map showing the changes in

the shoreline of Tsho Rolpa, the world's highest glacial lake (a testament to the ravages of climate change), with global events from past decades, which the artist saw as pivotal in human history.

33 Curiously, while most of the visual works avoided depicting his body as it was engulfed by flame, his fruit and vegetable cart was a rather common theme in many of them. A replica of the cart was the central element in *Hommage à Mohamed Bouazizi*, an installation created by French antiwar artist Effer Lecébé, which was shown at an unticketed exhibition at Centre d'art contemporain in Paris from 22 January 2011. Standing in the middle of a white space, the cart held fresh fruits and vegetables that were distributed to the attendees. The load was replenished every day on 7.15 pm, the hour of Bouazizi's death. Next to the makeshift stall sat a small mound of ash, providing a stark contrast to the life around it. Bouazizi's name, written out in large black block letters on the wall, further emphasised his absence.

34 It was translated into a number of languages, including Danish, English, German, Italian, and Spanish. In France, public readings of the novella were held at the Théâtre du Rond Point in Paris, with passages recited by actress Dominique Blanc (Ben Jelloun, "This Week").

35 Previously, a portion of the text was included in the anthology *Ten Years Later*. The chapter written for the book by Ben Jelloun, entitled *A Tale of Two Martyrs*, comprised *Spark* and a section dedicated to Egyptian Salafi Sayed Bilal, who was arrested on 5 January 2011 in Alexandria on suspicion of involvement in the suicide bombing of a Coptic church four days earlier, which left 23 people dead. Bilal was beaten to death by the police three weeks before the popular revolt broke out in Egypt.

References

The online resources identified below were consulted multiple times. All of them were active as of 1 December 2018.

A Single Spark. Directed by Park Kwang-su, performances by Moon Sung-keun, Kim Bo-kyeong, Hong Kyoung-in, produced by Yoo In-taek, 1995.

Abouzeid, Rania. "Bouazizi: The Man Who Set Himself and Tunisia on Fire." *Time*, 21 Jan. 2011. content.time.com/time/magazine/article/0,9171,2044723,00.html.

Aziz, Nahid. "What Self-Immolation Means for Afghan Women." *Peace Review. A Journal of Social Justice*, vol. 23, no. 1, 2011, pp. 45–51.

Bady, Aaron. "Spectators to Revolution: Western Audiences and the Arab Spring's Rhetorical Consistency." *Cinema Journal*, vol. 52, no. 1, 2012, pp. 137–142.

Bargu, Banu. "Why Did Bouazizi Burn Himself? The Politics of Fate and Fatal Politics." *Constellations*, vol. 23, no. 1, 2016, pp. 27–36.

Ben Hassine, Sami. "We Finally Have Revolution on Our Minds." *The Arab Spring: Rebellion, Revolution and a New World Order*, edited by Toby Manhire, Guardian Books, 2012, pp. 215–216.

Ben Jelloun, Tahar. *A Tale of Two Martyrs*. Translated by Linda Coverdale. *Ten Years Later*, edited by John Freeman, Granta, 2011, pp. 23–34.

———. *By Fire*. Translated by Rita S. Nezami, *The New Yorker*, 16 Sep. 2013. www.newyorker.com/magazine/2013/09/16/by-fire.

———. *By Fire: Writings on the Arab Spring*. Translated by Rita S. Nezami, Courbstone Books, Northwestern UP, 2016.

———. *Co to jest islam? Książka dla dzieci i dorosłych* [What Is Islam? The Book for Children and Adults]. Translated by Dorota Zańko and Helena Sobieraj, Karakter, 2015.

———. "Democracy Is Not Like an Aspirin You Dissolve in Water." Interview by Ruth Schneider, *Exberliner*, 17 Aug. 2011. www.exberliner.com/whats-on/%E2%80%9Cdemocracy-is-not-like-an-aspirin-you-dissolve-in-water%E2%80%9D/.

———. *Islam Explained*. New Press, 2002.

———. "This Week in Fiction." Interview by Deborah Treisman, *The New Yorker*, 6 Sep. 2013. www.newyorker.com/books/page-turner/this-week-in-fiction-tahar-ben-jelloun.

Burhani, Ahmad Najid. "Fatwās on Mohamed Bouazizi's Self-Immolation: Religious Authority, Media, and Secularization." *Sharia Dynamics: Islamic Law and Sociopolitical Process*, edited by Timothy P. Daniels, Palgrave Macmillan, 2017, pp. 63–89.

Caricature. 4.bp.blogspot.com/-dO4t28RXBGg/Tb6D1ajIMjI/AAAAAAAAACk/szfflwgfanM/s400/Caricature+005.jpg.

Cho, Young Cheon. *The Politics of Suffering in the Public Sphere: The Body in Pain, Empathy, and Political Spectacles*. Dissertation, U of Iowa, 2009.

Cho, Young-rae. *A Single Spark: The Biography of Chun Tae-il*. Translated by Chun Soon-ok, Dolbegae Publishers, 2003.

Chun, Soon-ok. *They Are Not Machines: Korean Women Workers and their Fight for Democratic Trade Unionism in the 1970s*. Ashgate, 2003.

Davies, Wyre. "Doubt Over Tunisian 'Martyr' Who Triggered Revolution." *BBC*, 17 Jun. 2011. www.bbc.com/news/world-middle-east-13800493.

De Soto, Hernando. "The Real Mohamed Bouazizi." *Foreign Policy*, 16 Dec. 2011. foreignpolicy.com/2011/12/16/the-real-mohamed-bouazizi/.

Doucette, Jamie. "Minjung Tactics in a Post-Minjung Era? The Survival of Self-Immolation and Traumatic Forms of Labour Protest in South Korea." *New Forms and Expressions of Conflict at Work*, edited by Gregor Gall, Palgrave Macmillan, 2013, pp. 212–232.

Ferguson, Niall. *The Great Degeneration: How Institutions Decay and Economies Die*. Allen Lane, 2014.

Fierke, Karin. *Political Self-Sacrifice: Agency, Body and Emotion in International Relations*. Cambridge UP, 2013.

Grojean, Olivier. "Self-Immolation by Kurdish Activists in Turkey and Europe." *Revue d'Etudes Tibétaines*, no. 25, 2012, pp. 159–168.

Hołyst, Brunon. *Suicydologia* [Suicidology], 2nd edition. LexisNexis, 2012.

Jacobson, Alec. "Duality in Bouazizi: Appraising the Contradiction." *SIT Digital Collection*, Independent Study Project, 2011, Spring. digitalcollections.sit.edu/cgi/viewcontent.cgi?article=2014&context=isp_collection.

Jallad, Zeina. "The Power of the Body: Analyzing the Logic of Law and Social Change in the Arab Spring." *Columbia Journal of Race and Law*, vol. 6, no. 2, 2016, pp. 139–168.

"Jeon Tae-il Bridge." Translated by David Carruth. *Seoul Magazine*. magazine.seoulselection.com/2013/05/10/jeon-tae-il-bridge/.

Khosrokhavar, Farhad. "The Arab Revolutions and Self-Immolation." *Revue d'Etudes Tibétains*, no. 25, 2012, pp. 169–179.

Kim, Heung-sook. "Mother Lee So-sun." *The Korea Times*. www.koreatimes.co.kr/www/news/opinon/2015/05/169_76652.html.

Kim, Hyojoung. "Micromobilization and Suicide Protest in South Korea, 1970–2004." *Social Research*, vol. 75, no. 2, 2008, pp. 543–578.

Kim, Kyung Hyun. "Post-Trauma and Historical Remembrance in Recent South Korean Cinema: Reading Park Kwang-su's 'A Single Spark' (1995) and Chang Son-u's 'A Petal' (1996)." *Cinema Journal*, vol. 41, no. 4, 2002, pp. 95–115.

"Korean Film 1990–95." www.koreanfilm.org/kfilm90-95.html.

Lagarde, Dominique. "Czy ktoś uratuje Ibn Alego?" [Can Anyone Save Ibn Ali?]. *Ostatnie dni dyktatorów* [The Dictators' Last Days], edited by Diane Ducret and Emmanuel Hecht. Translated by Anna M. Nowak, Znak Horyzont, 2014, pp. 241–249.

Lankov, Andrei. "Labor Activist Chon Tae-il's Death: A Wake-up Call." *The Korea Times*, 2011. www.koreatimes.co.kr/www/news/nation/2011/01/113_80158.html. Accessed on 9 Apr. 2019.

Lim, Merlyna. "Framing Bouazizi: 'White Lies,' Hybrid Network, and Collective/Connective Action in the 2010–11 Tunisian Uprising." *Journalism: Theory, Practice, and Criticism*, vol. 14, no. 7, 2013, pp. 921–941.

Lynch, Marc. *The Arab Uprising: The Unfinished Revolutions of the Middle East.* PublicAffairs, 2012.

"Meeting Chun Tae-il: The Memory of a Beautiful Young Man Comes Alive on the Chun Tae-il Bridge." *Korea Democracy Foundation*, 30 Nov. 2010. en.kdemo.or.kr/notification/news/page/10/post/45.

"Mohamed Bouazizi Héros Tunisian Révolution Tunisie." Uploaded by TheMuslimantifa, *YouTube*, 17 Jan. 2011. www.youtube.com/watch?v=5Nir6FcXDM8.

Nezami, Rita S. "Translator's Introduction." Tahar Ben Jelloun. *By Fire: Writings on the Arab Spring*, Courbstone Books, Northwestern UP, 2016.

Nti, Nana Bemma. "Lessons from the Death of a Tunisian Salesman: A Commentary." *African Security Review*, vol. 22, no. 2, 2013, pp. 78–84.

Othman, Nasih. "Suicide by Self-Burning in Iraqi Kurdistan: Description and Risk Factors." *Archives of Suicide Research*, vol. 15, no. 3, 2011, pp. 238–249.

Park, Ben B.C. "Sociopolitical Contexts of Self-Immolations in Vietnam and South Korea." *Archives of Suicide Research*, vol. 8, no. 1, 2004, pp. 81–97.

Pazurek, Marcin. "Samospalenie po tunezyjsku" [Self-Burning in the Tunisian Way]. *Tygodnik Powszechny* [Krakow], no. 8, 10 Feb. 2012, pp. 24–25.

Rasool, Izaddin A., and Joanne L. Payton. "Tongues of Fire: Women's Suicide and Self-Injury by Burns in the Kurdistan Region of Iraq." *The Sociological Review*, vol. 62, no. 2, 2014, pp. 237–254.

Ryan, Yasmine. "The Tragic Life of a Street Vendor." *Al Jazeera*, 20 Jan. 2011. www.aljazeera.com/indepth/features/2011/01/201111684242518839.html.

———. "How Tunisia's Revolution Began." *Al Jazeera*, 26 Jan. 2011. www.aljazeera.com/indepth/features/2011/01/2011126121815985483.html.

Schraeder, Peter J., and Hamadi Redissi. "Ben Ali's Fall." *Journal of Democracy*, vol. 22, no. 3, 2011, pp. 5–19.

Shneidman, Edwin S. "Suicide, Lethality, and the Psychological Autopsy." *Aspects of Depression*, edited by Edwin S. Shneidman and Magno J. Ortega, Little, Brown, 1969.

Spivak, Gayatri Ch. "Can the Subaltern Speak?" *Marxism and the Interpretation of Culture*, edited by Cary Nelson and Lawrence Grossberg, Macmillan, 1988, pp. 271–314.

The Noble Qur'an. quran.com.

Thomas, Anne. "Authors at Berlin Festival Talk About 'Writing the Arab Spring'." *Deutsche Welle*, 12 Sep. 2011. www.dw.com/en/authors-at-berlin-festival-talk-about-writing-the-arab-spring/a-6615878.

Yakoub, Joachim Ben. "Performing Self-Sacrifice, Despite Everything or Despite Oneself? Embodying a Necropolitical Space of Appearance in the Tunisian Revolution." *Shifting Corporealities in Contemporary Performance: Danger, Im/mobility and Politics*, edited by Marina Gržnić and Aneta Stojnić, Pallgrave Macmillan, 2018, pp. 251–274.

Figure PIII.4 Wolfgang Stiller *Matchstick Men* (2010).

Index

Note: *Italic* page numbers refer to figures and page numbers followed by n refer to notes.

Abdelhamid, Majd *227*, 270n32
Abe, Shinzō 90
Abouzeid, Rania 247
Acevedo Becerra, Sebastián 55–56
act-performance see performance
Adamec, Zdeněk 70, 220n33
Adnane, Noureddine 81
Afghanistan 73–74; Kabul 73
Agamben, Giorgio 6, 15n10
Ahvazi Arabs 90
Akihito, Emperor of Japan 45
Al Jazeera TV 229, 255–259, 261
Al Qaeda 73, 249
Aladár, Farkas 160n46
Alanssi, Mohamed 73
Albania 87; Tirana 87
Alcalay, Luna 221n37
Alekh, Hasan Ali 81
Algeria 36n11, 79–80, 258; Bordj
  Menaïel 80; M'Sila 36n11
Alinsky, Saul: *Rules for Radicals* 162n67
Allain, Paul 127–128
Allworth, Edward 52
Alter, Nora 103–106, 159n35
altruism 2, 14n1, 20–22, 40, 115, 170,
  180, 205, 229
altruistic suicide (Durkheim) *see* suicide
Améry, Jean (born Hans Mayer) 33
Amini, Khodayar 91
Amis, Kingsley 153
Ammar, Rachid 230
Ammari, Mohamed 256
Ánanda Margá 53
Andrews, William 45

Andriolo, Karin 3, 21, 23–24, 30,
  34, 36n2
Andrzejewski, Jerzy 181
anti-war activism 44, 60, 65, 74–75,
  160n53; against the war in Vietnam
  42, 44, 103–107, 128, 132–133, 136,
  138–142, 145, 147, 153, 161n58,
  161n61, 168, 170, 178; *see also*
  pacifism
Anwar, Ghazi 73–74
Anyık, Eşref 53
Aouichia, Mohamed 80
Apostolidis, Andreas 48
The Arab Spring 3, 26, 80, 229, 250, 262
Arden, John 147
Arendt, Hannah 32
Armenians 55
Army of the Republic of Vietnam
  (ARVN) 112, 114, 122–123, 157n19
Artaud, Antonin 6, 15n8, 127–128,
  159n34; *The Theatre and Its Double* 127
artivism (Taylor, Diana) 12–13, 65
ARVN *see* Army of the Republic of
  Vietnam
Asakereh, Younes 89–90
Al ash-Sheikh, Abdul-Aziz ibn Abdullah,
  Mufti 261
Ashton, John 53
Attar, Farīd ud-Dīn (born Abū Ḥamīd bin
  Abū Bakr Ibrāhīm): *The Conference of
  the Birds* 13
Australia 15n11, 53, 89, 91, 192; Brisbane
  92; Christmas Island 91; Melbourne 91
Austria: Vienna 204

276 Index

Aydın, Filiz Tutku 52
Aziz, Mohamed Ould Abdel 80
Aziz, Nahid 22, 259

Bà Đặng Thị Kim Liêng 86
Babeş, Liviu Cornel 57
Badal, Parkash Singh 76
Bady, Aaron 262
Badylak, Walenty 53, 218n6
Bahrain 79, 81
Balderstone, Simon 53
Baldwin, Alec (Alexander R.) 161n59
Baldwin, James 149
Balogh, Zsolt: *1968* 46
Bamford, Graham 61–62
Banionis, Raimundas 49
Banisadr, Seyyed Abolhassan 62
Banksy (pseud.): *Made in China. Tibet*
    159n39; *Napalm (Can't Beat That*
    Feeling) 131
Bansal, Shyam Sunder 76
Bảo Đại, Emperor of Vietnam 112
Barba, Eugenio 127
bare life (Agamben) 6
Bargu, Banu 8, 35; *biosovereignty* 9; on
    Bouazizi 4, 230, 263; *necroresistance* 2, 9,
    15n5, 20; *politicization of death* 2; *Starve*
    and Immolate 2, 9–10; *weaponization of*
    life 2
Barker, Ciph 221n37
Battersby, Lucy 131
Battikh, Othman, Mufti 261
Bauer, Sándor 46
Beaumont, Florence 42
Beauregard, Alexandrine: *Imaginary*
    Self-Immolation 84
Beck, András 213
Beckley, Connie 222n44
Becklund, Laurie 84
Bednáriková, Eva 201
Bejko, Lirak 87
Belgium: Brussels 220n34
Ben Ali, Zine El Abidine: downfall 80,
    229–230, 248, 252, 258–259, 269n19,
    269n21; reactions to Bouazizi's self-
    burning 79, 255, 257–258, 263; rule in
    Tunisia 248–250, 253, 265, 269n16
Ben Ammar, Tarak 230
Ben Amor, Hamada (pseud. El Général)
    259, 269n21
Ben Hassine, Sami 269n16
Ben Jelloun, Tahar 229, 263–264; on Al
    Jazeera TV 256; *Cette aveuglante absence*

de lumière 264–265; *Par le feu (By Fire)*
    230, 263–268; on self-burnings 261;
    on suicide in Islam 259; *A Tale of Two*
    Martyrs 271n35
Ben Mhenni, Lina 256
Benedetto, André: *Napalm* 159n35
Benedict XV, Pope (born Giacomo della
    Chiesa) 178
Benn, James 8, 15n7, 115–118
Beran, Josef, Archbishop 206
Béreš, Jan 202–203
Bergman, Ingmar: *Persona* 12, 16n15,
    159n33
Berrigan, Daniel, Father 105
Bezdíček, Vilibald 200, 204
Bhagavad Gītā 146
Bhund, Sarwar 72
Bhutto, Benazir 72
Biały, Ewa 173, 176, 179
Bieniasz, Maciej: *Płonący* 217n6
Biggs, Michael 2–4, 41, 59; on protest
    self-burnings and hunger strikes
    22–23; scrutiny of protest self-burnings
    23–27; on *suicide protests* 20–22; on
    Thích Quảng Đức's self-immolation
    107, 157n23, 159n32
Bilal, Sayed 271n35
Bilgee, Tuur 92
biopower (Foucault) 4, 9–10, 32
Blanc, Dominique 271n34
Blažek, Petr: on Palach 195–199, 201,
    204, 208–209, 215, 220n28, 221n37,
    223n54; on Plocek 219n16; on Siwiec
    45, 169, 172–175, 180–182, 217n4,
    218n15
Bolivia 210
Bond, James 160n46
Bondhus, Barry 149, 151, 155
Borissov, Boyko 87
Bosák, Emanuel 204
Bosnia and Herzegovina 62
Bouazizi, Ali 254, 256
Bouazizi, Mannoubia 248, 250, 258,
    269n21
Bouazizi, Mohamed (Tarek al-Tayyib
    Muhammad ibn Bu'azizi): biographical
    references 248, 250–251; in *By Fire*
    230, 263, 265–268; reception and
    recognition 229–230, 247, 252,
    254–255, 258, 261–263, 269n17,
    270n29, 270n31; responses in culture
    270–271n 32, 271n33; the self-burning
    and its consequences 3–4, 79–80,

229, 251–255, 258–260, 262, 269n14,
269n19; *see also* Ben Ali
Bourguiba, Habib 249, 255, 269n13
Brazee, Ronald 43
Brechtian poetics 148, 152
Brezhnev, Leonid 52, 200
Brook, Peter: *Battlefield* 162n64; *Tell
Me Lies* 107, 146, 151–155, 162n65,
162n66; *US* 107, 146–151, 162n65,
162n66
Brown, George 153
Brown, Timothy 60
Browne, Malcolm 108; account of
Thích Quảng Đức's self-immolation
108–111; *The New Face of War* 155,
156n2; photographs of Đức's act 3, 41,
103, 106, 108–110, 118–120, 124–125,
128, 130, 132, 156n2, 157n13, 158n26
Bruno, Giordano 205
Brüsewitz, Oskar 50
Buber, Martin 140
Buddha Shakyamuni (born Siddhārtha
Gautama) 88, 104, 107, 109, 116–117,
125, 156n1
Buddhism 157n16; attitude to
self-burnings in Chinese tradition
115–118; attitude to suicide 25,
36n9; versus Catholicism in Vietnam
112–113; Engaged Buddhism 103–104;
Vesak 104, 114; Vietnamese *sangha* 110,
114, 122–123, 154
The Buddhist crisis in Vietnam 114–115,
119–125
Buffetrille, Katia 84
Bukartyk, Piotr 93
Bulgaria 87; Varna 87
Bundt, Robert 137
Burešová, Dagmar 214–216, 224n53
Burhani, Ahmad Najid 252, 259,
261–262, 270n24
Burke, Edmund 33
The Burning Bush see Holland, Agnieszka
Burns, Alan: *Palach* 221n37
Bush, George W. 145
Businov, Yelena 73
By Fire see Ben Jelloun, Tahar

Cabot Lodge, Henry, Jr. 119, 135
Cambodia 42, 108
Camus, Albert 140
Canada 49, 55, 70–71, 218n13; Montreal
49, 84, 211
Cannan, Denis 162n66

Cao Ngọc Phương *see* Chân Không
Carlson, Marvin 10
Carmichael, Stokely S. Ch. (pseud.
Kwame Ture) 154
Castro, Fidel 132
Catholic Worker Movement 42, 105
Catholicism: attitude to other faiths
157n16; attitude to suicide 178; Vatican
65–66; *see also* Buddhism
Cavara, Paolo 124
CBS TV 120, 122, 144, 159n33
Ceaușescu, Elena 57
Ceaușescu, Nicolae 57
Cemilev, Reşat *see* Dzhemilev, Reshat
Černík, Oldřich 201
Cézanne, Paul: *La maison du pendu* 210
chaebol (Korean) 61, 243
Chaffin, Craig 160n46
Chaikin, Joseph 146
Chan, I-hua 36n7, 58
Chân Không (born Cao Ngọc Phương)
41, 44, 103, 110
Chang, Kathleen *see* Change, Kathy
Chang, Maria Hsia 69
Chang, Song-u: *Kkotnip* 243
Change, Kathy (born Kathleen Chang)
36n4, 64–65
Chanoff, David 108, 111, 113, 156n10
Charvát, Josef 202
Chary, Kasoju Srikanth 78
Chatfield, Charles 136, 139
Chauhan, Surinder Singh 59
Chen, Guo 67
Cheng, Nan-jung 57–58
Chile 55, 69; Conceptión 55; Santiago 69
Chin, Frank 64
China/People's Republic of China
6, 15n7, 44, 66–69, 71, 77, 81–84,
88, 115–117, 155, 157n21; Beijing
24, 67–69, 78, 131; Changchun 68;
Chengdu 71; Kaifeng 68; Nanjing 71;
Nanning 69; Qinghai 82; Shaanxi 44;
Sichuan 77, 82; *see also* Falun Gong
(Falun Dafa); Taiwan; Tibet
Chinnasamy 41
Chirac, Jacques 71
Cho, Young Cheon 30–34, 36n2, 61, 238,
240, 268n5
Cho, Young-rae 228, 231, 234–241,
268n6
Choi, Yeon-yeol 90
Chun, Doo-hwan 56, 228, 231, 241–242,
268n8

278 Index

Chun, Sang-soo 232
Chun, Soon-ok 231, 268n4
Chun Tae-il (Chŏn *or* Jeon Tae-il):
  biographical references 231–239; in
  Park Kwang-su's film 244–247; self-
  immolation and its consequences 4, 48,
  228–229, 239–242, 268n6
Chung, Won-shik 61
Cieślak, Ryszard 126–128, 146–147
Citton, Yves 81
Claiborne, Clay: *Vietnam: American
  Holocaust* 159n33
Clampit, Amy 160n46
Coburn, Jon 43, 139, 160n50, 160n51,
  160n52
Coleman, Loren 8, 53
Colotka, Peter 194
Comenius, John Amos 196
communitas (Turner, V.) 7
Confucianism 61, 116; in Vietnam 112
Cooper, Kim
copycat suicide see suicide
Costa-Gavras, Constantin: *Amen* 15n14;
  La Petite Apocalypse 15n14
Croatia: Rijeka 220n35
Cronkite, Walter L. 122
Crosby, Kevin 3
Cultural Revolution *see* revolution
Currien, Father 137
Cyprus 54
Czabańska-Rosada, Małgorzata 50, 52
Czabański, Adam 8, 20–21, 50, 52
Czapliński, Przemysław 12
Czech Republic/Czechia 46, 70, 198,
  210, 213, 217, 220n33, 222n42;
  Humpolec 70; Ostrava 70; Prague
  70, 171
Czechoslovakia/Czechoslovak Socialist
  Republic 3, 45–46, 170, 175, 179,
  192–198, 206–207, 209, 211, 214,
  217n3, 217n4, 217n6, 219n16, 221n37;
  Brno 200, 202–203, 220n30; Česká
  Lípa 214–215; České Budějovice
  200; Cheb 202; Jihlava 206, 219n16;
  Lány 197; Libiš 197; Mělník 196, 213,
  220n34; Plzeň 202; Prague 45, 168,
  171, 192, 195–197, 199–201, 203–204,
  206, 213, 215–216, 217n2, 217n3,
  217n6, 220n34; Staré Hory 219n16;
  Šumperk 171, 217n3; Vítkovo near
  Opava 217n; Všetaty 196–197, 204,
  208, 220n34, 222n51; *see also* Czech
  Republic; Slovakia

Dahoud, Yacoub Ould 80
Dalai Lama (religious name Tenzin
  Gyatso, born Lhamo Thondup) 66–67,
  77, 81–83
Đào Thị Yến Phi 42
Daoism 67; in Vietnam 112
Darabi, Homa 36n4, 62–63
Darabi, Parvin 63–64
Davidson, Helen
Davies, Wyre 247, 255
Day, Dorothy 105, 141
De Sica, Vittorio: *Ladri di biciclette* 265
De Soto, Hernando 230, 247–248,
  250–252, 262
Death of a Regime 159n33
DeBenedetti, Charles 136, 139
Dębska, Agnieszka 177
Delanoë, Bertrand 270n31
Delerium: *Faces, Forms & Illusions* 159n36
deliberate self-burning (DSB) 2, 14n2,
  15n6, 22–23, 25
Delvaux-Mufu, Maggy 36n11, 72
Demery, Monique 121, 156n10
Democratic People's Republic of Korea
  (North Korea) 6, 61, 236; *see also* Korea
Democratic Republic of Vietnam (North
  Vietnam) 124, 135–136, 142, 160n50,
  161n57; *see also* Vietnam
Deng, Annie 71
Denmark 53
Dera Sacha Sauda 76
Devine, Alexa 161n62
Devine, Sean: *Re: Union* 145–146, 161n62
Dhakal, Sadish: *Jamaraa Narahalaa*
  270–271n32
dharma (Sanskrit) 146
Dionisopoulos, George 119–120
discipline (Foucault) 9–10
Doan, Van Toai 108, 111, 113, 156n10
Doğan, Mazlum 54
Doherty, Ben
Dolak, Józef 218n6
Domańska, Ewa 8
Dommen, Arthur 118, 156n10
Dondzik, Michał 185, 188
Donnan, Stuart 53
Dorr, Jeanne
Dostoyevsky, Fyodor M. 150
Doucette, Jamie 240
Dress Code: *Flame* 88
Driberg, Thomas 153
Drygas, Maciej 169, 172, 175, 177, 179,
  182, 184, 217n4, 218n15; *Dzieci z*

Hotelu Ameryka 49; *Testament* 169,
171–172, 175, 184–185, 188–192;
Usłyszcie mój krzyk 45, 169, 171–172,
174–178, 181, 183–184, 186–188,
218n12; *Vaikai iš Amerikos viešbučio* 49
DSB *see* deliberate self-burning
Du Plessix Gray, Francine 136
Dubček, Alexander 181, 193, 201, 205
Duch-Dyngosz, Marta 173
Dufresne, Diane 49
Dunn, Katrina 162n62
Dương Văn Minh 123
Durkheim, Émile: *Le Suicide* 20, 25
Dušek, Otakar: *38 Nails for Josef Toufar and
Jan Palach* 220n36
Dzhemilev, Mustafa 52
Dzhemilev, Reshat 52

Egypt 79–80, 265, 271n35; Cairo 80; El
Qantara 80
Eichler, Patrik 195
Eisler, Jerzy 177, 180–181, 217n4
El Hadri, Chawki Belhoussine 256
Ellsberg, Daniel 143
Elósegi Odriozola, Joseba 36n8, 47
Elstner, Reinhold 64
Epydemye 221n37
Erdene, S. 92–93
Escoffier, Alain 50
Ethiopia 79; Dawro Zone 81; Tercha 81
Evers, Medgar 119
Ewart, Ewa: *Access to Evil* 6

Falhi, Houcine 256
Falun Gong (Falun Dafa) 67–69
Farley, Helen 69
Farrahi, Neusha 36n10, 56–57
fast to death 8–9, 14n1, 110; *see also*
hunger strike
Federal Bureau of Investigation (FBI) 73
Federal Republic of Germany *see*
Germany
Ferguson, David 160n46
Ferguson, Niall 250–251
Fertacz, Magda: *Nie gaście* 217n1, 221n37
Fierke, Karin 8, 35, 123, 251, 259–260,
270n30
Fijałek, Krzysztof 53
Fischer, Marc 75
Fisher, David 136
Fisher, Ian 65
Forest, Jim 105
Foucault, Michel 13, 32–33

Frames, Robin 140
France 70–71, 81; Labastide-Saint-
George 82; Paris 50, 70
Franco, Francisco 47
Frankenheimer, John: *Path to War* 161n59
Frayne, Evan 161n62
Freeman, William Th.: *The Spirit of Jan
Palach* 222n40
Funamoto, Shūji 45

Galili, Lily 73
Galindo, Regina José 12
Gandhi, Indira P. 53, 58, 204
Gandhi, Mohandas K. (Mahatma) 23, 51,
140–141, 161n54, 204
Gandhi, Rajiv 58, 77, 85
Gandhi, Sonia 85
Ganesan, Mohan 14n2, 22
'Gardzienice', Centre for Theatre
Practices 218n12
Gatti, Armand: *V comme Vietnam* 159n35
Gaudium et Spes, encyclical 178
Gaulin Bergeron, Huguette 49
Gauthier, Saskia 14n2
The Gaza Strip 73, 256
Gebre, Yenesew 81
Geertz, Clifford 8; *The Interpretation
of Cultures* 14; *thick description* 5
Georgakis, Kostas 47
Georgia 79; Abkhazia 79; Tbilisi 79
Germany: Falkenstein in Saxony 52;
Federal Republic of Germany
(FRG) 51–52, 53–54, 64, 161n61;
German Democratic Republic
(GDR) 50, 52; Hamburg 51; Munich
64; Nazi Germany 173; Zeitz near
Leipzig 50
Gernet, Jacques 157n21
Ginsberg, Allen 149, 156n4
Godard, Jean-Luc: *Camera Œil* 132,
159n42; *Loin du Vietnam* 159n40
Goldwater, Barry M. 135
Gomułka, Władysław 168, 175, 178,
181, 188
Goranov, Plamen 87–88
Górski, Kazimierz 183
Goswami, Rajiv 36n10, 37n12, 58–59
Gott, Karel 221n37
Gough, Richard 8, 32
Grabysa, Maciej 53
Gramsci, Antonio 219n16
Grass, Günther: *Max* 159n35

280 Index

Gray, Amlin: *How I Got That Story* 159n65

Great Britain 52–54, 70–71; London 54, 61–62, 70–71; Macclesfield 61

Greece: Athens 48; Kerkyra (Corfu) 48; Thessaloniki 87

Green, Peter 70

Grojean, Olivier 55, 270n26

Grotowski, Jerzy 125–128, 146–147; *The Constant Prince* 126–128; *Towards a Poor Theatre* 127

Gründler, Hartmut 36n11, 51

Gruppo Padovano di Protesta Nazionale 222n39

Gryglewicz, Tomasz 217n6

Guenther, Lisa 15n10

Guevara de la Serna, Ernesto (pseud. Che) 153, 210

Günther, Rolf 52

Gupta, Rishi 59

Ha Van Tran 108, 119

Habermas, Jürgen 31

Halberstam, David 41, 108, 110, 114, 156n2, 158n26

Hall, Michael 89

Hamas 73

Hamdi, Faida 251, 254–255, 269n19

Hammer, Ellen 112, 115, 157n23

han (Korean) 246

Hao, Huijin 67, 69

Harding, James M. 9, 109, 115, 118, 127–128, 156n5, 159n34, 159n35

Hariman, Robert 106

Harvie, Jen 127–128

Hasham, Nicole

Hassan II, King of Morocco 264

Hassani, Neda 70–71

Havel, Václav 182, 193, 207, 209, 211, 214, 220n31, 222n47

Hedges, Paul 30, 69

Hejduk, John: *The House of Suicide* and *The House of the Mother of the Suicide* 171, 209–213, 222n43, 222n44, 222n46

Hejduk, Renata 211

Helfer, Richard 162n65, 162n66

Hen, Józef (born Józef Henryk Cukier): *Western* 217n6

Hendrickson, Paul 144

Hendrix, Jimi (James M.) 129

Heni, Chams Eddine 252

Heo, Se-uk 75

Herekol, Yekta *see* Kahraman, Erdoğan

Herz, Alice 42, 105, 138–139, 141, 143, 160n49, 160n50, 160n51

Herz, Helga 160n49

Heschel, Abraham 141, 161n55

Higgins, Marguerite 120, 157n12

Himmel, Nieson 57

Hinduism 157n16; attitude to suicide 36n9

Hirnyk, Oleksa 51

Hitler, Adolf 16n14, 160n49

Hlavatý, Josef 202–203

Hồ Chí Minh (born Nguyễn Sinh Cung) 132, 142, 157n17

Hochhuth, Rolf: *The Representative* (*The Deputy*) 15n14

hogra (Arabic) 229

Holeček, Lubomír 197–198, 201, 214

Holland, Agnieszka 168, 171, 194, 198, 205, 208–209, 219n20, 219n22; *The Burning Bush* 171, 196, 209–210, 213–217, 222n50, 222n51

Hołyst, Brunon 20, 270n25

Hong, Ki-il 56

Hong, Kyoung-in 244

"honour killing" 260

Hood, James 119

Hope, Marjorie 156n9, 158n23

Hopkins, Peter 157n20

Horáková, Milada 221n37

Horchani, Mehdi 256

The House of Suicide and *The House of the Mother of the Suicide see* Hejduk, John

Hrubý, Tomáš 213

Hrůza, Michal 221n37

Huba, Martin 215

Huh, Jik 43, 237

Hulík, Štěpán 213–214

Hungary 46–47: Budapest 46

hunger strike 36n3, 41–42, 51, 73, 87, 54, 61, 66–67, 76, 78, 87, 89, 104, 114, 160n53, 200, 220n31, 240, 270n26; versus self-burning 8, 22–23, 31, 33; *see also* fast to death

Hunt, Albert 146, 148–149, 151, 162n65, 162n66

Hus, Jan 170, 198, 202, 205

Husák, Gustáv 193, 195, 200–201

Husni, Mariwan 55

Hussein, Saddam 260

Hutagalung, Sondang 85

ianfu (Japanese) 90–91
India 41, 52, 57–59, 66, 73–74, 76, 78, 81–82, 85, 116–117; Andhra Pradesh 58, 78–79; Bathinda, Punjab 76; Bhopal 57; Bihar 53; Chennai 76, 85; Cuttack, Orissa 59; Dharamsala 66–67; Jamnagar 74; Kanchipuram 85; Kashmir 73–74; Kizappazuvur, Madras 41; New Delhi 59, 66–67; Patna 53; Rajkot, Gujarat 74; Sirsa, Haryana 76; Sriperumbudur 85; Tamil Nadu 58, 76–77, 85; Telangana 78–79
Indochina 106, 146, 149–150, 158n23
Indonesia 85; Jakarta 85
intifada (Arabic) 230, 263, 268
Iran (Islamic Republic of Iran) 56, 62–63, 70–71, 81, 89–90, 265; Ahvaz 90; Arab Struggle Movement for the Liberation of Ahvaz (ASMALA) 90; diaspora 56–57, 71, 81, 92; Ilam 63; Kermanshah 63; Khorramshahr 89–90; National Council of Resistance of Iran (NCRI) 70–71; People's Mujahedin of Iran (MEK) 70–71; Tehran 62–63, 70; *see also* revolution
Iraq 70
Irving, David 64
Islam 67, 88, 157n16; attitude to self-annihilation 259–262, 270n23, 270n24, 270n25, 270n26, 270n30; Islamic Revolution *see* revolution; the Islamists 249; Shia 63, 259; Sunna 259, 261
Israel 46, 54, 73, 86; Kedumim 73; Tel Aviv 86
Italy 47, 70, 79; Bari 87; Florence 204; Genoa 47; Milan 204; Palermo 81; Rome 158n29, 204, 220n34; San Cataldo in Sicily 65
Iwaki, Kyoko 37n15

Jaafar, Abdou Abdel-Moneim 80, 261
Jáchimová, Veronika 221n37
Jackson, Glenda 148–150, 153
Jacobs, Hayes B. 160n50
Jacobs, Sally 162n66
Jacobs, Seth 110–111, 119, 156n10
Jacobson, Alec 230, 247, 250–252, 258, 260, 262–263
Jacopetti, Gualtiero: *Mondo cane 2* 124–126
Jallad, Zeina 230, 251–252
Jan, Yün-hua 8, 115–116

Janion, Maria 176
Jankowski, Celene 43, 160n52
Jan-Krukowska, Justyna: *Flame* 84
Japan 43–45, 90–91, 161n61, 228, 232–233, 237; Hiroshima 180; Ogasawara Islands 45; Okinawa 45; Osaka 45; Tokyo 37n15, 44, 91
Jareš, Jakub 195
Jedličková, Maria 208
Jehad, Mohamed 91
JFK *see* Kennedy, John F.
jihad (Arabic) 260–261
John XXIII, Pope (born Angelo Giuseppe Roncalli) 113, 118
John Paul II, Pope (born Karol Wojtyła) 178
Johnson, Charles 137
Johnson, Lyndon B. (LBJ) 43, 104, 123, 136, 138, 142–144, 161n61
Joiner, Charles 118, 122, 156n10
Jones, Howard 111, 121, 124, 156n10, 158n27
Jones, Mark 149–150, 152–155
Jones, Sam 77
Jordan 79, 81
Joshi, Pravin 74
Judaism 73, 157n16
Juncker, Jean-Claude 72
Jung, Krzysztof: *Całopalenie* 221n37

Kaczmarski, Jacek 221n37
Kaczyński, Lech 182
Kahraman, Erdoğan (pseud. Yekta Herekol) 55
Kąkolewski, Krzysztof 188
Kalanta, Romas 48–49, 217n6
Kaliski, Bartosz 173–175, 177–180, 205
Kallentoft, Mons 15n13
Kamiński, Tadeusz 173
Kang, Ki-hoon 60
Kang, Kyung-dae 60–61
Kańska, Stanisława 176
Kantor, Tadeusz 184
Kantůrková, Eva 208
Karami, Arash 90
Karcz, Zygmunt 169
Karnow, Stanley 41, 44, 112–113, 122, 136, 156n7, 156n10
Kasabian 221n37
Katsiaficas, Gregory 61
Katzenbach, Nicholas 119
Kaufman, Ami 86

282 Index

Kaźmierczak, Leszek (pseud. Eldo) 219n19
Keefer, Edward C. 114, 156n8, 156n10
Kelly, Brendan 8, 29
Kempton, Murray 152
Kennedy, John F. (JFK) 114, 119, 121–123, 143, 158n27
Khamenei, Ali, Ayatollah 56–57, 62
Khan, Amir 74
Khomeini, Ruhollah, Ayatollah 62
Khosrokhavar, Farhad 81, 259–262, 270n29
Kilgore, Charles 124
Kilroy, Kevin 75
Kim, Bo-kyeong 244
Kim, Cha-ho 268n6
Kim, Dae-jung 61, 238, 241–242, 268n8, 269n10
Kim, Heung-sook 241
Kim, Hyojoung 8, 31, 61, 228, 239, 268n1
Kim, Il-sung 232
Kim, Jae-joon, Pastor 240
Kim, Kyung Hyun 242–244, 246
Kim, Soomi 65
Kim, Young-kyun 60
Kim, Young-sam 242, 246, 268n8
King, Anita 65
King, Martin Luther, Jr. 104–105, 141, 156n3, 161n55
King, Sallie B. 14n1, 104, 118, 136, 140, 158n24
King, Tim 77
Kisielewski Stefan 177
Klaus, Václav 70
Kleyff, Jacek 93
Kmuníčková, Zdenka 195, 200
Kochanowski, Janusz 183
Koeppel, Matthias: *Die Selbstverbrennung des Pfarrers Brüsewitz* 50
Kohout, Pavel 214
Kohoutek, Luboš 220n34
Kokeš, Lukáš 219n19
Kolankiewicz, Leszek 128
Kolbe, Maksymilian Maria, Father 178, 183
Konwicki, Tadeusz: *Mała apokalipsa* 11, 217n6
Korea (Republic of Korea *or* South Korea) 25–26, 43, 48, 56, 60–61, 75, 90–91, 139, 230–233, 236–240, 242–243, 247, 268n1, 268n5; Daegu 232–233; the Gwangju Uprising

(massacre) 56, 60–61, 228, 243; the Korean War 232, 236, 240, 244; Panmunjom armistice 232; Pusan 91, 232; Seongnam 60; Seoul 6, 43, 48, 56, 60, 75, 90, 228, 231–234, 237–238, 242, 244, 268n6; *see also* Democratic People's Republic of Korea
Kościuszko, Tadeusz 183
Kosiński, Dariusz 34
Kosygin, Alexei 200
Kovan, Martin 30
Krauze, Krystyna: *Powrót Agnieszki H.* 222n47
Kryl, Karel 221n37
Kubečková, Pavla 213
Kubenko, Vladimír: *Tryzna* 220n26
Kubrick, Stanley: *Spartacus* 267
Kulmiński, Robert 9, 170, 179, 183, 195, 198–199, 201, 219n24, 221n37, 221n38
Kulthum, Umm (born Fāṭima 'Ibrāhīm es-Sayyid el-Beltāǧī) 265
Kundera, Milan 170, 205, 208, 214, 220n29
Kurds 36n6, 53–55, 270n26; Kurdistan Workers' Party (PKK) 53–55
Kurtay, Ferhat 54
Kurz, Iwona 9, 179
Kustow, Michael 162n65, 162n66
Kutyła, Julian 13
Kuwait 60
Kwapis, Robert 181, 193–194, 200–205, 207
Kwaśniewski, Aleksander 182
Kwon, Hyok 6

The Laboratory Theatre 125–126, 146–147, 218n12
Lagarde, Dominique 248–249
Lahiri, Simanti 8, 37n13, 161n54
Laing, Alexander 160n46
Laloë, Véronique 14n2, 22
Lamb of God 221n37
Lang, John 161n62
Lankov, Andrei 232
LaPorte, Roger A. 42, 105
Latvia: Riga 46; *see also* Latvian Soviet Socialist Republic
Latvian Soviet Socialist Republic 46
Laouri, Fadoua 81
Lawrence, Marjie 155
Lazarek, Gabriela 37n14
LBJ *see* Johnson, Lyndon B.

Lê Quang Tung 122
Lê Thị Tuyết Mai 88–89
Lebenstein, Jan 181
Lecébé, Effer: *Hommage à Mohamed Bouazizi* 271n33
Lederer, Jiří 195, 197, 202, 205
Lee, Kyung-hae 36n1
Lee, So-sun (Yi So-seon) 231–232, 240–242
Lenin (born Ulyanov), Vladimir I. 206
Lester, David 75
Levely, George 60
LeVine, Mark 81
Levittoux, Karol 218n11
Li, Hongzhi 67–68
Liangqing 44
Liber, Marcin: *Fuck… Sceny buntu* 218n12
Libera, Zbigniew 130
Libya 248, 262
Lilly, Alex 72
Lim, Merlyna 252–256, 258
Lina ci Rovina 221n37
Liu, Chunling 67
Liu, Siying 67–68
Lithuania: Kaunas 48; *see also* Lithuanian Soviet Socialist Republic
Lithuanian Soviet Socialist Republic 48–49
Litzinger, Ralph 84
Lloyd, Robert 149–152
Lobsang Tonden (born David Alain) 82
Loin du Vietnam see Marker, Chris
Loney, Glenn 162n65, 162n66
Lotus Sutra 116–118; *see also* Buddhism
Lucaites, John 106
Luo, Guili 69
Lux, Štefan 15n14
Luxembourg 72
Lynch, Marc 248

MacKenzie, Scott 152
Madame Nhu *see* Trần Lệ Xuân
Maghreb 81, 263
Maginnis, Kevin: *Self-Immolation* 11, *167*
Mahābhārata 146, 162n64
Mahler, Gustav 150
Maj, Bronisław 53
Makhlouf, Zouhayr 255
Makukh, Vasyl 170
Maksymowicz, Virignia: *Thirty Blocks* 161n58
Malaysia 76–77
Malinka, Miroslav 202

Malone, Vivian 119
Mamut, Musa 36n8, 51–52
Mandal, Bindheshwari Prasad 58
Mańka, Jarosław 53
Manus Island (Papua New Guinea) 91
March on the Pentagon *see* Pentagon
March on Washington 136
Marcuse, Herbert 42
Marker, Chris (born Christian François Bouche-Villeneuve): *Loin du Vietnam* 132, 159n40; *La sixième face du pentagone* 161n61
Marotti, William 45
Marowitz, Charles: *Palach* 221n37
Maruf, Harun 91
Marzouki, Moncef 262
Masaryk, Tomáš Garrigue 182, 196–197, 203, 222n47
Mašín, Josef 206
Masoumali, Omid 92
mass media 2, 9, 29, 41, 108, 252, 263
Mauritania 79–80, 229; Nouakchott 80
Mauss, Marcel 24
May, Karl F. 196
Mayakovsky, Vladimir V. 107
Mayrock, Bruce 46
Mazur, Władysław 175, 180–181
Mazurek, Bohdan: *Epitafium na śmierć Jana Palacha* 218n6
Mbembe, Achille 6
McCutcheon, Russell 106, 115
McDonagh, Martin: *Seven Psychopaths* 130
McGranahan, Carole 84
McGregor, Ewan: *American Pastoral* 158n31
McKelvey, Tara 169
McKenzie, Jon: *Perform or Else* 7–10
McNamara, Margaret 143
McNamara, Robert 135, 138, 143–146, 161n61, 162n63; in *Path to War* 161n59; in *Re:Union* 145, 162n62
McQueen, Steve (Steven): *Hunger* 36n3
Mehrjui, Dariush: *Bemani* 63
Memon, Dhani Bux 72
Memorial 73
MENA *see* Middle East and North Africa
Menard, Aubre 93
Merton, Thomas 104–105, 141
Messiah complex 29, 65
Michelsen, Nicholas 4, 8, 29–30
Mickiewicz, Adam: *Dziady* 218n11
Middle East 55, 65, 89, 259

284 Index

Middle East and North Africa (MENA) 2, 26, 37n11, 229–230, 260, 262–263, 265
Mieszko I, King of Poland 179
Mikołajewski, Jarosław 93
Mikulášek, Bohdan: *Ticho* 220n26
Miller, Edward 156n10
Miller, Jonathan 147
Miller, William 156n10
Milota, Stanislav: *Jan 69* 220n26
minjung (Korean) 233, 244, 246
Miño Pérez, Eduardo 69
Mitchell, Adrian 151, 162n66: *Skin of Flame* 107, 160n46; *To Whom It May Concern* 107, 148, 156n4
Al-Moayad, Mohammed Ali Hassan 73
Modi, Narendra Damodardas 74
Mohanty, Surendra 59
Mondo cane 2 see Jacopetti, Gualtiero; Prosperi, Franco
Mongolia 92; Ulaanbaatar 92
Moon, Ik-hwan, Pastor 269n10
Moon, Sung-keun 244, 269n10
Moore, Charles 89
Morawski, Piotr: *Tajne taśmy SB* 173
Morocco 79–81; Casablanca 81; Souk Sebt 81
Morris, Errol: *The Fog of War* 143, 161n60
Morrison, Benjamin 133, 137, 142
Morrison, Christina 133–134, 137, 142
Morrison, Emily 42, 133–134, 137–138, 142, 145, 154, 161n56
Morrison, Norman: biographical references and anti-war activism 135–136, 160n47; the influence of the act on Robert McNamara 143–145; in *Path to War* 161n59; reception in Vietnam 133–135, 142–143, 161n57; responses in culture 107, 132–133, 146, 148–149, 154–155, 160n46; in *Re:Union* 145, 161n62; the self-immolation and its consequences 3, 42–43, 106–107, 132–135, 137–142, 159n44, 160n52, 160n53; in *US* and *Tell Me Lies* 107, 146, 148–149, 154–155
Morrison Welsh, Anne 136–137, 140; *Held in the Light* 133–135, 137–138, 140–144, 160n46, 160n53; in *Loin du Vietnam* 133–135; in *Tell Me Lies* 154; in *US* 149
Moserová, Jaroslava: 192–193; *Letter to Wollongong* 192, 221n37

Moules, Raymond 60s
Mounier, Emmanuel 113
Moyses, Márton 47
Mrożek, Sławomir 179, 181
Mubarak, Muhammad Hosni El Sayed 80, 265
Munro, Pauline 152–154
Musharraf, Pervez 72
Muthukumar, Kumar 76–77
Myanmar 76; Rangoon 76
Mycielski, Zygmunt 181

Na, Kahn-chae 61
Nacházelová, Blanka 206
Nader, Luiza 11, 218n7
Nadesan, Balasingham 77
Naji, Lahseen 256
Nalankilli, Thanjai 41
National Liberation Front (NLF) 112–113, 119, 123, 132, 135
Nauru *see* Republic of Nauru
Ndreca, Gjergj 87
necroperformance (Sajewska) 7
necropolitical space (Mbembe) 6
Němcová, Dana 209
Nepal 81–82
Netanyahu, Benjamin 86
The Netherlands 79; Amsterdam 81, 85, 160n50, 204
The New York Times 108, 121, 142, 144, 156n2, 158n26, 158n27
Nezami, Rita S. 264
Ngô Đình Cẩn 157n17, 158n29
Ngô Đình Diệm 3, 41, 106, 108, 112–114, 118–123, 125, 157n12, 157n17, 159n33, 159n44
Ngô Đình Khôi 157n17
Ngô Đình Luyện 157n17, 158n29
Ngô Đình Nhu 3, 113, 115, 121–122, 159n44
Ngô Đình Thục 113, 158n29
Ngodup, Thupten 66–67
Nguyễn Cao Kỳ 43
Nguyễn Chánh Thi 43
Nguyễn Khánh 123
Nguyễn Kim Thành (pseud. Tố Hữu): *Emily, My Child* 142–143
Nguyễn Ngọc Rao 108
Nguyễn Văn Thông 108–111
Nguyễn Văn Trỗi 135
Nhất Chi Mai *see* Thích Nữ Diệu Huỳnh
Nhat Hanh *see* Thích Nhất Hạnh
Nierman, Leonardo 74

Index   285

Nigerian Civil War 46
Nixon, Richard 42
Niziołek, Grzegorz 11
NLF *see* National Liberation Front
non-violence 3, 22, 24, 27, 51, 82–83,
  104–105, 141
Norimatsu, Satoko Oka 45
North Korea *see* Democratic People's
  Republic of Korea
North Vietnam *see* Democratic Republic
  of Vietnam
Novotny, Antonín 198
Nový, Vilém 206, 214–215
Nowak-Jeziorański, Jan 180
Nti, Nana Bemma 248

Obama, Barack H. 77
Öcalan, Abdullah 54
Öcalan, Osman 54
Ogden, Hugh 160n46
Ogura, Toyofumi: *Letters from the End of
  the World* 180
Okasha, Ahmad 260
Old Believers 3
Olšany Cemeteries in Prague 203–204,
  217n3, 222n47
Oman 265
Öner, Necmi 54
Onyekachi, Chima 46
The Open Theatre 146; *Viet Rock*
  159n35
Ormando, Alfredo 65–66
Othman, Nasih 55, 259
Ownby, David 69

Pachman, Luděk 202, 214
pacifism 104–105; *see also* anti-war
  activism
Paget, Reginald 153
Pahlavi, Mohammad Reza 56, 62
Pakistan 72; Gilgit-Baltistan 73; Kashmir
  as contended with India 73–74
Palach, Jan: biographical references 195–
  197, 219n18, 219n20; followers 46–48,
  51, 70, 87, 171, 202–203, 219n16,
  220n30, 220n33; in *The Burning
  Bush* 213–217; responses in culture
  171, 209–217, 217–218n6, 218n9,
  220n26, 220–221n36, 221n37, 221n38,
  222n40, 222n42; the self-immolation,
  its consequences, appraisals, and
  recognition 3, 36n1, 45–46, 168,
  170–171, 180–181, 192–195, 197–209,

217n2, 219n25, 220n27, 220n28,
  220n29, 220n31, 220n34, 220n35,
  222n47
Palach, Jiří 196, 222n53
Palach, Josef 196
Palachová, Libuše 196, 208, 214–215,
  222n45, 223n53
Palata, Luboš 36n1
Panas, Jan: *Komandos* 217n1
Panchen Lama 82
Papadopoulos, Georgios 47
Paputsis, Costantinos 48
Paracel Islands 88
Park, Ben B. C. 14n1, 48, 56, 61, 228
Park, Chung-hee 43, 48, 228, 231, 233,
  237, 240–241
Park, Kwang-su 243; *Areumdaun
  cheongnyeon Jeon Tae-il (A Single Spark)*
  228, 231, 242–247
Park, Sung-hee 60
Pasolini, Pier Paolo 210; *Bestia da stile*
  221n37
Patil, Pratibha 85
Patler, Nicholas 140, 145, 160n48,
  161n61
Pauhofová, Tatiana 215
Paul VI, the Pope (born Giovanni
  Montini) 204
Pavlensky, Petr 12–13
Pawar, Kailash 57
Payton, Joanne L. 55, 259
Pazurek, Marcin 250
Peaslee, Richard 151, 162n66
Peer, Milan: *Ticho* 220n26
Pentagon 3, 42, 106, 133–134, 137, 140,
  143–146, 154; March on the Pentagon
  161n61
performance 6–7; *act-performance* 35,
  107–108, 117; *cultural performance* 7;
  necroperformance 7; self-burning as
  performance 6–8, 33–35
performance studies 6, 9–10; *performative
  turn* 8
Petrović, Lena 147, 150
Petrycki, Jacek: *Powrót Agnieszki H.*
  222n49
Phạm Văn Đồng 142
The Philippines 52, 89
Phillips, Lynette 52–53
Phuntsog, Rigzin 81
Piłsudski, Józef 173
Pink Floyd: *Wish You Were Here* 14n4
Pinochet, Augusto 55–56

286 Index

Pinter, Harold 147
Pipia, Nana 79
PKK *see* Kurds
Plamondon, Luc 49
Plank, Katarina 3
Plocek, Evžen 219n16
Płużański, Tadeusz 184
Pogonowska, Anna: *W świetle Jana Palacha* 218n9
Pokorná, Jaroslava 215
Poland/Polish People's Republic 9, 12–13, 15n6, 37n14, 45, 53, 93, 127, 169–171, 173, 175, 178, 180–181, 183–184, 186, 214, 217n4, 217n6, 218n13, 221n37; Cieszyn 37n14; Dębica 182; Krakow 53, 218n12; Opole 127; Przemyśl 45, 168, 172–175, 177, 182, 189, 219n15; Rzeszów 218n15; Tarnobrzeg 177; Warsaw 45, 93, 168, 171–172, 174–175, 177, 180–181, 189, 218n7, 218n12; Wrocław 84, 126, 146
Polásek, Jan 220n30
Poniatowski, Józef 183
Porcher, Jacqueline 154
Potter, Terry 148
Pownall, David: *Torch No. 1* 221n37
Prabhakaran, Velupillai 76
The Prague Spring 45, 169–170, 174, 180–181, 192–194, 196–197, 214, 220n29, 221n37
Pratt, Mike 148
ProART: *JAN* 221n37
Procházková, Lenka: *Slunce v úplňku* 221n37
Prosperi, Franco: *Mondo cane 2* 124–126, 154
Protestant (punk group) 221n37
Puhovski, Nenad: *Graham and I – a True Story* 62
punctum (Barthes) 128

al-Qaradawi, Yusuf 261
qigong (Chinese) 67
The Quakers' beliefs 135–136
Quảng Đức *see* Thích Quảng Đức

Raczak, Lech 176
Radio Free Europe (RFE) 46, 172–173, 180–181, 209, 217n2, 218n8
Rado, James (born James A. Radomski): *Hair* 159n35

Rage Against the Machine (RATM) 129
Ragni, Gerome (Jerome): *Hair* 159n35
Ragno, Fabio: *Jan Palach* 222n39
Rajaratnam, Thenmozhi (pseud. Dhanu) 85
Rajavi, Maryam 70–71
Rajavi, Massoud 70
Rao, Kalvakuntla Ch. 78
Rao, Srinivasa A. 79
Rasool, Izaddin A. 55, 259
Ratajczakowa, Dobrochna 203
RATM *see* Rage Against the Machine
Rázl, Stanislav 200
Read, David 162n66
Reagan, Ronald 57
Redgrave, Vanessa 147
Redissi, Hamadi 230, 248–250, 258
Reeves, Geoffrey 146, 149–151, 162n65, 162n66
Republic of China *see* Taiwan
Republic of Korea *see* Korea
Republic of Nauru 91–92
Republic of Somaliland *see* Somalia
Republic of Vietnam *see* Vietnam
Resnais, Alain 132, 159n41
restored behaviour (Schechner) 7
revolution: April (South Korea) 232, 240; Bolshevik (Russia) 199; Cultural (China) 44, 67; Hungarian 47; industrial 9; Islamic (Iran) 56, 62, 262; Jasmine (Tunisia) 230, 252–253, 263, 265, 267; museum in Hanoi 143; Velvet (Czechoslovakia) 199, 209, 213
Rex, Alejandro 51
Reynolds, Bryan 81
RFE *see* Radio Free Europe
Rhee, Syngman 232, 240
Richard, Ivor 153
Rips, Ilya Aronovich 46
Ritscher, Malachi (Mark D.) (pseud. Richter) 74–75
Robbins, Thomas 3
Robin, Françoise 84
Rodowicz-Czechowska, Jadwiga: *Dziady/Soreisai/*祖霊際 218n12
Roh, Jai-bong 61
Roh, Moo-hyun 75
Roh, Tae-woo 60–61, 228, 241–242, 268n8
Rojas, Gonzalo 56
Romania (Socialist Republic of Romania) 47, 57; Braşov 47, 57

Rose, Clifford 148
Roth, Phillip: *American Pastoral* 158n31
Rothschild, M. A. 14n2
Roustayi, Kambiz 81
Rumor, Mariano 204
Russia 3, 86; Moscow 88; Novosibirsk 86; *see also* Soviet Union
Ryan, Cheyney 43, 105, 139, 141
Ryan, Yasmine 247, 258, 269n12

Sabatos, Charles 70, 170, 192, 208, 210, 213, 220n29, 221n37
Sádecký, Josef 195
Saigon *see* Vietnam
Saikhanbileg, Chimed 92
Sajewska, Dorota 7
Sakharov, Andrei 52
Sands, Bobby (Roibeard Gearóid Ó Seachnasaigh) 36n3, 54
sangha see Buddhism
Sangdor 84
Sangko 78
Sangster, Leigh 84
Sarkar, Prabhat Ranjan 53
Sarkar, Shyamal 76
Sarkozy, Nicolas 213
sati (Hindi) 2
Satō, Eisaku 44
satyagraha (Sanskrit) 141, 161n54
Saudi Arabia 52, 268n2
Schechner, Richard 7
Schmidt, Helmut 51
Schneider, Ruth 264
Schraeder, Peter J. 230, 248–250, 258
Scofield, Paul 153
Scott, Michael 162n66
Securitate 47, 57
Seguir G. 36–37n11
Seifert, Jaroslav 202
self-burning *see* deliberate self-burning (DSB); suicide protest
self-harm 8, 13, 91; lip sewing 15n11
self-immolation (self-sacrifice by fire) 2, 14n1, 40; *see also* suicide protest
self-mortification 8
Senkodi 85
seppuku (Japanese) 27
Al-Shabbi, Abu al-Qasim 270n28
Shahadi, Joseph 8, 21, 32, 65
Shakya, Tsering 4
Shapiro, David 222n43; *The Funeral of Jan Palach* 210–211

Sharon, Ariel 73
Sharp, Gene: *Dictatorship to Democracy* 27
Shaw, Geoffrey 156n10
Shekhar, G. C. 85
Shelley, Martha
Shenork I Kaloustian, Patriarch 55
Shevchenko, Taras 51
Shibata, Shingo 160n50
Shilling, Chris 32
Shirakawa, Kazuo 45
Shneidman, Edwin S. 259
Shrikantha, Kanthar N. 77
Shrinan 85
Shizong, Emperor of China 117
Sienkiewicz, Karol 130
Sihanouk, Norodom, Ruler of Cambodia 108
Sikhs 76
Silman, Moshe 86
Singapore 85
Singer, Milton 7
Singh, Gurmeet R. R. 76
Singh, Guru Gobind 76
Singh, Jaswinder 76
Singh, Manmohan 59
Singh, S. P. 59
Singh, Vishwanath P. 58
A Single Spark see Park, Kwang-su
Sithu U Thant 138, 204
Šiuša, Andrius 49
Siwiec, Adam 191
Siwiec, Innocenta 168, 189, 191, 218n13
Siwiec, Maria 172, 177, 182, 190, 218–219n15
Siwiec, Mariusz 191
Siwiec, Ryszard (pseud. Jan Polak): biographical references 173–174, 218n14; reception and recognition 177–184, 218n8, 218n10; responses in culture 184–192, 217n1, 218n7, 218n12; the self-immolation and its consequences 3, 45, 174–179, 218–219n15
Siwiec, Wit 172, 176–177, 218n10, 218n14
Siwiec-Szabaga, Elżbieta 168, 174, 191, 218n14
Skoczek, Zbigniew 172
Skolarczyk, Katarzyna 173–174, 177–178, 218n14
Skow, Lisa 119–120
Škutina, Vladimír 214

288 Index

Slach, Miroslav 195–196, 198
Slezak, Victor 161n59
Śliskowski, Stanisław 185
Slovakia/Slovak Socialist Republic 219n25, 220n27; Bratislava 200, 219n17, 220n27; see also Czechoslovakia/Czechoslovak Socialist Republic
Smarzowski, Wojciech: *Kler* 12
Smith, Louis S. 114, 156n8, 156n10
Smolen, Michael 135
Smrkovský, Josef 194, 201
Sobolewski, Tadeusz 216, 222n50
social drama (Turner, V.) 7
Soheyli, Farzaneh 63
Solzhenitsyn, Aleksandr I. 197
Somalia 91; Hargeisa 91; Republic of Somaliland 91
Sontag, Susan: *On Photography* 157n13; *Regarding the Pain of Others* 28, 152; *Styles of Radical Will* 16n15, 161n57; *Under the Sign of Saturn* 127
South Korea see Korea
South Park 130
South Vietnam see Vietnam
sovereignty (Foucault) 4, 9, 31
Soviet Union 46, 48, 51, 180, 191, 193, 196, 200; Besh-Terek 51; Crimea 51; Moscow 205
Spagnola, Dustin 130
Spain: Basque Country 47; Gipuzkoa 47; San Sebastián (Donostia) 47
Spanish Civil War 47
Special Forces (After Banksy) see Van Thanh Rudd
Spellman, Francis, Cardinal 105
Spivak, Gayatri Ch. 228
Šrajer, Jindřich 219n18
Sri Lanka 76–77, 88; Colombo 88
Sriharan, S. Nalini 85
Stach, Sabine 179, 206–207
Stalin, Josef (born Ioseb Besarionis dze Jughashvili) 51
Staples, Amy J. 124
Starbuck, George 160n46
Stasi 50, 52
Steele, Jonathan 62
Stefanicki, Robert 24, 67, 83
Stiller, Wolfgang *Matchstick Men 1, 274*
Stojaspal, Jan 70
Stolarska, Bronisława 185
Stoltzfus, Randall 130

Strasz, Małgorzata 173, 219n15
Strzałka, Jan 178
Students for a Democratic Society 136
subaltern 5, 228
Subeliani, Koba 79
suicide 2, 8, 14n2, 15n6, 20–25, 36n1; *altruistic suicide* 8, 20–22; parasuicide 259; *performatic suicide* 21; *protest suicide* 21; *suicide mobilisation* 8; suicide terror attack 8, 20, 24, 54, 270n26; Werther effect (*copycat suicide*) 8, 26; see also *seppuku*
suicide protest 2–8, 10–11, 13, 15n6, 15n14, 20–35, 36n2, 40–41, 61, 83, 108, 130, 180, 201, 228, 237, 239, 254–255, 268n1; effectiveness 30, 37n14, 37n15; motivations 23; performative dimension 34–35; role of politics and religion 25; scrutiny 28–29; versus hunger strikes 22–23
Sulik, Bolesław 151–152, 155
Sullivan, Gerald 43, 106
suttee see sati
Svoboda, Ludvík 198, 201–202
Sweeney, George 14n1
Switzerland 70–71, 77; Geneva 52; Vevey 220n34
Sylvanus, Erwin: *Jan Palach* 221n37
Syria 55, 79, 81, 155, 229, 262; Qamishli 55; Rojava 55
Szczepanek, Tomasz (pseud. Pelson) 219n19
Szczepański, Tadeusz 12
Szczęsny, Piotr 13–14, 37n14, 93, 184, 218n12
Szczygieł, Mariusz: *Gottland* 70
Szekalski, Krzysztof: *Fuck… Sceny buntu* 218n12; *Samospalenie* 217n1
Szostało, Wiktor: *Performance for Freedom* 221n37
Szymański, Paweł 186–187, 189

Tạ Phong Tần 86–87
Tae, Jun-seek: *Eo-meo-ni* 242
Taiwan 57–58; Taipei 57
Takahashi, Suzi 65
Tamils 41, 76–77, 85; Liberation Tigers of Tamil Eelam (LTTE) 76–77
Tan, Yihui 69
Tang, Fuzhen 71
Tapey (born Lobsang Tashi) 77–78, 82
Tarkovsky, Andrei: *Nostalghia* 12

Index   289

Tasovská, Klára 70
Tatars 51–52
Taylor, Dan 2
Taylor, Diana 12–13
Techung 67
Telangana *see* India
Tell Me Lies see Brook, Peter
terrorism 20, 24, 27–29, 34, 70–71, 73,
  77, 83, 90, 92, 145, 253, 258, 261, 263;
  versus protest self-burnings 8
Testament see Drygas, Maciej
Thalib, Munir Said 85
Than, Shwe 76
Thatcher, Margaret 14n1, 36n3
Thaw, Zin Naing 76
Theatre of Cruelty *see* Artaud, Antonin
Theatre of the Eight Day 15n14
Thera, Bowatte Indarathana 88
Thích Đức Nghiệp 107–108
Thích Giác Đức 107
Thích Giác Thanh 42
Thích Hue Hien 44
Thích Nguyễn Hương 121
Thích Nhất Hạnh (born Nguyễn Xuân
  Bảo) 103–106, 113, 118, 145; *The Path
  of Return Continues the Journey* 105; *The
  Raft is Not a Shore* 105–106; *In Search
  of the Enemy of Man* 104, 158n24;
  Vietnam: Lotus in a Sea of Fire 103, 113
Thích Nữ Diệu Huệ 41
Thích Nữ Diệu Huỳnh (born Nhất Chi
  Mai) 44, 104
Thích Nữ Diệu Quang 121
Thích Nữ Thanh Quang 43
Thích Nữ Tu Diệu 41
Thích Quảng Độ 89
Thích Quảng Đức (born Lâm Văn Túc)
  3, 11, 41, 103, 106–112, 118–119,
  122–124, 127–131, 133, 145, 148,
  156n5, 156n8, 156n11, 158n26,
  159n34, 217n6, 254
Thích Quảng Hương 158n30
Thích Quảng Lien 108
Thích Thanh Tuệ 121
Thích Thiện Mỹ 12, 126, 158n30,
  159n32
Thích Tiêu Diêu 121, 156n9
Thích Tịnh Khiết 114, 121
Thích Trí Quang 43, 114, 122
Thomas, Anne 263
Thomson, Romin 63–64
Thoreau, David H. 140

Tiananmen Square 67–68, 71
Tibet 26, 36n1, 66, 77, 81–84; Lhasa
  78, 82; Ngawa 78, 81; Tibetan
  Government in Exile 66; Tibetan
  Youth Congress 66; Xigazê (Shigatse)
  66; *see also* China/People's Republic of
  China; Dalai Lama
Tischner, József, Father 178, 182–183, 185
Tlili, Sami: *Sans plomb* 270n27
Tố Hữu *see* Nguyễn Kim Thành
Todd, Michael 161n58
Tony, Mike 65
Topmiller, Robert 41, 44, 103, 112,
  156n10, 158n24
Toufar, Jan 221n36
Trabelsi, Layla 249
Trần Lệ Xuân (pseud. Madame Nhu *or*
  Dragon Lady) 115, 120–121, 125, 148,
  157n17, 158n25
Treisman, Deborah 263
Trewin, John C. 151, 162n65
Trimech, Abdesslem 252, 254, 269n15
Trojan, Jakub Schwarz, Pastor 197, 204
Trueheart, William 114
Từ Đàm Pagoda 114, 156n9
Từ Nghiêm Pagoda 44, 104
Tunisia 79–80, 229, 247–250, 252–257,
  259, 261, 263, 265, 269n13, 269n18;
  1968 rebellion 13; Ben Arous 251,
  257, 263; Djerba 249; El Marsa 247;
  Gafsa riots 253–254, 257; the Internet
  253–255, 269n16; Kasserine 256–258;
  Meknassy 256; Menzel Bouzaiane 256;
  Métlaoui 252; Monastir 252; Regueb
  256; Sfax 251, 269n12; Sidi Bouzid 79,
  229, 247–248, 252–253, 255–258, 262;
  Sousse 263; Thala 256–257; Tunis 251,
  257, 262–263
Turkey 53–55; Ankara 55; Istanbul 55
Turner, Bryan 33
Turner, Victor 7
Twain, Mark 149
Twohig, Niall 161n58

Uehling, Greta 52
Uhl, Petr 206
Ukraine/Ukrainian Soviet Socialist
  Republic 51; Kaniv 51; Kyiv 170; Lviv
  173; Odessa 73
United Nations (UN) 46, 52, 56, 73, 121
United States of America 3, 9, 42–43, 46,
  52–53, 55–56, 60, 62, 64, 67, 73–75,

290 Index

77, 87, 89, 103–105, 113, 118, 121, 123–124, 128, 132–133, 135–136, 138, 140–141, 154–155, 158n26, 158n27, 160n49, 160n50, 161n58, 171, 218n13, 221n37, 233, 236; Amherst, Massachusetts 60; Arlington 106; Atlanta 211; Austin 89; Chicago 74–75; Cuyahoga River 14n3; Detroit 42, 138; Florida 75; Grand Saline, Texas 89; Isleton, California 60; Los Angeles 42, 56; New York City 42, 46, 65, 68, 103–105, 119, 132, 139, 146, 151, 211, 222n43, 222n44, 222n46; Ohio 42, 64; Philadelphia 64; Princeton 103; South Bend, Indiana 43; Springfield, Massachusetts 60; Syracuse, New York 43; Washington, D.C. 73, 122, 136, 139, 161n61, 230
Urbankowski, Bohdan 217n2
The US *see* United States of America
US see Brook, Peter
Usłyszcie mój krzyk see Drygas, Maciej
Ut, Nick (born Huỳnh Công Út): *Terror of War* 131

Vaculík, Ludvík 197, 207
Vågnes, Øyvind 130
Van Thanh Rudd: *No Nauru 40,* 91; *Special Forces (After Banksy) 101,* 130–132
Vardys, Stanley 49
Vasagar, Jeevan 71
Vatican 65–66
Verhovek, Sam Howe 60
Vesak *see* Buddhism
Việt Cộng 112, 120, 122, 136–137, 155
Việt Minh 113, 135
Vietnam (Republic of Vietnam *or* South Vietnam) 3, 14n1, 22, 26, 41–45, 47, 86, 88–89, 103–108, 112–114, 118–126, 129–130, 132–136, 138–150, 152–155, 156n2, 156n9, 156n10, 157n12, 157n14, 157n15, 157n21, 160n46, 160n48, 160n52, 160n53, 161n58, 161n61, 168, 170, 178, 198, 217n6, 237; Bạc Liêu 86; Cần Thơ 44; Đà Lạt 103, 113; Đà Nẵng 42, 44, 136; Huế 44, 107, 113–115, 121, 123, 125, 156n9, 156n11; Nha Trang 42, 121; Saigon (*later* Hồ Chí Minh City) 12, 41, 44, 88, 103–104, 106–108, 112, 114, 119–121, 123–125, 130–131, 135,

137, 148; Tinh Gia Định 42; *see also* Democratic Republic of Vietnam
Vietnam war *see* war in Vietnam
Vilkaite, Ruta 44
Vlachová, Kristina 196
Vyoral, Petr: *Poslední Čech* 221n38

Wainwright, Loudon 140
Walaszkowski, Patryk 13
Wallace, George 119
Wang, Dan 66
Wang, Jindong 67–68
Wang, Lixiong 83
Waniek, Eugeniusz 53
war in Vietnam 3, 41–45, 104–105, 112, 132, 136, 138, 145–147, 150, 154, 161n58
The Warsaw Pact invasion in Czechoslovakia 3, 45, 168–170, 179, 181, 189, 192, 197, 199
Warsaw's Decennial Stadium 168, 171–172, 182–183, 217n5
Weibgen, Lara 208, 221n37
Weiler, Christel 6
Weinberger-Thomas, Catherine 2
Wenceslas Square 45, 168, 171, 196, 198–199, 201, 203–204, 207, 209, 216
Weng, Biao 71
Werner, Andrzej 168
Werther effect *see* suicide
The West Bank 73, 270n32
Westmoreland, William 144
Whalen-Bridge, John 84
Wheeler, Andrew 162n62
Whitehead, Peter 151, 156n4
Whitman, Walt (Walter) 149
Wierzyński, Kazimierz: *Na śmierć Jana Palacha* 217n6
Williams, David 162n65
Williams, Tyrone 75
Williamson, James 211
Willson, Brian 160n53
Wilson Abrahams, Andy: *Alfredo's Fire* 66
Winne, George 42, 161n58
Woeser, Tsering 36n1, 36n5, 78, 82, 84
Wojciechowski, Zbigniew 178
Women for Peace 138
Women Strike for Peace 138
Women's International League for Peace and Freedom 138
Woolf, Henry 148

World War II 47, 90, 162n63, 173, 181, 219n21, 232
Worsthorne, Peregrine 153
Wyrzykowski, Piotr: *Self-Immolation* 11, *19*

Xá Lợi Pagoda 108, 111, 122,

Yakoub, Joachim Ben 269n15, 270n27, 270n28
Yang Murray, Michelle 128, 158n26, 158n27, 158n28
Yasi, Hodan 92
Yemen 73, 91, 262, 265
Yoon, Yong-ha 61
Yordanov, Kiril 87
Yu, Hua 71
Yu, Jimmy 157n23
Yudhoyono, Susilo Bambang 85
Yui, Chūnoshin 44
Yushchenko, Viktor 51

Zajíc, Jan 171, 200, 216, 219n16; Palach and Zajíc's monument 212, 217n3
Zambrowski, Antoni 182

Zandinejad, Samaneh 63
Zardari, Asif Ali 72
Zaroulis, Nancy 43, 106
Zátopek, Emil 214
Zborník, Dobroslav: *Příběh Palachova hrobu* 220n32
Zbrożyna, Barbara: *Sarkofag pamięci Jana Palacha* 218n6
Zeiger, Mimi 211
Zeler, Bogdan 218n11
Zenawi, Meles 81
Zengin, Mahmut 54
Zero Jigen 45
Zhang, Li 71
Zhao, Yuezhi 69
Zi, Jun Toong 119, 121
Zieliński, Jerzy Ryszard (pseud. Jurry) 218n7
Zimmer, Ben 162n67
Zippo Band 221n37
Žižka, Ladislav 197
Zoubek, Olbram 201, 204, 217n3
Żuk, Paweł 93
Żuk, Piotr 93
Żuromski, Andrzej (pseud. Żurom) 15n12

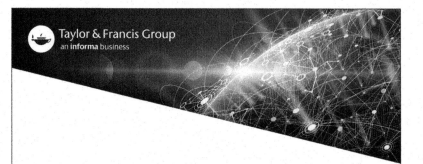